Student Hints and Solutions

to accompany

Mathematics
for
Elementary Teachers

A CONTEMPORARY APPROACH

9th Edition

Gary L. Musser
Oregon State University

William F. Burger

Blake E. Peterson
Brigham Young University

Prepared by
Lynn E. Trimpe
Linn-Benton Community College
Vikki R. Maurer
Linn-Benton Community College
Roger J. Maurer
Linn-Benton Community College

WILEY
JOHN WILEY & SONS, INC.

COVER PHOTO: Quinn Peterson/© Media Bakery

CONTENTS

PREFACE

This resource guide contains hints, additional hints, and complete solutions for all of the Part A problems in the text, *Mathematics for Elementary Teachers*, by Gary L. Musser, William F. Burger, and Blake E. Peterson. It is designed to help you improve your problem-solving ability by providing hints to get you started on each of the problems, as well as complete solutions that model one correct solution for each problem.

How to Use the *Student Hints and Solutions Manual*

Your textbook contains some challenging problems. You will probably be able to solve many of them without referring to this resource, but there will be some that may "stump" you at first. To make the best use of this resource, you should make your best effort to solve a problem before you turn to the solutions manual. The only way to become a better problem-solver is by solving problems yourself. Therefore, you should first try solving each problem by referring to the suggestions and examples given in class and in your text. If, after a reasonable period of time, you are unsuccessful in your efforts to solve a problem, we suggest following these steps:

1) Go on to another problem or take a break from your studying. Come back to the problem later and give it another try.

2) Read the hint for that problem in Part 1 of this manual, and try the problem again.

3) Read the additional hint for the problem (if there is one), and try again.

4) Read *part* of the solution to the problem in Part 2 of this manual, and see if you can complete the solution yourself.

5) Read the rest of the solution, and see if you can determine where your difficulty lay.

NOTE: Even if you have solved a problem correctly, you may find the hints and solutions useful, as they may show you another correct solution to the problem or a completely different approach to the problem.

Lynn E. Trimpe
Vikki R. Maurer
Roger J. Maurer

PART 1 - HINTS FOR PART A PROBLEMS

from

Mathematics for Elementary Teachers

A CONTEMPORARY APPROACH

by Gary L. Musser, William F. Burger,
and Blake E. Peterson

prepared by Lynn E. Trimpe

HINTS - PART A PROBLEMS

Chapter 1
Section 1.1

1. There are two different-sized triangles possible.

2. Try using a variable to represent each of the original numbers. You can then write two equations. *

3. Use a variable to represent the width of the tennis court.

4. The square of what one-digit number is also a perfect cube?

5. Any even number can be represented as $2n$, for some integer n. How could you represent an odd number?

6. Try the Guess and Test strategy. *

7. Use variables to represent the numbers in the circles and write equations representing the sums of the numbers in the circles.

8. Draw a picture. *

9. Draw a picture and try the Guess and Test strategy.

10. Use the Systematic Guess and Test strategy. Try starting with possibilities for the corners first.

11. Consider what kind of number the sum of two, three, or four consecutive integers might be.

12. Notice that the circle in the upper left has no arrows leaving it. What can you conclude from this observation?

13. Consider starting the timers at the same time. *

14. (a) You want larger digits in high-place-value positions.
    (b) You want to find two three-digit numbers that are as close to the same value as possible. *

15. UseGuess and Test.*

16. Try systematic guess and test. You might first consider the possible values for the letter P. *

17. Try using variables to represent the weights of the three objects.

18. Draw a picture and use guess and test.

19. Use a variable to represent the original number and perform the given operations.

20. Use the Systematic Guess and Test strategy. *

21. You might first make a list of the perfect cubes.

22. Use the Systematic Guess and Test strategy,first placing numbers in the corner slots.

23. Use the Inferential Guess and Test strategy and start by considering the possibilities for two overlapping circles. *

24. Try using a variable to represent the number of dots on a side. *

An additional hint for this problem is given in the next section.

Section 1.2

1. Compare the number of terms in the sum to the answer.

2. Compare successive terms in each sequence and look for a pattern. *

3. Compare successive figures and look for patterns in each component of the drawing.

4. Consider the number of 4s and 5s in each line of the sequence.

5. What arithmetic operations will make true statements with the numbers in each row?

6. (f) It might be helpful to add a third column to the table you made for part (a). In the new column list the number that is twice the number of dots in the figure. How is this number related to the triangular number?

7. Consider placing more than one coin in each pan. For example, what might you conclude if there were three coins in each pan?

8. Draw a picture. Try starting at one point on the circle and counting the number of unduplicated segments that can be drawn.

9. Consider differences between successive terms and look for a pattern. *

10. A three-column table may be helpful here. Let the columns be: square number (n), number of dots in the nth triangular number, and number of dots in the nth square number.

11. What do all of the amounts paid to date have in common? *

12. How does each perimeter compare to the number of triangles?

13. Look for a pattern in the columns of numbers. Where are the even numbers located? Where are the odd numbers located? *

14. Write out the dimensions of each collection of cubes.

15. Compare the factors in the product with the terms in the sum and with the terms in the Fibonacci sequence.

16. How does the sum in each example relate to the Fibonacci sequence?

17. Look for a pattern in the sequence of sums.

18. Look at the numbers in the row beneath the circle.

19. (d) Try writing the number of squares at each step as a sum, rather than as a single term. That is, write $1 + 4 + 8$ rather than 13 at step 3. *

20. Make a list of the positive integers. Determine which of those integers can be written as a sum of 4s and 9s and which ones cannot. *

21. Count the small points on each larger point of the star.

22. Look for a pattern in the sequence of marble colors that appear in the eManipulative activity.

*** An additional hint for this problem is given in the next section.**

Chapter 2
Section 2.1

33. Draw various Venn diagrams.

34. Draw a diagram showing the possible pairings. *

35. Make up sets with the appropriate number of elements and list all possible subsets in each case. *

36. What must be true in order for two sets to be equal? To be equivalent?

37. Draw a Venn diagram or make up several examples of sets D and E.

38. Write out a set of eight skirts and a set of seven blouses. Then find the Cartesian product of the two sets you have written.

39. Try a simpler problem. Start with fewer entries first; for example, suppose there were only five entries.

40. You must find a systematic way to pair up each point on $\overline{AC}$ and $\overline{CB}$ with a unique point on $\overline{AB}$. *

41. Draw a picture. You must find a way to connect each point on the chord to a unique point on the arc of the circle.

42. Draw a Venn diagram of these three sets: TV watchers, newspaper readers, and radio listeners. Indicate the number of persons in each region of the diagram. *

43. Draw a Venn diagram of the three sets A, B, and C and indicate the number of persons in each region.

44. What do the elements of $A \times B$ look like?

Section 2.2

15. When is the additive principle applied and when is the subtractive principle applied in the Roman numeration system? Does position matter in the Egyptian system?

16. (a) Write out the corresponding Egyptian numerals and count the symbols used.
    (b) Look for a pattern in your answers to (i) - (iv) in part (a).

17. When would a new 1999 model car have first been advertised?

18. Imagine section A of the newspaper opened flat. What numbers would appear on the full pages directly above and directly below the page described?

19. Try rewriting the sum inside the parentheses in each case. *

20. Try comparing two coins at a time, one per pan. What are the possible outcomes and what conclusions can you draw?

21. (a) Add the values of the individual numerals.
    (b) You will need accent marks for numerals larger than 1000.

Section 2.3

26. Write the numerals on both sides of each equation in expanded form. *

27. Make a list of numerals in each base and examine the ones digits.

* An additional hint for this problem is given in the next section.

28.   First look at a simpler problem. For example, how many digits would be used for a book of 25 pages?

29.   Use the expanded form of the numeral. *

30.   (b) Represent the month, day, and year of birth as two-digit numbers in expanded notation. For example, let the month be $10a + b$.

Chapter 3
Section 3.1

15.   Remember that if a set is closed under addition, the sum of any two elements of the set (not necessarily different elements) must also be an element of the set.

16.   Since only three signs can be used, at least some of the numerals must have more than one digit.

17.   Remember the sums of all four rows are the same and the numbers 10 - 25 will fill the grid. Use these facts to determine the sum in any row of the magic square.*

18.   What is "magic" about a magic square is the common sums. Use the numbers given in the hexagon to calculate a few sums. Do you see any patterns?

19.   (b) Notice that if no "carries" are involved, a palindrome will result after one addition. Try a 2-digit number that will involve "carries." *

20.   Let n = youngest daughter's age. What algebraic expression would represent the next-youngest daughter's age?

21.   Think about what numbers might go in the corners. These numbers will each be used in two of the sums.

Section 3.2

18.   If a team consists of 4 pairs, how many dancers are on each team?

19.   Use the Repeated-Addition Approach.

20.   Try using measurement division or the Repeated-Subtraction Approach.

21.   Consider the Missing-Factor Approach.

22.   What number multiplied times 12,349 will yield an answer of 12,349?

23.   Remember that multiplication can be thought of as repeated addition.

24.   (a) To find the sum of the numbers in a row, first find the sum of all the numbers in the magic square. *
      (b) Choose a base and use digits 1 - 9 as exponents. *

25.   Look for a pattern in the number and type of whole numbers added together.

26.   Use systematic guess and test. Start by considering which products are possible.

27.   Let n = original number. Write an algebraic expression representing the operations performed on the number.

* **An additional hint for this problem is given in the next section.**

28. Use direct reasoning. A table or a list is helpful for keeping track of possibilities that you eliminate.

29. Use variables or use the Guess and Test strategy. *

30. Make a list comparing the number of days elapsed and the number of creatures on Earth.

31. Use direct reasoning. See the solution to the initial problem at the beginning of this chapter.

32. Can you find examples of whole numbers a, b, and c for which $ac = bc$ but $a \neq b$?

Section 3.3

15. Use the definition of a whole-number exponent to expand the expression on the left-hand side of the equation.

16. (a) Write 6 as a product of factors and use properties of exponents.
     (b) Write 9 as a product of factors and use properties of exponents.
     (c) Write 12 as a product of factors and use properties of exponents.

17. Make a table listing the number of five-year periods since 2000 in one column and the price of a candy bar at that time in another column of the table. *

18. Remember that if $n(A) < n(B)$, then A matches a proper subset of B.

19. What pattern do you notice in the sum of two cubes on the right-hand side? What patterns do you observe in the terms that appear on the left-hand side? *

20. Each size of pizza could have 0, 1, 2, 3, or all 4 toppings on it. *

21. Use systematic guess and test. A list of the perfect squares would be helpful here.

22. Consider all possible products in each case and compare answers to perfect squares.

23. (a) If $a < b$, then $a + n = b$ for some nonzero whole number n. *
     (b) Rewrite the Property of Less Than and Addition for the operation of subtraction by replacing each addition with subtraction.

Chapter 4
Section 4.1

25. Start by rounding each number to the nearest thousand.

26. Notice that 2(246,913,578) = 493,827,156.

27. Use the Guess and Test strategy. *

28. You want a low estimate and a high estimate for the differences.

29. Rewrite 13,333,333 as a sum and use the distributive property to find its square.

30. Try writing 99 as 100 − 1.

31. Compare the tens digit in the number to be squared with the first two digits in the answer. Do you see a relationship? *

* An additional hint for this problem is given in the next section.

32. You might first calculate the number of minutes required for sound to reach the moon.

33. Look at the last digit (ones digit) of each of the factors.

34. Rewrite each factor in the product by adding to or subtracting from the same number.

35. Rewrite each number on the right as a sum and then multiply using the distributive property.

36. Rewrite the larger number as a sum and then apply the distributive property.

37. Be careful with the order of operations.

38. Compare the digits in the products to the digits in each factor. *

39. To use the "round a 5 up" method, what digit of the number do you look at? *

40. Try the Guess and Test strategy.

41. Fill the smaller, 3-liter pail first.

Section 4.2

35. Work the problem correctly yourself, and compare your steps with the "student" versions.

36. Try systematic guess and test. Many solutions are possible. *

37. Where must the largest digits in the set be placed in order to yield the largest sum? To yield the smallest sum?

38. Use systematic guess and test. Start with two-digit numbers whose sum is close to 100.

39. Use systematic guess and test. Notice that the digits remaining in a column (plus any "carries") must add up to 1, 11, or 21.

40. (d) Try other pairs of numbers such as 21 and 52, or 22 and 51. Look at sums and differences again. Consider also products of such pairs of numbers. Do you see a pattern?

41. Compare the number of rows and columns in the figure to the terms in the sum.

42. Use systematic guess and test. Notice that not all of the digits 0 - 9 can be used and that the possibilities for R are limited. *

43. Work each problem yourself, and compare your steps to the answer obtained by each student. Look for a pattern in each student's answers.

44. Notice that each digit in one factor is multiplied by each digit in the other factor, and each of the resulting products occupies a particular place-value position.

45. Try several different four-digit numbers. Keep in mind that digits may be repeated and that 0 may be used as a digit. Look for a pattern.

Section 4.3

19. Look at the digits used and the sum of the digits in the units places. *

20. Let x = the amount of money Steve has.

* *An additional hint for this problem is given in the next section.*

21. What digits can appear in the units place of a perfect square?

22. Make a list of perfect squares larger than 100. When the difference between one of these squares and 100 is added to 164, is the result a perfect square?

Chapter 5
Section 5.1

15. (a) Use a factor tree.
    (b) Consider tests for divisibility.
    (d) Compare the prime factors of each divisor to the prime factors of the original number. Also compare the exponents on those prime factors.

16. Let $n = a \times 10^2 + b \times 10 + c$. You want to show that 5 divides n if and only if 5 divides c. *

17. Write out or imagine what each factorial looks like. For example, $20! = 20 \times 19 \times 18 \times \cdots \times 3 \times 2 \times 1$. You do *not* need to multiply the factors together to get a numerical answer. *

18. (a)-(b) See the hint for problem 17.
    (c) How do the numbers 8 and 7 differ?

19. What are the prime numbers less than 30? Check to see which of them is a factor of one of the given numbers.

20. Continue to substitute whole numbers for n. You will not need to check any counting numbers greater

than 17 since $p(17) = 17^2 + 17 + 17$ is not prime.

21. (a) List your results in a table as you do part (b). Use divisibility tests to check for primes.

22. One of the tests for divisibility will give you a factor of a group of these numbers. *

23. Consider the fact that, except for 2, all the prime numbers are odd. So the sum of two primes, both different from 2, would be even.

24. A list of the first 10 or 12 perfect squares might be useful here.

25. Keep in mind that of two consecutive counting numbers, one must be even and one must be odd.

26. Refer to the beginning of this section to see how the Sieve of Eratosthenes might be used to locate prime numbers less than 200.

27. (b) Think about the fact that each odd number can be obtained by adding an odd number to an even number.

28. To save time in testing pairs of numbers, notice that the same two primes may work for several pairs. For example, the primes 11 and 13 lie between 7 and 14 and also between 8 and 16.

29. Use the prime factorization of 1,234,567,890 to determine all of its possible factors.

30. Examine the kind of factors each product in the set has. Do you see any common factors?

An additional hint for this problem is given in the next section.

31. Look at the prime factorizations of the numbers 2 through 10. What different factors must a multiple of these numbers have?

32. Look at the prime factorizations of the numbers 2, 4, 5, 6, and 12. What different factors must a multiple of these numbers have?

33. Try several sets of three consecutive counting numbers to get an idea of what the divisor might be. To prove your answer is correct, use a variable. *

34. Use variables to prove that your observation is true. *

35. (a) Use the property of whole numbers that says that if $a \mid m$ and $a \mid n$, then $a \mid (m + n)$.
    (b) Notice that the numbers in part (a) are four consecutive composite numbers.

36. Use variables to represent the unknown prices and write an expression for the total cost. *

37. Solve a simpler problem: Find a 2-digit number such that when 7 is subtracted from it, the result is divisible by 7, and when 8 is subtracted from it, the result is divisible by 8. *

38. One cupcake left over each time means that if the number of cupcakes were divided by 2, 3, 4, 5, or 6, the remainder would be 1 in each case. *

39. Write the 6-digit number abc,abc in expanded form:
    $100,000a + 10,000b + 1000c + 100a + 10b + c$.*

40. (a) Write the palindrome as $abba$. Which digits have place values that are odd powers of 10? *
    (b) Try a few examples of other palindromes with an even number of digits. Can you write a proof as in part (a)? Do you see a pattern?

41. Each of the annual sales amounts must be a multiple of the cost of the calculator.

42. Try writing the two related numbers that are divisible by 7 in expanded form. *

43. Be sure you understand how the sums are obtained. Compare the answer in one step with the sum in the next step.

44. Use the distributive property to expand the given expression. *

45. Use your calculator to show that 11 divides 1,111,111,111, 13 divides 111,111,111,111, and 17 divides 1,111,111,111,111,111.

46. (a) How many 3s occur in the prime factorization of 24!?
    (b) The prime factorization of the desired factorial will contain six 3s as factors.
    (c) Remember that $12 = 2^2 \times 3$.

47. Use the formula $p(n) = n^2 + n + 17$ to fill the $p(n)$ column in your spreadsheet.

---

* An additional hint for this problem is given in the next section.

Section 5.2

18. Make a list. For each number, starting with 2, how many factors does it have and what is their sum?

19. Start by determining all the proper divisors of each number.

20. Start by determining all the proper divisors of each number. Be sure to exclude 1 from each list.

21. Use the relationship between LCM(a, b), GCF(a, b), a, and b. *

22. Look at the method presented in this section for finding the number of different factors of any given whole number. *

23. Look at the method presented in this section for finding the number of different factors of any given whole number. *

24. For what values of n is $2^n - 1$ a prime number? NOTE: n must be a counting number.

25. GCF(24, x) = 1 means the largest whole number that is a factor of both 24 and x is 1.

26. The price of a candy bar and the price of a can of pop must each be a factor of the total amount of money earned.

27. If c = the price of one chicken, d = the price of one duck, and g = the price of one goose, then $3c + d = 2g$. *

28. Look at the prime factorization of each number. *

29. Start with the largest possible 3-digit number.

30. Write the numbers in their expanded form, i.e., $1000a + 100b + 10b + a$. *

31. What must the sum of the primes in any row equal?

32. What is the least number of cards that could be divided exactly into 2 equal piles, 3 equal piles, or 5 equal piles?

33. Write $100a + 10b + a$ in terms of a and determine whether the resulting expression is divisible by 7.

34. Look at the prime factorization of each of the numbers.

35. Consider how much is left in the large container when juice is poured from the large container to the smaller one.

Chapter 6
Section 6.1

16. To find a fraction with a denominator of 100, write an equation setting two fractions equal to one another.

17. (a) Are the listed fractions getting larger or smaller?
    (b) Consider improper fractions.

18. For each year, create a fraction that compares the number of tons of waste recycled with the total number of tons of waste generated.

19. You will subdivide the hexagon differently for parts of this problem.

An additional hint for this problem is given in the next section.

20. Look at several other fractions of this same form. Examine the factors of the numerator and denominator in each case.

21. What are the one-digit squares that are possible sums of the numerator and denominator?

22. Try several examples in each case. If the numerator is said to be fixed, then the two fractions being compared must have the same numerators. Otherwise, you may choose any numbers you like for the two numerators.

23. Recall the theorem which states that for fraction $\dfrac{a}{b}$ and nonzero whole number n, $\dfrac{an}{bn} = \dfrac{a}{b}$.

24. Use cross products or try substituting values for a, b, c, and d.

25. Using a variable, write another fraction equivalent to $\dfrac{3}{5}$.

26. Using a variable, write anotherfraction equivalent to $\dfrac{1}{11}$.

27. Using a variable, write anotherfraction equivalent to $\dfrac{7}{8}$.

28. Using a variable, write another fraction equivalent to $\dfrac{5}{12}$.

29. Draw pictures of the possible paths. Be systematic in the routes you try.

30. Use systematic guess and test. Think about what numbers are multiples of 5, 3, or 6.

31. Rewrite the fractions $\dfrac{4}{7}$ and $\dfrac{1}{2}$ with a common denominator. *

Section 6.2

20. What fraction of the restaurant do Sally and her brother together own?

21. Altogether, what fraction of his life did John spend growing up, in college, and as a teacher? *

22. Find a common denominator.

23. What fraction of the garden is already planted in potatoes and carrots?

24. One whole golf course is the sum of its parts. What fraction of the golf course is in fairways and greens?

25. Examine carefully how David "borrowed" in the subtraction problem.

26. (c) What kind of numbers are 6, 28, and 496? *

27. If there are n terms in the numerator and denominator of the fraction, then the numerator can be written $1 + 3 + 5 + \ldots + (2n - 1)$.

28. Make a list of the sums with 1 term, 2 terms, 3 terms, and so on. Do you see a pattern in the answers?

---

* **An additional hint for this problem is given in the next section.**

29. (e) Compare the sums
$$\frac{15}{50} + \frac{3}{6} \text{ and } \frac{15}{50} + \frac{1}{2}.$$

30. Find the least common denominator by factoring all the denominators. Then add the fractions.

31. Look carefully at the sum $\frac{1}{3} + \frac{1}{6} = \frac{1}{2}$. Notice that the least common multiple of 2 and 3 is 6.

32. Draw a regular octagon and count the number of segments that would be required to connect each vertex with every other vertex. *

33. You might start by counting the zeros that precede nonzero digits.

Section 6.3

25. Perform division to solve each equation.

26. How do you determine the average of two numbers? There are two ways.

27. Solve a simpler problem to determine what operation is required. For example, how would you solve the problem if each load required 2 cups of detergent?

28. Use a variable. *

29. Use a variable. *

30. Try solving a simpler problem. *

31. What fraction of the original group was still participating on July 2? *

32. Draw a diagram showing Tammy's trip to school together with the times. *

33. First determine what operation is required. In part (a), if the recipe is doubled, then twice as much flour is needed.

34. Use guess and test or use a variable.*

35. (b) What fraction of the previous year's value does the equipment have at the end of a year? *

36. Write one equation for each of the two numbers and then solve for the numbers. *

37. (b) How would you perform $\frac{a}{b} \div n$ using the invert-the-divisor-and-multiply approach? What would the result be?

    (c) Think of $5\frac{3}{8}$ as $5 + \frac{3}{8}$ and $10\frac{9}{16}$ as $10 + \frac{9}{16}$.

38. In Sam's case, watch what he does with the denominators of the fractions. In Sandy's case, look at her second step.

39. Use a variable. Let x represent the number of apples in the store.

40. Use two variables. *

41. How many $\frac{3}{5}$'s are in 1 whole? *

An additional hint for this problem is given in the next section.

Chapter 7
Section 7.1

18. Use systematic guess and test. *

19. Consider the total amount of lost wages due to the strike and the number of hours Kathy works during one year. *

20. Rewrite each decimal as a fraction. What is the common denominator?

Section 7.2

15. You want to calculate the time in light years. How are distance, rate, and time related?

16. What are the only possible prime factors of the denominator of a fraction in simplest form whose decimal expansion terminates? *

17. Work backward. Consider some familiar terminating decimals, for example, $0.5 = \dfrac{1}{2}$.*

18. Beginning with the equality $0.\bar{1} = \dfrac{1}{9}$, we can multiply both sides by any nonzero number we choose.

19. This is the same as problem 18, except begin with $0.\overline{01} = \dfrac{1}{99}$.

20. This is the same as problem 18, except begin with $0.\overline{001} = \dfrac{1}{999}$.

21. (a) Count the number of decimal places and compare with similar decimals in problems 18 - 20.
     (b) Remember that to find the fractional representation of a number such as $0.\overline{65}$, we can start by letting $n = 0.\overline{65}$, or $n = 0.656565\ldots$

22. (a) Look at problems $18 - 20$ to determine what the denominator of the fraction must be. *
     (b) When might it be possible to simplify a fraction such as the one you wrote in part (a) to one that will have a decimal representation with fewer than five digits in the repetend?

23. Write out the decimal so that the repetend appears several times. Looks for a pattern in the digits. *

24. Try a simpler problem. For example, compare $\dfrac{1}{13}$ to $\dfrac{10}{13} = 10 \times \dfrac{1}{13}$.*

25. On an inexpensive, four-function calculator an overflow error usually occurs when the result of a calculation is too large or too small. *

26. Let x represent the amount of money Gary had before cashing the check from Joan.

27. Let x represent the original value of the car. Then what was its value after one year?

28. Convert the time to minutes.

---

*   **An additional hint for this problem is given in the next section.**

29. What was the total distance traveled on the trip?

30. How many U.S. dollars would you receive for 121 yen?

31. How many centimeters are in one inch?

32. How many times would the price have increased by 0.03? *

33. How many liters per cylinder does each engine have?

34. Draw a grid and use guess and test. Record the number of moves you make for each try.

Section 7.3

12. Remember to calculate the amount of juice - that is, water and concentrate.

13. You could set up a proportion like:
$$\frac{\text{acres}}{\text{days}} = \frac{\text{acres}}{\text{days}}.$$

14. You could set up a proportion like:
$$\frac{\text{peaches}}{\text{servings}} = \frac{\text{peaches}}{\text{servings}}.$$

15. You could set up a proportion like:
$$\frac{\text{ounces}}{\text{weeks}} = \frac{\text{ounces}}{\text{weeks}}.$$

16. What fraction of each day has the man spent sleeping?

17. You could set up a proportion like:
$$\frac{\text{Earth weight}}{\text{Moon weight}} = \frac{\text{Earth weight}}{\text{Moon weight}}.$$

18. You could set up a proportion like:
$$\frac{\text{miles}}{\text{year}} = \frac{\text{miles}}{\text{year}}.$$

19. You could set up a proportion like:
$$\frac{\text{altitude gained}}{\text{horizontal distance traveled}} = \frac{\text{altitude gained}}{\text{horizontal distance traveled}}. *$$

20. Ignore the extraneous information in the problem and set up a proportion. *

21. (a) If the teacher : student ratio is 1 : 35 and there are 1400 students, how many teachers are there at this time? *
    (b) What is the total cost for all of the teachers in the school? *

22. (a) Use the fact that the ratio of the distance from Earth to Mars to the distance from Earth to Pluto is 1:12.37.
    (b) Use the fact that Pluto is 30.67 AU from Earth, as was given in part (a). *
    (c) Use your result from part (a), which gives the AU distance from Earth to Mars.

23. You can solve each part by writing a proportion in a form such as one of the following:
$$\frac{\text{years}}{\text{years}} = \frac{\text{hours}}{\text{hours}} \text{ or } \frac{\text{hours}}{\text{years}} = \frac{\text{hours}}{\text{years}}. *$$

An additional hint for this problem is given in the next section.

24. Let d = distance to the airport. Use distance = rate × time to solve for time. *

25. If the ratios of successive amounts are whole numbers, each amount of money must be divisible by the preceding amount of money.

26. Compare the fractions $\dfrac{\text{hits}}{\text{at bats}}$ in simplest form.

27. Use a variable.

28. If the man had 0 dollars after the final purchase, he must have had exactly $20 before that purchase. Half of that $20 he had in his pocket and half had been given to him by his father. How much had been in his pocket before the second purchase? *

29. You could have more than one dollar's worth of change.

30. Consider the last subtraction. What number would you want to leave your opponent with so that he/she is sure to lose? What about your opponent's second-to-last subtraction? *

31. Notice that the 11-minute timer lasts 4 minutes longer than the 7-minute timer.

32. Draw a picture of the racetrack and the posts. *

Section 7.4

14. What are the "part" and the "total" in this case?

15. Is the unknown quantity the "part" or the "total"?

16. (a) Remember that the value of the account is the original balance plus interest earned. *

17. How much total interest would you pay for the 15 days if you pay 0.04839% each day? *

18. 2 is what percent of 35?

19. (a) If contributions increased by 73% from 1990 to 1997, what percent of the 1990 contributions were the contributions in 1997?

20. (b) Use your result from part (a) to determine what percent each energy source is of the total.

21. Is the dollar amount of the discount 15% of the original price?

22. Use a variable. Let x = selling price of the car.

23. Consider this relationship: 20% of 50 is 10% of 100.

24. If you received an 8% discount on the car, what percent of the original price did you pay? *

25. (a) You want to determine what percent 8.5×10^{13} is of 5.2×10^{14}.

26. Use a variable. Let x = number of grams of protein recommended (U. S. RDA). *

* *An additional hint for this problem is given in the next section.*

27. If the slacks were made 10% longer than 40 inches, what would be their length before washing? *

28. Try a few examples by working the problem both ways. For example, suppose a $100 item is marked up 10% and then down 10%. What would the final price be? *

29. Suppose that Cathy has 100 baseball cards. How many do Joseph and Martin have?

30. The range is from 70% of the difference to 80% of the difference.

31. The number of outputs provided by the unit must be a whole number.

32. Try the calculation both ways. Suppose that the doctor had charged you $100 before any discounts.

33. Use a variable or start with an arbitrary number of people. For example, let x = the population of the country at the start of 2004. *

34. Simulate the game with a partner, using toothpicks, coins, etc. *

35. Try the calculation both ways. To make the arithmetic easier, suppose an item cost $100 originally.

36. Elaine will earn 3.5% interest twice a year for the next 3 years.

37. Each year she needs to earn 11% more than during the previous year.

38. Each year the value of their savings will be worth 8.25% more than the previous year. What percent of the previous year's savings is the value of their savings in any one year? *

39. What is the percent of increase from the CPI in 2000 to the CPI in 2001?

40. Make a table containing a number of examples. Compare salary, taxes and net earnings. *

41. Write an equation relating the average wage this year to the average wage last year.

42. Use systematic guess and test. Since you are asked the man's age in 1949, you know he must have been born prior to 1949. *

43. Make a table comparing dimensions and perimeters.

44. Use the fact that Distance = Rate × Time to calculate the total time for a round trip in each case.

Chapter 8
Section 8.1

18. Try making a table of the account balance after each check or deposit.

19. (a)-(c) Try a few examples. Pay close attention to the parentheses in part (c).
    (d) Remember that the identity property must hold in both directions. For example, in the case of addition, $a + 0 = a$ and $0 + a = a$.

20. Assuming that the adding-the-opposite approach works means assuming that $a - b = a + (-b)$. So this equality can be used at any time in the proof. *

21. Try several examples for each part. Be sure to also consider cases where one or both numbers are negative or zero.

* An additional hint for this problem is given in the next section.

22. Remember that the sums of the rows are equal and that the nine given numbers must fill the grid. Use these facts to find the sum for any row. *

23. (a) Since A is closed under subtraction, to show that a number is an element of A, you must show that it can be written as a difference using 4s and 9s.
    (b) Are there any numbers that cannot be obtained using 4s and 9s and the operation of subtraction?
    (c) Again, consider whether there are numbers that you cannot obtain using 4s and 9s.
    (d) Try some more examples as in part (c). Vary your choices of elements. *

24. Work from the bottom up.

25. Try a few examples first. To test whether the procedure will always work, write each number in expanded form, as in $10a + b$.

26. Look for two (or more) squares whose sides together make up the side of another square. *

27. In each circle, look for combinations of numbers that add up to the opposite of the number that is already in the circle.

Section 8.2

24. What number must be in the first square of the bottom row?

25. Remember that the set of integers is an infinite set, containing all the whole numbers and their opposites.

It does not, however, contain decimal numbers like 6.9.

26. (b) First consider which cases always give a positive or always give a negative.

27. How does $|x|$ compare to x if x is a negative integer?

28. See the theorem about multiplying an integer by -1 in the textbook.

29. Consider how much must be added in each case to get out of debt.

30. To start, consider the product of integers in the bottom row. *

31. If $x<y$, you may multiply both sides of the inequality by a positive number and the inequality is preserved. See the Property of Less Than and Multiplication by a Positive in your textbook. *

32. You want to calculate the number of grams in one atom of carbon.

33. (a) It might be easiest to first convert the rate of hair growth into scientific notation. *

34. There is more than one possible answer. You might make a table with columns for numbers of cows, sheep, and rabbits, as well as total cost. Try some combinations of 100 animals. *

35. If x^2 is a perfect square, then x^2 must be of the form $3n$ or $3n +1$, where n is a whole number. *

An additional hint for this problem is given in the next section.

36. Try guess and test. Remember that the price is expressed in terms of cents *per dozen*.

37. If $ab = 0$, and $b \neq 0$, what can you conclude about a?

Chapter 9
Section 9.1

32. The definition of equality of rational numbers states that two rational numbers are equal if, and only if, the "cross-products" are equal. So you must show that the "cross-products" are equal in this case.

33. See Section 6.2 for a proof that addition of fractions is commutative. Notice that proof uses the fact that addition of whole numbers is commutative. Similarly, to prove properties of rational number multiplication, you may use properties of integers or fractions.

34. (b) By the adding-the-opposite approach, $\dfrac{a}{b} - \dfrac{c}{d} = \dfrac{a}{b} + \left(-\dfrac{c}{d}\right)$. Start with this definition of subtraction and show that the result you found in part (a) holds. Remember there will be two parts to the proof since the result is given as an if-and-only-if statement.
   (c) Same as part (b) except you start by using the definition of subtraction given in part (a) and must show this means
   $$\frac{a}{b} - \frac{c}{d} = \frac{a}{b} + \left(-\frac{c}{d}\right).$$

35. You may use the distributive properties of multiplication over addition for fractions and/or integers. *

36. Remember that if $\dfrac{a}{b} < \dfrac{c}{d}$, where $b > 0$ and $d > 0$, then there must be a positive fraction $\dfrac{m}{n}$ such that this condition holds: $\dfrac{a}{b} + \dfrac{m}{n} = \dfrac{c}{d}$. *

37. Find some $\dfrac{e}{f}$ so that this condition holds: $-\left(-\dfrac{a}{b}\right) + \dfrac{e}{f} = \dfrac{a}{b} + \dfrac{e}{f}$. *

38 The six-minute period may not start until one or both timers have gone off at least once. *

Section 9.2

26. See the proof that there is no rational number whose square is 2 in this section of the textbook. *

27. Look at the prime factorization of 9. How does this affect the argument about prime factors of both sides?

28. Begin by assuming that $\sqrt[3]{2}$ is a rational number. Then cube each side of the equation. *

29. If $\dfrac{a}{b}$ is a rational number, what kind of number is $\dfrac{a}{5b}$? *

An additional hint for this problem is given in the next section.

30. (a) Assume that $1 + \sqrt{3}$ is rational and then isolate $\sqrt{3}$. Show that a contradiction results.

31. Use the results proved in problems 29(b) and 30(b).

32. Try several other examples, such as: $\sqrt{36} + \sqrt{64} \stackrel{?}{=} \sqrt{100}$. Is the result ever true?

33. For what kinds of numbers is $\sqrt{a}$ defined in this section? See the definition in the textbook.

34. Look at multiples of the Pythagorean Triple $(3, 4, 5)$. For example, is $(9, 12, 15)$ a Pythagorean Triple?

35. Try several pairs of values for u and v. Read the conditions for u and v carefully.

36. Use a variable. Let $x =$ the smallest of the three consecutive integers. What expressions represent the other two integers? *

37. Use variables to represent the numerator and denominator of the rational number. *

38. Draw a picture. Imagine putting the two pieces of wire together and then cutting. *

39. It may be helpful to arrange the professions in order of salary. *

40. Make a list of all factor pairs of 1280.

Section 9.3

16. To show that a relation is an equivalence relation, you must show that it is reflexive, symmetric, and transitive. *

17. (c) If degrees Celsius equals degrees Fahrenheit, then $g(m) = m$, and $f(n) = n$. Solve one of these equations.

18. Look at the difference between successive terms.

19. (c) You want $C(x) > 1000$. Consider only whole numbers of months.

20. (a) Use the formula for the terms of a geometric series and the two given terms to write two equations in two unknowns.

21. (c) Use the formula for the nth term of a sequence of this type to write your function $T(n)$.

22. (b) Is there a common ratio or common difference between successive terms?
    (c) Consider the number of triangles formed in each step and the number of toothpicks in each triangle. *

23. Use the formula for the nth term of an arithmetic or geometric sequence to write the function $A(n)$.

24. Use the formula for the nth term of an arithmetic or geometric sequence to write the function $A(n)$.

25. The flight of the clown ends when she lands on the ground, that is, when $h(t) = 0$.

---

* ***An additional hint for this problem is given in the next section.***

26. Solve a simpler problem. Consider two 3-digit numbers, one in base two and one in base ten. Which could a friend guess, digit-by-digit, in the fewest guesses?

27. Is there a common ratio or difference between successive terms in each sequence?

28. What kind of sequence do the numbers form? *

29. Look for a pattern in the inputs and outputs of each function to determine how the outputs were generated.

Section 9.4

17. (a) Remember that $f(1)$ means Thevalue of y when $x = 1$.
    (b) The domain is the set of possible values of which variable?
    (c) If $f(x) = 2$, which variable has a value of 2?

18. (a) Remember that $d(4)$ means the value of d when $h = 1$.
    (b) Be careful with units.
    (c) The domain in this case is the set of possible values of which variable?

19. (a) Which variable is represented bywhich axis?
    (b) If her age is 30, then $a = 30$.
    (c) How does the graph change as you move from left to right?

20. (a) Look at the graphs of the basic function types presented in this section.
    (c) Locate 100m on the vertical axis.
    (d) What physical limitations are there to this problem?

21. (b) When is $s = 90$?
    (c) When the ball hits the ground, $s(t) = 0$.
    (d) What is the maximum value of s?

22. (b) What is the value of t in the year 2006?
    (c) Locate 8 on the vertical axis or use a graphics calculator to locate the point with a y-coordinate of 8.
    (d) Choose any point on your graph. Then find the point on the graph where the value of P is twice as large. Compare the values of t.

23. At what point on the route would the cyclist's speed begin to decrease? *

24. Think about who must ride the elevator first. A picture might help.

25. Start by trying some positive values of b, and see how the graph changes. Then trysome negative values of b.

Chapter 10
Section 10.1

18. (b) Can you make the intervals small enough that no data points fall into some intervals?

19. (a) Which kinds of graphs can be used effectively to show the enrollment in each type of school? Which would best compare the types of schools?

20. (a) Since the sources are listed by percent of the total budget, how might you show how much of the total each source represents?

*** An additional hint for this problem is given in the next section.**

21. (a) Which kind of graph could best show how tuition costs changed over time?
    (c) Which kind of college had the greatest percent increase over the whole time period?

22. (a) What type of graph would best show the comparison between the two groups?

23. (a) Which types of graph would best show the change in subscribers over time?

24. (a) Which types of graphs might show the relationship between the three types of funding and, at the same time, the way those relationships changed over the years?

25. (b) Your regression line may come close to many of the data points, but it may actually pass through only a few. It might not even pass through any of the points in the scatter plot. *

26. Make a scatter plot of the data and sketch a regression line. *

Section 10.2

15. (a) If the circle for Company *B* has radius 2 inches, how would its area compare to the area of the circle for Company *A*?
    (b) If the sphere for Company *B* has a radius of 2 inches, how would its volume compare to the volume of the sphere for Company *A*?

16. Notice that the scale on the vertical axis begins at 0. How might you change it?

17. How might you modify the scale on the vertical axis to emphasize the difference in bar heights?

18. How might you modify the scale on the vertical axis to de-emphasize the difference in bar heights?

19. Notice the scale on the vertical axis. How might you modify it?

20. What factors might affect the number of fish that are captured?

21. How might the company select the 20 doctors for the study? How might those 20 doctors *not* be representative?

Section 10.3

19. Use the formula for a *z*-score.

20. Use the formula for a *z*-score.

21. The data values in Set 2 will need to be twice as "spread out" as the values in Set 1.

22. Think backward. To find the average, you divide the total points earned by the number of students in the class. So what must you do to find the total number of points earned?

23. Find the total number of points scored by the original 100 students. See hint for problem 22. *

24. You have been given some unnecessary information in this problem.

25. Find the mean, standard deviation, and Lora's *z*-score for each set of test scores.

* An additional hint for this problem is given in the next section.

26.   What should the manager consider when reordering shoes? *

27.   (a) What will two graphs look like if they have the same mean?
      (b) What will two graphs look like if they have the same variance?

28.   (a)-(b) Remember that $z = \dfrac{x - m}{s}$,

      where m is the mean of all scores and s is the standard deviation.
      (c) What percent of scores lie to the left of the z-score you found in part (b)?

Chapter 11
Section 11.1

22.   (a) It would be helpful to list the possible outcomes as ordered pairs.
      (b) To calculate $P(D)$, it may be easier to use the complement of D.

23.   Draw a picture of the region consisting of all points within 10 miles of Albany. Do the same for Binghamton. Label the cities and the distances between them in your drawing.

24.   See the examples and description of the probability of a "geometric" event in problem 23. *

Section 11.2

14.   Use the Fundamental Counting Property in each case. *

15.   (a)-(b) Use the Fundamental Counting Property. *
      (c) Use your results from parts (a) and (b).

16.   (c) Compare your results from part (b) to Pascal'sTriangle.

17.   (a) Refer to Pascal's Triangle.
      (b) Compare probabilities using the table given for 3 shots and the table you completed for 4 shots in part (a).

18.   (b) Which outcomes correspond to Los Angeles winning in 2 straight games? Which correspond to Portland winning after losing the first game?
      (c) If an event has several outcomes, corresponding to the ends of several branches, the probabilities at the ends of the branches should be added.

19.   (a) The probability that LA wins or Portland wins is 1.
      (d) What outcome corresponds to LA losing the second game but winning the series?
      (e) It might be easier to determine the probability that the series does *not* go for 3 games.

20.   (b) To determine the probability that A wins in 4 games, consider all the possible ways in which that might occur.
      (c) One way in which A could win the series in 5 games is the outcome $ABABA$.
      (d) Use your results from parts (a) - (c).

21.   (b) Use the Fundamental Counting Property.
      (c) How many different sequences of answers are correct?
      (d) Use your answers from parts (b) and (c).

22.   (a) There should be nine branches in the final stage of the tree.

*** An additional hint for this problem is given in the next section.**

(d) Use the probabilities assigned in your tree diagram, not just the number of elements in the event or sample space. *

23. What is the greatest number of *unmatched* socks you could pull out?

24. If there are three puppies, how many possibilities are there for the sexes of the puppies? That is, if each puppy is either male or female, how many elements are in the sample space?

25. Construct a two-stage probability diagram. Notice that the probability of choosing a black ball or a white ball from box two depends on what was chosen from box one. *

26. (a) There will be six different sizes of equilateral triangles. *

Section 11.3

15. (a) Try rewriting the right-hand side of the equation.

16. (a) Think of the ID number as a series of 9 blanks, each to be filled with one of the letters. You might start by assuming that all nine letters look different. *
    (b) Given that the first three letters must be GHS, there are only six positions left to consider. *

17. (a) In how many ways can three letters be placed on the license plate? *
    (b) In how many ways can Edwardo's initials be placed on the license plate in the right order?

18. Think of the lock's combination as a series of four blanks, each to be filled with one of the numbers.

19. (a) Try writing an equation that relates $_mP_n$ and $_{10}C_7$.
    (b) Try using Pascal's triangle and the value of $_{15}P_2$.

20. If order does not matter, are you looking for a number of combinations or permutations?

21. Think about how passengers will be assigned to particular seats.

22. In each case, start by thinking about how many choices there are for the first chip selected. *

23. In each case, start by thinking about how many choices there are for the first letter of the "word". *

24. (a) What do $_{20}C_5$ and $_{20}C_{15}$ mean (using the formula for $_nC_r$)?

25. (a) Do not worry about making the sum on each side 17. In how many ways can the 9 digits be placed in the circles?
    (b) In how many ways can digits be placed in the corners?
    (c) Which pairs of numbers add up to 14?
    (d) Think about what the two open slots in each row must add up to.
    (e) In how many ways can the digits 1, 2 and 3 be placed in the corners?

*** An additional hint for this problem is given in the next section.**

26. (a) Does the order of selection matter in this case?
    (b) If Glenn is chosen, how many selections remain to be made?
    (c) If Glenn and Mickey are chosen, how many selections remain to be made?

27. Does the order of the cards matter?
    (a) In how many ways can 4 aces be chosen from one deck?
    (b) 3 kings would be selected from how many kings?
    (c) 5 diamonds would be selected from how many diamonds?
    (d) How many aces, kings, etc., would you be selecting "one" from?

28. Does the order in which the people are selected matter?
    (a) The five persons will be selected from how many people?
    (b) In how many ways can one person be selected from the group of exposed persons?
    (c) If you know the probability that one person has been exposed and you know the probability that two persons have been exposed, how can you determine the probability that one *or* two persons have been exposed?

Section 11.4

22. (a) Event A can occur in three ways, so there are three branches of the probability tree diagram to consider.
    (c) What are the elements of the event $A \cap B$?
    (d) Use the property of probability that gives a formula for calculating $P(A \cup B)$.

(e) Use the definition of conditional probability given in this section.

23. (a) How many students won awards?
    (f) Use the definition of conditional probability given in this section of the text.

24. (b) For the American League team to win in four games, they must win the first and win the second and win the third and win the fourth games. Think of a tree diagram.
    (d) If the series ends in four games, it means the American League team won in four games or the National League team won in four games.
    (e) Remember that if the odds in favor of an event are $a{:}b$, then the probability of the event occurring is $\dfrac{a}{a+b}$.

25. (a) The probability of each sequence is the same. Think of a probability tree diagram.
    (c) If the series ends in five games, it means the American League team won in five games or the National League team won in five games.

26. (a) The probability of any sequence of 4 As and 2 Ns is the same. Think of the probability tree diagram described in the problem.
    (c) If the series ends in six games, it means the American League team won in six games or the National League team won in six games.

* An additional hint for this problem is given in the next section.

27. (a) Same as the hints for problem 26 except the sequences will consist of 4 As and 3 Ns.

28. (b) Remember that if the odds in favor of an event are $a : b$, then the probability of the event occurring is $\dfrac{a}{a+b}$.

   (c) Remember that the expected value of an experiment is given by the following sum:
   $$E = v_1 p_1 + v_2 p_2 + \cdots + v_n p_n.$$
   In this problem, $v_i =$ number of games in the series and $p_i =$ probability that the series endsin that many games.

29. When performing the simulation many times, find the average number of selections needed to get all five toys.

30. Starting with any one point, how many possible segments can be drawn from that point? *

Chapter 12
Section 12.1

12. In each case analyze what has been done to the first picture in order to obtain the second.

13. If the given image was flipped across the dotted line, what would the resulting figure look like?

14. Try looking at just one half of the figure.

15. Try drawing just one half of the figure at a time.

16. (a) Try drawing just one half of the figure at a time. *

   (b) Think backward. Consider how the final figure was obtained in part (a). *

17. Try using a ruler or folding the paper to check your answer.

18. Try covering up part of the figures when comparing lengths.

19. Copy each map and try coloring or numbering each region.

20. Use a ruler and/or protractor to attempt to draw the parallel or perpendicular lines on triangular dot paper.

21. Copy the triangular lattice on your paper. Using a ruler and/or protractor, draw parallel or perpendicular sides of quadrilaterals as needed. Be sure to check the lengths of sides. *

22. Examine one row of the lattice at a time. How many figures of each type can be drawn, for example, using as vertices the points in the first row? *

23. Rotate your tracing to see if the diagonals coincide.

Section 12.2

11. You might find graph paper useful here. *

12. Try cutting the shapes out of graph paper and fitting them together. Or you might draw a 5 by 8 rectangle on graph paper and try to fill it with tetrominos. *

*** An additional hint for this problem is given in the next section.*

13. Rotate your tracing until it coincides with the original figure. In how many ways can you turn it so that the two figures coincide?

14. Rotate your tracing until it coincides with the original figure. In how many ways can you turn it so that the two figures coincide?

15. Consider all properties of the diagonals, not just length.

Section 12.3

13. Which angle measures add up to equal $m(\angle AFD)$? *

14. How can $m(\angle 1)$ be represented in terms of $m(\angle 2)$?

15. What angles are congruent to $\angle 1$? Use the parallel lines and vertical angles. *

16. You may use the Corresponding Angles Property. That is, if corresponding angles are congruent, then the lines are parallel. *

17. (a)-(b) Use vertical angles and the Corresponding-Angles Property.

18. The Corresponding Angles Property states that if lines are cut by a transversal so that corresponding angles are congruent, then the lines are parallel. What are some pairs of corresponding angles? *

19. How do the measures of the angles compare?

20. Make a table and look for a pattern. *

21. Does the measure of $\angle ADB$ depend upon the location of point D?

22. Review the definitions of acute, obtuse, and equiangular triangles. Carefully check the triangles you draw to see if they fit the criteria.

Section 12.4

22. Tracing paper may be helpful here.

23. Notice that each small triangle in the figure is a right triangle. *

24. Use the fact that the sum of the angle measures in a triangle is 180°. Look at both large and small triangles in the figure. *

25. Draw pictures to complete the table. Be careful not to count diagonals more than once. *

26. Try a simpler problem. What if there were only 4 people in the room? Only 5 people? *

27. What is the measure of each angle of the regular pentagon in the center of the star? *

28. Use the fact that the angles meeting at any vertex add up to 360°.

29. Draw the polygons on tracing paper so they can be overlapped and viewed easily. Do not limit your investigation to regular polygons.

30. (a) Does the sum of the measures of the five angles vary as the shape of the star changes?
    (b) What is the sum of the measures of the angles of the polygon in the interior of the star?

31. In each part you might find it helpful to start drawing from the center of the hexagon. *

*** An additional hint for this problem is given in the next section.**

Section 12.5

17.   Do you see the small cube inside or outside the larger figure?

18.   You might count the cubes in each layer, keeping in mind that some cubes are hidden.

19.   Notice the direction of each letter shown on the original cube.

20.   It might be helpful to use blocks or dice to build the stacks of cubes. Then look at the stack from each direction.

21.   The bottom row of each base design describes how many cubes lie above each square in the front row of the figure.

22.   You might look at the shape on top of the cube. What side would be adjacent to it if the figure at the left were folded? Consider the orientation, too. You might also find it helpful to construct a paper model and fold it to form a model of a cube.

23.   Use a piece of clay, a block, a die, or a sugar cube as a model. Not all of the planes of symmetry are horizontal or vertical.

24.   Notice that the axis of rotational symmetry shown passes through two opposite faces of the cube. You may find a block, a die, a sugar cube, or other model of a cube helpful.

25.   (a) Try turning a block, a die, or other model of a cube to check this out. Mark the top face, if necessary.

(b)   How many pairs of opposite vertices are there in a cube?

26.   (a) Use a block, a die, a sugar cube, or other model of a cube in order to try rotating on this axis. Mark the top face, if necessary.
      (b) How many different pairs of opposite edges are there in a cube?

27.   Cut the cardboard center of a paper towel roll along the lines and see what shape results when you unroll the tube.

28.   It might be helpful to start by making a cube out of clay. Experiment by making some slices to see what shapes result.   *

Chapter 13
Section 13.1

23.   Use dimensional analysis. You can form a unit ratio using the fact that 1 gallon of water weighs about 8.3 pounds.

24.   Use dimensional analysis. How many microliters of blood are in one liter?

25.   Use dimensional analysis to perform the necessary conversion in each part of the problem.

26.   See the descriptions of portability, convertibility, and interrelatedness in your textbook.   *

27.   (a) Use dimensional analysis to convert from miles per second to miles per year.

---

*   *An additional hint for this problem is given in the next section.*

28. Since both trains are moving at 50 mph, the resultant rate is actually 100 mph. *

29. (a) How many square feet are in one acre? Use dimensional analysis to convert from acres to square feet.
    (b) Use dimensional analysis to convert from cubic feet to pounds.
    (c) Use dimensional analysis to convert from pounds to gallons.

30. (a) Draw a new ruler with marks at only 1, 4, and 6 units. How can you measure with it?
    (b)-(c) Consider the new ruler you made for part (a). How might a similar ruler be constructed for each of these two problems?

31. (a) First determine the number of cubic feet in a cord of wood. *
    (b) How much money would the son make in one day?
    (c) How many cubic feet of wood are cut in one day?
    (d) You could solve this problem using a proportion:
    $$\frac{\$85}{100\,\text{ft}^3} = \frac{?}{?}. \ *$$

32. How does the time required to hike uphill compare to the time required to hike downhill? *

33. Use dimensional analysis. Express your final answer in years, not minutes.

34. Use dimensional analysis to convert the height of the stack of hamburgers to miles.

Section 13.2

27. Because the building is perpendicular to the ground, you may apply the Pythagorean theorem.

28. Express the area of the enclosure in terms of x and y. *

29. Visualize the hypotenuse of a right triangle.

30. The area of the large figure equals the sum of the areas of its parts. *

31. Use the Pythagorean theorem.

32. Use the Pythagorean theorem. *

33. (b) Determine the number of boundary points, b, and the number of inside points, i.

34. Use a variable for the width of the rectangle. What variable expression would represent the length of the rectangle?

35. Is it possible to draw a triangle with two sides congruent? With all three sides congruent?

36. If $a^2 + b^2 = c^2$, then a triangle with sides of lengths a, b, and c is a right triangle. What type of triangle is it if $a^2 + b^2 > c^2$?

37. Remember that Hero's formula uses the lengths of the sides of a triangle to find the area of a triangle. *

38. (a) How are the 7.5° angle and the angle at the center of the earth related?

An additional hint for this problem is given in the next section.

(b) You can use a proportion here:

$$\frac{500 \text{ mi}}{7.5°} = \frac{?}{?}.$$

39. The diameter of the hole is also the diagonal of the square. Use a variable to find the length of the sides of the square.

40. Draw a right triangle in the figure by connecting the center of the smaller circle to point *B*. Label the lengths of the sides of the triangle using a variable. *

41. What is the total area of all four semicircles in the drawing? What is the total area of the square? *

42. Find the total area inside the circle(s) and inside the square. *

43. Use a variable to represent the width of one ring.

44. Note that the price *per square centimeter* is the same.

45. For each triangle draw the height to the horizontal base. Notice that right triangles are formed.

46. Use dimensional analysis. Be careful when using square units.

47. Use right triangles and squares to cover the white-filled shape and then compare areas.

Section 13.3

13. First find the areas of all surfaces to be painted. Then use dimensional analysis.

14. Use dimensional analysis. Remember that surface area is

measured in square units, so the scale must be adjusted.

15. Use wooden cubes, plastic cubes, or sugar cubes, if available. *

16. Use variables or choose any dimensions you like for the original box. Then determine its surface area. What happens to the surface area of the box if you double the dimensions?

17. Remember that the volume of a sphere is given by $V = \frac{4}{3}\pi r^3$ and the surface area is given by $S = 4\pi r^2$. *

18. Use a variable or choose any radius for the sphere. Then calculate its surface area. What happens to the surface area when you reduce the radius by half?

19. What is the circumference of the cylinder?

20. The sphere must touch the top, bottom, and sides of the cylinder. *

Section 13.4

12. Use wooden cubes, plastic cubes, or sugar cubes, if available. When you are calculating the surface area, remember to count only the exposed faces.

13. Each shape has a cut made in it. Find the volume of the figure without the cut.

14. (a) Use a variable to represent the radius of one tennis ball. How

An additional hint for this problem is given in the next section.

might you represent the height of the can?

(b) First find the volume of the can and of the tennis balls.

15. How do you calculate the volume of any prism?

16. Find the volume of the cylinder.

17. The Great Wall of China forms a giant prism. *

18. How do you calculate the volume and lateral surface area of any pyramid?

19. (a)-(b) Think of the pipe as a cylinder. Be sure to use consistent units when calculating the volumes.

20. Use dimensional analysis. Remember that volume is measured in cubic units, so the scale must be adjusted.

21. (a) If the inside diameter is 60 feet, what is the capacity of the spherical tank?

22. What is the inside radius of the sphere? *

23. (a) By how much did the volume of water in the aquarium increase? *

    (b) What is the total volume of the marbles?

24. Draw a picture of a right square prism, labeling the dimensions. Write expressions representing the volume and surface area. Do the same for a new prism in which all dimensions have been doubled.

25. (a) Assume the height is unchanged. Try an example or

use variables for the radius and height of the cylinder.

26. Which arrangement provides the largest opening for water to pass through?

27. (b) Use the formula for the volume of a cube and solve for s, where s = length of an edge of the cube.

28. How much larger is the big circle cut by the post hole digger than the small circle?

29. First find the volume of the original tank.

30. For which solid does the volume formula contain only one variable? Use the fact that each solid has the same volume. *

31. Be sure that you have the correct dimensions for each piece of lumber. That is, are the dimensions exact?

32. (a)-(c) Use a model. Experiment with ten blocks, dice, or sugar cubes, summarizing your results in a table.

Chapter 14
Section 14.1

9. Check corresponding sides and angles. If there is only angle or one side marked, is it *included*?

10. Check corresponding sides and angles. If there is only angle or one side labeled, is it *included*?

An additional hint for this problem is given in the next section.

11.   Check corresponding sides and angles. If there is only angle or one side marked, is it *included*?

12.   (a) Is the given angle included?
       (c) Refer to your answer in part (b).

13.   Use a protractor and a ruler to draw these triangles accurately.

14.   (a) What distances did the hikers step off to be equal? *
       (b) Which congruence property holds?
       (c) Use congruent triangles. *

15.   (a) Try to draw two noncongruent triangles with three corresponding angles congruent or with two sides and an angle congruent.
       (b)-(d) Consider the possibilities. For example, with four corresponding parts congruent, you might have three sides and one angle. What would that tell you about the two triangles?

16.   (b) Use the fact that you were given $\angle ABC \cong \angle WXY$. Also, from part (a) you know that $\angle 2 \cong \angle 6$.
       (c) From part (b) and the given information, you have two corresponding parts congruent. What other congruent parts would show the triangles congruent?
       (d) Use the same kind of argument you used for part (b).

17.   Use a variable. Let $m(\angle D) = x$. Then what could be used to represent $m(\angle E)$? *

18.   Use the result proved in Example 14.3 of this section.

19.   Pay careful attention to whether the given angle is *between* the two given sides as you construct different triangles.

Section 14.2

10.   (a) What conditions must be satisfied for a quadrilateral to be a parallelogram?
       (b) Use your result from part (a).
       (c) Use your result from part (b).

11.   (a) What similar triangles are formed by the parallel lines and transversals?
       (b) Write a proportion using corresponding sides of ΔPAD and ΔPBE.
       (c) Write a proportion using corresponding sides of ΔPAD and ΔPCF.
       (d) Use your results from parts (b) and (c).
       (e) Use your results from parts (b) and (d).

12.   (a) What segments on transversals n and o correspond to $\overline{AB}$ and $\overline{BC}$?

13.   Draw a picture and use similar triangles.

14.   When light is reflected, the angle of incidence is congruent to the angle of reflection.

15.   (b) Draw a picture and label the known measures. You will have two right triangles embedded in the same figure.

16.   (a)-(b) Form a proportion using the distance from the projector and the thumb height.

***   An additional hint for this problem is given in the next section.***

17. Draw a picture. Remember that the triangle will be at eye level and lines up with the point on the trunk at which you will cut the tree. *

18. What triangles are similar in the drawing? What corresponding sides include the segment $\overline{BD}$?

19. Try several examples of pairs of right triangles. Compare the areas of the triangles. *

20. There are three pairs of similar triangles contained in the drawing. Can you name them? Which pair yields a proportion involving the sides with lengths x, a, and 1?

21. First use a proportion to find CE. *

22. There are three right triangles in the figure. Use the AA Similarity Property to show the triangles are similar. *

23. (d) Make a table and examine what happens to one side of the original triangle as n increases.*

24. (d) Make a table and examine what happens to the area added on to one side of the original triangle as the value of n increases. *

Section 14.3

10. There is more than one way to construct some of these angles.
    (a) If lines are perpendicular, then a right angle is formed.
    (b) An angle of $45°$ is half of a $90°$ angle.
    (c) An angle of $135°$ is half of a $270°$ angle.
    (d) An angle of $67.5°$ is half of a $135°$ angle.

11. Construct perpendicular bisectors to locate the midpoints of the sides.

12. Start by choosing a side and constructing a perpendicular to that side through the vertex opposite the side.

13. First choose a length to represent one unit. *

14. (a) Use compass and straightedge to copy $\overline{BC}$ three times to create a segment of length $3a$.
    (c) How are the sides of the two triangles related?

15. To construct a new triangle with $\angle P \cong \angle A$, use the Copy an Angle construction.

16. Draw medians and angle bisectors in several types of triangles such as scalene triangles, isosceles triangles, etc.

17. Keep in mind that an angle bisector is a segment through a vertex that cuts the vertex angle in half, while a median is a segment through a vertex that cuts the opposite side in half.

18. Draw perpendicular bisectors and medians in several types of triangles such as scalene triangles, isosceles triangles, etc.

19. A perpendicular bisector passes through the midpoint of a side and is perpendicular to it. A median also passes through the midpoint of a side but is drawn from the opposite vertex.

An additional hint for this problem is given in the next section.

20. Construct the perpendicular bisector of a segment $\overline{AB}$ following the procedure given in the textbook. Note the radii used for your arcs. Label the points of intersection as in the given figure. Draw in segments $\overline{AP}$, $\overline{BP}$, $\overline{AQ}$, and $\overline{BQ}$. *

21. The bisector of $\angle A$ divides the triangle into two triangles. By what congruence property will the two triangles be congruent? *

Section 14.4

12. There is more than one way to construct some of these angles.
    (a) An angle of 15° is half an angle of 30°.
    (b) How might 75° be written as the sum of two angles you know how to construct?
    (c) How might 105° be written as the sum of two angles you know how to construct?

13. First construct a perpendicular bisector to create a right angle.

14. Recall that the golden ratio is

    $\dfrac{1+\sqrt{5}}{2}$.

15. (c) Does the circumcenter lie inside, outside, or on a side of the triangle in each case?

16. (c) Does the circumcenter lie inside, outside, or on a side of the triangle in each case?

17. Measure each side and angle of the triangle $C_1C_2C_3$.

18. Examine the construction given in Example 14.10 in the textbook. Notice that if $PQ = a$ and $PS = b$, then $PT = ab$. If the product of the lengths (or ab) and the length of one of the segments (say a) were known, then the other length (b) could be constructed. *

19. (a) If $\dfrac{a}{x} = \dfrac{x}{b}$, $a = 1$, and $b = 2$, then what is the value of x?
    (b) What segments in the drawing or in your construction are congruent by construction? What triangles in the drawing are congruent? *

20. Think of the edge of the lined paper as a transversal. The parallel lines on the page intercept congruent segments on that transversal. *

Section 14.5

1. (b) What do you know about the base angles of an isosceles triangle?
   (f) What is the definition of the perpendicular bisector of a line segment?

2. Use the definition of a rhombus.

3. What is the definition of a square? That is, what must be shown to verify that $STUV$ is a square? *

4. Show that $\triangle ABE \cong \triangle CDE$. *

5. Since the diagonal of a parallelogram cuts it into two triangles, you can complete part of the construction of the parallelogram by using the SSS construction for a triangle.

---

*   *An additional hint for this problem is given in the next section.*

6. Use congruent triangles to show that $\angle STU \cong \angle TSV$.

7. See the hint for problem 5.

8. Try sketching an isosceles trapezoid first. Label the bases and the legs. If you draw perpendiculars from the endpoints of the shorter base to the longer base, what do you notice about the triangles formed? *

9. What does it mean for AC to be the geometric mean of AD and AB? How can this fact be stated in terms of ratios of corresponding sides of triangles? *

10. (a)-(c) What additional conditions must be met for a parallelogram to be a rectangle, rhombus, or square? How do those conditions affect the diagonals of $PQRS$?

11. Identify congruent angles in the drawing in order to determine which pairs of corresponding sides are referred to in the proportions given, such as, $\dfrac{b}{x} = \dfrac{x+y}{b}$. *

12. (a) What is the geometric definition of a kite? *
    (b) Find the area of the kite by dividing the kite into triangles whose areas are easily found.

13. You are given that $\triangle ABC$ and $\triangle A'B'C'$ have three pairs of corresponding sides congruent. But, you must show that the triangles are congruent without using the SSS Congruence Property. *

14. Assume that $\dfrac{AC}{AB} \neq \dfrac{A'C'}{A'B'}$. As stated, there must be a point D' on $\overline{A'C'}$ where $\dfrac{AC}{AB} \neq \dfrac{A'D'}{A'B'}$. What triangles must then be similar by the SAS Similarity Property? Remember you were given that $\angle A \cong \angle A'$ and $\angle B \cong \angle B'$. *

15. When finding the areas of the triangles, let the base in each case be the side of the square. What is the height in each case? *

16. Be sure to try several different sizes and types of quadrilaterals and their midquads.

Chapter 15
Section 15.1

15. What conditions must be met in order for a quadrilateral to be a rectangle?

16. Remember that a rectangle is also a parallelogram, a square is also a rhombus, and so on.

17. Consider both the lengths of the sides and the measures of the angles in the triangles.

18. Click and drag to change the slope of one line.

19. (a) Redraw the picture on graph paper, placing the base of the pole at the origin.
    (b) Use the Pythagorean theorem.

20. First find the slope of the ramp and then express that result as a percent grade.

An additional hint for this problem is given in the next section.

21. (a) Note that $\overline{PO}$ and $\overline{RT}$ are both horizontal and thus parallel.
    (b) What do you know about the corresponding sides of similar triangles?

22. Remember that if P, M, and Q are collinear with M between P and Q, then $PM + MQ = PQ$. Use the distance formula and the given coordinates for P, M, and Q to show that this relationship holds.

23. Draw x-, y- and z-axes as shown. Mark units on each of your axes. If the x-coordinate of a point is positive, move forward that many units along the x-axis. If the y-coordinate is positive, move right.

Section 15.2

22. The center of the circle is the circumcenter of the triangle, the point of intersection of the perpendicular bisectors of the sides of the triangle. *

23. For each pair of vertices, write the equation of the line that passes through those points.

24. Point D is the midpoint of side $\overline{BC}$.

25. The altitude $\overline{PT}$ is perpendicular to the line containing side $\overline{RS}$. *

26. (b) Look at your last entry in the table of part (a).
    (c)-(d) Remember that if the equation of a line is written as $y = mx + b$, then the slope is the coefficient of x, which is m.

27. What do you know about the slopes and y-intercepts of the two lines if the system of two linear equations has no solution, exactly one solution, or infinitely many solutions?

28. Sketch x- and y-axes. Remember that the initial side of the angle lies on the positive x-axis; that is, you will measure the angle starting from the positive x-axis.

29. Note that the distance from P to D will be $\sqrt{x^2 + (b - y)^2}$. You need to find the value of this expression. You do *not* need to determine the values of x, y, or b. *

30. Use a variable and write equations to represent total cost and total revenue. *

31. What are the shapes of the graphs of the two equations? In how many points might the graphs intersect?

Section 15.3

1. Start by plotting the three given points. *

2. There is only one correct position for the fourth vertex for each set of coordinates.

3. Keep in mind the lengths of the sides of each figure when finding the missing coordinates.

4. Use the lengths of the sides of the triangle to specify the coordinates of the vertices. Remember that it is a right triangle.

---

* An additional hint for this problem is given in the next section.

5. (a) Start by plotting point X at the origin. *
    (b) First plot points X and Z on the x-axis. *

6. Determine the slopes of all four sides of $RSTU$.

7. First determine the slopes of all four sides of $ABCD$. *

8. You will need to use the midpoint formula, the slope formula, and the coordinate distance formula here.

9. Use the coordinate distance formula and the given coordinates to show the lengths of the diagonals are the same.

10. (a) To find the equation of the line containing the median from vertex A, first find the midpoint of side $\overline{CB}$. *
    (d) Solve simultaneous equations.

11. Find the lengths of the diagonals by using the coordinate distance formula.

12. (a) Write $AB = BC$ using the distance formula and the given coordinates for points A, B, and C.
    (b) Find the slopes of $\overline{AC}$ and the median from vertex B. *

13. (a) Remember that the altitude from vertex R will be perpendicular to side $\overline{ST}$. What does this mean in terms of slope? *
    (d) Solve simultaneous equations.

14. What does it mean for the diagonals of a parallelogram to "bisect each other"? *

15. (a)-(c) Remember that if a line has slope a, where $a \neq 0$, then any line perpendicular to it must have slope $\dfrac{-1}{a}$.
    (b) Solve simultaneous equations.

16. Consider the possible lengths of the horizontal side. *

17. Try using variables to represent each of the girls' ages.

18. Try using variables. For example, let $x=$ number of bicycles that passed the house.

19. Try using a variable to represent Mike's investment and a variable to represent Joan's investment.

20. Try letting $x =$ number of quarters spent and $y =$ number of dimes spent.

21. Try a simpler problem. Examine a smaller grid or look at a portion of the grid shown. *
    (c) Use your results from parts (a) and (b).

Chapter 16
Section 16.1

29. What will each type of transformation do to point A? *

30. Not all of these are possible. *

31. (a)-(c) Plot the triangle and its image in each case. *

32. Try moving the center of rotation to various positions, being sure to

An additional hint for this problem is given in the next section.

place it at different distances from the original figure.

33. Try several examples with the same scale factor, but move the center of the size transformation closer to the original figure. Then choose a new scale factor and again move the center.

Section 16.2

15. (a) See the argument associated with figure 16.26 in the textbook.
    (b) Think about how to show that three points are collinear using slopes. This argument will be similar.

16. See the argument in the textbook that isometries preserve angle measure.

17. Remember that rotations are isometries and that isometries preserve angle measure. See the argument in the textbook. *

18. Remember that points A, B, and C are collinear and point B is between points A and C if, and only if, $AB + BC = AC$.

19. Sketch lines p' and q' and then draw a transversal that intersects them. Which angles must be congruent to angles 1 and 2? *

20. See the argument associated with Figure 16.30 of the textbook, which shows that $\triangle PQR \cong \triangle P'Q'R'$.

21. Draw several examples for each case, if possible. Note angles and centers of rotation, etc. *

22. How do you locate the center of the size transformation? The figures showing size transformations in this section of the textbook might be helpful here.

23. First find the center of the size transformation, point P. *

24. What segments are congruent if l is the line of reflection? Can you use those segments to show a pair of triangles congruent? *

25. What happens when an object is reflected twice, across two parallel lines?

Section 16.3

1. (a) First find P', the image of point P under half-turn, H_A.*
   (b) Note that these are the same half-turns as in part(a) applied in reverse order.

2. Remember that any isometry preserves distance.

3. What is a rotation followed by a size transformation?

4. To verify that $\triangle ABC \cong \triangle ADC$, you must show that $\triangle ABC$ is mapped onto $\triangle ADC$ under the transformation.

5. What lines of symmetry does the rectangle have?

6. What lines of symmetry does the regular hexagon have?

7. What line(s) of symmetry does the isosceles trapezoid have?

8. (a) How have the two red regions been shifted?

---

* *An additional hint for this problem is given in the next section.*

(b) How has the entire red region been shifted?

(c) Consider the bases and heights of the two parallelograms in Figure (3) and Figure (4).

(d) Where did the red regions in Figure (5) originally come from?

9. Let M be the midpoint of diagonal $\overline{AC}$. What are the images of points A, C, and D, under the half-turn centered at M? *

10. Use corresponding parts of congruent triangles.

11. What is the image of point A under the reflection M_{BP}?

12. (a) Draw in the diagonals of the kite. Look at one of the triangles formed and use the result from problem 11.

(b) What does it mean for a polygon to have reflection symmetry? *

13. (a) What is the image of A' under the reflection M_S? How does this point relate to point A? *

(b) Use the variables x and y. *

14. (a) Choose two intersecting sides, say the bottom and the right-hand side. Reflect B across the right-hand side to a point B'. Then reflect B' across the extension of the bottom of the pool table.

(b) Refer to Example 16.14. *

15. What size transformation could be used to "shrink" square $ABCD$ so that its image $A'B'C'D'$ is congruent to $EFGH$? *

*** An additional hint for this problem is given in the next section.**

ADDITIONAL HINTS - PART A PROBLEMS

Chapter 1
Section 1.1

2. You can also use the Guess and Test strategy here.

6. Remember that you might not use all of the symbols.

8. The stools need not be evenly spaced along the walls.

13. The timers can be run repeatedly.

14. (b) By how much can the hundreds digits of the two numbers differ? Which digits in the tens and units place will make the two numbers have close to the same value?

15. Notice that the inner two squares touch more squares than squares in any other position. What might you conclude about which digits to place there?

16. What values could the letter U have?

20. Try using the first few terms to get a sum that differs from 100 by only 1 or 2.

23. In your lists of possibilities for each circle, notice the numbers that work for both of the overlapping circles.

24. Notice that each corner dot belongs to two sides.

Section 1.2

2. How does each term compare to the previous one? Is there a common difference or a common ratio?

9. You will need to look at more than one set of differences.

11. Try adding 1 to each total paid to date. Do you see a pattern in the results?

13. For each column, consider the difference between every other number.

19. (d) What do all terms but the first term have in common?

20. In attempting to write a positive integer as a sum of 9s and 4s, you might first consider how many 9s could be in the sum.

Chapter 2
Section 2.1

34. How many different elements of B could be paired with one in A?

35. Make a table comparing the number of elements in the set to the number of subsets and look for a pattern.

40. Try drawing line segments connecting some points on $\overline{AC}$ with points on $\overline{AB}$.

42. Start with the innermost region and be sure not to count any persons twice.

Section 2.2

19. See the formula developed in problem 6(f) of Section 1.2A.

Section 2.3

26. More than one answer is possible for part (d).

29. Let the number be represented by $10a + b$, where a and b are the tens and units digits, respectively.

Chapter 3
Section 3.1

17. Choose a row, column, or diagonal containing two numbers. What must be the sum of the two missing numbers? Look for combinations of unused numbers with this sum.

19. (b) See if you can find a relationship between the sum of the two digits in a number and the number of steps required to obtain a palindrome.

Section 3.2

24. (a) Remember that each row sum is the same. Once you know what that sum is, use guess and test to place the digits.
     (b) Remember that when you multiply powers together, you add the exponents.

29. In this problem there are actually three unknowns: the number of cups of tea per person, the number of cakes per person, and the number of persons in the group.

Section 3.3

17. What kind of sequence do the candy bar prices form?

19. How can you relate the number of terms on the left-hand side of each equation to the terms on the right-hand side?

20. You might name your four toppings and consider that each topping either is or is not included on a given pizza.

23. (a) What happens if you add c to both sides of this equation?

Chapter 4
Section 4.1

27. Consider the magnitude of the factors and look at the final digit in the product.

31. To verify the result in general, represent the number as $10a + 5$ and then square.

38. Look for a pattern in the kinds of products for which this shortcut works. How are the units digits related?

39. Be sure to specify what happens to every digit of the number when you round using this method.

Section 4.2

36. Notice that the sum of the first two digits must be 9 or less.

42. "Carries" will be required in each column so that the sums in each column will differ.

Section 4.3

19. Imagine base pieces: units, longs, and flats.

Chapter 5
Section 5.1

16. See the justification for divisibility by 2 in this section of the text.

17. Examine what factors appear on the right-hand side. How do they compare with the number you are testing as a divisor, or with the factors of that number?

22. Look for a pattern in the relationship between the number of 1s in the number and its factors.

33. Let n = the first of the three consecutive counting numbers. Then what expressions would represent the next two counting numbers? The next three numbers?

34. Let a = the first number and b = the second number. Then the sequence of numbers will look like this: $a, b, a + b, a + 2b,$....What is the seventh number? What is the sum of all ten numbers?

36. What factor do all the terms in your expression have in common?

37. If you subtract 7 from a number and the result is divisible by 7, then the original number must have been divisible by 7.

38. If 1 were subtracted from the number of cupcakes, the result would be divisible by 2, 3, 4, 5, and 6.

39. Combine like terms and factor.

40. (a) To use the divisibility test for 11, add the digits with place values that are odd powers of 10 and add the digits with place values that are even powers of 10.

42. If 7 divides 1001, then 7 will divide any number or expression that has 1001 as a factor.

44. Look for terms that have a common factor of 11.

Section 5.2

21. Refer to the theorem stated in this section.

22. Remember you are to find the smallest number with a certain number of factors. So you want to choose the smallest possible prime factors and the fewest of them.

23. To characterize the sets of numbers, look at the prime factorization of the numbers.

27. Use systematic guess and test to find the solution. There is only one whole-number solution to the problem. Remember that the price cannot be a fraction of a dollar nor can it be negative.

28. What do you know about the prime factors of a perfect square?

30. Find the sum of the two numbers and combine like terms.

Chapter 6
Section 6.1

31. Try using a common denominator other than the least common denominator.

Section 6.2

21. Let t = number of years John lived.

26. (c) Compare the last term in the denominator to n.

32. Another approach might be to solve a simpler problem. Suppose there were only four players. Name them and list all the pairings that would be required.

Section 6.3

28. Let x = the number of barrels of oil refined in the U.S. in 2007.

29. Let x = the total number of students enrolled.

30. Suppose that each gallon of water required exactly two ounces of concentrate. What operation would you perform to determine the number of gallons of mix that could be made?

31. Use a variable. Let x = the number of employees originally enrolled in the fitness program.

32. What fraction of the trip does Tammy make between the grocery store and the bicycle shop?

34. To use a variable, try letting x = the total number of games played.

35. (b) Calculate the value of the equipment for each of several years until the value is less than $40,000.

36. If n = the first number, then the first number divided by one more than itself will be represented by the expression $\dfrac{n}{n+1}$. What must this equal?

40. Let s = the son's current age. Then his age seven years ago was $s - 7$.

41. What part of $\dfrac{3}{5}$ is left over?

Chapter 7
Section 7.1

18. What must the sum in each row be?

19. You can use a variable to represent the necessary increase in her hourly wage.

Section 7.2

16. If a number is divisible by only 2 or 5, what digits must it end in?

17. Write the prime factorization of the denominators of some fractions in simplest form whose decimal representations terminate. Look for a pattern.

22. (a) If a decimal has 1, 2, 3, or 4 digits in the repetend, what must the denominator of the corresponding fraction be when it is completely simplified?

23. Make a table listing which digit appears in which position. For example, for $\dfrac{1}{13}$:

Position of digit	digit
First	0
Second	7
Third	6
$\vdots$	$\vdots$

Look for a pattern in when the 6s appear, etc.

24. What happens when you multiply a decimal by 10 or 100?

25. Think of how you multiply fractions: $\dfrac{a}{b} \times \dfrac{c}{d} = \dfrac{ac}{bd}$.

32. If the price of a book has increased by 0.03 since last year, what multiple of last year's price is this year's price?

Section 7.3

19. Be sure to be consistent with the units in the problem.

20. You could use a proportion like:

$$\frac{\text{length of model}}{\text{wingspan of model}} = \frac{\text{length of plane}}{\text{wingspan of plane}}.$$

21. (a) How many teachers would be needed for a teacher : student ratio of 1 : 20?
    (b) Cost per pupil = (total cost) ÷ (number of pupils).

22. (b) You can write a proportion in a form such as one of the following:

$$\frac{\text{AU distance}}{\text{AU distance}} = \frac{\text{distance in miles}}{\text{distance in miles}}$$
or
$$\frac{\text{AU distance}}{\text{distance in miles}} = \frac{\text{AU distance}}{\text{distance in miles}}.$$

23. (d)-(f) Use your results from parts (a) - (c). For example, you know the number of years corresponding to one second. So, for part (e), you could write:

$$\frac{\text{seconds}}{\text{years}} = \frac{\text{seconds}}{\text{years}}.$$

A time line labeled in both years and hours might be helpful.

24. How does the time required for the trip at 60 mph compare to the time required for the trip at 30 mph?

28. You could also solve this problem by using a variable. Let x = amount of money in the man's pocket when he entered the store. Work forward in this case.

30. You might find it helpful to solve a simpler problem first. Suppose you started with 20 or 30 instead of 100.

32. How many lengths between posts have been covered in the 8 seconds?

Section 7.4

16. (a) Use a variable to determine the amount of the original investment.

17. If you pay 15 days before the due date, you pay no interest.

24. Use a variable. Let x = the original price of the car.

26. If 3 grams of protein is 4% of the U. S. RDA, how many grams are recommended per day?

27. Once the slacks were made longer, what would be the length of the slacks after washing, assuming that they shrink by 10%?

28. If you want to verify your result in general, use a variable. Let x = the initial price of an item.

33. If the population increased by 2.8% during 2004, what percent of the population at the start of 2004 was the population at the start of 2005?

34. Try going first and going second. What configurations do you want to leave your partner in order to win?

38. How many times will their savings increase by 8.25%?

40. Is there a salary that gives a maximum net earnings?

42. If the man's age at death was $\dfrac{1}{29}$ of his birth year, the year of his birth must be divisible by 29.

Chapter 8
Section 8.1

20. To show that the missing-addend approach holds, you must show:
    (1) If $a - b = c$, then $a = b + c$.
    (2) If $a = b + c$, then $a - b = c$.

22. Start with the middle row. What must be the sum of the two missing numbers?

23. (d) What relationship do you see between the set A and the two numbers that were given as elements of A?

26. Remember that the large figure is a rectangle, and the opposite sides of a rectangle have the same length.

Section 8.2

30. Remember that all rows, columns, and diagonals must yield the same product.

31. Notice that the problem states that both x and y are positive integers.

33. (a) How many seconds are there in one month?

34. What is the maximum number of cows that could be purchased with $1000?

35. Each whole number x must be of the form $3n$, $3n + 1$, or $3n + 2$. Try each possibility to see what form x^2 takes in each case.

Chapter 9
Section 9.1

35. Begin with the left-hand side of the equality and show it is equal to the right-hand side.

36. Start by assuming $\dfrac{a}{b} < \dfrac{c}{d}$, and try to show that $\dfrac{a}{b} + \dfrac{e}{f} < \dfrac{c}{d} + \dfrac{e}{f}$.

37. What fraction, $\dfrac{e}{f}$, added to $\dfrac{a}{b}$ gives 0?

38. You might find a diagram useful here. Try drawing line segments to represent time on each of the two timers.

Section 9.2

26. Start by assuming that $\sqrt{3}$ is rational, i. e., that there is a rational number $\dfrac{a}{b} = \sqrt{3}$. Then square both sides and look at prime factors.

28. If a number is a perfect cube, what will its prime factorization look like?

29. Use the fact that $\sqrt{3}$ has already been shown to be irrational.

36. Notice that you do not know which two numbers to add, so you must consider three cases. Write equations to represent each case. You will obtain quadratic equations.

37. How would you represent the sum of the rational number and its reciprocal?

38. You might try using variables to represent the lengths of the original two pieces of wire.

39. It might by helpful to use a variable. Try letting x represent Mr. Milne's income. How might you represent Mr. Smith's income?

Section 9.3

16. Fraction equality is reflexive if $\dfrac{a}{b} = \dfrac{a}{b}$. What condition must besatisfied in order for this statement to be true?

22. (c) Try thinking of the number of triangles formed as a sum, rather than as a single number. That is, in step 2, think of $1 + 2$, rather than 3.

28. Use the formula for the nth term of a sequence of this type to solve for n.

Section 9.4

23. When would the cyclist's speed begin to increase?

Chapter 10
Section 10.1

25. (b) To write an equation of your regression line, choose two points on the line. They may or may not be data points in the scatter plot.

26.   Because you want to use the man's salary to predict the woman's salary, put the men's salaries on the *x*-axis.

Section 10.3

23.   You must recalculate the class average for 102 students.

26.   What information does each measure of central tendency convey?

Chapter 11
Section 11.1

24.   Let S = sample space and A = event the dart hits the bull's eye. Find $m(S)$ and $m(A)$.

Section 11.2

14.   In how many ways can the first digit be chosen? The second digit?

15.   (a) In how many ways can the winning horse be chosen? The second-place horse?

22.   (d) Remember that there is more than one way to get a matched pair.

25.   When a ball is picked at random from the second box, there are eleven balls in the box. Notice that there are two ways to choose a white ball from the second box.

26.   (a) Make a table. It may be helpful to consider the number of equilateral triangles of each size that are upright and the number that are upside down. Try to recognize a pattern.

Section 11.3

16.   (a) How can you avoid duplication in the ID numbers? That is, how can you account for the fact that there are three Gs, three Hs, and three Ss?

       (b) To avoid duplication you will need to divide out any arrangements that look the same.

17.   (a) In how many ways could Edwardo's initials be selected in *any* order?

22.   Remember that once the first chip is selected, it is not replaced. Thus, there are fewer choices for the second chip.

23.   Because all the letters must be different, once the first letter of the "word" is chosen, there are fewer choices for the second letter.

Section 11.4

30.   What happens when you draw all possible segments from a second point?

Chapter 12
Section 12.1

16.   (a) Remember that the paper will be unfolded in the opposite order from which it was folded.

       (b) There is more than one way to fold and punch to obtain these figures.

21. Remember that a rhombus is a parallelogram and a square is a rectangle.

22. Remember that a square is a rhombus, a rectangle, and a parallelogram. Also, remember that a rectangle is a parallelogram.

Section 12.2

11. More than one solution is possible.

12. More than one solution is possible.

Section 12.3

13. Remember that $m(\angle AFE) = 180°$.

15. Remember that the sum of the angle measures in a triangle is 180°.

16. Use vertical angles to find another angle that is congruent to $\angle 1$ or $\angle 2$.

18. What must you show to verify that quadrilateral *ABCD* is a parallelogram?

20. As each new line is added, how many lines does it intersect? How many regions does it divide?

Section 12.4

23. How do the areas of the shaded squares compare?

24. Notice that the angle with measure *a* is one angle of an isosceles triangle.

25. To find a general formula, compare the entries in the first two columns to the entries in the third column.

26. Make a table and look for a pattern in the relationship between the number of people and the number of handshakes.

27. What is the measure of the base angles in each triangle forming an "arm" of the star?

31. (b) Remember that a kite is not necessarily a rhombus.

Section 12.5

28. Remember that a regular tetrahedron has four congruent edges. An edge of the tetrahedron will be longer than an edge of the cube.

Chapter 13
Section 13.1

26. What is the standard for length in the English system? In terms of convertibility, consider the relationships between feet and inches, miles and feet, etc. Are similar ratios used?

28. Use dimensional analysis or use the formula Distance = Rate × Time.

31. (a) You can use dimensional analysis and perform all of the needed conversions at once. Start with the 48 ft^3 of wood cut per hour.
     (d) You can also solve this problem by using dimensional analysis.

32. Remember that you cannot average the speeds (2 kph and 6 kph) to find the average speed. You must divide the total distance traveled by the total elapsed time.

Section 13.2

28. Make a table listing possible values of x and y and the areas that would result.

30. What is the area of one of the right triangles? What is the area of the small square?

32. Take a look at your solution to the preceding problem.

37. Divide the quadrilateral into two triangles. To apply Hero's formula you will need to know the lengths of all three sides of each triangle.

40. Use the radii shown in your drawing to find the difference in the areas of the two circles.

41. If the sum of the areas of all four semicircles is calculated, what areas have been counted twice?

42. What fraction of the area inside the square is the area inside the circle(s)? What percent is that?

Section 13.3

15. When you calculate the surface area, remember to count only the faces of the cubes that are on the outside of the prism.

17. Notice that both formulas involve the radius, not the diameter, of a sphere.

20. How will the height of the cylinder be related to the diameter of the sphere?

Section 13.4

17. Remember that you were asked to find the answer in cubic yards.

22. What is the volume of the metal in the sphere?

23. (a) Be sure to be consistent with units.

30. In the cone, how are the radius, height, and slant height related?

Chapter 14
Section 14.1

14. (a) If D, B, and T are collinear, what pair of congruent angles is formed?
    (c) The width of the river is AT. What side of $\triangle CBD$ corresponds to side $\overline{AT}$ in $\triangle ABT$?

17. Use the fact that angles D and E are supplementary to write an equation in terms of x.

Section 14.2

17. What two triangles are similar in your picture?

19. Try using two variables. If b = base and h = height of the smaller triangle, what expressions could be used to represent the base and height of the larger triangle? Calculate the areas of the two triangles.

21. Notice that both triangles are right triangles. So, given two sides of one of the triangles, the third side can be found.

22.   Corresponding sides of similar triangles are proportional.

23.   (d) At each step in the process, a segment is broken into four shorter segments. How is the length of each of the shorter segments related to n?

24.   (d) At each step in the process, four smaller triangles are added on to each section of the figure. How is the area of one of these small triangles related to n?

Section 14.3

13.   To create a right angle, you can construct a perpendicular bisector.

20.   (a) Which segments must be congruent because of the radii used during your construction?
      (b) What pairs of angles are congruent because of the fact that $\triangle APQ \cong \triangle BPQ$, as found in part (a)?
      (c) What can be said about $\angle APR$ and $\angle BPR$ as a result of (b)?
      (d) What can be said about $\overline{AR}$ and $\overline{BR}$ as a result of part (b)?

21.   Remember that if two angles of a triangle are congruent to two corresponding angles of another triangle, then the third pair of corresponding angles is also congruent.

Section 14.4

18.   What is the product of a and its reciprocal, $\dfrac{1}{a}$? Use that product in place of the product ab in the construction. Consider two separate cases: (1) $a > 1$ and (2) $a < 1$.

19.   (b) What triangles in the figure are similar? You might find it helpful to look carefully at the proportion $\dfrac{a}{x} = \dfrac{x}{b}$, which is what you want to show. What triangles might lead to this proportion?

20.   What must be true about segments formed on any other transversal?

Section 14.5

3.   Example 14.12, in this section, may be useful here.

4.   Remember that opposite sides of a parallelogram are congruent.

8.   What is the length of the shorter leg of the right triangle at each end of the trapezoid?

9.   You might want to review the similarity properties of triangles. Which one can be applied here?

11.   (c) To show $a^2 + b^2 = c^2$, write $a^2 + b^2$ in terms of x and y, substituting the given expressions. Use algebra to simplify the resulting expression.

12.   (a) First show that $\triangle ABC \cong \triangle ADC$.

13.   Show that both $\triangle B'A'C'$ and $\triangle BAC$ are congruent to $\triangle BAD$, which you constructed, by using the SAS Congruence Property.

14. If $\triangle ABC \sim \triangle A'B'D'$, what angles must be congruent? Why does this create a contradiction?

15. Note that the height of $\triangle ABD$ plus the height of $\triangle ACE$ equals BC.

Chapter 15
Section 15.2

22. Write equations for the perpendicular bisectors of two of the sides of the triangle.

25. Use the fact that the product of the slopes of perpendicular lines (neither one vertical) is −1.

29. Represent the lengths of the line segments forming the rectangle in terms of x, y, a, and b. Use the Pythagorean theorem to write three equations in x, y, a, and b. Solve simultaneous equations.

30. The break-even point is when revenue = cost.

Section 15.3

1. The fourth vertex can be in any of three positions. It can be opposite any of the three given vertices.

5. (a) Next plot point Z on the x-axis. What must the coordinates of Z be?
   (b) If the y-axis is a line of symmetry and $XZ = 8$, what do you know about the coordinates of X and Z?

7. What condition must be met for a parallelogram to be a rectangle?

10. (a) Find the equation of the line through two points: A and the midpoint of $\overline{CB}$.

12. (b) Use your result from part (a).

13. (a) You must find the equation of the line that contains point R and that is perpendicular to $\overline{ST}$.

14. What are the midpoints of the diagonals?

16. Use the distance formula or Pythagorean theorem to determine the lengths of the non-horizontal sides.

21. Determine the number of possible paths of the same length from A to each point in the grid, starting with the upper right corner. Label each point with the number of paths to that point and look for a pattern.

Chapter 16
Section 16.1

29. More than one answer is possible for parts (b) and (d).

30. (c) How does the line of reflection relate to each point and its image?
    (d) Think about your answer to part (c).

31. How do the images of points A, B, and C compare to the original points?

Section 16.2

EFGH? Check the orientations of the two squares.

17. To show that two lines are parallel, you could show that corresponding angles are congruent.

19. You might find the argument you used for problem 17 helpful here.

21. (b) How do you locate the center of a rotation? Example 16.8 may be useful here.

23. You need to find R' such that $\dfrac{PQ}{PQ'} = \dfrac{PR}{PR'}$. Use similar triangles here.

24. If $\overline{PP'}$ intersects l in R and $\overline{QQ'}$ intersects l in point S, you might try drawing segments RQ and RQ'.

Section 16.3

1. (a) Remember that P'' is the image of P', not P, under half-turn H_B.

9. Remember that a half-turn is an isometry and so has all the properties of an isometry.

12. (b) Consider the image of each vertex under the reflection M_{AC}.

13. (a) Remember that point A represents any point.
     (b) What is the distance between r and s in terms of x and y?

14. (b) Remember that the angle of incidence will equal the angle of reflection.

15. What isometry or combination of isometries will map $A'B'C'D'$ to

PART 2 - SOLUTIONS TO PART A PROBLEMS

from

Mathematics for Elementary Teachers

A CONTEMPORARY APPROACH

by Gary L. Musser, William F. Burger, and Blake E. Peterson

prepared by Vikki R. Maurer and Roger J. Maurer

SOLUTIONS - PART A PROBLEMS

Chapter 1: Introduction to Problem Solving

Section 1.1

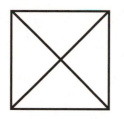

1. (a) Draw a picture like the one shown. Notice that there are four small triangles formed by the intersection of the diagonals. Upon further inspection, we see that any two adjacent triangles form another larger triangle. Therefore, there are eight triangles formed.

   (b) Step 1: Understand the problem - Triangles are formed by the diagonals and sides of the square, and triangles of different sizes are formed. The total number of triangles of all sizes formed is desired.

   Step 2: Devise a plan - Draw a square along with its diagonals. Decide on a systematic way of counting triangles. You might start by counting all possible small triangles first. Then count triangles formed by combining two triangles, etc.

   Step 3: Carry out the plan - Systematically count triangles of all sizes.

   Step 4: Look back - Consider whether the solution makes sense. Have you counted triangles of all sizes?

Section 1.1

2. Let x and y represent the two original whole numbers. Since Scott subtracted the two numbers and got 10, we know $x - y = 10$. Since Greg multiplied the two numbers and got 651, we know $xy = 651$. We need to solve the equations $x - y = 10$ and $xy = 651$ simultaneously.

$x - y = 10$	Solve for x.
$x = 10 + y$	Substitute into $xy = 651$.
$(10 + y)y = 651$	Distribute
$10y + y^2 = 651$	
$y^2 + 10y - 651 = 0$	Factor.
$(y - 21)(y + 31) = 0$	Set each factor to zero.
$y = 21$ or $y = -31$	

   Since y is a whole number, we have $y = 21$. Therefore, $x = 10 + 21 = 31$. The correct sum is $21 + 31 = 52$.

Section 1.1

3. Let w = the width of the tennis court. Since the length of the court is 6 feet more than twice the width, the length of the court, l, is $2w + 6$. Since the perimeter of a rectangle is $2w + 2l$, and the perimeter of the rectangular tennis court is 228 feet, we know

$$2w + 2l = 228$$

$$2w + 2(2w + 6) = 228 \quad \text{since } l = 2w + 6$$

$$2w + 4w + 12 = 228$$

$$6w + 12 = 228$$

$$6w = 216$$

$$w = 36 \text{ feet}$$

$$l = 2(36) + 6 = 78 \text{ feet.}$$

Therefore, the dimensions of the tennis court are 36 feet by 78 feet.

Section 1.1

4. If the number is a multiple of 11 and there are only two digits, a pair, then the two digits must be the same. Our options are 11, 22, 33, 44, 55, 66, 77, 88, and 99. The number is also even so our options become 22, 44, 66, and 88. When we multiply the pair, we automatically have a perfect square so we need to look for the square that is also a cube.

$2^2 = 4$ This is not a cube.

$4^2 = 16$ This is not a cube.

$6^2 = 36$ This is not a cube.

However, $8^2 = 64 = 4^3$. The number must be 88.

Section 1.1

5. The number 9 can be expressed as $4 + 5$. Since any even number can be represented as $2n$ for some n, then any odd number can be represented as $2n + 1$ for some n. Further, $2n + 1$ can be written as $(n + n) + 1$ or $n + (n + 1)$, which represents two consecutive numbers.

Section 1.1

6. Since we can use a symbol more than once, we need not use all the symbols. Use the Guess and Test strategy and remember the order of operations. The solution can be written three ways: $6 \div 6 + 6 + 6 = 13$, $6 + 6 \div 6 + 6 = 13$, or $6 + 6 + 6 \div 6 = 13$.

Section 1.1

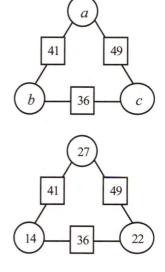

7. Let a = the number in the top circle, b = the number in the left circle, and c = the number in the right circle. Since the number in each square is the sum of the numbers in the circles on each side of it, we have the following equations:
$$a + b = 41 \quad a + c = 49 \quad b + c = 36$$
Since $a + b = 41$, we know $b = 41 - a$. Since $a + c = 49$, we know $c = 49 - a$. Substituting these into the equation $b + c = 36$ yields the following:
$$41 - a + 49 - a = 36$$
$$90 - 2a = 36$$
$$54 = 2a$$
$$27 = a.$$
So, $b = 41 - 27 = 14$ and $c = 49 - 27 = 22$.

Section 1.1

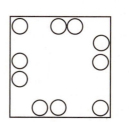

8. Draw a picture and use the Guess and Test strategy. Your first instinct may be to place a stool in each of the four corners. In that case, the six remaining stools cannot be placed along the four walls so that each wall has the same number of stools. Continue guessing by placing stools in fewer corners. Also, notice that ten stools divided by four walls yields two stools per wall with two stools left over. By placing these two leftover stools in opposite corners, each wall has three stools.

Section 1.1

9. Assume it is possible to do and give it a try. If we have one pocket that contains zero dollars, say the first pocket, then we must put at least one dollar in each remaining pocket. Place one dollar in the second pocket. This forces us to

place at least two dollars in each remaining pocket. Place two dollars in the third pocket. Continue in this manner, adding one more dollar to each pocket.

The total number of dollars needed is $0 + 1 + 2 + 3 + 4 + 5 + 6 + 7 + 8 + 9 = 45$. We have only $44. Notice we have used the fewest number of dollars possible at each step so we can do no better. We conclude it cannot be done.

Section 1.1

10.   We should use a Systematic Guess and Test strategy. Since each corner affects two sides, we should try to determine the corners first. Place the smallest number, 2, in a corner. Consider all possible three-number combinations that, with the 2, add to 21. The only options are 10, 6, 3; 10, 5, 4; 9, 7, 3; and 9, 6, 4. Since we cannot repeat numbers, the only two combinations that will work are 10, 5, 4 and 9, 7, 3. The two unused digits, 6 and 8, add to 14, so must be placed on the remaining side with corner digits that add to 7. One solution is shown.

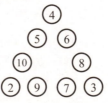

Section 1.1

11.   Use the spreadsheet activity, *Consecutive Integer Sum*, to help you guess and test possible sums quickly.

(a)   2 Integers: It is impossible to add two consecutive integers to obtain a sum of 84, since the sum of any two consecutive integers will be odd.

3 Integers: The sum of any three consecutive integers will be a multiple of 3, and since 84 is a multiple of 3, try possible sums in the spreadsheet. Divide 84 by 3 to obtain a good first guess. $27 + 28 + 29 = 84$ is the solution.

4, 5, and 6 Integers: There are no solutions.

(b) 2 Integers: Divide 213 by 2 to obtain a good first guess.
The solution is $106 + 107 = 213$.
3 Integers: Divide 213 by 3 to obtain a good first guess.
The solution is $70 + 71 + 72 = 213$.
4 and 5 Integers: There are no solutions.
6 Integers: Divide 213 by 6 to obtain a good first guess.
The solution is $33 + 34 + 35 + 36 + 37 + 38 = 213$.

(c) 2 and 3 Integers: There are no solutions.
4 Integers: Divide 154 by 4 to obtain a good first guess.
The solution is $37 + 38 + 39 + 40 = 154$.
5 and 6 Integers: There are no solutions.

Section 1.1

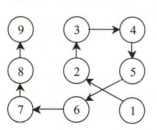

12.   Looking at the diagram, we notice the circle in the upper left hand corner has no arrow leaving it. This circle must contain the 9 since it is a dead end. Notice the circle in the lower right hand corner has arrows only leaving it. This circle must contain 1, since it is a beginning point. Furthermore, you may notice the circle directly below the 9 has only one arrow leaving it leading to the 9. This circle must contain the 8. Now use the Guess and Test strategy. Only two circles could contain the number 2. Placing it above the 1 eventually forces us to cross the middle circle twice. Placing the 2 in the middle circle leads to the solution shown.

Section 1.1

13.   Consider possible sums and differences involving 5 and 8. Notice that $5 + 5 + 5 = 15$ and $8 + 8 = 16$. You would like to measure 1 minute, and since $16 - 15 = 1$, it is possible to devise a plan to measure 1 minute. Begin the 5-minute timer and the 8-minute timer at the same time. Run the 5-minute timer a total of three times at the same time that you run the 8-minute timer two times. After the 5-minute timer stops, there will be 1 minute left on the 8-minute timer.

Section 1.1

14.   (a) To maximize the sum, put the largest digits in the greatest place value positions. Put the 9 and 8 in the hundreds places. It follows that the next largest digits should be put in the tens positions. Put the 7 and 6 in .

the tens places The 5 and 4 are forced into the ones places. One possible solution is given next.

$$975$$
$$+ \ 864$$
$$\overline{1839}$$

There are 8 possible solutions. These are found by switching digits of the same place value such as the 9 and the 8. Since addition is commutative, the sum of each of the solutions is the same: 1839.

(b) We want the hundreds digits to differ by 1 to minimize the difference. This difference can be reduced further by arranging the remaining digits so that we are forced to borrow as much as possible. Consider the tens and ones places. We want to subtract the largest possible number, 98, from the smallest possible number, 45. This leaves the 7 and 6 to the hundreds places. Therefore, the smallest possible difference is $745 - 698 = 47$.

Section 1.1

15. Because the two inner squares touch more squares than any others, we should place in them the numbers which contact the fewest numbers, i.e., the most extreme: 1 and 8.

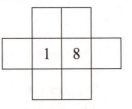

The 1-square touches every other square except the one to the right of the 8. Place the 2 in the square to the right of the 8. Place the 7 in the square to the left of the 1.

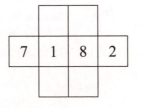

Out of the remaining digits, we must place the 3 and 5 together and the 4 and 6 together. Note that the 3 cannot touch the 2-square, and the 6 cannot touch the 7-square. We end up with two solutions:

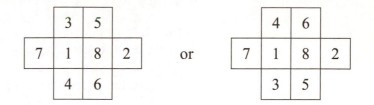

Other solutions are possible. When the 1 and the 8 were placed in the two inner squares, their order could have been switched so the 1 was to the right of the 8. This new placement would have led to two more solutions.

Section 1.1

16. Notice the P in the sum is alone in the ten thousands place so we can consider it first. P = 1 since it must be the result of carrying. U = 9 since we could not have carried to obtain P = 1 if U was less than 9. E = 0 since E results from U plus a carry. Notice R + A = 10 and C is odd, since S + S is even and S + S + 1 is odd. So far we have used 0, 1, and 9. Use the Guess and Test strategy to solve the rest. R and A could be 2 and 8, 3 and 7, or 4 and 6. If we try R = 8 and A = 2, we see S must be 3 and C must be 7. So we have the following solution.

$$\begin{array}{r} 9338 \\ + 932 \\ \hline 10270 \end{array}$$

Section 1.1

17. Let s = the weight of one spool, t = the weight of one thimble, and b = the weight of one button. Since two spools and one thimble balance eight buttons, $2s + t = 8b$. Since one spool balances one thimble and one button, we have $s = t + b$. Since we want an equation relating buttons and spools, we can isolate t in each of the equations above and set them equal to each other.

$t = 8b - 2s$ and $t = s - b$

So, $8b - 2s = s - b$

$$9b = 3s$$

$$3b = s.$$

Thus, three buttons will balance one spool.

Section 1.1

18. We do not want consecutive digits next to each other. The numbers in consecutive circles must differ by at least 2. Using the Inferential Guess and Test strategy, consider the top four circles. Place in them the odd digits since they differ by multiples of 2.

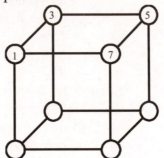

Now we can place the even numbers in order clockwise in the bottom circles as long as the 2 is not directly below the 1 or the 3. One solution is shown next.

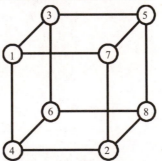

Many solutions are possible. Another solution involves placing the numbers 4, 8, 5, and 1 in the top circles. The numbers 2, 6, 3, and 7 are then placed clockwise in the bottom circles, making sure the 2 is directly below the 4.

Section 1.1

19. The Use a Variable strategy will be helpful. Let n be the original number. Perform the following operations:

(1) Add 10: $n + 10$

(2) Multiply by 4: $4(n + 10) = 4n + 40$

(3) Add 200: $4n + 40 + 200 = 4n + 240$

(4) Divide by 4: $(4n + 240)/4 = n + 60$

(5) Subtract the original number: $n + 60 - n = 60$

Therefore, no matter what the original number is, the result will always be 60 after performing the given set of operations.

Section 1.1

20. The digits must be used in decreasing order. Use the Systematic Guess and Test strategy by beginning with a number close to 100. We can then add or subtract smaller digits to close in on 100. Begin with 98. Some combination of additions and subtractions on the remaining digits must yield 2. Since the sum of the digits 1 through 7 is 28 we need to subtract somewhere. Since $15 + 13 = 28$ and $15 - 13 = 2$, we want some of the digits to add to 15 and the remaining digits to add to 13. (These will be subtracted.) Notice that $7 + 5 + 3 = 15$, so one solution is $98 + 7 - 6 + 5 - 4 + 3 - 2 - 1 = 100$. Also, since we know $6 + 5 + 4 = 15$, another solution is $98 - 7 + 6 + 5 + 4 - 3 - 2 - 1 = 100$. Many solutions are possible. Continue to explore number combinations. Another solution is $98 - 7 + 6 + 5 - 4 + 3 - 2 + 1 = 100$.

Section 1.1

21. Use the Make a List strategy and list the perfect cubes that are smaller than 1729. These are $1^3 = 1$, $2^3 = 8$, $3^3 = 27$, $4^3 = 64$, $5^3 = 125$, $6^3 = 216$, $7^3 = 343$, $8^3 = 512$, $9^3 = 729$, $10^3 = 1000$, $11^3 = 1331$, and $12^3 = 1728$. Find any two of these cubes that have a sum of 1729. We see that $1^3 + 12^3 = 1729$ and $9^3 + 10^3 = 1729$. Thus, $a = 1$, $b = 12$, $c = 9$, and $d = 10$.

Section 1.1

22. For the eManipulative activity, *Number Puzzles*, use the Systematic Guess and Test strategy. Since each corner affects two sides, we should try to determine the corners first.

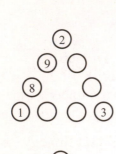

(i) Try small numbers in the corners as shown at left. Keeping in mind that each side must add to 23, we see that even if we use our largest remaining numbers, 9 and 8, we cannot obtain a side which totals 23.

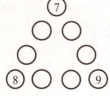

(ii) Try large numbers in the corners as shown at left. For the side containing 8 and 9, we need $23 - 8 - 9 = 6$. The options are 5 and 1 or 2 and 4. For the side containing 8 and 7, we need $23 - 8 - 7 = 8$. The options are 6 and 2 or 5 and 3. For the side containing 9 and 7, we need $23 - 9 - 7 = 7$. The options are 1 and 6, 2 and 5, or 3 and 4. The only way to *not* repeat numbers is to use the combinations 1 and 5, 2 and 6, 3 and 4, respectively. A solution is given next.

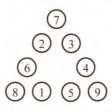

Section 1.1

23. In the eManipulative activity, *Circle 21*, five of the numbers will already be placed in the figure. Begin by considering a pair of overlapping circles in which one of the missing numbers is in the overlap position. Use the Make a List strategy and list all possible options for that position. For example, suppose the numbers 10 and 11 are placed as shown next. In the circle containing 10, the only possibilities for the remaining two positions are 2 and 9, 3 and 8, 4 and 7, or 5 and 6. In the circle containing 11, the only possibilities for the remaining two positions are 1 and 9, 2 and 8, 3 and 7, or 4 and 6.

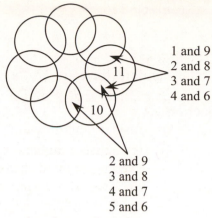

1 and 9
2 and 8
3 and 7
4 and 6

2 and 9
3 and 8
4 and 7
5 and 6

Use the Inferential Guess and Test strategy to place numbers in the overlap position between the 10 and 11. If the number 2 is placed in that position, then two other positions are forced to contain 9 and 8 as shown next.

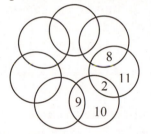

Continue using the Inferential Guess and Test strategy. A solution is shown next.

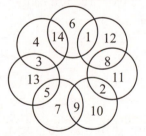

Section 1.1

24. The Use a Variable strategy will be helpful. Let n represent the number of dots on each side of the hexagon. Notice that each corner dot is a part of two different sides. The expression $6n$ represents the total number of dots with each corner dot counted twice. Since there are six corners that are counted twice, the total number of dots can be expressed as $6n - 6 = 126$. Solve this equation for n.

$$6n - 6 = 126$$
$$6n = 132$$
$$n = 22.$$

Therefore, there are 22 dots on each side.

Section 1.2

1. (a) Consider the following table:

Sum	Answer
1	$1 = 1^2$
$1 + 3$	$4 = 2^2$
$1 + 3 + 5$	$9 = 3^2$
$1 + 3 + 5 + 7$	$16 = 4^2$
$1 + 3 + 5 + 7 + 9$	$25 = 5^2$

   Each sum is the square of the number of consecutive odd terms added together, so each number in the answer column is a perfect square.

   (b) Nine are required since $9^2 = 81$:
   $$1 + 3 + 5 + 7 + 9 + 11 + 13 + 15 + 17 = 81.$$

   (c) Thirteen are required since $13^2 = 169$:
   $$1 + 3 + 5 + 7 + 9 + 11 + 13 + 15 + 17 + 19 + 21 + 23 + 25 = 169.$$

   (d) Twenty-three are required since $23^2 = 529$:
   $$1 + 3 + 5 + 7 + 9 + 11 + 13 + 15 + 17 + 19 + 21 + 23 + 25 + 27 + 29 + 31 + 33 + 35 + 37 + 39 + 41 + 43 + 45 = 529.$$

Section 1.2

2. Compare successive terms in each sequence. Look for a common difference or ratio.

   (a) Each term is half as large as the previous term. The ratio of consecutive terms is 2:1. Therefore, the missing term is $64 \div 2 = 32$.

   (b) Each term is one third as large as the previous term. The ratio of consecutive terms is 3:1. Therefore, the missing term is $\frac{1}{9} \div 3 = \frac{1}{9} \times \frac{1}{3} = \frac{1}{27}$.

(c) Consider the difference between successive terms.

Term

7   9   12   16

2   3   4

Difference

Notice that the difference increases by 1 each time. Therefore, the difference between 16 and the next term should be 5. The missing term is $16 + 5 = 21$.

(d) One possibility is that each term is formed by using the previous term. In the previous term, the sum of the last two digits is found. To this sum add the previous term after the last two digits have been replaced with a single zero.

new term =

$$\begin{pmatrix} \text{sum of the last} \\ \text{two digits of the} \\ \text{previous term} \end{pmatrix} + \begin{pmatrix} \text{previous term with the} \\ \text{last two digits replaced} \\ \text{by a zcro} \end{pmatrix}$$

For example: $12{,}789 = (6 + 3) + (12{,}780) = 9 + 12{,}780$. Therefore, the missing term is $(8 + 9) + (1270) = 17 + 1270 = 1287$.

Section 1.2

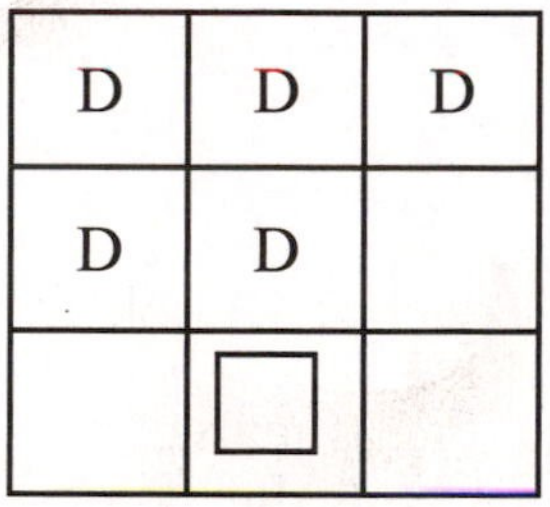

3. (a) Notice the letters are in alphabetical order, and the letters increase by one in each figure. The next figure should contain the letter D five times. Notice also in the original figure, which contains two of the letter A, a segment is drawn (a single side). In the figure with three of the letter B, an angle is drawn (two sides). In the figure with four of the letter C, a triangle is drawn (three sides). Therefore, in the figure that will contain five of the letter D, a four-sided figure, or a square, should be drawn. The figure that best completes the sequence is shown.

(b) Consider the three types of objects in the figures. First consider the triangle. In successive figures, the triangle in the upper left-hand square becomes smaller and then changes color. In the last figure given, the triangle has moved to the upper right-hand square. The next figure in the sequence should show a smaller triangle in the upper right-hand square.

Next, consider the arrow. In successive figures, the arrow moves along the second row of squares, first pointing right, then pointing up in the middle square, then pointing left, and then pointing down in the middle square. The next figure in the sequence should show the arrow pointing right.

Finally, consider the circle. In successive figures, the circles fill diagonal sets of squares moving from the lower right to upper left. If this pattern continues, the next figure in the sequence will have a single circle in the upper left square. The figure that best completes the sequence is shown.

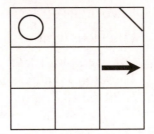

Section 1.2

4. $6^2 - 5^2 = 36 - 25 = 11$

$56^2 - 45^2 = 3136 - 2025 = 1111$

$556^2 - 445^2 = 309,136 - 198,025 = 111,111$

(a) Since the number of 5s in the first squared number increases by 1 in each difference, and the number of 4s in the second squared number increases by 1 in each difference, we predict that the next difference should be

$5556^2 - 4445^2 = 30,869,136 - 19,758,025$

$$= 11,111,111.$$

(b) In order to determine the eighth line, we should use the Make a List and Look for a Pattern strategies.

Line	Number of 5s in First Squared Number	Number of 4s in Second Squared Number	Number of 1s in the Difference
1	0	0	$2 = 2 \times 1$
2	1	1	$4 = 2 \times 2$
3	2	2	$6 = 2 \times 3$
4	3	3	$8 = 2 \times 4$
⋮	⋮	⋮	⋮
8	7	7	$16 = 2 \times 8$

Therefore, from the table we see the eighth line will be

$$55{,}555{,}556^2 - 44{,}444{,}445^2 = 1{,}111{,}111{,}111{,}111{,}111.$$

Section 1.2

5. In the first two number grids, notice that each digit in the first column is the product of the two digits directly to the right of it, and each digit in the first row is the product of the two digits directly below it. Consider the third number grid. Since row 2, row 3, column 2 and column 3 each have two missing numbers, begin with row 1.

60	6	?
?	?	5
2	?	?

60	6	10
30	6	5
2	1	2

Consider row 1: $60 = 6 \times ?$ The missing number is 10.

Consider column 3: $10 = 5 \times ?$ The missing number is 2.

Consider column 1: $60 = ? \times 2$ The missing number is 30.

Consider row 2: $30 = ? \times 5$ The missing number is 6.

Consider column 2: $6 = 6 \times ?$ The missing number is 1.

Fill in the missing numbers. The third grid is shown.

Section 1.2

6. (a) Count the dots in each array.

Triangular Number	Number of Dots in the Array
1	1 = 1
2	3 = 1 + 2
3	6 = 1 + 2 + 3
4	10 = 1 + 2 + 3 + 4
5	15 = 1 + 2 + 3 + 4 + 5
6	21 = 1 + 2 + 3 + 4 + 5 + 6

The nth triangular number is the sum of the first n whole numbers.

(b) The sketch that represents the seventh triangular number is given next:

(c) The 10th triangular number will contain 1 + 2 + 3 + 4 + 5 + 6 + 7 + 8 + 9 + 10 = 55 dots.

(d) The 11th triangular number will have 55 + 11 = 66 dots. The 12th triangular number will have 66 + 12 = 78 dots. The 13th triangular number will have 78 + 13 = 91 dots. Therefore, the triangular number with 91 dots is the 13th such number.

(e) The 14th triangular number has 91 + 14 = 105 dots. The 15th triangular number has 105 + 15 = 120 dots. The 16th triangular number has 120 + 16 = 136 dots. The 17th triangular number has 136 + 17 = 153 dots. Therefore, there is no triangular number that has 150 dots in its shape.

(f) Consider the table we made in part (a). Add a third column labeled "Twice the Number of Dots", as shown in the following table.

Triangular Number	Number of Dots in the Array	Twice the Number of Dots
1	1	$2 = 1 \times 2$
2	3	$6 = 2 \times 3$
3	6	$12 = 3 \times 4$
4	10	$20 = 4 \times 5$
5	15	$30 = 5 \times 6$
6	21	$42 = 6 \times 7$
$\vdots$	$\vdots$	$\vdots$
n	?	$n \times (n + 1)$

The pattern appears to be that number of dots in the *n*th triangular number is $\dfrac{n(n+1)}{2}$.

(g) The sum of the first 100 counting numbers is the same as the number of dots in the 100th triangular number. If $n = 100$, then we have $\dfrac{100(101)}{2} = 5050$. Therefore the sum of the first 100 counting numbers is 5050.

Section 1.2

7. Access the Chapter 1 eManipulative, *Counterfeit Coin*. Notice, in the eManipulative, the counterfeit coin could be heavier or lighter. Select the 8-coin or 9-coin option to get a feel for this type of problem.

   For the problem of detecting the heavier counterfeit coin out of a set of 12 coins, begin by placing four coins on each side of the scale. If they balance, then the counterfeit coin is among the remaining four coins. Place two of the remaining coins on each side of the scale. The counterfeit coin will be on the heavier side and will be determined in one more weighing. If the original four coins on each side of the scale do not balance, then the counterfeit coin is among the heavier four coins. Place two coins of the four on each side of the scale. The counterfeit coin will be on the heavier side and will be determined in one more weighing. Thus, the counterfeit coin can be found in three weighings.

Section 1.2

8. Use the Draw a Picture and Look for a Pattern strategies. Select any point at random and notice that there are only 19 other points to which it can be connected using a segment.

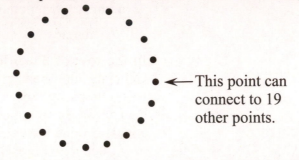

←—This point can connect to 19 other points.

Draw in the 19 segments. Move to an adjacent point and notice that there are only 18 other points to which it has not already been connected, so 18 additional segments can be formed.

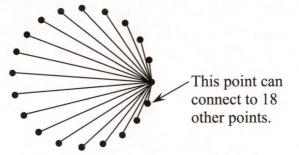

This point can connect to 18 other points.

Continue in this manner. The total number of segments drawn will be the sum of the segments formed at each stage: $19 + 18 + 17 + 16 + 15 + 14 + 13 + 12 + 11 + 10 + 9 + 8 + 7 + 6 + 5 + 4 + 3 + 2 + 1 + 0 = 190$.

Section 1.2

9. (a) Consider the differences between terms.

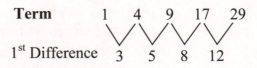

Term 1 4 9 17 29

1st Difference 3 5 8 12

There is no clear pattern in the differences, so find the second and third difference, if necessary, and use the Look for a Pattern strategy.

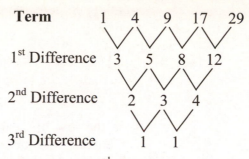

In the row of 3rd differences, there is a pattern of 1s. Generate the next three terms in the sequence by working backward. The row of 3rd differences will contain all 1s so we can add three more 1s to that row and determine the values that will occur above until the next three terms in the sequence are generated.

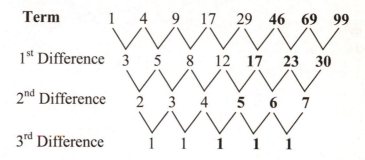

Therefore the next three terms in the sequence are 46, 69, and 99.

(b) Consider the differences between terms.

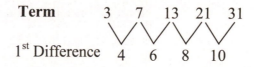

There seems to be a pattern in the differences. They all differ by 2. Listing the row containing the second differences makes that fact obvious.

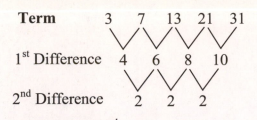

In the row of 2nd differences, there is a pattern of 2s. Generate the next three terms in the sequence by working backward. The row of 2nd differences will contain all 2s so we can add three more 2s to that row and determine the values that will occur above until the next three terms in the sequence are generated.

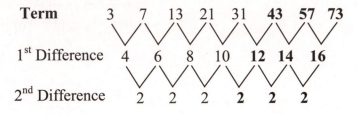

Therefore the next three terms in the sequence are 43, 57, and 73.

Section 1.2

10. Construct a table comparing the number of dots in each triangular number to the number of dots in each square number.

Square Number	Number of Dots in the nth Triangular Number	Number of Dots in the nth Square Number
1	1	1
2	3	4
3	6	9
4	10	16
5	15	25
6	21	36
7	28	49
8	36	64
9	45	81
10	55	100
$\vdots$	$\vdots$	$\vdots$

(a) The third square number is 9. The two triangular numbers whose sum is 9 are the second and third, which have 3 and 6 dots, respectively.

(b) The fifth square number is 25. The two triangular numbers whose sum is 25 are the fourth and fifth, which have 10 and 15 dots, respectively.

(c) The 10th square number is 100. It is the sum of the 10th and 9th triangular numbers ($55 + 45 = 100$). The 20th square number is $20^2 = 400$. It is the sum of the 20th and 19th triangular numbers ($210 + 190 = 400$). The nth square number is n^2. It is the sum of the nth and $(n - 1)$st triangular numbers as follows:

nth Triangular Number + $(n - 1)$st Triangular Number

$$= \frac{n(n+1)}{2} + \frac{(n-1)n}{2}$$

$$= \frac{n^2 + n}{2} + \frac{n^2 - n}{2}$$

$$= \frac{2n^2}{2}$$

$$= n^2$$

Thus, the sum of the nth and $(n - 1)$st triangular numbers is the nth square number.

(c) From the table, we notice that 36 is the 8th triangular number and is also a perfect square. Therefore, the 8th triangular number is the 6th square number.

(e) Consider the differences between pairs of square numbers. The following differences yield triangular numbers. There are others. $4 - 1 = 3$, $49 - 4 = 45$, $64 - 36 = 28$, $100 - 64 = 36$, $25 - 4 = 21$, $64 - 49 = 15$, $64 - 9 = 55$, and $169 - 64 = 105$.

Section 1.2

11. Make a table of the amount paid each day and the sum of the payments up to that day and use the Look for a Pattern strategy.

Day	Pay for Day (cents)	Pay to Date (cents)
1	1	$1 = 2^1 - 1$
2	2	$3 = 2^2 - 1$
3	4	$7 = 2^3 - 1$
4	8	$15 = 2^4 - 1$
5	16	$31 = 2^5 - 1$

Notice each entry in the "Pay to Date" column can be generated from $2^{\text{day}} - 1$. On day 30, the total will be $2^{30} - 1 = 1,073,741,823$ cents. If we convert this from cents to dollars, we see the total will be $10,737,418.23. This amount is much greater than 1 million dollars.

Section 1.2

12. For 1 triangle, the perimeter is 3. For 2 triangles, the perimeter is 4. For 3 triangles, the perimeter is 5. For 4 triangles, the perimeter is 6. Notice that the perimeter is always 2 more than the number of triangles. This relationship can be summarized in a table.

Number of Triangles	Perimeter
1	3
2	4
3	5
4	6
5	7
6	8
⋮	⋮
10	12
⋮	⋮
38	40
⋮	⋮
n	$n + 2$

Section 1.2

13. Continue the number arrangement and use the Look for a Pattern strategy.

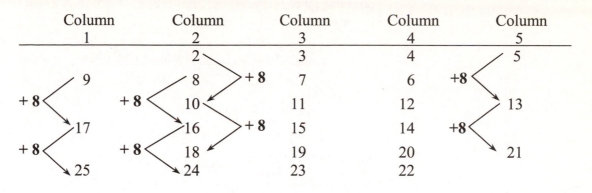

(a) Notice that 100 is an even number, and there are only two even columns, 2 and 4. Consider column 2. In it the difference between every other element is 8. The integers in column 2 are either $2 + 8n$ or $0 + 8n$, for some whole number n. If 100 fell in column 2, it would have to be the result of one of these two forms. Because $100 = 4 + 8 \times 12$, it cannot be in this column. Thus we see, 100 must be in column 4.

(b) Similarly, 1000 must either be in column 2 or 4. Notice that $1000 = 0 + 8 \times 125$, so it must be in column 2.

(c) Because 1999 is an odd number, we have three columns to consider. Notice column 1 contains integers of the form $9 + 8n$, and column 5 contains integers of the form $5 + 8n$, for some whole number n. Notice that $1999 = 7 + 8 \times 249$. Thus, it cannot be in column 1 or 5. The number 1999 must fall in column 3.

(d) By the same reasoning, 99,997 must be in column 5 because $99,997 = 5 + 8 \times 12,499$.

Section 1.2

14. To find the number of cubes in the 100th collection of cubes, make a list of the number of cubes found in the 1st, 2nd, 3rd, ... collections. Look for a relationship between the dimensions of the solid and the number of $1 \times 1 \times 1$ cubes in the solid. Notice that the first solid is a single $1 \times 1 \times 1$ cube. The second solid contains two layers of four cubes for a total of eight $1 \times 1 \times 1$ cubes. The third solid

contains three layers of nine cubes each for a total of twenty-seven $1 \times 1 \times 1$ cubes.

Dimensions	Number of Cubes
$1 \times 1 \times 1$	$1 = 1^3$
$2 \times 2 \times 2$	$8 = 2^3$
$3 \times 3 \times 3$	$27 = 3^3$

Notice the number of cubes in each solid is the product of the dimensions. In other words, the number of cubes is the cube of the length of a side. For the 100th collection of cubes, the number of $1 \times 1 \times 1$ cubes is $100(100)(100) = 100^3 = 1,000,000$.

Section 1.2
15. The next six terms of the Fibonacci sequence are 34, 55, 89, 144, 233, and 377. Notice the sum of the squares of the first n Fibonacci numbers is the product of the nth and $(n + 1)$st terms of the Fibonacci sequence. To predict the sum of $1^2 + 1^2 + 2^2 + 3^2 + ... + 144^2$, find the Fibonacci number that is one term beyond 144. The desired sum is equal to $144 \times 233 = 33,552$.

Section 1.2
16. Sixteen terms of the Fibonacci sequence are: 1, 1, 2, 3, 5, 8, 13, 21, 34, 55, 89, 144, 233, 377, 610, and 987.
Observe the following pattern:
$1 + 2 = 3$
$1 + 2 + 5 = 8$
$1 + 2 + 5 + 13 = 21$
$1 + 2 + 5 + 13 + 34 = 55$
$1 + 2 + 5 + 13 + 34 + 89 = 144$
Compare each equation with the Fibonacci sequence. Notice the total for each set of additions is the element in the Fibonacci sequence that is one term beyond the largest Fibonacci number in the sum. Therefore, the answer to $1 + 2 + 5 + 13 + 34 + 89 + 233 + 610$ should be 987. Check this using your calculator.

Section 1.2

17. (a) Consider the following table.

Numbers in the Diagonals of Pascal's Triangle	Sum
1	1
1	1
1 1	2
1 2	3
1 3 1	5
1 4 3	8
1 5 6 1	13

(b) Notice that the sequence of numbers in the "Sum" column is the Fibonacci sequence. Therefore, the next three sums should be 21, 34, and 55. If entries are added to Pascal's triangle, we have the following:

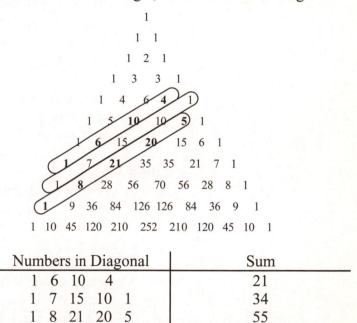

Numbers in Diagonal	Sum
1 6 10 4	21
1 7 15 10 1	34
1 8 21 20 5	55

Section 1.2

18. (a) The encircled numbers are 1, 2, 1, 3, 3, 4, and 6. The sum is 20.

(b) In the following figure, notice that several sets of seven numbers in Pascal's Triangle have been circled. Pay attention to the number in bold print below each circle.

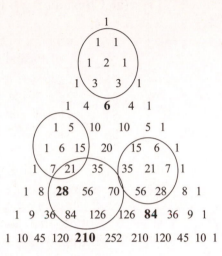

Encircled Numbers	Sum
1, 1, 1, 2, 1, 3, 3	12 = 2(6)
1, 5, 1, 6, 15, 7, 21	56 = 2(28)
15, 6, 35, 21, 7, 56, 28	168 = 2(84)
21, 35, 28, 56, 70, 84, 126	420 = 2(210)

Notice the sum of each set of seven numbers is twice the number that is directly below the center term in each circle.

Section 1.2

19. (a) The next two figures in the sequence are sketched next.

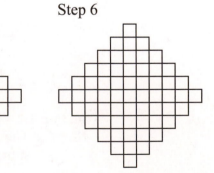

(b) Consider the following table.

Step Number	Number of Squares	Number of New Squares Attached
1	1	
2	$5 = 1 + 4$	$4 = 4(1)$
3	$13 = 1 + 4 + 8$	$8 = 4(2)$
4	$25 = 1 + 4 + 8 + 12$	$12 = 4(3)$
5	$41 = 1 + 4 + 8 + 12 + 16$	$16 = 4(4)$
6	$61 = 1 + 4 + 8 + 12 + 16 + 20$	$20 = 4(5)$

Each new figure is formed by adding to the original square. Notice that the number of new squares attached at each step is a multiple of 4. Consider the "Number of New Squares Attached" column of the table above. If a 4 is factored out of each term, with the exception of the 1, we obtain the triangular numbers. This factorization is illustrated in the next table.

Step Number	Number of Squares
1	1
2	$5 = 1 + 4 = 1 + 4(1)$
3	$13 = 1 + 4 + 8 = 1 + 4(1 + 2)$
4	$25 = 1 + 4 + 8 + 12 = 1 + 4(1 + 2 + 3)$
5	$41 = 1 + 4 + 8 + 12 + 16 = 1 + 4(1 + 2 + 3 + 4)$
$\vdots$	$\vdots$
n	$1 + 4(1 + 2 + 3 + ... + (n - 1))$

Because the sum of the first $n - 1$ counting numbers is $\dfrac{(n - 1)(n)}{2}$, the number of squares in the nth step is

$$1 + 4(1 + 2 + 3 + ... + (n - 1)) = 1 + \frac{4(n - 1)(n)}{2}$$

$$= 1 + 2n(n - 1).$$

(c) At step 7, the sum is $1 + 2(7)(7-1) = 1 + 2(7)(6) = 85$.

Step 7

(d) In the 10th figure, there would be $1 + 2(10)(9) = 1 + 180 = 181$ squares. In the 20th figure, there would be $1 + 2(20)(19) = 1 + 760 = 761$ squares. In the 50th figure, there would be $1 + 2(50)(49) = 1 + 4900 = 4901$ squares.

Section 1.2

20. There is an unlimited supply of darts. Begin by listing integers. Notice which integers can be obtained using some combination of 9s and 4s. Make a table. For each possible score note the number of 9s and 4s used, in the table on the next page.

Integer	Possible Score?	Number of 9s Used	Number of 4s Used
1	No		
2	No		
3	No		
4	Yes	0	1
5	No		
6	No		
7	No		
8	Yes	0	2
9	Yes	1	0
10	No		
11	No		
12	Yes	0	3
13	Yes	1	1
14	No		
15	No		
16	Yes	0	4
17	Yes	1	2
18	Yes	2	0
19	No		
20	Yes	0	5
21	Yes	1	3
22	Yes	2	1
23	No		
24	Yes	0	6
25	Yes	1	4
26	Yes	2	2
27	Yes	3	0
28	Yes	0	7
29	Yes	1	5
30	Yes	2	3
31	Yes	3	1
⋮	⋮	⋮	⋮

The largest score you can obtain is 23. Notice a pattern in the number of 9s used. Once the score of 27 is reached, each of the following scores is formed by adding zero, one, two, or three 9s and a multiple of 4.

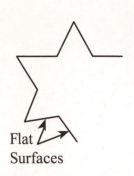

Flat
Surfaces

Section 1.2

21. Notice that a new point is added to any flat surface to create a new star.

   (a) For the third star, notice that each of the 6 points of the second star receives 2 new points so that each appears to be made up of 3 small points. Therefore, the third star is made up of $3 \times 6 = 18$ points. One of the six clusters of three points from the third star is enlarged and is shown to the left. Notice that there are 8 flat surfaces.

   (b) To form the fourth star, notice that there are 8 flat surfaces for each of the 3-point clusters from the third star. Add a new point to each of the flat surfaces so that each cluster in the fourth star has 11 points. One of the six clusters of 11 points from the fourth star is enlarged and is shown below. Since there are six of these clusters of 11 points on the fourth star, the fourth star will have a total of $11 \times 6 = 66$ points.

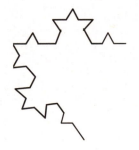

Section 1.2

22. Use the eManipulative activity, *Color Patterns*. In the first exercise the pattern is Lt Blue, Lt Blue, Blue, Lt Blue. In the second exercise the pattern is Green, Blue, Green, Yellow. In the third exercise the pattern is Red, Blue, Blue, Purple.

SOLUTIONS - PART A PROBLEMS

Chapter 2: Sets, Whole Numbers, and Numeration

Section 2.1

33. (a) $X \cap Y$: Consider the following Venn diagram.

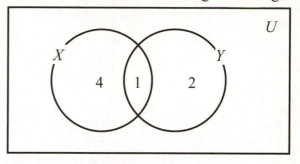

Set X has 5 elements. Set Y has 3 elements. Set $X \cap Y$ has 1 element. Notice that all of the elements in Y could also be in X, which would maximize the number of elements in the intersection. Therefore, the greatest number of elements possible in $X \cap Y$ is 3.

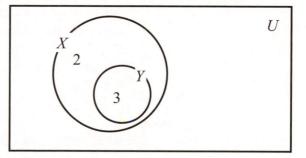

$X \cup Y$: Consider the following Venn diagram.

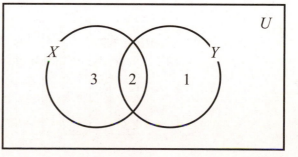

The sum of the number of elements in $X \cup Y$ is 6. If there were fewer elements in $X \cap Y$, then there would be more in $X \cup Y$. The greatest number of elements possible in $X \cup Y$ is 8.

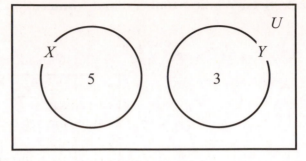

(b) $X \cap Y$:

The number of elements in the intersection of X and Y cannot be larger than the number of elements in either set individually. Recall part (a). Suppose set Y is completely contained in set X. In that case, the maximum number of elements in $X \cap Y$ is y, which represents the number of elements in set Y. Let x represent the number of elements in set X. From part (a), we see that the greatest number of elements in the union occurs when the sets have no elements in common, in which case the number of elements in $X \cup Y$ is the sum of the number of elements in their individual sets. The maximum number of elements in $X \cup Y$ is $x + y$.

Section 2.1

34. Consider sets A and B. The element 1 in set A can be paired with any of the four elements in set B.

After the initial pairing, element 2 in set A could be paired with any of the three remaining elements in set B. Likewise, element 3 in set A could be paired with either of the two remaining elements in set B, and element 4 in set A must be paired with the remaining element in set B. Therefore, the total number of one-to-one correspondences possible between A and B is $4 \times 3 \times 2 \times 1 = 24$.

Section 2.1

35. (a) Consider the set { }. Its only subset is itself: { }, so it has 1 subset.
    (b) Consider the set $\{x\}$. Its subsets are { } and $\{x\}$, so it has 2 subsets.
    (c) Consider the set $\{x, y\}$. Its subsets are { }, $\{x\}$, $\{y\}$, and $\{x, y\}$, so it has 4 subsets.
    (d) Consider the set $\{x, y, z\}$. Its subsets are { }, $\{x\}$, $\{y\}$, $\{z\}$, $\{x, y\}$, $\{x, z\}$, $\{y, z\}$, and $\{x, y, z\}$, so it has 8 subsets.
    (e) Construct a table and notice the relationship between the number of elements in a set and the number of subsets it contains.

Number of Elements	Number of Subsets
0	$1 = 2^0$
1	$2 = 2^1$
2	$4 = 2^2$
3	$8 = 2^3$

Notice that the number of subsets appears to always be 2 raised to a power. The exponent is the number of elements in the set. Therefore, for a set of 5 elements, the number of subsets is $2^5 = 32$.

    (f) We can generalize to the case of n elements. The number of subsets is 2^n.

Section 2.1

36. (a) This is possible. For example, consider set $A = \{1, 2, 3\}$ and set $B = \{x, y, z\}$. Sets A and B are equivalent since we can find a 1-1 correspondence between them. However, sets A and B cannot be equal since they do not contain exactly the same elements.
    (b) This is not possible. Two sets that are equal contain exactly the same elements, thus the same number of

elements. We can always find a 1-1 correspondence between sets with the same number of elements.

Section 2.1

37. (a) $D \cap E = D$ only when $D \subseteq E$.
    (b) $D \cup E = D$ only when $E \subseteq D$.
    (c) Considering parts (a) and (b), $D \cap E = D \cup E$ if and only if $D = E$.

Section 2.1

38. Consider a set of eight skirts, $S = \{S1, S2, S3, S4, S5, S6, S7, S8\}$ and a set of seven blouses, $B = \{B1, B2, B3, B4, B5, B6, B7\}$. Since any outfit Carmen chooses will consist of a single skirt and a single blouse, the concept of Cartesian product can be applied.

$$S \times B = \begin{cases} (S1, B1) & (S1, B2) & (S1, B3) & ... & (S1, B7) \\ (S2, B1) & (S2, B2) & (S2, B3) & ... & (S2, B7) \\ \vdots & \vdots & \vdots & \vdots & \vdots \\ \vdots & \vdots & ... & ... & \vdots \\ (S8, B1) & (S8, B2) & ... & ... & (S8, B7) \end{cases}$$

The number of outfits Carmen can wear is $8 \times 7 = 56$, which is the number of elements in the Cartesian product.

Section 2.1

39. Use the Solve a Simpler Problem strategy. Suppose we begin with 8 participants. In the first round, there would be 4 matches. In the second round, there would be 4 participants in 2 matches. In the third round, there would be 2 participants in one match. This yields a total of $4 + 2 + 1 = 7$ matches. Alternatively, consider beginning with 5 participants. In round one, 4 of the 5 participants compete in 2 matches, eliminating 2 players. Two of the 3 remaining participants compete in one match, eliminating 1 player. The two remaining participants compete in one final match. This yields a total of $2 + 1 + 1 = 4$ matches. Notice that there is a pattern. The number of matches in each case is one less than the number of original participants since every participant loses except the

champion. Thus, if we begin with 32 participants, the total number of matches is 31.

Section 2.1

40. Draw a picture. Construct line segments that connect points on base $\overline{AB}$ to points on the sides. If you use line segments perpendicular to the base, then a 1-1 correspondence can be found.

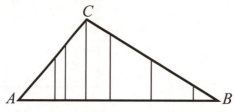

If we continue in the same manner, no points on the base or the sides will be left out.

Section 2.1

41. Draw a picture. Systematically construct line segments from $\overline{AB}$ to $\overset{\frown}{ACB}$. One way to do this is to use line segments that are perpendicular to $\overline{AB}$.

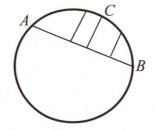

Continuing to draw line segments in this way will yield a 1-1 correspondence between the points on $\overline{AB}$ and the points on $\overset{\frown}{ACB}$.

Section 2.1

42. Draw a Venn diagram. The three sets are T, the set of people who watched television, N, the set of people who read the newspaper, and R, the set of people who listened to the radio. Begin filling the Venn diagram from the center and work out. Begin with $T \cap N \cap R$ which represents

the set of people who watched television *and* read the newspaper *and* listened to the radio. We are given that the number of voters in $T \cap N \cap R$ is 6.

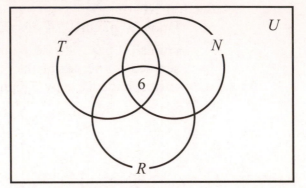

Now consider the region $N \cap R$ which represents the set of people who read the newspaper *and* listened to the radio. Notice that $N \cap R$ also contains people who fall in the set $T \cap N \cap R$, so be careful not to count some of the voters twice. Since the set $N \cap R$ contains 9 voters, and we have already accounted for 6 of them, there must be 3 in the remaining portion of $N \cap R$.

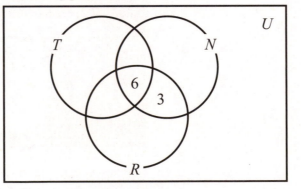

Similarly, in the remaining portion of $N \cap T$, there would be $20 - 6 = 14$ people, and in the remaining portion of $T \cap R$, there would be $27 - 6 = 21$ people. We know 65 people belong in set T. Notice that set T overlaps other sets so we have already accounted for $21 + 6 + 14 = 41$ of them. Thus, there are $65 - 41 = 24$ voters in the remaining portion of T. Similarly, there are $39 - (14 + 6 + 3) = 16$ in the remaining portion of N, and $39 - (21 + 6 + 3) = 9$ in the remaining portion of R. Since there were 100 voters altogether, and we accounted for only 24 + 14 + 16 + 21 + 6 + 3 + 9 = 93 of them, there must be 7 voters who do not rely on any of these methods to keep up with current events.

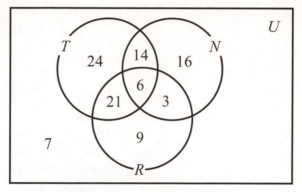

(a) Those voters who kept up with current events by some means other than the three sources belong to the set $\overline{T \cup N \cup R}$ which is shaded in the following Venn diagram. There are 7 voters in $\overline{T \cup N \cup R}$.

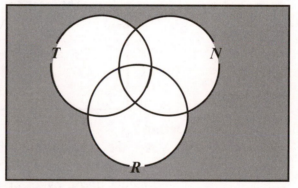

(b) Those voters who kept up with current events by reading the paper but not by watching television belong to the set $N \cap \overline{T}$ which is shaded in the following Venn diagram. There are 19 voters in $N \cap \overline{T}$.

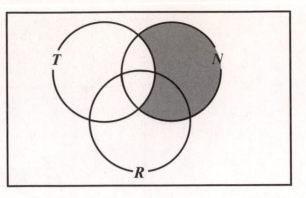

(c) Those voters who use only one of the three sources to keep up with current events belong in the following shaded region of the Venn diagram. There are 49 voters in this region.

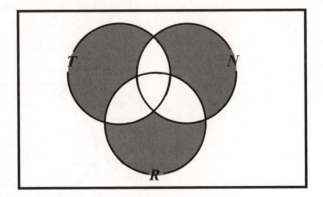

Section 2.1

43. At the convention there are butchers, bakers, and candlestick makers. Realize that someone could be both a butcher *and* a baker or some other combination. For each description, consider a Venn diagram and shade the described region. The fact that 50 people were in both B and A, but not in set C means that 50 people were in the set $(A \cap B) - C$. This region is shaded in the following Venn diagram.

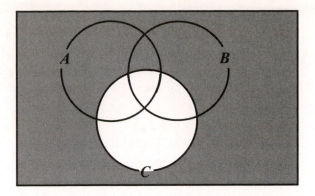

The total number represented is 50 + 70 + 60 + 40 + 50 + 80 = 350. Since there were 375 people at the convention, there must have been 375 − 350 = 25 people who were butchers, bakers, *and* candlestick makers. Therefore, there were 25 people in *A*, *B*, and *C*.

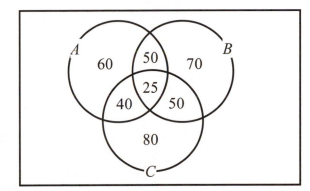

Section 2.1

44. The student is incorrect. *A* × *B* is the Cartesian product. All possible pairs are formed where the first element comes from set *A* and the second element comes from set *B*. While the symbol "×" looks like the familiar multiplication symbol, with sets it takes on a new meaning. Multiplication rules do not apply in this situation. Know the context in which symbols are used.

Section 2.2

15. The Roman System is a positional (additive and subtractive) system. Confusion can occur anytime there is an additive versus a subtractive case, such as IV versus VI, where in the first instance the 1 is subtracted from the 5 and

in the second, it is added. There are many such examples: IX versus XI, CM versus MC, and so on. The Egyptian System is not positional. It is a completely additive system. Reversing symbols will not change the value of the number.

Section 2.2

16. (a) Translate each problem into Egyptian symbols and count the symbols used.

    (i) ∩∩∩∩∩IIIIIIIII + ∩∩∩∩∩∩∩IIIIIII, 30 symbols.

    (ii) 9∩∩∩∩ − ∩∩∩∩∩∩∩∩IIIIIIIII, 24 symbols.

    (iii) ⌐⌐⌐⌐⌐⌐⌐999999999∩∩∩∩∩∩∩IIIIIII +
    999999999∩∩∩IIII, 47 symbols.

    (iv) ⌐⌐⌐⌐⌐⌐⌐⌐⌐999999∩∩∩∩∩∩∩∩IIIIIIII −
    ⌐⌐⌐⌐⌐999∩∩∩∩∩∩∩IIIIIIIII, 57 symbols.

    (b) Each digit tells us the number of symbols needed of a particular value. The sum of the digits in the number in our system corresponds to the number of symbols needed to represent the number in the Egyptian System. Therefore, to find the number of symbols needed to represent the sum or difference we need to add the digits of the addends (or subtrahend and minuend).

Section 2.2

17. Since the 1999 Lincoln Mark VIIs came out on December XXVI (December 26th), the advertisement probably ran in a 1998 paper. (It is not likely that the dealer would begin advertising his new 1999 model at the end of 1999). Write 1999 in Roman numerals. Recall that the Roman system has a subtractive principle.

$$\underset{}{M} \quad \underset{\text{subtract}}{\underbrace{C \quad M}} \quad \underset{\text{subtract}}{\underbrace{X \quad C}} \quad \underset{\text{subtract}}{\underbrace{I \quad X}}$$

M = 1000, CM = 900, XC = 90, and IX = 9. Therefore, 1999 = MCMXCIX.

Section 2.2

18. On the sheet Linda pulled out, the left half was numbered A4, and the right half was numbered A15. On the backside of the left half, the number must be A3. Therefore, the sheet containing A1 and A2 is still in the paper. By the same reasoning, if A15 is the number on the right half, the other side of the right half must be numbered A16. Since there is one sheet after this one, the two sides would be numbered A17 and A18. Therefore, there are 18 pages in section A of the newspaper.

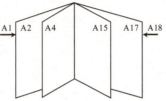

A1 A2   A4   A15   A17 A18

Section 2.2

19. Notice that the sums in parentheses are triangular numbers. Recall that the sum of the first n counting numbers is $\dfrac{n(n+1)}{2}$. Rewrite each triangular number in parentheses using this formula.

$$1993 \times (1+2+3+...+1994) = 1993 \times \frac{(1994)(1995)}{2} = \frac{(1993)(1994)(1995)}{2}$$

$$1994 \times (1+2+3+...+1993) = 1994 \times \frac{(1993)(1994)}{2} = \frac{(1993)(1994)(1994)}{2}$$

Since $\dfrac{(1993)(1994)(1995)}{2} > \dfrac{(1993)(1994)(1994)}{2}$, we see that $1993 \times (1+2+3+...+1994)$ is larger.

Section 2.2

20. Consider the simpler problem of finding the counterfeit coin given three coins. Begin by weighing two coins. If they weigh the same, the third coin is the counterfeit coin, and we can tell if it is heavier or lighter by comparing it to one of the original coins. If the first two coins do not balance, then switch the heavier one with the third coin. If the third coin is heavier, then the counterfeit coin is the

lighter one. If they balance, then the heavy coin is counterfeit. Now we return to the problem of five coins. Choose any two coins to weigh. If they balance, use the method from the three-coin problem on the remaining three coins. If they do not balance, then select one of the remaining three coins and complete the three-coin test.

Section 2.2

21. Ionian numerals are found by adding the values of the various basic numerals. Remember to use an accent before a symbol to represent a multiple of 1000.

   (a) (i) $\mu\beta = 40 + 2 = 42$

   (ii) $\chi\kappa\epsilon = 600 + 20 + 5 = 625$

   (iii) Notice γ represents 3000. The accent mark is omitted because the size of the number being represented is clear without it.
   $\gamma\phi\lambda\gamma = 3000 + 500 + 30 + 3 = 3533$

   (iv) Notice π represents 80,000 because $'\theta$ represents 9000.
   $\pi'\theta\omega\alpha = 80,000 + 9000 + 800 + 1 = 89,801$

   (b) (i) $85 = 80 + 5 = \mu\epsilon$

   (ii) $744 = 700 + 40 + 4 = \psi\mu\delta$

   (iii) Use $'\beta$ to represent 2000.
   $2153 = 2000 + 100 + 50 + 3 = '\beta\rho\nu\gamma$

   (iv) Use $'\kappa$ to represent 20,000 and $'\alpha$ to represent 1000. $21,534 = 20,000 + 1000 + 500 + 30 + 4 = '\kappa'\alpha\phi\lambda\delta$

Section 2.3

26. Write out the numbers on both sides of the equation using expanded form. Use a variable for the missing base.

   (a) $32 = 44_b$

   $3 \times 10 + 2 \times 1 = 4b + 4 \times 1$ Solve for the unknown base.

   $30 + 2 - 4 = 4b$

   $28 = 4b$

   $7 = b$

   So, $32 = 44_{seven}$.

   (b) $57_{eight} = 10_b$

   $5 \times 8 + 7 \times 1 = 1 \times b + 0 \times 1$

$$40 + 7 = b$$
$$47 = b$$

So, $57_{\text{eight}} = 10_{\text{forty-seven}}$.

(c) $31_{\text{four}} = 11_b$

$$3 \times 4 + 1 \times 1 = 1 \times b + 1 \times 1$$
$$12 + 1 - 1 = b$$
$$12 = b$$

So, $31_{\text{four}} = 11_{\text{twelve}}$.

(d) $15_x = 30_y$

$$1x + 5 \times 1 = 3y + 0 \times 1$$
$$x + 5 = 3y$$
$$x = 3y - 5$$

Notice that $x = 3y - 5$ is an equation for a line, so there are an infinite number of solutions. However, the original equation puts restrictions on the solution. Consider base y. The digit 3 is used so y must be at least 4 since base 4 uses only the digits zero through three. If $y = 4$, then $x = 3(4) - 5 = 7$. Therefore, $x = 3y - 5$ and $x \geq 7$.

Section 2.3

27. List numerals in each base to determine the ones digit.
    (a) Base 10: 0, 2, 4, 6, 8, 10, 12, 14, 16, ...
        Notice the ones digit in each case is 0, 2, 4, 6, or 8.
    (b) Base 4: $0 = 0_{\text{four}}$, $2 = 2_{\text{four}}$, $4 = 10_{\text{four}}$, $6 = 12_{\text{four}}$, $8 = 20_{\text{four}}$, $10 = 22_{\text{four}}$, ...
        Notice the ones digit is always 0 or 2.
    (c) Base 2: $0 = 0_{\text{two}}$, $2 = 10_{\text{two}}$, $4 = 100_{\text{two}}$, $6 = 110_{\text{two}}$, $8 = 1000_{\text{two}}$, $10 = 1010_{\text{two}}$, ...
        Notice that the ones digit is always 0.
    (d) Base 5: $0 = 0_{\text{five}}$, $2 = 2_{\text{five}}$, $4 = 4_{\text{five}}$, $6 = 11_{\text{five}}$, $8 = 13_{\text{five}}$, $10 = 20_{\text{five}}$, $12 = 22_{\text{five}}$, ...
        Notice that the ones digit is always 0, 1, 2, 3, or 4. Base five uses only digits 0, 1, 2, 3, and 4 so there can be no others.

Section 2.3

28. Consider a simpler problem. How many digits would be used in a 25-page book? (Note: The front and back of each sheet of paper in a book are separate pages.) The page numbers are 1, 2, 3, 4, 5, 6, 7, 8, 9, 10, 11, 12, 13, 14, 15, 16, 17, 18, 19, 20, 21, 22, 23, 24 and 25. Notice that the page numbers from 1 to 9 each have 1 digit. The page numbers from 10 to 25 each have 2 digits. Therefore, the total number of digits used is found as follows:

(9 pages)(1 digit/page) + (16 pages)(2 digits/page) = 41 digits in all. To solve the given problem, set up a table relating page numbers to digits used.

Page Number	Digits/Page	Total Digits
$1-9$	1	$9 \times 1 = 9$
$10-99$	2	$90 \times 2 = 180$
$100-999$	3	$900 \times 3 = 2700$
$1000-9999$	4	$9000 \times 4 = 36,000$

Our book used 2989 digits. By adding the total number of digits on pages numbered from 1 to 999, we see that we have used only 2889 digits. There are 100 digits left to use. Each page from 1000 on uses 4 digits. Since $100 \div 4 = 25$, there are 25 pages left. These would be pages 1000 through 1024. Thus, there are 1024 pages in the book.

Section 2.3

29. Use expanded form to represent the two-digit number. Let the two-digit number be ab. In expanded form, the number would be $10a + 1b$. Set up two equations using the information given.

    (1) The sum of the digits is 12, so $a + b = 12$.

    (2) If the digits are reversed, the new number, ba, is 18 greater than the original, ab, so we have $10b + 1a = 10a + 1b + 18$.

Collecting like terms in (2), we have $-9a + 9b = 18$. Solving the system of equations, $a + b = 12$ and $-9a + 9b = 18$, simultaneously yields $a = 5$ and $b = 7$. Thus, the original two-digit number was 57.

Section 2.3

30. (a) Let's try this sequence of operations using my birthday which is 03/17/66.

    (1) Multiply the month by 4: $4(03) = 12$
    (2) Add 13: $12 + 13 = 25$
    (3) Multiply by 25: $25(25) = 625$
    (4) Subtract 200: $625 - 200 = 425$
    (5) Add the day of the month: $425 + 17 = 442$
    (6) Multiply by 2: $442(2) = 884$
    (7) Subtract 40: $884 - 40 = 844$
    (8) Multiply by 50: $844(50) = 42,200$
    (9) Add last two digits of birth year: $42,200 + 66 = 42,266$
    (10) Subtract 10,500: $42,266 - 10,500 = 31,766$

    If the final answer is of the form *abcdef*, then the digits in the tens and ones places, *ef*, are the last two digits of the birth year. The digits in the thousands and hundreds places, *cd*, are the digits of the day of the month. The digits in the hundred thousands and ten thousands places, *ab*, are the digits in the month of the year.

    (b) Use expanded notation. If the birthday is *ab/cd/ef*, then the final answer should be $100,000a + 10,000b + 1000c + 100d + 10e + f$.

(1) Multiply month by 4: $4(10a + b) = 40a + 4b$
(2) Add 13: $40a + 4b + 13$
(3) Multiply by 25: $25(40a + 4b + 13) = 1000a + 100b + 325$
(4) Subtract 200: $1000a + 100b + 325 - 200 = 1000a + 100b + 125$
(5) Add the day: $1000a + 100b + 125 + 10c + d = 1000a + 100b + 10c + d + 125$
(6) Multiply by 2: $2(1000a + 100b + 10c + d + 125) = 2000a + 200b + 20c + 2d + 250$
(7) Subtract 40: $2000a + 200b + 20c + 2d + 250 - 40 = 2000a + 200b + 20c + 2d + 210$
(8) Multiply by 50: $50(2000a + 200b + 20c + 2d + 210) = 100,000a + 10,000b + 1000c + 100d + 10,500$
(9) Add the last two digits of the year:
$100,000a + 10,000b + 1000c + 100d + 10e + f + 10,500$

(10) Subtract 10,500: $100,000a + 10,000b + 1000c + 100d + 10e + f + 10,500 - 10,500 = 100,000a + 10,000b + 1000c + 100d + 10e + f$

Since the expanded form of *abcdef* is $100,000a + 10,000b + 1000c + 100d + 10e + f$, we see this technique will always work.

SOLUTIONS - PART A PROBLEMS ≡≡≡≡≡≡≡≡

Chapter 3: Whole Numbers: Operations and Properties

Section 3.1

15. At this point, we know only that 1 is in the set. For the set to be closed under addition, we must be able to select any two elements, not necessarily different, add them and end up with an element in the set. Since 1 is in the set, and $1 + 1 = 2$, we know 2 must be in the set. It follows that since $1 + 2 = 3$, 3 must be in the set. Since $1 + 3 = 4$, 4 must be in the set. If we continue in this manner, we will generate the set of counting numbers.

Section 3.1

16. We can use only three plus or minus signs. This means we can have only four terms with one of them being at least a three-digit number. If we keep the digits in order and consider possible three-digit numbers, then we notice that any three-digit number besides 123 will yield a number too large to get back to 100. Therefore, the other six digits must form the following two-digit numbers: 45, 67, and 89. Trial and error with the signs leads to the solution $123 - 45 - 67 + 89 = 100$.

Section 3.1

17. Since the magic square will contain all the numbers from 10 to 25 exactly once, and each row has the same sum, if we add the numbers from 10 to 25 and divide by 4 (the number of rows), then we will find the sum for each row.

$$(10 + 11 + 12 + ... + 23 + 24 + 25) \div 4 = \frac{280}{4} = 70$$

Consider column 2. The sum of the missing numbers must be $70 - 16 - 23 = 31$. The only unused pair of numbers that add to 31 are 11 and 20.

25	11		
14	20	19	17
18	16		
13	23	24	10

Consider row 2. The sum of the missing numbers must be $70 - 19 - 17 = 34$. The only possible pairs of unused numbers that add to 34 are 12 and 22, 13 and 21, 14 and 20. Since column 2 and row 2 contain a common number, we must choose the pair 14 and 20 since 20 is also in column 2. Fill in these numbers, placing 20 at the intersection of row 2 and column 2.

Consider column 1. The missing number must be $70 - 25 - 14 - 18 = 13$.

Consider row 4. The missing number must be $70 - 13 - 23 - 10 = 24$.

Consider column 3. The missing numbers must add to $70 - 19 - 24 = 27$. The only unused pair of numbers that add to 27 are 12 and 15. In order to figure out which squares to place them in, we need to consider another row.

25	11	12	22
14	20	19	17
18	16	15	21
13	23	24	10

Consider row 1. The missing numbers must add to $70 - 25 - 11 = 34$. The only unused pair of numbers that add to 34 are 12 and 22. Since 12 must also be in column 3, place 12 at the intersection of row 1 and column 3. Then we know that 15 belongs at the intersection of column3 and row 3. The final unused numbers, 21 and 22, must be placed at the intersections of row 3 and column 4, and row 1 and column 4, respectively. The final solution is shown.

Section 3.1

18. Notice that when the three diagonals of a hexagon are drawn in, the hexagon looks like a collection of six equilateral triangles. What is "magic" about the magic hexagon is that the sum of the numbers along each side of each equilateral triangle is the same, 22.

Section 3.1

19. (a) Use the method given:

(i)	(ii)	(iii)
39	87	32
+93	+78	+23
132	165	55
231	561	
363	726	
	627	
	1353	
	3531	
	4884	

(b) In part (a) two-digit numbers were used. Notice that when the sum of the two digits of the original number is less than 10, the procedure takes one step because there are no carries. If the sum of the two digits is 15 or greater, then the procedure can take more than three steps because there is a carry in the first sum, causing the total to exceed 150. This, in turn, causes a carry in at least the next two steps. Thus, two-digit numbers, whose digits add to at least 15, such as 69, 78, 79, or 89, will take more than three steps. Verify this with one of the numbers.

Section 3.1

20. Let n = the youngest daughter's age. Since the number of years between the youngest daughter's age and the next youngest daughter's age is equal to the youngest daughter's age, the next youngest daughter must be $n + n = 2n$ years old. Since the daughters' ages are spaced evenly, the other daughters must be $3n$, $4n$ and $5n$ years old respectively. The oldest daughter is 16 years older than the youngest daughter, so $n + 16 = 5n$. Solving, we see that $4n = 16$ and $n = 4$. The ages are 4, 8, 12, 16, and 20.

Section 3.1

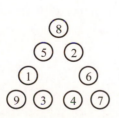

21. Access the eManipulative, *Number Puzzles*. Consider the corner circles first. They are important because numbers placed in corner circles are added along two sides. Place the number 9 in a corner. The remaining three circles on each of the two sides of the triangle containing the 9 must be filled with numbers that add to 23. The possible combinations are 1, 5, 8; 1, 6, 7; 2, 4, 8; 2, 5, 7; 3, 4, 7; and

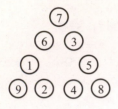

3, 5, 6. Remember that we can use each digit only once.

The only three sets of combinations that do not repeat numbers are 1, 5, 8 and 3, 4, 7 or 1, 7, 6 and 2, 4, 8 or 2, 4, 8 and 3, 5, 6. If we try to use 1, 7, 6 and 2, 4, 8 then a solution is possible. If we try to use 1, 5, 8 and 3, 4, 7, then a solution is possible. If we try to use 2, 4, 8 and 3, 5, 6, then the remaining side will add to at most 22. Two possible solutions are shown.

Section 3.2

18. A single team is made up of 4 pairs of dancers. A pair is 2, so there are $2 \times 4 = 8$ dancers per team. The contest has 213 teams so (213 teams)(8 dancers per team) = 1704 dancers. Thus, there are 1704 dancers participating in the contest.

Section 3.2

19. Each stamp costs 32¢. Using the Repeated-Addition Approach, twelve 32¢ stamps would cost $3.84 because $0.32 + 0.32 + 0.32 + 0.32 + 0.32 + 0.32 + 0.32 + 0.32 + 0.32 + 0.32 + 0.32 + 0.32 = 12(0.32) = 3.84$.

Section 3.2

20. We want to know how many dollars can be purchased with 300 yen. We know $1 is worth 121 yen so every 121 yen can be viewed as a single group corresponding to $1. We need to figure out how many groups of 121 yen there are in 300 yen. This is a measurement division problem. We see $300 \div 121 \approx 2.48$. Therefore, we see that $2.48 can be purchased with 300 yen.

Section 3.2

21. The estate valued at $270,000 is to be divided into three parts with the same amount of money in each. By the Missing-Factor Approach, since $270,000 = 3 \times 90,000$, we know $270,000 \div 3 = 90,000$. Each heir will receive $90,000 before taxes.

Section 3.2

22. In order for Shirley to avoid reentering the number 12349, she needs to input some number, *a*, such that $12349 \times a = 12349$. Shirley should enter the number 1 since 1 is the identity for multiplication. She would be using the Identity Property for Whole-Number Multiplication.

Section 3.2

23. Yes, set *A* is closed under multiplication. For a set to be closed under multiplication, the product of any two elements (not necessarily different elements) from the set must be in the set. Remember that in the set of whole numbers multiplication can be thought of as repeated addition. Because set *A* is closed under addition, any product, (i.e., repeated sum) is also in the set *A*.

Section 3.2

24. (a) To determine the sum for each row, we need to find the sum of all the numbers in the magic square. Since the sum of the numbers from 1 to 9 is 45, the total for each row must be $45 \div 3 = 15$. Since the numbers on the diagonal must also add to 15, the bottom left corner must be 2. Consider the row and column containing the number 8. Out of the remaining digits, our only options are 6 and 1 or 4 and 3 if the sum is to be 15. Similarly, in the row and column containing the number 2, our only options are 9 and 4 or 6 and 7. One possible magic square is shown.

4	3	8
9	5	1
2	7	6

(b) A base must be selected. We can, for example, choose base 2. We will let the digits 1 through 9 be used as exponents. Since we add exponents when we multiply numbers with exponents, we can use the arrangement of numbers in the magic square from (a) to form the multiplicative magic square. Each row, column and diagonal has a product of 2^{15}.

2^4	2^3	2^8
2^9	2^5	2^1
2^2	2^7	2^6

Section 3.2

25. Notice that each line contains consecutive odd numbers beginning, in the first line, with 1. Each new line contains one more number than the previous line. The sum of the numbers in each line is the cube of the number of terms in

the line. Therefore, the next three lines in the pattern must be as follows:

$$31 + 33 + 35 + 37 + 39 + 41 = 6^3 = 216$$
$$43 + 45 + 47 + 49 + 51 + 53 + 55 = 7^3 = 343$$
$$57 + 59 + 61 + 63 + 65 + 67 + 69 + 71 = 8^3 = 512.$$

Section 3.2

26. Consider multiplication and division, the most restrictive operations, first. The two numbers that are multiplied must result in a single digit answer. Our only options are $2 \times 3 = 6$ or $2 \times 4 = 8$. The only division problems that result in whole numbers are $8 \div 4 = 2$, $8 \div 2 = 4$, $6 \div 2 = 3$, or $6 \div 3 = 2$. Through trial and error, we find that $6 \div 3 = 2$ is the only appropriate division problem. The solution is shown next.

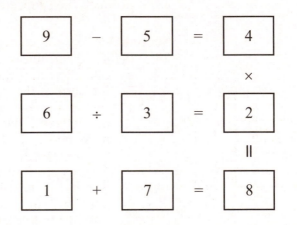

Section 3.2

27. Use a variable. Let n = the original number. Perform the operations.

   (1) Add 10: $n + 10$

   (2) Multiply by 2: $2(n + 10) = 2n + 20$

   (3) Add 100: $2n + 20 + 100 = 2n + 120$

   (4) Divide by 2: $(2n + 120) \div 2 = n + 60$

   (5) Subtract the original number: $n + 60 - n = 60$

No matter what the original number is, the result will always be 60 after performing the given set of operations. Sixty is the number of minutes in an hour.

Section 3.2

28. We need to find out who owned each frog and how each frog placed. From clue 1, we know that since Michelle's frog finished ahead of Bounce and Hoppy, her frog must be either Hippy or Pounce. From clue 2, since Hippy and Hoppy tied for second, Michelle's frog must have finished first and must be Pounce. Also, since Hippy and Hoppy tied for second, Bounce must have been third.

From clue 3, since Kevin and Wendy recaptured Hoppy after he escaped from his owner, we know neither of them owned Hoppy. Since Michelle owns Pounce, the only person left to own Hoppy is Jason. From clue 4, Kevin's frog earned a red ribbon for second place. Since the other second-place frog was owned by Jason, we know Kevin owns Hippy.

Finally, the only frog and owner left are Wendy and Bounce. Thus, the solution is as follows:

Place	Frog	Owner
First	Pounce	Michelle
Second	Hippy	Kevin
Second	Hoppy	Jason
Third	Bounce	Wendy

Section 3.2

29. Notice there are three unknowns. Let

    p = number of people in the group,
    t = number of cups of tea each drank, and
    c = number of cakes each ate.

The total number of cups of tea is pt, so $30pt$ is the cost of the tea in cents. Similarly, pc is the total number of cakes, so $50pc$ is the cost of the cakes in cents. Therefore, since the total bill came to 1330 cents, we know

$$30pt + 50pc = 1330$$

$$10p(3t + 5c) = 1330$$

$$p(3t + 5c) = 133.$$

We have two factors, p and $(3t + 5c)$, which when multiplied yield 133. The factors of 133 are 1 and 133 or 7 and 19. We can eliminate 1×133 since a "group" implies more than one person so the factors are 7 and 19. We know $3t + 5c \neq 7$ when t and c are whole numbers. Therefore, $p = 7$ and $3t + 5c = 19$. By guessing and checking, we find $c = 2$ and $t = 3$. Each of the 7 people had 3 cups of tea and 2 cakes.

Section 3.2

30. When a single creature reproduces itself, it divides itself into three new creatures (not three *additional* creatures). Construct a table and compare the number of days elapsed to the number of creatures on earth.

Days Elapsed	Number of Creatures
1	$1 = 3^0$
2	$3 = 3^1$
3	$9 = 3^2$
4	$27 = 3^3$

Notice that the number of creatures on any given day is 3 raised to a power that is 1 less than the number of days elapsed. Thus, on day 30, there must be 3^{29} or almost 70 trillion creatures.

Section 3.2

31. Consider the simpler problem of finding one counterfeit coin out of three coins in a single weighing. Place one coin in each pan. If they balance, then the extra coin is counterfeit. If not, the lighter coin is counterfeit. In the case of 8 coins, place 3 coins on each pan. If they balance, weigh the remaining two coins to find the counterfeit one. If three of the coins are lighter, apply the simpler problem scenario to find the counterfeit coin. (For the case where one coin out of five is counterfeit, see problem 20 in Section 2.2A.)

Section 3.2

32. We want to know whether the property "If $ab = bc$, then $a = b$ for all whole numbers" is true. Recall the set of whole numbers is $\{0, 1, 2, 3, 4, \ldots\}$. Try a few examples. Suppose that $ac = bc$. If we let $a = 6$, $b = 11$, and $c = 0$, then $6 \times 0 = 11 \times 0$, so $0 = 0$ is true, but $6 \neq 11$. Therefore, the property is not true for all whole numbers.

Section 3.3

15. Let a, m, and n be whole numbers where a is not zero. Use the Definition of the Whole-Number Exponent and the theorem that states $a^m a^n = a^{m+n}$ in the following proof.

$$\left(a^m\right)^n = \underbrace{\left(a^m\right)\left(a^m\right)\cdots\left(a^m\right)}_{n \text{ factors}} \quad a^{\overbrace{m+m+\cdots+m}^{n \text{ addends}}} = a^{m \cdot n}$$

Section 3.3

16. We can distribute exponentiation over a product:

$$(ab)^m = a^m \times b^m$$

Any exponent can be written as a sum of exponents, and a number raised to a sum can be broken up into a product:

$$a^{m+n} = a^m \times a^n$$

(a) $6^{10} = (2 \times 3)^{10} = 2^{10} \times 3^{10}$ and $3^{20} = 3^{10+10} = 3^{10} \times 3^{10}$.

Compare to see that $6^{10} = 2^{10} \times 3^{10} < 3^{10} \times 3^{10} = 3^{20}$.

(b) $9^9 = (3 \times 3)^9 = 3^9 \times 3^9 = 3^{18}$. Since $18 < 20$, we know $9^9 = 3^{18} < 3^{20}$.

(c) $12^{10} = (3 \times 4)^{10} = 3^{10} \times 4^{10}$ and $3^{20} = 3^{10+10} = 3^{10} \times 3^{10}$.

Compare to see that $12^{10} = 3^{10} \times 4^{10} > 3^{10} \times 3^{10} = 3^{20}$.

Section 3.3

17. Make a table to show how the price changed over the period of a few years. Here $n =$ the number of 5-year periods since 2000.

Year	Price (in dollars)	n
2000	0.25	0
2005	0.50	1
2010	1.00	2
2015	2.00	3
2020	4.00	4
2025	8.00	5
2030	16.00	6
2035	32.00	7
2040	64.00	8

(a) In 2015, the price of the candy bar would be $2.00.

(b) In 2040, the price of the candy bar would be $64.00.

(c) Notice that since the price doubles, or is 2 times as large, at each increase, the sequence of prices is a geometric sequence, where $a = 0.25$, $r = 2$, and begins with $n = 0$. Therefore, $P(n) = 0.25(2)^n$ dollars or $P(n) = 25(2)^n$ cents.

Section 3.3

18. Consider an example. Let $n(A) = 3$, $n(B) = 5$, and $n(C) = 6$. The fact that $3 < 5$ means that we can find a 1-1 correspondence between set A and a proper subset of set B.

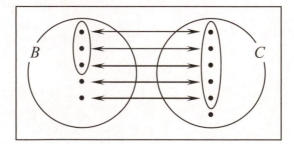

Also, $5 < 6$ means that we can find a 1-1 correspondence between set B and a proper subset of set C.

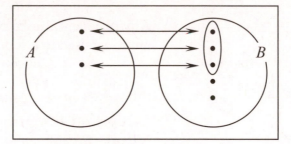

Notice that the elements in A can be matched with a proper subset of the elements of B. Furthermore, this proper subset can be matched with a proper subset of the previous proper subset of C.

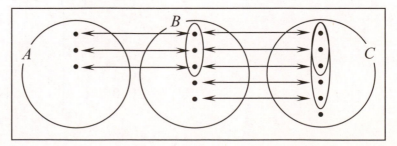

Thus, since there is a 1-1 correspondence between set *A* and a proper subset of *C*, we have 3 < 6. This can be generalized to the case where $a = n(A)$, $b = n(B)$, and $c = n(C)$.

Section 3.3

19. $2 + 3 + 4 = 9 = 1 + 8 = 1^3 + 2^3$
    $5 + 6 + 7 + 8 + 9 = 35 = 8 + 27 = 2^3 + 3^3$
    $10 + 11 + 12 + 13 + 14 + 15 + 16 = 91 = 27 + 64 = 3^3 + 4^3$

    (a) The next two lines in the sequence are:

    $17 + 18 + 19 + 20 + 21 + 22 + 23 + 24 + 25 = 4^3 + 5^3$ and
    $26 + 27 + 28 + 29 + 30 + 31 + 32 + 33 + 34 + 35 + 36 = 5^3 + 6^3$.

    Notice that the number of terms in the sum is the same as the sum of the base numbers to the right of the equal sign. The first number in each sum is one more than the square of the smaller base number. The last number in the sum is the square of the larger base number.

    (b) $9^3 + 10^3$ will have $9 + 10 = 19$ terms in the sum. The first term in the sum will be $9^2 + 1 = 82$, and the last term will be $10^2 = 100$. Therefore, $82 + 83 + 84 + \ldots + 99 + 100 = 9^3 + 10^3$.

    (c) $12^3 + 13^3$ will have $12 + 13 = 25$ terms in the sum. The first term will be $12^2 + 1 = 145$, and the last term will be $13^2 = 169$. Therefore, $145 + 146 + 147 + \ldots + 168 + 169 = 12^3 + 13^3$.

    (d) $n^3 + (n + 1)^3$ will have $n + n + 1 = 2n + 1$ terms in the sum. The first term in the sum will be $n^2 + 1$, and the last term will be $(n + 1)^2$. Therefore, we know that $(n^2 + 1) + (n^2 + 2) + (n^2 + 3) + \ldots + (n + 1)^2 = n^3 + (n + 1)^3$.

Section 3.3

20.   Suppose the four toppings are pepperoni, onion, sausage, and anchovies. For each size pizza we decide how many toppings to put on: 0, 1, 2, 3, or 4. For example, for each of the pizza sizes (S, M, L, XL), we may or may not include pepperoni.

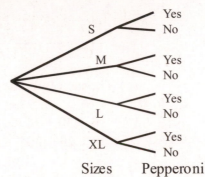

At this stage, there are $4 \times 2 = 8$ possible pizza choices. For each additional topping, we may include it or not include it. This doubles the number of pizza types for every topping considered. Thus, there are 64 different pizza combinations since $4 \times 2 \times 2 \times 2 \times 2 = 4 \times 2^4 = 64$.

Section 3.3

21.   (a)   The only one-digit perfect squares are 0, 1, 4, and 9. The only two-digit perfect squares are 16, 25, 36, 49, 64, and 81. Notice that only 49 consists of digits that are each perfect squares. None of the other two-digit perfect squares have perfect squares for both digits.

   (b)   List all three-digit perfect squares. Find any that include a single one-digit perfect square and a two-digit perfect square. The lists we made from part (a) will be helpful.

Three-Digit Perfect Squares		
100	289	576
121	324	625
144	**361**	676
169	400	729
196	441	784
225	484	841
256	529	900
		961

Since 169 is made up of 16 (a two-digit square) and 9 (a one-digit square), and 361 is made up of 36 (a two-digit square) and 1 (a one-digit square), both 169 and 361 have the desired property.

For parts (c) - (f), it will be helpful to have a list of all four-digit perfect squares.

Four-Digit Perfect Squares

1024	2116	3600	5476	7744
1089	2209	3721	5625	7921
1156	2304	3844	5776	8100
1225	2401	3969	5929	8281
1296	2500	4096	6084	8464
1369	2601	4225	6241	8649
1444	2704	4356	6400	8836
1521	2809	4489	6561	9025
1600	2916	4624	6724	9216
1681	3025	4761	6889	9409
1764	3136	4900	7056	9604
1849	3249	5041	7225	9801
1936	3364	5184	7396	
2025	3481	5329	7569	

(c) Use the lists from part (a) to find the desired numbers.

Four-Digit Square	Two One-Digit Squares	Two-Digit Square
1369	1, 9	36
1600	0, 0	16
1936	1, 9	36
2500	0, 0	25
3600	0, 0	36
4900	0, 0	49
6400	0, 0	64
8100	0, 0	81
9025	9, 0	25

(d) Use the list from part (b) to find the desired numbers.

Four-Digit Square	Three-Digit Square	One-Digit Square
1225	225	1
1444	144	4
3249	324	9
4225	225	4
4900	900	4

(e) Use the list from part (a) to find the desired numbers.

Four-Digit Square	Two Two-Digit Squares
1681	16, 81

(f) Since the only single-digit perfect squares are 0, 1, 4, and 9, the only four-digit perfect squares made up of four one-digit squares are 1444, 4900, and 9409.

Section 3.3

22. Consider all possible products and compare them to perfect squares.

Mathematician One:

$2 \times 4 = 8 \qquad 2 \times 12 = 24 \qquad 2 \times 22 = 44$

$8 + 1 = 9 \qquad 24 + 1 = 25 \qquad 44 + 1 = 45$

$\quad 9 = 3^2 \qquad\quad 25 = 5^2 \qquad\quad 45 = \text{Not Square}$

Mathematician One is incorrect.

Mathematician Two:

$\quad 2 \times 12 = 24 \qquad\quad 2 \times 24 = 48 \qquad\quad 2 \times 2380 = 4760$

$24 + 1 = 25 \qquad\qquad 48 + 1 = 49 \qquad\quad 4760 + 1 = 4761$

$\quad 25 = 5^2 \qquad\qquad\quad 49 = 7^2 \qquad\qquad 4761 = 69^2$

$12 \times 24 = 288 \qquad 12 \times 2380 = 28,560 \qquad 24 \times 2380 = 57,120$

$288 + 1 = 289 \qquad 28,560 + 1 = 28,561 \qquad 57,120 + 1 = 57,121$

$\quad 289 = 17^2 \qquad\quad 28,561 = 169^2 \qquad\qquad 57,121 = 239^2$

Mathematician Two is correct.

Section 3.3

23. (a) Prove: If $a < b$, then $a + c < b + c$.

Suppose that $a < b$. Then we know there exists a number n such that $n > 0$ and $a + n = b$. If we add c to both sides of this equation, we have the following:

$(a + n) + c = b + c$

$a + (n + c) = b + c$ Associative Property for Addition

$a + (c + n) = b + c$ Commutative Property for Addition

$(a + c) + n = b + c$ Associative Property for Addition

So, by the definition of less than, we see $a + c < b + c$.

(b) Prove: If $a < b$, then $a - c < b - c$.

Suppose $a < b$. Then we know there exists a number, n, such that $n > 0$, and $a + n = b$. If we subtract c from both sides of this equation, we have

$(a + n) - c = b - c$

$(a + n) + (-c) = b - c$

$a + [n + (-c)] = b - c$ Associative Property for Addition

$a + (-c + n) = b - c$ Commutative Property for Addition

$[a + (-c)] + n = b - c$ Associative Property for Addition

$(a - c) + n = b - c$

So, by the definition of less than, we see $a - c < b - c$.

SOLUTIONS - PART A PROBLEMS

Chapter 4: Whole-Number Computation – Mental, Electronic, and Written

Section 4.1

25. Round each of the numbers to the nearest thousand and add them.
$$5000 + 14,000 + 8000 + 20,000 + 9000 + 39,000 = 95,000$$
The desired sum is 87,000, which is 8000 less than 95,000. The number that rounded to 8000 was 7782. Therefore, the number 7782 was not included.

Section 4.1

26. Rewrite the expression, $493,827,156^2$, using properties of exponents and factors.
$$
\begin{aligned}
493,827,156^2 &= (493,827,156)(493,827,156) \\
&= \big[(2)(246,913,578)\big]\big[(2)(246,913,578)\big] \\
&= (246,913,578)\big[(2)(2)(246,913,578)\big] \\
&= (246,913,578)(987,654,312)
\end{aligned}
$$
Thus, the equation is true.

Section 4.1

27. Use rounding techniques and the guess and test method to estimate possible products.
    (a) $13 \times 6000 = 78,000$ is too small.
    $140 \times 800 = 112,000$ is too small.
    $1400 \times 90 = 126,000$ is too big, but each number was rounded up. So $1357 \times 90 = 122,130$.
    (b) $6 \times 70,000 = 420,000$ is too small.
    $70 \times 7,000 = 490,000$ is too big, but each number was rounded up. So check $66 \times 6666 = 439,956$.
    (c) Notice the ones digit is a 4. Using one multiplication sign, this could only result from the 9, 6 or 4, 6 combination. So try $789 \times 3,456 = 2,726,784$, which is too small and $78,934 \times 56 = 4,420,304$, which is too big. Since we did not find the solution, we should try multiplying three numbers using two multiplication signs. Notice $8 \times 3 \times 6$ ends in a 4, so we use these as the ones digits. Therefore, $78 \times 93 \times 456 = 3,307,824$.

(d) We use the same procedure as in (c). We see that to obtain a 5 in the ones place, we are forced to split the digits after the 5 when using only one multiplication sign. $12,345 \times 67 = 827,115$ is too big. Use two multiplication signs and notice we must break the digits at odd numbers. Therefore, $123 \times 45 \times 67 = 370,845$.

Section 4.1

28. To find a range for subtraction problems for three-digit numbers, we look for a way to obtain a high estimate and a low estimate. Consider two cases: borrowing or not borrowing.

(i) When it is necessary to borrow in the hundreds place, we should round both numbers down for the high estimate. For the low estimate, we should round the minuend down and the subtrahend up. For example, consider $742 - 281$. For the high estimate, round both numbers down to $700 - 200 = 500$. For the low estimate, round the minuend down and the subtrahend up to $700 - 300 = 400$. Thus, the answer is between 400 and 500.

(ii) When no borrowing is needed, round the minuend up and the subtrahend down for the high estimate. Round both of them up for the low estimate. For example, consider $742 - 222$. For the high estimate, round the minuend up and the subtrahend down to $800 - 200 = 600$. For the low estimate round both up to $800 - 300 = 500$. Thus, the answer is between 500 and 600.

Section 4.1

29. On most hand-held calculators, squaring a number greater than 99,999 produces an answer in scientific notation. Information can be lost since not all the digits are necessarily displayed. When squaring a number that is greater than 99,999 it is possible to rewrite the number as a sum that can be squared easily using the distributive property. Consider the number 13,333,333. We can rewrite it as $13,000,000 + 333,000 + 333$. Therefore, the number $13,333,333^2$ can be written as follows:

$(13{,}000{,}000 + 333{,}000 + 333)(13{,}000{,}000 + 333{,}000 + 333) =$
169,000,000,000,000 + 4,329,000,000,000 + 4,329,000,00
+ 4,329,000,000,000 + 110,889,000,000 + 110,889,000 +
4,329,000,000 + 110,889,000 + 110,889 =
177,777,768,888,889.

Although $13{,}000{,}000 \times 13{,}000{,}000$ would be converted to scientific notation on the calculator, we can use the fact that $13 \times 13 = 169$ *will* fit in the display, and then we can add on the appropriate number of zeros.

Section 4.1

30. $99 \times 36 = 3564$

$99 \times 23 = 2277$

If we think of 99 as $100 - 1$, then

$99 \times 36 = (100 - 1) \times 36 = 3600 - 36 = 3564$

$99 \times 23 = (100 - 1) \times 23 = 2300 - 23 = 2277.$

So, $99 \times 57 = (100 - 1) \times 57 = 5700 - 57 = 5643$ and $99 \times 63 = (100 - 1) \times 63 = 6300 - 63 = 6237.$

Section 4.1

31. (a) Consider $25^2 = 625$, $35^2 = 1225$, $45^2 = 2025$, and $55^2 = 3025$. Notice that each number to be squared is of the form $a5$ where a is the tens digit and 5 is the ones digit. Squaring any number of the form $a5$ results in a number whose first digit(s) are $a(a + 1)$ and whose final digits are always 25. In general, $(a5)^2 = 100a(a + 1) + 25$. Using this method, we can find the values of

65^2: $6 \times 7 = 42$,   so $65^2 = 100(42) + 25 = 4225$
75^2: $7 \times 8 = 56$,   so $75^2 = 100(56) + 25 = 5625$
95^2: $9 \times 10 = 90$,   so $95^2 = 100(90) + 25 = 9025$

(b) Let $a5$ be any two-digit number, where a is the tens digit and 5 is the ones digit. Use expanded form to find the square.

$$\begin{aligned}
(a5)^2 &= (10a + 5)(10a + 5) \\
&= 100a^2 + 50a + 50a + 25 \\
&= 100a^2 + 100a + 25 \\
&= 100a(a + 1) + 25
\end{aligned}$$

Section 4.1

32. Yes, George was correct. To calculate the time for the inhabitant of the moon to hear the battle of Waterloo, we need to first calculate the time in minutes required for sound to reach the moon. For sound to travel 123,256 miles at 4 miles per minute it would take $123,256 \div 4 = 30,814$ minutes. Now convert this time to days, hours, and minutes. Since 1 day = 24 hours = 1440 minutes, 30,814 minutes is $30,814 \div 1440 = 21$ days, with a remainder of 574 minutes. Since 1 hour = 60 minutes, the 574 minutes is $574 \div 60 = 9$ hours, with a remainder of 34 minutes. Thus, the total time required is 21 days, 9 hours, and 34 minutes.

Section 4.1

33. Recall that when multiplying numbers, the ones digit in the solution is the same as the ones digit of the product of the ones digits of the original factors. Consider the given numbers. The ones digits are 8 and 9. Since $8 \times 9 = 72$, the ones digit of the solution is 2. This means that the given numbers could not possibly be the factors of the number consisting of 71 consecutive 1s because it has a 1 in the ones place.

Section 4.1

34. For each product, we need to find the number that is halfway between the factors. Then we can rewrite each factor by adding to or subtracting from this number.

(a) $54 \times 46 = (50+4)(50-4) = 50^2 - 4^2 = 2484$

(b) $81 \times 79 = (80+1)(80-1) = 80^2 - 1^2 = 6399$

(c) $122 \times 118 = (120+2)(120-2) = 120^2 - 2^2 = 14,396$

(d) $1210 \times 1190 = (1200+10)(1200-10)$

$$= 1200^2 - 10^2$$
$$= 1,439,900$$

Section 4.1

35. Notice that the result of $898{,}423 \times 112{,}303$ will not fit into the display of the calculator. Rewrite each factor as a sum and use the distributive property: $898{,}423 \times 112{,}303 = (898{,}000 + 423)(112{,}000 + 303) = 100{,}576{,}000{,}000 + 272{,}094{,}000 + 47{,}376{,}000 + 128{,}169 = 100{,}895{,}598{,}169.$

Section 4.1

36. We can rewrite $439{,}268 \times 6852$ as $(439{,}000 + 268) \times 6852$ and distribute. Then we can multiply 439×6852 on the eight-digit calculator and add on 3 zeros (or multiply by 1000).

$$(439{,}000 + 268) \times 6852 = (439 \times 6852) \times 1000 + 268 \times 6852$$
$$= 3{,}008{,}028 \times 1000 + 1{,}836{,}336$$
$$= 3{,}008{,}028{,}000 + 1{,}836{,}336$$
$$= 3{,}009{,}864{,}336$$

Section 4.1

37. (a) If we apply the order of operations to the given expression, that is, multiply first and add last, we obtain $76 \times 54 + 97 = 4104 + 97 = 4201$. In order to obtain 11,476, we must insert parentheses so that we add first: $76 \times (54 + 97) = 76 \times 151 = 11{,}476$.

    (b) The order of operations requires that we square 13 first and then multiply by 4: $4 \times 13^2 = 4 \times 169 = 676$. In order to obtain 2704, we need to first multiply 4×13 and then square the result: $(4 \times 13)^2 = 52^2 = 2704$.

    (c) The standard order of operations produces $13 + 59^2 \times 47 = 13 + 3481 \times 47 = 13 + 163{,}607 = 163{,}620$. No parentheses are necessary.

    (d) The order of operations requires that we square first and then divide, followed by subtraction and addition, respectively.

$$79 - 43 \div 2 + 17^2 = 79 - 43 \div 2 + 289$$
$$= 79 - 21.5 + 289$$
$$= 57.5 + 289$$
$$= 346.5$$

Since the desired answer, 307, is a whole number, insert parentheses to ensure that a whole number results from the division.

$$(79-43)\div 2 + 17^2 = (79-43)\div 2 + 289$$
$$= 36 \div 2 + 289$$
$$= 18 + 289$$
$$= 307$$

Section 4.1

38. (a) Notice that each product is of the form $ab \times ac$, where a is the tens digit and b and c are the ones digits. The resulting product is of the form $a(a+1)\times 100 + b \times c$. Using this form, we see that
$$57 \times 53 = 5 \times 6 \times 100 + 7 \times 3$$
$$= 3000 + 21$$
$$= 3021.$$

(b) Notice that the factors ab and ac are related further in that $b + c = 10$ so $c = 10 - b$. Thus, the factors can be written as $ab \times a(10 - b)$, where a is the tens digit, and b and $10 - b$ are the ones digits. (Note: In the expression $a(10 - b)$, the parentheses do NOT indicate multiplication but instead are used to separate the tens digits from the ones digit.)
$$ab \times a(10 - b) = (10a + b)(10a + 10 - b)$$
$$= 100a^2 + 100a - 10ab + 10ab + 10b - b^2$$
$$= 100a^2 + 100a + 10b - b^2$$
$$= 100a(a + 1) + b(10 - b) \qquad \text{Factoring}$$
$$= 100a(a + 1) + bc \qquad \text{Since } c = 10 - b$$

Thus $ab \times a(10 - b)$ has the desired form.

(c) Problem 31 is a special case where b and c are 5.

Section 4.1

39. To use the "round a 5 up" method, we must first identify the digit in the place to which we are rounding. Once this digit is identified, consider the digit to its right. If that digit is a 5, 6, 7, 8, or 9, then add 1 to the digit to which we are rounding. (Note: If the digit in the place to which we are

rounding is a 9 and we add 1, then we must also perform any necessary carrying that this may cause.) If the digit to the right is a 4 or less, then leave the digit in the place to which we are rounding alone. Finally, put zeros in all the places to the right of the digit to which we are rounding to obtain the "rounded" number.

Section 4.1

40. Begin by trying any eight consecutive odd numbers, such as 7, 9, 11, 13, 15, 17, 19, and 21. Their product is 916,620,705, which is much too big. Rather than randomly guessing another set of numbers, eliminate the largest, 21, and include 5. The new product is 218,243,025. This is still too big. When we eliminate the 19 and include 3, the product is the number we were looking for. Therefore, the eight consecutive odd numbers are 3, 5, 7, 9, 11, 13, 15, and 17.

Section 4.1

41. In order to obtain exactly one liter of water, we must pour water from one pail to the other. Notice two 3-liter pails are equal to 6 liters, which is one liter more than a 5-liter pail. Fill the 3-liter pail. Pour it into the 5-liter pail. Fill the 3-liter pail again. Pour as much as you can into the 5-liter pail. This leaves the desired one liter of water in the 3-liter pail.

Section 4.2

35. The correct solution to the problem is

$$
\begin{array}{r}
1 \\
29 \\
+83 \\
\hline
112
\end{array}
$$

Larry is not carrying at all. He should carry the 1 when he adds 9 and 3. He just writes down the 12. As a result, when he adds the 8 and the 2 (the 80 and 20), he places the 1 in the thousands place rather than in the hundreds place. Curly adds the 9 and 3 which is 12, but he carries the ones digit instead of the tens digit. Moe fails to carry the tens digit after adding 9 and 3, but what can you expect from three stooges?

Section 4.2

36. Guess and test but look for restrictions on the sums first. In the hundreds place the numbers must total 9 or less since there is no digit in the thousands place of the solution (that is, no carry). Also, you may check for yourself to see that there must be at least one carry since each digit is used once. Two possible solutions are given next.

	359	and	281
	+127		+673
	486		954

Section 4.2

37. (a) To obtain the greatest sum, place the largest digits in the hundreds places. The largest of the remaining digits must be placed in the tens places. The last two remaining digits are placed in the ones places.

$$863$$
$$+742$$
$$1605$$

(b) To obtain the least sum, place the smallest digits in the hundreds places. The smallest of the remaining digits must be placed in the tens places. The last two remaining digits are placed in the ones places.

$$347$$
$$+268$$
$$615$$

Section 4.2

38. There is no restriction on the number of additions that can be used. In order to obtain a sum of 100, at most two digits can be paired up at a time. Since the digits must be kept in order, begin on one side and rule out possible number combinations.

Begin by pairing digits from smallest to largest: $12 + 34 + 56 + 7 = 109$. Since this sum is greater than 100, try to split up one of the pairs. Notice that $34 + 56 = 90$, which means we still need to add 10. By splitting the number 12 into $1 + 2$ and adding 7, we obtain the 10 we need. One solution is $1 + 2 + 34 + 56 + 7 = 100$.

If we worked with pairs from largest to smallest, we would consider $1 + 23 + 45 + 67 = 136$. Notice that $23 + 67 = 90$. By splitting the number 45 into $4 + 5$, we obtain another solution: $1 + 23 + 4 + 5 + 67 = 100$.

Section 4.2

39. In order to replace 7 digits with zeros and obtain a sum of 1111, each column must add to 1, 11, or 21. Notice that the digits in the hundreds column must always add to 11.

(a) First consider the hundreds column since it must add to 11. This total might result after carrying 2, 1, or 0 from the tens column. Make a list of the possible sums of the digits in the hundreds column involving each of the carries.

<u>If we carry 2</u> from the tens column, we need to find combinations of digits that add to 9. The choices are $9 + 0 + 0 + 0 + 0$ or $0 + 0 + 5 + 3 + 1$.

<u>If we carry 1</u> from the tens column, we need to find combinations of digits that add to 10. The choices are $9 + 0 + 0 + 0 + 1$ or $0 + 7 + 0 + 3 + 0$.

<u>If we carry 0</u> from the tens column, then the combination of digits must add to 11. The only choice is $0 + 7 + 0 + 3 + 1$.

Try one of these possibilities and continue. For example, use $9 + 0 + 0 + 0 + 0$. The tens column must add to 21. Make a list of the possible tens digit combinations that total 21 after possible carries of 2, 1, or 0 from the ones column.

<u>If we carry 2</u> from the ones column, find combinations of digits to add to 19. Use $9 + 7 + 0 + 3 + 0$. Notice that we have replaced 6 digits with zeros. We can only replace one more digit with a zero. It is impossible to replace one digit in the ones column and total 21.

<u>If we carry 1</u> from the ones column, find combinations of digits that add to 20. Use $9 + 7 + 0 + 3 + 1$. Five digits have been replaced with zeros. We need to replace 2 digits in the ones column with zeros and also obtain a total of 11. Use $0 + 7 + 0 + 3 + 1$.

Therefore, the solution is:

$$990$$
$$077$$
$$000$$
$$033$$
$$\underline{+011}$$
$$1111$$

(b) Consider part (i). In this case, we need to replace eight digits with zeros. Notice that $999 + 111 = 1110$ is close to the desired total of 1111, but nine digits have been replaced with zeros. Since the total is off by 1, consider the ones column. By replacing only two digits with zeros, we need to obtain a total of 11. We try $0 + 7 + 0 + 3 + 1$. The solution is:

$$990$$
$$007$$
$$000$$
$$003$$
$$\underline{+111}$$
$$1111$$

Consider part (iii). In this case, we must replace ten digits with zeros. Consider the possible ways to obtain totals of 1, 11, or 21 in the ones column.

$$1: 0 + 0 + 0 + 0 + 1$$
$$11: 0 + 7 + 0 + 3 + 1$$
$$21: 9 + 7 + 5 + 0 + 0.$$

Since we need to replace so many digits with zeros, try the case that uses the greatest number of zeros for the ones column.

$$0$$
$$0$$
$$0$$
$$0$$
$$\underline{+1}$$

Consider the tens column. We must obtain a total of 1, 11, or 21 without any carries from the ones column. Since we still must replace six more digits with zeros, use the case with the greatest number of zeros for the tens column.

```
    00
    00
    00
    00
  +11
```

Is it possible to obtain a total of 1111 by replacing only two digits in the hundreds column with zeros? Yes, if we use $0 + 7 + 0 + 3 + 1$.

```
   000
   700
   000
   300
 +111
  1111
```

Consider part (ii). Since we want to replace nine digits with zeros, see if it is possible to change part (iii) slightly. In the hundreds column, is it possible to obtain a total of 11 by replacing one digit with a zero? No, so consider the tens column. Try using $0 + 7 + 0 + 3 + 1$. Then in the hundreds column we must replace three digits and obtain a total of 10 since there is a carry from the tens column. Use $0 + 7 + 0 + 3 + 0$. One solution is:

```
    000
    770
    000
    330
 + 011
   1111
```

Section 4.2

40. (a) $26 + 37 = 63$ and $36 + 27 = 63$. Notice that the sum is the same in each case.

(b) $37 - 26 = 11$ and $36 - 27 = 9$. Notice that the differences differ by 2.

(c) If we pick any such pairs from two consecutive columns, then the sums are always the same, and when we subtract, the answers always differ by 2. Consider several examples: For the pairs 21, 52 and 51, 22, we have $21 + 52 = 73 = 51 + 22$. We also have $52 - 21 = 31$ and $51 - 22 = 29$.

For the pairs 4, 45 and 44, 5, we have $4 + 45 = 49 = 44 + 5$. Also, $45 - 4 = 41$ and $44 - 5 = 39$.

(d) Since we see patterns for addition and subtraction, consider possible patterns for multiplication and division. Note, however, that division often results in fractions, so we consider only multiplication. For the given pairs 26, 37 and 36, 27, we have $26 \times 37 = 962$ and $36 \times 27 = 972$. Notice that there is a difference of 10 and that the tens digits in each pair differ by 1. For the pairs 21, 52 and 51, 22, we have $21 \times 52 = 1092$ and $51 \times 22 = 1122$. Notice that the products differ by 30 and that the tens digits in each pair differ by 3. Test this pattern on other pairs. For example, for the pairs 4, 45 and 44, 5, we have $4 \times 45 = 180$ and $44 \times 5 = 220$. The products differ by 40 and the tens digits in each pair differ by 4. Therefore, the difference of the products is always 10 times the difference in the tens places in each pair.

Section 4.2

41. (a) Our figure must be a 4×5 array of Xs.

    | X | X | X | X | X |
    | X | X | X | X | X |
    | X | X | X | X | X |
    | X | X | X | X | X |

    (b) The sum of the Xs in half of the figure can be expressed in a similar way.

    $$1 + 2 + 3 + 4 = \frac{1}{2}(4 \times 5)$$

    $10 = 10$ The sum is correct.

    Recall that the sum of the first n natural numbers is $\frac{1}{2} n(n + 1)$.

    (c) $1 + 2 + \ldots + 50 = \frac{1}{2}(50 \times 51) = 1275$

    $1 + 2 + \ldots + 75 = \frac{1}{2}(75 \times 76) = 2850$

Section 4.2

42. Notice that only seven of the ten digits are used in each problem. Since none of the digits in the total are the same, we must carry in each column *and* each carry must be different. (If we did not carry in the ones column, we would not carry in *any* column, and a 4-digit solution would not result.) Since adding any three different digits will result in a sum between 3 and 24, the only possible carries are 1 and 2. Consider the ones column. In order to carry a 1 into the tens column *and* carry a 2 into the hundreds column, the ones column must total 19. This forces the tens column to total 20 and the hundreds column to total 21. So RSTU must equal 2109. All possible digit combinations which add to 19 without repeating digits are $8 + 7 + 4$ or $8 + 6 + 5$. Two solutions are given next.

$$
\begin{array}{r}
888 \\
777 \\
+444 \\
\hline
2109
\end{array}
\qquad
\begin{array}{r}
888 \\
666 \\
+555 \\
\hline
2109
\end{array}
$$

Section 4.2

43. Bob: Although Bob does not show his carries, he seems to add them correctly. His problem is that he only multiplies ones digits with ones digits, tens digits with tens digits, hundreds digits with hundreds, and so on, as long as both numbers have that digit. Otherwise, he just brings the digit down. For the last question, Bob's solution would be:

$$
\begin{array}{r}
84 \\
\times\ 26 \\
\hline
184
\end{array}
$$

Jennifer: Notice that she never includes the carries in the sum, although she does carry correctly. For the last question, Jennifer's solution would be:

$$
\begin{array}{r}
3 \\
25 \\
\times\ \ 6 \\
\hline
120
\end{array}
$$

Suzie: Suzie carries correctly, however she adds the tens digit and the carry before multiplying. Her solution for the last question would be:

$$3$$
$$29$$
$$\times\ \underline{4}$$
$$206$$

Tom: Any multiplication by a single digit number is done correctly. Tom does show his carries correctly. However, he has the same problem as Bob. Tom's final solution would be:

$$2$$
$$517$$
$$\times\ \underline{463}$$
$$2081$$

Consider algorithms and models that might help each student overcome his or her problems. Bob and Tom might benefit from using expanded form and the distributive property. This would force them to remember that you need to multiply each digit in the first number by each digit in the second number no matter what their place value. Jennifer might benefit from using a concrete model that would force her to add in the carries. Suzie needs to use one of the intermediate algorithms so that she is forced to multiply the digits in the factors first and then add the carry.

Section 4.2

44. In this algorithm it is necessary to locate each product in the correct place value position. To do this, recall some general multiplication facts.

When multiplying digits in the following place values:	Place the last digit of the number in the
ones × tens	tens place
ones × hundreds	hundreds place
ones × thousands	thousands place
tens × tens	hundreds place
tens × hundreds	thousands place
tens × thousands	ten thousands place

In the algorithm, the digits in one factor are systematically multiplied by the digits in the other factor. In each of the following steps, the bold number(s) in the 35 is multiplied by the bold number(s) directly below it. Use the table above to determine where the product should be positioned by place value.

<u>Product</u>

Step 1:   **35**

         4967   21 (1 in the tens place)

Step 2:   **35**   1835 (8 in the hundreds place)

         4967   (5 in the ones place)

Step 3:   **35**   2730 (7 in the thousands place)

         49**6**7   (0 in the tens place)

Step 4:   **35**   1245 (2 in the ten thousands place)

         4967   (5 in the hundreds place)

Step 5:   3**5**   20 (0 in the thousands place)

         4967

We can calculate the product 4967 × 35 as follows:

$$
\begin{array}{r}
2\ 1 \\
1\ 8\ 3\ 5 \\
2\ 7\ 3\ 0 \\
1\ 2\ 4\ 5 \\
2\ 0 \\
\hline
1\ 7\ 3\ 8\ 4\ 5
\end{array}
$$

Using the same steps, we can multiply 5314 and 79.

<u>Product</u>

Step 1:   **79**

         5314   28 (8 in the tens place)

Step 2:   **79**   736 (7 in the hundreds place)

         531**4**   (6 in the ones place)

Step 3:   **79**   2109 (1 in the thousands place)

         53**1**4   (9 in the tens place)

Step 4:   **79**   3527 (5 in the ten thousands place)

         5314   (7 in the hundreds place)

Step 5:   7**9**   45 (5 in the thousands place)

         5314

We can calculate the product 5314×79 as follows:

```
            2 8
          7 3 6
        2 1 0 9
      3 5 2 7
        4 5
    _____
    4 1 9 8 0 6
```

Section 4.2

45. Consider an example. Select any four-digit number, such as 4126. The largest possible number formed using these digits is 6421. The smallest is 1246. Subtract the smallest from the largest to get $6421 - 1246 = 5175$. Using this new four-digit number, repeat the process.

Four-Digit Number	Largest Number	Smallest Number	Difference
4126	6421	1246	5175
5175	7551	1557	5994
5994	9954	4599	5355
5355	5553	3555	1998
1998	9981	1899	8082
8082	8820	0288	8532
8532	8532	2358	6174
6174	7641	1467	6174

Notice that eventually the number 6174 is obtained and once it is, no new numbers are generated by the process.

Section 4.3

19. Notice that the smallest base in which this addition problem could be done is base 6, since the digits 1 through 5 are used. Consider the sum of the digits in the units' places. $5 + 2$ yields 1 in the unit's place of the sum. This would not happen in base 7 or a base larger than 7. In a base of at least 8, we would have $5 + 2 = 7$. If the problem were done in base 7, we would have $5 + 2 = 10$, so there would be a 0 in the unit's place of the sum. Therefore, this problem must have been done in base 6. Alternately, consider base blocks. In that case, we would have 5 units + 2 units = 1 long + 1 unit in base 6.

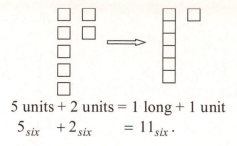

5 units + 2 units = 1 long + 1 unit

$$5_{six} + 2_{six} = 11_{six}.$$

Section 4.3

20. Steve has the least amount of money. We can find out how much money each person has if we know how much Steve has. Use a variable. Let x = the amount of money Steve has. Since Tricia has $21 more than Steve, Tricia has $(x + 21)$ dollars. Since Bill has $17 more than Tricia, Bill has $((x + 21) + 17)$ dollars. Since Jane has $10 more than Bill, Jane has $(((x + 21) + 17) + 10)$. Together, they have $115.

$$115 = x + (x + 21) + (x + 21 + 17) + (x + 21 + 17 + 10)$$
$$115 = 4x + 107$$
$$8 = 4x$$
$$2 = x$$

Therefore, Steve has $2, Tricia has $23, Bill has $40, and Jane has $50.

Section 4.3

21. To determine which of the numbers is a perfect square, consider the digit in the ones place of each number. Could that digit be the result of a number times itself? To answer that question, notice that when any number is squared, the ones digit is always the same as the ones digit of one of the following: 0^2, 1^2, 2^2, 3^2, 4^2, 5^2, 6^2, 7^2, 8^2, or 9^2 (i.e., the ones digit of the square of the ones digit). In general, when multiplying numbers if we are only interested in the resulting ones digit, we do not need to calculate the whole product. It is only necessary to look at the product of the digits in the ones places. The unit's digit in that product is the ones digit in the original product.

Possible Ones Digits	Square	Ones Digit of Square
0	0	0
1	1	1
2	4	4
3	9	9
4	16	6
5	25	5
6	36	6
7	49	9
8	64	4
9	81	1

For a perfect square, the only digits that could be in the ones place are 0, 1, 4, 5, 6, or 9. Therefore, 39,037,066,084 is the only possible perfect square in the list, and it is the square of 192,578.

Section 4.3

22. Make a list of the perfect squares greater than 100. Calculate what number had to be added to 100, in each case, to obtain the perfect square. Add that number to 164 and see if a new perfect square is created.

Perfect Square	Square − 100	(Square − 100) + 164
121	21	185 Not a square
144	44	208 Not a square
169	69	233 Not a square
196	96	260 Not a square
225	125	$289 = 17^2$

If 125 is added to 100 and to 164, the results are 225 and 289. Both are perfect squares.

Section 4.3

23. Base four has the four basic numerals 0, 1, 2, and 3. The calculation shows the numeral 4 used, which is not a possible numeral in base four.

Section 4.3

24. Use the standard subtraction algorithm. In order to subtract 234_{five} from 421_{five} note that regrouping is needed from the five's place. The 2 becomes a 1 and one group of five is moved into the one's place so 4 can be subtracted.

$$
\begin{array}{r}
\overset{\scriptstyle 1\ \ 11}{4\ \cancel{2}\ \cancel{1}}\,_{five} \\
-\ 2\ 3\ 4\,_{five} \\
\hline
2\,_{five}
\end{array}
$$

Again regrouping is needed from the twenty-five's place. The 4 becomes a 3 and the one group of twenty-five is moved into the five's place so the 3 can be subtracted.

$$
\begin{array}{r}
\overset{\scriptstyle 3\ \ 11\ \ 11}{\cancel{4}\ \cancel{2}\ \cancel{1}}\,_{five} \\
-\ 2\ 3\ 4\,_{five} \\
\hline
1\ 3\ 2\,_{five}
\end{array}
$$

The final answer is 132_{five}.

SOLUTIONS - PART A PROBLEMS

Chapter 5: Number Theory

Section 5.1

15. (a) Use a factor tree to write 36 in prime factorization form.

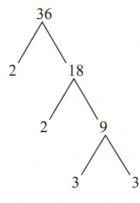

Therefore, $36 = 2 \times 2 \times 3 \times 3 = 2^2 \times 3^2$.

(b) Recall that any number that divides 36 must also be a factor of 36. We can use tests for divisibility to determine the factors of 36.

$2 \mid 36$ because 36 is even and $2 \times 18 = 36$.

$3 \mid 36$ because the sum of the digits of 36 is a multiple of 3 and $3 \times 12 = 36$.

$4 \mid 36$ because $4 \times 9 = 36$.

$6 \mid 36$ because both 2 and 3 divide 36.

Therefore, the numbers 1, 2, 3, 4, 6, 9, 12, 18, and 36 are all divisors of 36.

(c) A factor tree may be helpful when writing each divisor from part (b) in prime factorization form: 1, 2, 3, $4 = 2^2$, $6 = 2 \times 3$, $9 = 3^2$, $12 = 2^2 \times 3$, $18 = 2 \times 3^2$, $36 = 2^2 \times 3^2$.

(d) Because 36 has only two factors of 2 and two factors of 3, the prime factorization of each divisor contains at most two factors of 2 and at most two factors of 3. No prime factors of the divisors differ from the prime factors of the original number.

(e) If m divides n, then m must be a factor of n. The prime factorization of m must contain at most two 13s and at most five 29s. It will contain no other prime factors.

Section 5.1

16. **Divisibility by 5**: If abc is any three-digit number, then let $n = a \times 10^2 + b \times 10 + c$ be the number in expanded form. Observe that $a \times 10^2 + b \times 10 = 10(10a + b)$. Since $5|10$, it follows that $5|[10(a \times 10 + b)]$ or $5|[a \times 10^2 + b \times 10]$ for digits a and b. So, if $5|c$, then $5|[10(a \times 10 + b) + c]$, and $5|(a \times 10^2 + b \times 10 + c)$. Therefore, $5|n$. Conversely, let $5|(a \times 10^2 + b \times 10 + c)$. Since $5|(a \times 10^2 + b \times 10)$, we see $5|[(a \times 10^2 + b \times 10 + c) - (a \times 10^2 + b \times 10)]$, so $5|c$.

Divisibility by 10: If abc is any three-digit number, then let $n = a \times 10^2 + b \times 10 + c$ be the number in expanded form. Observe that $a \times 10^2 + b \times 10 = 10(a \times 10 + b)$. Since $10|10$, it follows that $10|[10(a \times 10 + b)]$ or $10|(a \times 10^2 + b \times 10)$ for any digits a and b. So, if $10|c$, then it follows that $10|[10(a \times 10 + b) + c]$ or $10|(a \times 10^2 + b \times 10 + c)$ Thus, $10|n$. Conversely, let $10|(a \times 10^2 + b \times 10 + c)$. Since $10|(a \times 10^2 + b \times 10)$, we see that $10|[(a \times 10^2 + b \times 10 + c) - (a \times 10^2 + b \times 10)]$. Therefore, $10|c$. (Note: For 10 to divide c, a single-digit number, c would have to be zero.)

Section 5.1

17. (a) True. Since $6! = 6 \times 5 \times 4 \times 3 \times 2 \times 1$ has 6 as a factor, $6\,|6!$.
    (b) True. Since $6! = 6 \times 5 \times 4 \times 3 \times 2 \times 1$ has 5 as a factor, $5\,|6!$.

(c) False. 6! does not contain 11 as a factor and 11 is a prime. Therefore, it cannot be the result of some product of factors of 6!.

(d) True. Since 30! = 30 × 29 × ... × 3 × 2 × 1 has 30 as a factor, 30 |30! .

(e) True. Since 40 = 10 × 4 and 30! = 30 × 29 × ... × 11 × 10 × 9 × ... × 4 × 3 × 2 × 1, we see 30! contains 10 and 4 as factors. Therefore 40|30! .

(f) False. 30! has 5 as a factor so 30! must end in a 0 or 5. It follows that 30! + 1 must end in 1 or 6. Notice that 30 has 5 as a factor. Therefore, 30 cannot be divisor of 30! + 1 since 30! + 1 does not end in a 0 or 5.

Section 5.1

18. (a) It is true that 8 divides 7!. Notice that 8 = 2 × 4, and 7! = 7 × 6 × 5 × 4 × 3 × 2 × 1. 7! contains both 2 and 4 as factors. Therefore, 7! contains 8 as a factor.

(b) No, 7 does not divide 6! = 6 × 5 × 4 × 3 × 2 × 1. Since 7 is a prime, it cannot be the result of a product of factors of 6!. Therefore, 6! does not have 7 as a factor.

(c) Notice how the numbers are related in parts (a) and (b). In part (a), 8 is a composite number and can be written as a product of factors of 7!. In part (b), 7 is a prime number and cannot be written as a product of factors of 6!. In general, if n is a composite number greater than 4, then n divides $(n-1)!$. If n is prime, then n does not divide $(n-1)!$.

Section 5.1

19. If the one composite number in the list has a factor less than 30, we know we only need to check the primes 2, 3, 5, 7, 11, 13, 17, 19, 23, and 29 to see if they are factors of the number. No number in the set is even, so no number has a factor of 2. Since each number consists of 3s and a 1, the total of the digits cannot be divisible by 3. Therefore, none has a factor of 3. No number ends in 0 or 5, so no number has a factor of 5. Use a calculator to check for divisibility by 7, 11,..., 29. The composite number is 333,333,331 = 17(19,607,843).

Section 5.1

20. $P(n) = n^2 + n + 17$

n	$P(n)$	
0	17	Prime
1	19	Prime
2	23	Prime
3	29	Prime

Continue the list until $P(n)$ yields a composite number. Since $P(17) = 17^2 + 17 + 17 = 17 \times 19$, we know we need to try only whole numbers up to 17.

4	37	Prime
5	47	Prime
6	59	Prime
7	73	Prime
8	89	Prime
9	107	Prime
10	127	Prime
11	149	Prime
12	173	Prime
13	199	Prime
14	227	Prime
15	257	Prime
16	$289 = 17 \times 17$	Composite

16 is the smallest whole number for which $P(n)$ yields a composite number.

Section 5.1

21. (a) Consider the following table:

n	$n^2 + n + 41$
0	41
1	43
2	47
3	53
4	61
5	71
6	83
7	97
8	113
9	131
10	151

All the numbers are prime. Using divisibility tests, it is only necessary to check primes up to 13 to see if 151 is a prime number.

(b) Consider the following table which was formed by continuing the spiral.

131	130	129	128	127	126	125	124	123	122	
132	97	96	95	94	93	92	91	90	121	
133	98	71	70	69	68	67	66	89	120	
134	99	72	53	52	51	50	65	88	119	
135	100	73	54	43	42	49	64	87	118	
136	101	74	55	44	41	48	63	86	117	
137	102	75	56	45	46	47	62	85	116	
138	103	76	57	58	59	60	61	84	115	
139	104	77	78	79	80	81	82	83	114	
140	105	106	107	108	109	110	111	112	113	
141	142	143	144	145	146	147	148	149	150	151

All the prime numbers generated from the formula in part (a) are in the main diagonal (upper left to lower right).

Section 5.1

22. Recall the divisibility test for 11. Notice that any repunit number, consisting of an even number of ones, will be divisible by 11. Factor and look for a pattern.

	Number	Factors
2 1s	11	11×1
4 1s	1111	11×101
6 1s	111,111	$11 \times 10,101$
8 1s	11,111,111	$11 \times 1,010,101$
10 1s	1,111,111,111	$11 \times 101,010,101$
12 1s	111,111,111,111	$11 \times 10,101,010,101$
14 1s	11,111,111,111,111	$11 \times 1,010,101,010,101$
16 1s	1,111,111,111,111,111	$11 \times 101,010,101,010,101$
18 1s	111,111,111,111,111,111	$11 \times 10,101,010,101,010,101$

Each of these repunit numbers is divisible by 11. Notice that the other factor always contains half as many ones as the repunit number. Next, recall the divisibility test for 3.

Any repunit number made up of 3 ones or a multiple of 3 ones will be divisible by 3. Factor and look for a pattern.

	Number	Factors
3 1s	111	3×37
6 1s	111,111	$3 \times 37,037$
9 1s	111,111,111	$3 \times 37,037,037$
12 1s	111,111,111,111	$3 \times 37,037,037,037$
15 1s	111,111,111,111,111	$3 \times 37,037,037,037,037$

Each of these repunit numbers is divisible by 3. Notice that the other factor contains one less digit than the repunit number, repeats the combination 370, and ends in 37. The only repunit numbers left to factor are those with 5, 7, 11, 13, and 17 ones.

	Number	Factors
5 1s	11,111	41×271
7 1s	1,111,111	239×4649
11 1s	11,111,111,111	$21,649 \times 513,239$
13 1s	1,111,111,111,111	$53 \times 79 \times 265,371,653$
17 1s	11,111,111,111,111,111	$2,071,723 \times 5,363,222,357$

Section 5.1

23. The only number in the list that can be written as the sum of two primes is 7 since $7 = 2 + 5$. Notice all the numbers in the list are odd, and the sum of an odd number and an even number is always odd. Since the only even prime is 2, all the numbers must be the result of adding 2 and some other prime. If 2 is subtracted from each number in the list, the resulting number ends in 5. With the exception of the number 5 itself, any number ending in 5 will not be a prime.

Section 5.1

24. (a) List prime numbers less than 100 and note which primes are one more than a multiple of 4.

Prime	Prime
2	43
3	47
5 = 4(1) + 1	53 = 4(13) + 1
7	59
11	61 = 4(15) + 1
13 = 4(3) + 1	67
17 = 4(4) + 1	71
19	73 = 4(18) + 1
23	79
29 = 4(7) + 1	83
31	89 = 4(22) + 1
37 = 4(9) + 1	97 = 4(24) + 1
41 = 4(10) + 1	

(b) Since each prime of the form $4x + 1$, where x is a whole number, is to be written as the sum of two square numbers, it may be helpful to list the perfect squares less than 100. Perfect squares: 1, 4, 9, 16, 25, 36, 49, 64, and 81.

5 = 1 + 4	37 = 1 + 36	73 = 9 + 64
13 = 4 + 9	41 = 16 + 25	89 = 25 + 64
17 = 1 + 16	53 = 4 + 49	97 = 16 + 81
29 = 4 + 25	61 = 25 + 36	

Section 5.1

25. No, there is not another pair of consecutive primes. In each pair of consecutive whole numbers, one is even and one is odd. Any even number is divisible by 2. Therefore, with the exception of the number 2, no even number can be prime. The whole numbers 2 and 3 are the only consecutive primes.

Section 5.1

26. Access the eManipulative, *Sieve of Eratosthenes*. All numbers from 2 to 200 are displayed. The goal is to eliminate all nonprime numbers and locate all the prime numbers that are left which differ by two. By clicking on a number, all of its multiples can be removed. Begin with the number 2. Click and delete all the multiples of 2, but keep 2 since it is the smallest prime number. Click and delete all the multiples of 3, but keep 3 since it is prime.

Continue in this manner until only prime numbers are left. Scan the prime numbers and locate all twin primes. The twin primes less than 200 are 3 and 5, 5 and 7, 11 and 13, 17 and 19, 29 and 31, 41 and 43, 59 and 61, 71 and 73, 101 and 103, 107 and 109, 137 and 139, 149 and 151, 179 and 181, 191 and 193, and 197 and 199.

Section 5.1

27. (a)

$14 = 3 + 11$	$24 = 7 + 17$	$32 = 3 + 29$
$16 = 5 + 11$	$26 = 3 + 23$	$34 = 5 + 29$
$18 = 7 + 11$	$28 = 5 + 23$	$38 = 7 + 31$
$20 = 3 + 17$	$30 = 7 + 23$	$40 = 3 + 37$
$22 = 5 + 17$		

(b) Let n be any odd number greater than 6. Consider the prime number 3. Because $n - 3$ must be an even number, $n - 3$ can be expressed as the sum of two prime numbers by Goldbach's conjecture. If p and q are prime numbers, then $n - 3 = p + q$. Therefore, we have that $n = 3 + p + q$, so any odd number can be expressed as the sum of three primes.

Section 5.1

28. Make a list of primes. When a pair of primes is found between a number and its double, see if that pair of primes falls between other numbers and their doubles. The primes 7 and 11 fall between 6 and its double 12.

Consider primes 11 and 13. Each of the numbers 7, 8, 9 and 10 falls below 11, and each double, 14, 16, 18, and 20 is larger than 13.
Consider primes 17 and 19. Each of the numbers 11 through 16 is less than 17. Each double is greater than 19.
Consider primes 29 and 31. Each of the numbers 17 through 28 is less than 29. Each double is greater than 31.
Consider primes 31 and 37. The numbers 29 and 30 are both less than 31. Their doubles are greater than 37.
Consider primes 53 and 59. Each of the numbers 31 through 49 is less than 53. Each double is greater than 59.

Section 5.1

29. Factor 1,234,567,890 into primes. We find that 1,234,567,890 = $2 \times 3^2 \times 5 \times 3607 \times 3803$. In order to obtain two factors as close together as possible, multiply 3607 and 3803 by some combination of the remaining factors. The remaining factors are $2 \times 3^2 \times 5$. Notice that $2 \times 5 = 10$ and $3^2 = 9$. If we multiply $3607 \times 10 = 36,070$ and $3803 \times 9 = 34,227$, then the two factors with the smallest difference whose product is 1,234,567,890 are 34,227 and 36,070.

Section 5.1

30. (a) Six divides every number in the set. Notice that every number in the set is formed from the product of three consecutive counting numbers. Of the three consecutive counting numbers, at least one is even (has a factor of 2) and one is a multiple of 3. Therefore, since $2 \times 3 = 6$, we know 6 divides each number in the set. Since the smallest number in the set is $1 \times 2 \times 3 = 6$, no number larger than 6 could divide each number.

   (b) Three divides every number in the set. Notice that each number in the set is formed from the product of three consecutive odd numbers or three consecutive even numbers. If n is any counting number, then each number in the set is of the form $n(n + 2)(n + 4)$. When any number is divided by 3, the only possible remainders are 0, 1, and 2. Consider n. If n divided by 3 has a remainder of 0, then it is a multiple of 3, and the product has a factor of 3. If n divided by 3 has a remainder of 1, then $n + 2$ must be divisible by 3. If the remainder is 2, then $n + 4$ is divisible by 3. Therefore, one of the factors of each number in the set is divisible by 3.

Section 5.1

31. The smallest counting number that is divisible by the numbers 2, 3, 4, 5, 6, 7, 8, 9, and 10 must contain each of them as a factor. Consider the prime factorization of each number: 2, 3, 2^2, 5, 2×3, 7, 2^3, 3^2, 2×5. The desired number must contain at least 3 factors of 2, 2 factors of 3, 1

factor of 5, and 1 factor of 7. Therefore, the smallest counting number that is divisible by the numbers 2 through 10 is $2^3 \times 3^2 \times 5 \times 7 = 2520$.

Section 5.1

32. The smallest counting number that is divisible by 2, 4, 5, 6, and 12 must have each number as a factor. Consider the prime factorization of each number: 2, 2^2, 5, 2×3, $2^2 \times 3$. The desired number must contain at least 2 factors of 2, 1 factor of 3, and 1 factor of 5. The smallest number divisible by 2, 4, 5, 6, and 12 is $2^2 \times 3 \times 5 = 60$.

Section 5.1

33. Let n be any counting number. Then n, $n + 1$, and $n + 2$ are any three consecutive counting numbers. The sum of these numbers is $n + (n + 1) + (n + 2) = 3n + 3 = 3(n + 1)$. Notice that 3 is a factor of the sum. Thus, the sum of three consecutive counting numbers always has a divisor of 3.

Section 5.1

34. Try some examples:

$$3, 8, 11, 19, 30, 49, \underline{79}, 128, 207, 335$$

The sum is $869 = 11(79)$, and 79 is the seventh number.

$$17, 28, 45, 73, 118, 191, \underline{309}, 500, 809, 1309$$

Here the sum is $3399 = 11(309)$, and 309 is the seventh number.

Let a and b be any two counting numbers. If a sequence of ten numbers is formed so that each new term is the sum of the two preceding numbers, then the seventh number is a factor of the sum. That is, if the ten numbers are a, b, $a + b$, $a + 2b$, $2a + 3b$, $3a + 5b$, $5a + 8b$, $8a + 13b$, $13a + 21b$, and $21a + 34b$, then $5a + 8b$ is the seventh term. The sum is $55a + 88b = 11(5a + 8b) = 11$(seventh number).

Section 5.1

35. (a) Recall that for whole numbers a, m, and n, where $a \neq 0$, if $a|m$ and $a|n$ then $a|(m + n)$. Since $2|5!$ and $2|2$ then $2|(5! + 2)$. Therefore, $5! + 2$ is a composite number. Similarly, $5! + 3$, $5! + 4$, and $5! + 5$ are also composite.

    (b) Note that by using $5!$, we obtained 4 consecutive composite numbers. If we want 1000 consecutive composite numbers, then we should use $1001!$ and follow the example set in (a). The numbers $1001! + 2$, $1001! + 3$, $1001! + 4$, . . . , $1001! + 1001$ are all composite numbers. If m is a counting number and $2 \leq m \leq 1001$, then $m|1001!$ and $m|m$, so $m|(1001! + m)$.

Section 5.1

36. Calculate the cost of the apples and potatoes. The apples cost 5×27 cents $= 135$ cents $= \$1.35$. The potatoes cost 2×78 cents $= 156$ cents $= \$1.56$. Together they cost $\$1.35 + \$1.56 = \$2.91$. Since the total cost calculated by the cashier was $\$3.52$, the cantaloupes and lemons would have cost $\$3.52 - \$2.91 = \$0.61$. If $c = $ cost of one cantaloupe and $l = $ the cost of one lemon, then $3c + 6l = 61$ cents.

$$3(c + 2l) = 61$$

Notice that 3 is a factor of the cost of the fruit, but 61 is not divisible by 3. Since nothing costs a fraction of a cent, the cashier must have made a mistake.

Section 5.1

37. Let n be the three-digit number. Then we have $7|(n - 7)$, $8|(n - 8)$, and $9|(n - 9)$. Since $7|7$ and $7|(n - 7)$, we know $7|(n - 7 + 7)$, so $7|n$. Similarly, $8|n$ and $9|n$. Therefore, n is divisible by 7, 8, and 9. The only three-digit number that has 7, 8, and 9 as factors is $7 \times 8 \times 9 = 504$.

Section 5.1

38. There is always one cupcake left over when cupcakes are arranged in groups of 2, 3, 4, 5, or 6. Let n represent the number of cupcakes. Then since $n - 1$ cupcakes can be

arranged in groups of 2 we know that $n-1$ is a multiple of 2. We know that $2|(n-1)$. Similarly $3|(n-1)$, $4|(n-1)$, $5|(n-1)$, and $6|(n-1)$. We want one number, $n-1$, that contains 2, 3, 4, 5, and 6 as factors. Consider the prime factorization of each number: 2, 3, 2^2, 5, and 2×3. The smallest number containing each number as a factor must contain at least 2^2, 3, and 5. Thus, $n-1 = 2^2 \times 3 \times 5 = 60$ and $n = 61$ cupcakes.

Section 5.1

39. Consider any number of the form $abcabc$, where a, b, and c are whole numbers. In expanded form, the number is $100{,}000a + 10{,}000b + 1000c + 100a + 10b + c = 100{,}100a + 10{,}010b + 1001c = 1001(100a + 10b + c) = 11 \times 13 \times 7(100a + 10b + c)$. Note that 13 is a factor of this number, so any number of the form $abcabc$ is divisible by 13. The numbers 7 and 11 are also factors of $abcabc$.

Section 5.1

40. (a) Let $abba$ be any four-digit palindrome. Apply the divisibility test for 11 to any four-digit palindrome, $abba$. The sum of the odd-numbered digits is $b + a$. The sum of the even-numbered digits is $a + b$. The difference is $(a + b) - (b + a) = 0$, which is divisible by 11. Thus, any four-digit palindrome is divisible by 11.

(b) An argument similar to the one in part (a) can be used to show any palindrome with an even number of digits is divisible by 11, since the difference of the odd-numbered digits and the even-numbered digits will always be 0, which is a multiple of 11.

Section 5.1

41. Let c = the cost of one calculator. Then $c|2567$ and $c|4267$. Consider the theorem which states that for whole numbers a, m, n, where $a \neq 0$ and $m \geq n$, if $a|m$ and $a|n$, then $a|(m-n)$. By this theorem we know that $c|(4267 - 2567)$, so $c|1700$. (Notice $1700 = 2^2 \times 5^2 \times 17$.) Since neither 2567 nor 4267 is even or ends in 0 or 5, neither number contains 2 or 5 as a factor. The only other number that could possibly divide 2567, 4267, and 1700 is 17. Therefore, the cost of one calculator is $17. In the first

year, $2567 \div 17 = 151$ calculators were sold. In the second year, $4267 \div 17 = 251$ calculators were sold.

Section 5.1

42. Notice that $7|2149$ since $2149 = 7 \times 307$, and $7|149,002$ since $149,002 = 7 \times 21,286$. Try some examples.

$$7|7231 \text{ and } 7|231,007$$
$$7|5964 \text{ and } 7|964,005$$

Conjecture: If $7|abcd$, then $7|bcd00a$.

Proof: Suppose $7|abcd$. Add $abcd$ and $bcd00a$ in expanded form and simplify:

$$(1000a + 100b + 10c + d) + (100,000b + 10,000c + 1000d + a)$$
$$= 1001a + 100,100b + 10,010c + 1001d$$
$$= 1001(a + 100b + 10c + d)$$
$$= 7 \times 143(a + 100b + 10c + d).$$

Therefore, $7|(abcd + bcd00a)$. Since $7|abcd$ and $7|(abcd + bcd00a)$, then $7|[(abcd + bcd00a) - (abcd)]$ so $7|bcd00a$.

Section 5.1

43. Notice that the first number in each sum is the total from the previous equation. Continue the list by adding the next consecutive even number to the total from the previous equation, as shown next.

$$37 + 10 = 47$$
$$47 + 12 = 59$$
$$59 + 14 = 73$$
$$73 + 16 = 89$$
$$89 + 18 = 107$$
$$107 + 20 = 127$$
$$127 + 22 = 149$$
$$149 + 24 = 173$$
$$173 + 26 = 199$$
$$199 + 28 = 227$$
$$227 + 30 = 257$$
$$257 + 32 = 289 = 17^2 \quad \text{not a prime}$$

Section 5.1

44. Let $a \times 10^3 + b \times 10^2 + c \times 10 + d$ be any four-digit number. Then we have the following:

$$a \times 10^3 + b \times 10^2 + c \times 10 + d$$
$$= a(1001 - 1) + b(99 + 1) + c(11 - 1) + d$$
$$= 1001a - a + 99b + b + 11c - c + d$$
$$= 1001a + 99b + 11c - a + b - c + d$$
$$= 11(91a + 9b + c) - a + b - c + d$$
$$= 11(91a + 9b + c) - (a - b + c - d).$$

Notice that $11 | 11(91a + 9b + c)$. For 11 to divide $abcd$, 11 must also divide $a - b + c - d$, since we know that if $a | m$ and $a | n$, then $a | (m - n)$. This corresponds to the test for divisibility for 11. A number is divisible by 11 if and only if 11 divides the difference of the sum of the digits whose place values are odd powers of 10 and the sum of the digits whose place values are even powers of 10. In $abcd$, a and c are in the place values 10^3 and 10^1, respectively, and b and d are in the place values 10^2 and 10^0, respectively. Therefore, the test says that if $11 | ((a + c) - (b + d))$, then $11 | abcd$.

Section 5.1

45. Since $11 \times 101,010,101 = 1,111,111,111$, we know that $11 | 1,111,111,111$.
Since $13 \times 8,547,008,547 = 111,111,111,111$, we know that $13 | 111,111,111,111$.
Since $17 \times 65,359,477,124,183 = 1,111,111,111,111,111$, we know that $17 | 1,111,111,111,111,111$.

Section 5.1

46. (a) Recall that $24! = 24 \times 23 \times 22 \times 21 \times \ldots \times 3 \times 2 \times 1$. Notice that 3 is a factor of each of the numbers 3, 6, 9, 12, 15, 18, 21, and 24 in the expansion of 24!. If we factor out as many 3s as we can from each of these numbers, then we can determine the total number of factors of 3 in 24!. We

have $3 = 3 \times 1$, $6 = 3 \times 2$, $9 = 3^2$, $12 = 3 \times 4$, $15 = 3 \times 5$, $18 = 3^2 \times 2$, $21 = 3 \times 7$, and $24 = 3 \times 8$. Thus, there are 10 factors of 3 in 24!, or we can say that 3^{10} is a factor of 24!. Therefore, $n = 10$ and $3^{10}|24!$.

(b) We want to find $n!$ such that the expansion of $n!$ contains 6 factors of 3. Begin by listing counting numbers, noting how many factors of 3 each one contains.

$$1 \times 2 \times \mathbf{3} \times 4 \times 5 \times \mathbf{6} \times 7 \times 8 \times \mathbf{9} \times 10 \times 11 \times \mathbf{12} \times 13 \times 14 \times \mathbf{15}$$
$$\quad\;\; 1 \text{ factor} \qquad 1 \text{ factor} \qquad 2 \text{ factors} \qquad\;\; 1 \text{ factor} \qquad 1 \text{ factor}$$

Therefore, in 15! there are 6 factors of 3, so $3^6|15!$.

(c) Notice that $12 = 2^2 \times 3$. From the expansion of 24!, find all numbers that contain factors of 2 or 3. Numbers from 1 to 24 that contain factors of 2 or 3 are as follows: 2, 3, 4, 6, 8, 9, 10, 12, 14, 15, 16, 18, 20, 21, 22, and 24. Now factor each of these numbers: 2, 3, 2^2, 2×3, 2^3, 3^2, 2×5, $2^2 \times 3$, 2×7, 3×5, 2^4, 2×3^2, $2^2 \times 5$, 3×7, 2×11, $2^3 \times 3$. There are 22 factors of 2 and 10 factors of 3. Each factor of 12 will contain two 2s and one 3. Since there are only 10 factors of 3, we can only use 20 of the factors of 2 to make 10 factors of 12. Therefore, the largest n is 10, so $12^{10}|24!$.

Section 5.1

47. Use a spreadsheet to create a table. Label the columns "n" and "$p(n)$". See the solution to Problem 20 to view the table. The smallest whole number, n, for which $p(n)$ is not prime is 16. Let $n = 16$. Evaluate $p(n + 1) = p(16 + 1) = p(17) = 323$. Since 323 is divisible by 17, it is composite. Evaluate $p(n + 2) = p(16 + 2) = p(18) = 359$. 359 is a prime number.

Section 5.2

18. Make a table of all the numbers from 2 through 25. Do not consider the number 1 since it has no proper factors.

Number	Proper Factors	Sum of Proper Factors
2	1	1
3	1	1
4	1, 2	3
5	1	1
6	1, 2, 3	6
7	1	1
8	1, 2, 4	7
9	1, 3	4
10	1, 2, 5	8
11	1	1
12	1, 2, 3, 4, 6	16
13	1	1
14	1, 2, 7	10
15	1, 3, 5	9
16	1, 2, 4, 8	15
17	1	1
18	1, 2, 3, 6, 9	21
19	1	1
20	1, 2, 4, 5, 10	22
21	1, 3, 7	11
22	1, 2, 11	14
23	1	1
24	1, 2, 3, 4, 6, 8, 12	36
25	1, 5	6

(a) All of the numbers except 6, 12, 18, 20, and 24 are deficient.

(b) The numbers 12, 18, 20, and 24 are abundant.

(c) Only the number 6 is perfect.

Section 5.2

19. Use tests for divisibility or factor trees to help you generate all divisors of each pair of numbers.

(a) 1184 and 1210 are amicable.

The sum of the proper divisors of 1184 is 1210: $1 + 2 + 4 + 8 + 16 + 32 + 37 + 74 + 148 + 296 + 592 = 1210$.

The sum of the proper divisors of 1210 is 1184: $1 + 2 + 5 + 10 + 11 + 22 + 55 + 110 + 121 + 242 + 605 = 1184$.

(b) 1254 and 1832 are not amicable.

The sum of the proper divisors of 1254 is 1626: $1 + 2 + 3 + 6 + 11 + 19 + 22 + 23 + 33 + 38 + 57 + 66 + 114 + 209 + 418 + 627 = 1626$.

The sum of the proper divisors of 1832 is 1618: $1 + 2 + 4 + 8 + 229 + 458 + 916 = 1618$.

(c) 5020 and 5564 are amicable.

The sum of the proper divisors of 5020 is 5564: $1 + 2 + 4 + 5 + 10 + 20 + 251 + 502 + 1004 + 1255 + 2510 = 5564$.

The sum of the proper divisors of 5564 is 5020: $1 + 2 + 4 + 13 + 26 + 52 + 107 + 214 + 428 + 1391 + 2782 = 5020$.

Section 5.2

20. For each pair of numbers consider only the proper factors greater than 1.

(a) The numbers 140 and 195 are betrothed. The sum of the proper factors of 140 is $2 + 4 + 5 + 7 + 10 + 14 + 20 + 28 + 35 + 70 = 195$. The sum of the proper factors of 195 is $3 + 5 + 13 + 15 + 39 + 65 = 140$.

(b) The numbers 1575 and 1648 are betrothed. The sum of the proper factors of 1575 is $3 + 5 + 7 + 9 + 15 + 21 + 25 + 35 + 45 + 63 + 75 + 105 + 175 + 225 + 315 + 525 = 1648$. The sum of the proper factors of 1648 is $2 + 4 + 8 + 16 + 103 + 206 + 412 + 824 = 1575$.

(c) The numbers 2024 and 2295 are betrothed. The sum of the proper factors of 2024 is $2 + 4 + 8 + 11 + 22 + 23 + 44 + 46 + 88 + 92 + 184 + 253 + 506 + 1012 = 2295$. The sum of the proper factors of 2295 is $3 + 5 + 9 + 15 + 17 + 27 + 45 + 51 + 85 + 135 + 153 + 255 + 459 + 765 = 2024$.

Section 5.2

21. Recall the theorem that states $\text{GCF}(a, b) \times \text{LCM}(a, b) = ab$.

    (a) By substituting the known values into the equation, we have the following:

    $$(2 \times 3)(2^2 \times 3^3 \times 5) = a(2^2 \times 3 \times 5)$$

    $$2^3 \times 3^4 \times 5 = a(2^2 \times 3 \times 5)$$

    $$\frac{2^3 \times 3^4 \times 5}{2^2 \times 3 \times 5} = a$$

    $$2 \times 3^3 = a$$

    Therefore, $a = 2 \times 3^3 = 54$.

    (b) By substituting the known values into the equation, we have the following:

    $$(2^2 \times 7 \times 11)(2^5 \times 3^2 \times 5 \times 7^3 \times 11^2) = a(2^5 \times 3^2 \times 5 \times 7 \times 11)$$

    $$2^7 \times 3^2 \times 5 \times 7^4 \times 11^3 = a(2^5 \times 3^2 \times 5 \times 7 \times 11)$$

    $$\frac{2^7 \times 3^2 \times 5 \times 7^4 \times 11^3}{2^5 \times 3^2 \times 5 \times 7 \times 11} = a$$

    $$2^2 \times 7^3 \times 11^2 = a$$

    Therefore, $a = 2^2 \times 7^3 \times 11^2 = 166{,}012$.

Section 5.2

22. Consider the method for finding the number of divisors of any number. Write the number in prime factored form, add 1 to each exponent, and multiply the new exponents. We can create a number with a certain number of divisors by manipulating the exponents when the number is in prime factored form. The **smallest** number will use the smallest prime factors.

    (a) Since 1 is the only number having exactly one divisor, 1 must be the smallest number having exactly one divisor.

    (b) To create a number with exactly two divisors, the prime factorization of the number must have one prime factor with an exponent of 1. $(1 + 1 = 2$ divisors.) The smallest prime is 2, and $2^1 = 2$, so 2 is the smallest number with exactly two divisors.

(c) The smallest whole number having three divisors is $2^2 = 4$. Since 3 is prime, the only product that yields 3 is 1×3. Therefore, the exponent on the number in prime factored form must be 2 since $2 + 1 = 3$.

(d) Since 4 can result from 1×4 or 2×2, the small whole numbers having exactly four divisors are $2^3 = 8$ $(3 + 1 = 4$ divisors) and $2^1 \times 3^1 = 6$ $[(1 + 1)(1 + 1) = 4$ divisors]. The smallest such number is 6.

(e) Since 5 is prime, the exponent on the prime factor must be 4. Therefore, the smallest whole number with exactly five divisors is $2^4 = 16$ $(4 + 1 = 5$ divisors).

(f) Since 6 can result from 1×6 or 2×3, small whole numbers having six divisors are $2^5 = 32$ $(5 + 1 = 6$ divisors) and $2^2 \times 3^1 = 12$ $[(2 + 1)(1 + 1) = 6$ divisors]. The smallest number with six divisors is 12.

(g) Since 7 is prime, the exponent on the prime factor must be 6. The smallest whole number with seven divisors is $2^6 = 64$ $(6 + 1 = 7$ divisors).

(h) Since 8 can result from 1×8, $2 \times 2 \times 2$, or 2×4, small whole numbers having exactly eight divisors are $2^7 = 128$ $(7 + 1 = 8$ divisors), $2^1 \times 3^1 \times 5^1 = 30$ $[(1 + 1)(1 + 1)(1 + 1) = 8$ divisors], and $2^3 \times 3^1 = 24$ $[(3 + 1)(1 + 1) = 8$ divisors]. The smallest number with exactly eight divisors is 24.

Section 5.2

23. (a) Whole numbers with exactly two factors are called prime numbers. The following are examples of numbers with exactly two factors. The numbers are listed together with their factors.

2: 1, 2
3: 1, 3
5: 1, 5
7: 1, 7
11: 1, 11
13: 1, 13

(b) Squares of prime numbers have exactly three factors. The following are examples of numbers with exactly three factors.

4: 1, 2, 4
9: 1, 3, 9
25: 1, 5, 25
49: 1, 7, 49
121: 1, 11, 121
169: 1, 13, 169

(c) Whole numbers with exactly four factors are perfect cubes or numbers that are the product of two primes. The following are a few examples of numbers with exactly four factors.

6: 1, 2, 3, 6
8: 1, 2, 4, 8
10: 1, 2, 5, 10
14: 1, 2, 7, 14
15: 1, 3, 5, 15
21: 1, 3, 7, 21
22: 1, 2, 11, 22
27: 1, 3, 9, 27

(d) Whole numbers with exactly five factors must be generated by raising prime numbers to the fourth power. By the theorem that provides a method of finding the number of factors of a given number, we would add 1 to the exponent ($4 + 1 = 5$) to determine the number of factors. Some examples of numbers with exactly five different factors are shown next:

16: 1, 2, 4, 8, 16
81: 1, 3, 9, 27, 81
625: 1, 5, 25, 125, 625
2401: 1, 7, 49, 343, 2401
14,641: 1, 11, 121, 1331, 14641
28,561: 1, 13, 169, 2197, 28561

Section 5.2

24. $2^{n-1}(2^n - 1)$ is a perfect number when $2^n - 1$ is prime and $n = 1, 2, 3,...$ Generate the first four such perfect numbers by substituting $n = 1, 2, 3,...$ into the formula and checking to see whether $2^n - 1$ is prime.

n	$2^n - 1$
1	1 Not Prime
2	3 Prime
	Perfect Number $2^{2-1}(2^2 - 1) = 2(3) = 6$
3	7 Prime
	Perfect Number $2^{3-1}(2^3 - 1) = 4(7) = 28$
4	15 Not Prime
5	31 Prime
	Perfect Number $2^{5-1}(2^5 - 1) = 16(31) = 496$
6	63 Not Prime
7	127 Prime
	Perfect Number $2^{7-1}(2^7 - 1) = 64(127) = 8128$

Therefore, the first four such perfect numbers are 6, 28, 496, and 8128.

Section 5.2

25. Since the prime factorization of 24 is $2^3 \times 3$, 24 and any number which is a multiple of 2 or 3 will have a common factor different from 1. All whole numbers from 1 to 24 that are not multiples of 2 or 3 will share at most a common factor of 1 with 24. These numbers are 1, 5, 7, 11, 13, 17, 19, and 23.

Section 5.2

26. Since George had no money left over, the price of a candy bar and the price of a can of pop must each be a factor of the total amount of money earned. To find the fewest number of candy bars, we need to find the LCM(15, 48). LCM(15, 48) = LCM (3×5, $2^4 \times 3$) = $2^4 \times 3 \times 5$ = 240. The total amount of money earned was 240 cents. George sold candy bars at 15 cents each. Since 240 = 15×16, we know that 16 candy bars were sold.

Section 5.2

27. Let c = the price of one chicken, d = the price of one duck and g = the price of one goose. Since three chickens and one duck sold for as much as two geese, we know $3c + d = 2g$. Since one chicken, two ducks and three geese together sold for \$25.00, we know that $c + 2d + 3g = 25$. Solving for d in the first equation yields $d = 2g - 3c$. Substitute into the second equation and simplify:

$$c + 2(2g - 3c) + 3g = 25$$
$$c + 4g - 6c + 3g = 25$$
$$7g - 5c = 25$$
$$7g = 25 + 5c$$
$$7g = 5(5 + c)$$

Since the exact dollar amount is asked for, assume that means only whole numbers need to be considered. Notice that $7g$ must be a multiple of 5 since $7g = 5(5 + c)$. Since 7 is not a multiple of 5, then it must be that g is a non-zero multiple of 5. If g = \$5 then $7(5) - 5c = 25$ and c = \$2. Therefore, we see that $d = 2(5) - 3(2) = 10 - 6 = \$4$. The prices of one chicken, one duck, and one goose are \$2, \$4, and \$5, respectively. This is the only possible solution since, if g were a multiple of 5 any greater than 5 itself, one of the other variables would be negative, which is not allowed.

Section 5.2

28. Write each number in the set in prime factored form. $\{10, 20, 40, 80, 160, ...\} = \{2 \times 5, 2^2 \times 5, 2^3 \times 5, 2^4 \times 5, 2^5 \times 5, ...\}$ Any perfect square can be written as a product of some number and itself. This means that if the perfect square were written in prime factored form, each prime factor would have an even exponent. Since each number in the set has only one factor of 5, none of them can be perfect squares.

Section 5.2

29. Since each of the three digits in the number must be prime, it is only necessary to consider digits 2, 3, 5, and 7. We seek the largest prime number, so make a list of possible three-digit numbers using the largest prime digits first. Stop when the first three-digit prime number has been found.

Three Digit Number	Prime or Composite
777	Composite, $777 = 7 \times 111$
775	Composite, $775 = 5 \times 155$
773	Prime

Section 5.2

30. (a) Since we want to find a divisor greater than 1 for every such number, we use variables. Let *abba* be any four-digit palindrome. Then *baab* is a new palindrome formed by interchanging unlike digits. Add these two numbers using expanded form, as follows:

$abba + baab$

$= 1000a + 100b + 10b + a + 1000b + 100a + 10a + b$

$= 1111a + 1111b$

$= 1111(a + b).$

Since $1111 = 11 \times 101$, we know that 11, 101, and 1111 all divide the sum.

(b) $1111 \times$ GCF(a, b) is the largest whole number that divides the sum.

Section 5.2

31. In an additive magic square, all rows, columns, and diagonals must add to the same number. Adding row 1 yields a total of 120. Row 2 contains one empty spot. The missing prime must be $120 - 43 - 31 - 5 = 41$. Now, column 4 contains one empty spot, so it must be $120 - 37 - 41 - 29 = 13$. The missing prime in column 3 is $120 - 19 - 5 - 23 = 73$.

3	61	19	37
43	31	5	41
		73	29
		23	13

Consider row 3. There are two missing prime numbers. Their total must be $120 - 73 - 29 = 18$. The only primes that have not been used and that add to 18 are 11 and 7. Placing 7 at the intersection of row 3 and column 1 forces the missing prime in column 1 to be $120 - 3 - 43 - 7 = 67$. Placing 11 at the intersection of row 3 and column 2 forces the missing prime in column 2 to be $120 - 61 - 31 - 11 = 17$. The numbers in the magic square are as follows:

$$
\begin{array}{cccc}
3 & 61 & 19 & 37 \\
43 & 31 & 5 & 41 \\
7 & 11 & 73 & 29 \\
67 & 17 & 23 & 13
\end{array}
$$

Section 5.2

32. If the number of cards minus 1 is divisible by 2, 3, and 5, then the fewest number of cards that could satisfy the conditions is 1 more than the LCM of 2, 3, and 5. LCM$(2, 3, 5) = 2 \times 3 \times 5 = 30$. Thus, the fewest number of cards possible is $30 + 1 = 31$.

Section 5.2

33. $343 = 7 \times 49$, so 343 is divisible by 7. Notice, in the number 343, the digits in the tens and ones places add to 7, and the hundreds digit and the ones digit are the same. The number $252 = 7 \times 36$, so 252 is divisible by 7. Notice, in the number 252, the digits in the tens and ones places add to 7, and the hundreds digit and the ones digit are the same. Consider any three-digit number of this type in expanded form. That is, consider $100a + 10b + a$. If we assume $a + b = 7$ then $b = 7 - a$. Substituting $7 - a$ for b in the three-digit number, we have the following:

$$100a + 10(7 - a) + a = 100a + 70 - 10a + a$$
$$= 91a + 70$$
$$= 7(13a + 10).$$

Therefore, since 7 is a factor, the number is divisible by 7.

Section 5.2

34. Write each number in the set in prime factored form.
    $\{18, 96, 54, 27, 42\} = \{2 \times 3^2, 2^5 \times 3, 2 \times 3^3, 3^3, 2 \times 3 \times 7\}$.
    To find the pair with the greatest GCF, consider the GCF for all possible pairs.

    GCF(18, 96) = $2 \times 3 = 6$
    GCF(18, 54) = $2 \times 3^2 = 18$
    GCF(18, 27) = $3^2 = 9$
    GCF(18, 42) = $2 \times 3 = 6$
    GCF(96, 54) = $2 \times 3 = 6$
    GCF(96, 27) = 3
    GCF(96, 42) = $2 \times 3 = 6$
    GCF(54, 27) = $3^3 = 27$
    GCF(54, 42) = $2 \times 3 = 6$
    GCF(27, 42) = 3

    The pair with the greatest GCF is 54 and 27. GCF(54, 27) = 27. To find the pair with the smallest LCM, consider the LCM for all possible pairs.

    LCM(18, 96) = $2^5 \times 3^2 = 288$
    LCM(18, 54) = $2 \times 3^3 = 54$
    LCM(18, 27) = $2 \times 3^3 = 54$
    LCM(18, 42) = $2 \times 3^2 \times 7 = 126$
    LCM(96, 54) = $2^5 \times 3^3 = 864$
    LCM(96, 27) = $2^5 \times 3^3 = 864$
    LCM(96, 42) = $2^5 \times 3 \times 7 = 672$
    LCM(54, 27) = $2 \times 3^3 = 54$
    LCM(54, 42) = $2 \times 3^3 \times 7 = 378$
    LCM(27, 42) = $2 \times 3^3 \times 7 = 378$

    Three pairs have a least common multiple (LCM) of 54, which is the smallest: 18 and 54, 18 and 27, 54 and 27.

Section 5.2

35. Access the eManipulative, *Fill 'n Pour*.
    (a) In order to measure exactly 4 ounces, fill the 12 ounce container. Pour the liquid from the 12 ounce container into the 8 ounce container. There will be exactly 4

ounces left in the 12 ounce container. Other solutions are possible.

(b) In order to measure exactly 1 ounce, fill the 11 ounce container. Pour the liquid from the 11 ounce container into the 7 ounce container. There will be exactly 4 ounces left in the 11 ounce container. Empty the 7 ounce container. Pour the 4 ounces from the 11 ounce container into the 7 ounce container. Fill the 11 ounce container and pour it into the 7 ounce container (which already contains 4 ounces of liquid). There will be 8 ounces remaining in the 11 ounce container. Empty the 7 ounce container. Pour the liquid from the 11 ounce container into the 7 ounce container. This will leave 1 ounce in the 11 ounce container.

SOLUTIONS - PART A PROBLEMS

Chapter 6: Fractions

Section 6.1

16. (a) In 2005 the fraction of U.S. households that were married-couple households was

$$\frac{58,000,000}{113,000,000} = \frac{58 \cdot 1,000,000}{113 \cdot 1,000,000} = \frac{58}{113}.$$

To find the closest fraction with a denominator of 100, let x be the numerator and create an equation that shows the two fractions are equal.

$$\frac{x}{100} = \frac{58}{113}$$

Using an alternate version of cross-multiplication, the two fractions are equal if and only if $x = \frac{100 \cdot 58}{113} \approx 51.33$. Thus, the fraction $\frac{51}{100}$ is closest.

(b) In 2005 the fraction of U.S. households consisting of individuals living alone was

$$\frac{30,000,000}{113,000,000} = \frac{30 \cdot 1,000,000}{113 \cdot 1,000,000} = \frac{30}{113}.$$

To find the closest fraction with a denominator of 100, let x be the numerator and create an equation that shows the two fractions are equal.

$$\frac{x}{100} = \frac{30}{113}$$

Using an alternate version of cross-multiplication, the two fractions are equal if and only if $x = \frac{100 \cdot 30}{113} \approx 26.55$. Thus, the fraction $\frac{27}{100}$ is closest.

(c) In 2005 the fraction of U.S. households headed by a woman was

$$\frac{14,000,000}{113,000,000} = \frac{14 \cdot 1,000,000}{113 \cdot 1,000,000} = \frac{14}{113}.$$

To find the closest fraction with a denominator of 100, let x be the numerator and create an equation that shows the two fractions are equal.

$$\frac{x}{100} = \frac{14}{113}$$

Using an alternate version of cross-multiplication, the two fractions are equal if and only if $x = \dfrac{100 \cdot 14}{113} \approx 12.39$. Thus, the fraction $\dfrac{12}{100}$ is closest.

Section 6.1

17. (a) The fractions $\dfrac{1}{2}$, $\dfrac{1}{3}$, and $\dfrac{1}{4}$ are in decreasing order.
   Continuing the pattern would imply saving even **less**.

   (b) Improper fractions are greater than one. Paying only a "fraction" of the list price could result in paying **more**.

Section 6.1

18. In 2000, the fraction of the waste recycled was $\dfrac{68,000,000 \text{ tons}}{234,000,000 \text{ tons}} = \dfrac{34}{117} \approx 0.29$. In 2003, the fraction of the waste recycled was $\dfrac{72,000,000 \text{ tons}}{236,000,000 \text{ tons}} = \dfrac{18}{59} \approx 0.31$.

   Therefore, the greater fraction of the waste was recycled in the year 2003.

Section 6.1

19. (a) There are many ways to divide the hexagon into two equal pieces. Notice that if it is folded down the center vertically, then the two halves match exactly.

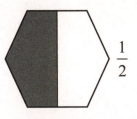

   (b) Construct three segments extending from the center perpendicular to every other side.

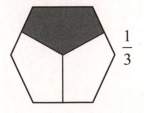

(c) Consider our picture from part (a). We can divide each half into two equal parts by constructing a horizontal segment through the center of the hexagon. This will divide the hexagon into four equal pieces.

$\dfrac{1}{4}$

(d) Consider our picture from part (b). We can divide each third into two equal parts by constructing three more segments from the center perpendicular to the three remaining sides. This will divide the hexagon into six equal parts as shown.

$\dfrac{1}{6}$

Alternatively, consider the hexagon that has been divided into thirds in the problem statement. Each third can be divided into two equal parts by constructing three more segments from the center to the three remaining vertices. This will divide the hexagon into six equal parts as shown next.

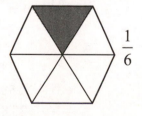

$\dfrac{1}{6}$

(e) Consider the first figure from part (d). Each sixth can be divided into two equal pieces by constructing six segments from the center to each vertex. This divides the hexagon into 12 equal pieces.

$\dfrac{1}{12}$

(f) Consider the second figure from part (d). The hexagon is divided into six equal pieces. Consider one triangular piece. We can divide it into four equal pieces by connecting midpoints for the sides, as shown next.

Doing this for each of the six triangles in the hexagon will divide it into 24 equal pieces.

$\dfrac{1}{24}$

Section 6.1

20. Consider several examples:

$$\frac{286}{583} = \frac{11 \times 26}{11 \times 53}$$

$$\frac{2886}{5883} = \frac{111 \times 26}{111 \times 53}$$

$$\frac{28,886}{58,883} = \frac{1111 \times 26}{1111 \times 53}$$

$$\frac{288,886}{588,883} = \frac{11,111 \times 26}{11,111 \times 53}$$

Notice that the number common to the numerator and denominator in each case has one more 1 than the number of 8s in the numerator and the denominator of the original fraction.

$$\frac{288...86}{588...83} = \frac{26 \times 111...1}{53 \times 111...1} = \frac{26}{53}$$

So, yes, the method always works.

Section 6.1

21. The sum of the numerator and denominator is a one-digit perfect square. The only one-digit squares are 1, 4, and 9. Consider all proper fractions whose numerators and denominators add to 1, 4, or 9. From this list, find the fraction such that the product of its numerator and denominator is a cube.

Fractions	Sum	Product
$\frac{1}{3}$	4	3
$\frac{1}{8}$	9	$8 = 2^3$
$\frac{2}{7}$	9	14
$\frac{3}{6}$	9	18
$\frac{4}{5}$	9	20

Therefore, $\frac{1}{8}$ is the desired fraction.

Section 6.1

22. Explanations will vary.

(a) False. Compare $\frac{23}{100}$ to $\frac{230}{10,000}$. In this case the numerator increased, but the fraction decreased because the denominator was increased by a larger power of 10. $\frac{23}{100} > \frac{230}{10,000}$.

(b) False. Compare $\frac{77}{100}$ to $\frac{7777}{1000}$. In this case, the denominator increased, but the fraction increased

because the numerator was also significantly increased.
$$\frac{77}{100} < \frac{7777}{1000}.$$

(c) True. Compare fractions with the same denominator: $\frac{5}{17} < \frac{9}{17} < \frac{13}{17}$. If the denominator remains the same and the numerator increases, then the fraction increases.

(d) True. Compare fractions with the same numerator: $\frac{3}{10} < \frac{3}{20} < \frac{3}{30}$. If the numerator remains the same and the denominator increases, then the fraction decreases.

Section 6.1

23. Since we know from our calculator that $\frac{12}{18} = \frac{2}{3}$, we also know that $\frac{12}{18} = \frac{2n}{3n}$ for some natural number n. In the fraction $\frac{2}{3}$, 2 and 3 have no common factors, so n must be the GCF(12, 18). Now we solve for n. Since $\frac{12}{18} = \frac{2n}{3n}$, we know $2n = 12$ and $3n = 18$. Therefore, $n = 6$.

(a) With the fraction calculator, $\frac{72}{168}$ simplifies to $\frac{3}{7}$.
We know that for some natural number n, $\frac{72}{168} = \frac{3n}{7n}$.
Solving for n yields $3n = 72$, so $n = 24$.

(b) With the fraction calculator, $\frac{234}{442}$ simplifies to $\frac{9}{17}$.
We know that for some natural number n, $\frac{234}{442} = \frac{9n}{17n}$.
Solving for n yields $9n = 234$, so $n = 26$.

Section 6.1

24. (a) This is incorrect. Consider the cross products.

$$\frac{ab + c}{b} = a + c$$

$$ab + c = b(a + c)$$

$$ab + c = ab + cb$$

$$c = cb$$

Notice that this last statement is only true when $b = 1$ or $c = 0$. In general, this method of cancellation is incorrect. Recall the theorem that states $\dfrac{an}{bn} = \dfrac{a}{b}$.

($\dfrac{a}{b}$ is any fraction and n is any nonzero whole number.)

In this case, b is not a factor of the entire numerator. Therefore, b cannot be cancelled.

(b) This is incorrect. Consider the cross products.

$$\frac{a + b}{a + c} = \frac{b}{c}$$

$$(a + b)c = b(a + c)$$

$$ac + bc = ba + bc$$

$$ac = ba$$

For this statement to be true, either $a = 0$ or $c = b$.

In general, this method of cancellation is incorrect since the variables that were cancelled were terms and not factors. We can only cancel common factors.

(c) This is correct. Since $\dfrac{b + c}{d} = \dfrac{a(b + c)}{a(d)} = \dfrac{ab + ac}{ad}$, this

method of cancellation works in general.

Section 6.1

25. Use a variable. Let n represent the number of girls in the class. Since $\dfrac{3}{5}$ of the class is made up of girls, $\dfrac{n}{25} = \dfrac{3}{5}$.

Solve for n using the cross products.

$$5n = 3(25)$$

$$5n = 75$$

$$n = 15$$

Therefore, there must be 15 girls in the class.

Section 6.1

26. Use a variable. Let n represent the number of votes received by the Independent party. Since $\frac{1}{11}$ of the votes were cast for the Independent party, $\frac{n}{6,186,279} = \frac{1}{11}$.

Solve for n using the cross products.
$$11n = 6,186,279$$
$$n = 562,389$$

Therefore, there must have been 562,389 votes cast for the Independent party.

Section 6.1

27. Use a variable. Let r represent the number of adult relatives of the students who attended the school bazaar. Since $\frac{7}{8}$ of the adults attending the bazaar were relatives of students, $\frac{r}{328} = \frac{7}{8}$. Solve for r using the cross products.

$$\frac{r}{328} = \frac{7}{8}$$
$$8r = 7(328)$$
$$8r = 2296$$
$$r = 287$$

Therefore, 287 of the 328 adults at the bazaar were relatives of students, and so $328 - 287 = 41$ adults were **not** relatives.

Section 6.1

28. Use a variable. Let P represent the number of books for the primary grades in the library. Since $\frac{5}{12}$ of the books are for the primary grades, $\frac{P}{5280} = \frac{5}{12}$. Solve for P using the cross products.

$$\frac{P}{5280} = \frac{5}{12}$$
$$12P = 5(5280)$$
$$12P = 26,400$$
$$P = 2200$$

Therefore, there are 2200 books in the library for the primary grades.

Section 6.1

29. Systematically draw all possible paths she could take from point *A* to point *B*. The paths Talia could take are shown next. In each case, Talia begins her trip at *A*, and she ends her trip at *B*.

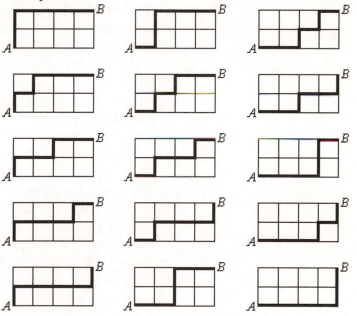

There are 15 paths Talia could take from *A* to *B*.

Section 6.1

30. (a) Using Systematic Guess and Test, begin by considering numbers with a 1 as the leftmost digit. For example, consider 10, 11, 12, 13, 14, 15, ... Of these, consider only multiples of three since they are the only numbers that could be three times as large as the number with the leftmost 1 removed. Some of the ones that are multiples of 3 are 12, 15, and 18. Of these, only 15 is

three times the number with 1 removed ($15 = 3 \times 5$). To find another number with this property, notice that if we add zeros to the numbers under consideration, we still have multiples of three that have 1s as their leftmost digits: 120, 150, and 180. Of these, only 150 is three times the number with the 1 removed ($150 = 3 \times 50$). We can generate infinitely many of these types of numbers by adding 0s, such as 1500; 15,000; and 150,000. Thus, numbers such as 50, 500, 5000, etc., will work.

(b) We know from part (a) that we only need to check numbers that have 1 as the leftmost digit and that are also multiples of 5: 15, 105, 110, 115, 120, 125, 130, 135... Of these, only 125 is 5 times the number with the 1 removed ($125 = 5 \times 25$). Once again, if we add zeros, then we can find other such numbers, such as 1250; 12,500; and 125,000. Thus, numbers such as 25, 250, 2500, etc., will work.

(c) We need to consider numbers that have 2 as the leftmost digit and that are also multiples of 6: 24, 204, 210, 216... Of these, only 24 is 6 times the number with the 2 removed ($24 = 6 \times 4$). By adding zeros, we can find other such numbers, such as 240 and 2400. Thus, numbers such as 4, 40, 400, etc., will work.

(d) We need to consider numbers that have 3 as the leftmost digit and are also multiples of 5: 30, 35, 300, 305, 310, 315, 320, 325... Of these, only 375 is 5 times the number with the 3 removed ($375 = 5 \times 75$). Adding zeros, we can find other such numbers, such as 3750 and 37,500. Thus, numbers such as 75, 750, 7500, etc., will work.

Section 6.1

31. Explore the eManipulative, *Comparing Fractions*. Create equivalent fractions by adjusting the number of division pieces until they are the same for both fractions. Adjust the denominators once the number of division pieces is the same, since a common denominator has been found. Adjust the numerators after counting the number of shaded pieces in each fraction representation. We are asked to find

two fractions between $\dfrac{4}{7}$ and $\dfrac{1}{2}$. While $\dfrac{4}{7} = \dfrac{8}{14}$ and $\dfrac{1}{2} = \dfrac{7}{14}$, the numerators of the new, equivalent fractions only differ by one. Create equivalent fractions with larger denominators. We practiced this already when we increased the number of line divisions for each fraction representation. Since $\dfrac{1}{2} = \dfrac{14}{28} = \dfrac{28}{56}$ and $\dfrac{4}{7} = \dfrac{16}{28} = \dfrac{32}{56}$, two fractions between $\dfrac{1}{2}$ and $\dfrac{4}{7}$ are $\dfrac{15}{28}$ and $\dfrac{31}{56}$.

Section 6.2

20. Sally, her brother, and a third person each own a fraction of one whole restaurant. Together, Sally and her brother own $\dfrac{1}{3} + \dfrac{1}{4} = \dfrac{4}{12} + \dfrac{3}{12} = \dfrac{7}{12}$ of the restaurant. The third person owns the rest, or $1 - \dfrac{7}{12} = \dfrac{12}{12} - \dfrac{7}{12} = \dfrac{5}{12}$. Therefore, the third person owns $\dfrac{5}{12}$ of the restaurant.

Section 6.2

21. Let $t =$ John's age at death, or the number of years John lived. John's life can be broken down into non-overlapping time periods, as shown next.

Childhood: one-quarter of his life $= \dfrac{1}{4}t$

College: one-sixth of his life $= \dfrac{1}{6}t$

Teaching: one-half of his life $= \dfrac{1}{2}t$

Retirement: last six years $= 6$

If all of these periods are added, the total is t years.

$$\frac{1}{4}t + \frac{1}{6}t + \frac{1}{2}t + 6 = t$$

$$\frac{3}{12}t + \frac{2}{12}t + \frac{6}{12}t + 6 = t$$

$$\frac{11}{12}t + 6 = t$$
$$11t + 72 = 12t$$
$$72 = t$$

Therefore, John was 72 years old when he died.

Section 6.2

22. We need to find the total amount of pizza eaten (that is, the sum of the fractional parts eaten by each person). Rafael ate $\frac{1}{4}$ of the pizza, and Rocco ate $\frac{1}{3}$. Notice that the denominators of the fractions are not the same.

$$\frac{1}{4} + \frac{1}{3} = \frac{1\times3}{4\times3} + \frac{1\times4}{3\times4} = \frac{3+4}{4\times3} = \frac{3+4}{12} = \frac{7}{12}.$$

Together, they ate $\frac{7}{12}$ of a pizza.

Section 6.2

23. Since Greg plants $\frac{2}{5}$ of his garden in potatoes and $\frac{1}{6}$ of his garden in carrots we have the following:

$$\frac{2}{5} + \frac{1}{6} = \frac{2\times6}{5\times6} + \frac{1\times5}{6\times5} = \frac{12}{30} + \frac{5}{30} = \frac{17}{30}.$$

He used a total of $\frac{17}{30}$ of his garden space. Since we know that $\frac{17}{30}$ of 1 complete garden is being used, we subtract to find the fraction of garden which remains for the other crops.

$$1 - \frac{17}{30} = \frac{30}{30} - \frac{17}{30} = \frac{13}{30}.$$

Therefore, $\frac{13}{30}$ of the garden remains.

Section 6.2

24. If we consider one whole golf course to be made up of fairways, greens, and tees, then all together the fraction in fairways, the fraction in greens, and the fraction in tees

must add to 1 whole golf course. Letting T represent the fraction of the golf course in tees, we have the following:

$$\frac{11}{12} + \frac{1}{18} + T = 1.$$

To solve for T, find the least common denominator of 12 and 18.

$$T = 1 - \frac{11}{12} - \frac{1}{18}$$

$$T = \frac{36}{36} - \frac{33}{36} - \frac{2}{36}$$

$$T = \frac{1}{36}.$$

Therefore, $\frac{1}{36}$ of the golf course is in tees.

Section 6.2

25. David is subtracting as if he is using base 10 numbers. When he borrowed, he thought he borrowed 10 rather than 5. If David could use base 5 blocks, he could see that when he borrows 1 long, it is equal to $\frac{5}{5}$.

Section 6.2

26. (a) $\frac{1}{2} + \frac{1}{3} + \frac{1}{6} = \frac{3}{6} + \frac{2}{6} + \frac{1}{6} = \frac{6}{6} = 1$

    (b) $\frac{1}{2} + \frac{1}{4} + \frac{1}{7} + \frac{1}{14} + \frac{1}{28} = \frac{14}{28} + \frac{7}{28} + \frac{4}{28} + \frac{2}{28} + \frac{1}{28}$

    $$= \frac{28}{28}$$

    $$= 1$$

    (c) This result is true for 496. Consider the divisors (other than 1) of 496: 2, 4, 8, 16, 31, 62, 124, 248, and 496. Adding the corresponding fractions, we have the following:

$$\frac{1}{2}+\frac{1}{4}+\frac{1}{8}+\frac{1}{16}+\frac{1}{31}+\frac{1}{62}+\frac{1}{124}+\frac{1}{248}+\frac{1}{496}=$$

$$\frac{248}{496}+\frac{124}{496}+\frac{62}{496}+\frac{31}{496}+\frac{16}{496}+\frac{8}{496}+\frac{4}{496}+\frac{2}{496}+\frac{1}{496}=\frac{496}{496}=1$$

Notice that $1+2+4+8+16+31+62+124+248=496$. A number whose proper factors have a sum equal to the number is called a perfect number. Thus, 496 is a perfect number. The result described in parts (a) through (c) is true for all perfect numbers.

Section 6.2

27. Yes, they are all the same fraction.

$$\frac{1+3}{5+7}=\frac{4}{12}=\frac{1}{3}, \quad \frac{1+3+5}{7+9+11}=\frac{9}{27}=\frac{1}{3}, \text{ and}$$

$$\frac{1+3+5+7}{9+11+13+15}=\frac{16}{48}=\frac{1}{3}$$

Two other such fractions are:

$$\frac{1+3+5+7+9}{11+13+15+17+19}=\frac{25}{75}=\frac{1}{3} \text{ and}$$

$$\frac{1+3+5+7+9+11}{13+15+17+19+21+23}=\frac{36}{108}=\frac{1}{3}$$

Notice from the hint, the sum of the first n odd numbers is n^2. If there are n terms in the numerator, we can write the numerator as $1+3+5+\cdots+(2n-1)$. Since the denominator is the sum of the next n odd numbers, we can write it as $(2n+1)+(2n+3)+\cdots+(2(2n)-1)$. Notice that if the denominator had been the sum $1+3+5+\cdots+(2(2n)-1)$, then its value would have been $(2n)^2=4n^2$. But remember, the first n terms of this sum are in the numerator, and we know that is n^2. Therefore, the sum of the terms in the denominator is $4n^2-n^2=3n^2$. Thus, the fraction can be written $\frac{n^2}{3n^2}=\frac{1}{3}$.

Section 6.2

28. Consider a simpler problem with fewer terms. Make a list and find a pattern.

Terms	Sum
1	$\dfrac{1}{2}$
2	$\dfrac{1}{2}+\left(\dfrac{1}{2}\right)^2 = \dfrac{1}{2}+\dfrac{1}{4}=\dfrac{3}{4}$
3	$\dfrac{1}{2}+\left(\dfrac{1}{2}\right)^2+\left(\dfrac{1}{2}\right)^3 = \dfrac{1}{2}+\dfrac{1}{4}+\dfrac{1}{8}=\dfrac{7}{8}$
4	$\dfrac{1}{2}+\left(\dfrac{1}{2}\right)^2+\left(\dfrac{1}{2}\right)^3+\left(\dfrac{1}{2}\right)^4 = \dfrac{1}{2}+\dfrac{1}{4}+\dfrac{1}{8}+\dfrac{1}{16}=\dfrac{15}{16}$
5	$\dfrac{1}{2}+\left(\dfrac{1}{2}\right)^2+\left(\dfrac{1}{2}\right)^3+\left(\dfrac{1}{2}\right)^4+\left(\dfrac{1}{2}\right)^5 = \dfrac{1}{2}+\dfrac{1}{4}+\dfrac{1}{8}+\dfrac{1}{16}+\dfrac{1}{32}=\dfrac{31}{32}$

Notice that there is a relationship between the number of terms and the numerator and denominator. For n terms, the numerator is 2^n-1 and the denominator is 2^n. For the sum $\dfrac{1}{2}+\dfrac{1}{2^2}+\cdots+\dfrac{1}{2^{100}}$, the numerator is $2^{100}-1$ and the denominator is 2^{100}. Therefore, the sum is $\dfrac{2^{100}-1}{2^{100}}$.

Section 6.2

29. (a) Compare 3 hits to 6 at-bats, $\dfrac{3}{6}=\dfrac{1}{2}$. Therefore, half of the at-bats are hits in this game.
   (b) He now has 18 hits this season.
   (c) He now has 56 at-bats this season.
   (d) Compare his hits this season to his at-bats this season, $\dfrac{18}{56}=\dfrac{9}{28}$.
   (e) Compare $\dfrac{15}{50}\oplus\dfrac{3}{6}$ and $\dfrac{15}{50}\oplus\dfrac{1}{2}$ using baseball addition.

$$\frac{15}{50} \oplus \frac{3}{6} = \frac{(15+3)}{(50+6)} = \frac{18}{56} = \frac{9}{28}$$

$$\frac{15}{50} \oplus \frac{1}{2} = \frac{(15+1)}{(50+2)} = \frac{16}{52} = \frac{4}{13}$$

When fractions are replaced by equivalent fractions, the answers are not the same.

Section 6.2

30. It is possible to add unitary fractions with different odd denominators to obtain 1. Find the least common denominator for the given sum: LCD $= 3^3 \times 5 \times 7 = 945$. Now adding the unitary fractions, we have the following:

$$\frac{1}{3} + \frac{1}{5} + \frac{1}{7} + \frac{1}{9} + \frac{1}{15} + \frac{1}{21} + \frac{1}{27} + \frac{1}{35} + \frac{1}{63} + \frac{1}{105} + \frac{1}{135} =$$

$$\frac{315}{945} + \frac{189}{945} + \frac{135}{945} + \frac{105}{945} + \frac{63}{945} + \frac{45}{945} + \frac{35}{945} + \frac{27}{945} + \frac{15}{945} + \frac{9}{945} + \frac{7}{945} =$$

$$\frac{945}{945} = 1$$

Thus, the sum is 1.

Section 6.2

31. In the example, $\frac{1}{2} = \frac{1}{3} + \frac{1}{6}$. Notice that the least common multiple of 2 and 3 is 6. The unitary fractions are related as follows: $\frac{1}{n} = \frac{1}{n+1} + \frac{1}{n(n+1)}$.

    (a) $\frac{1}{5} = \frac{1}{6} + \frac{1}{30}$ (b) $\frac{1}{7} = \frac{1}{8} + \frac{1}{56}$ (c) $\frac{1}{17} = \frac{1}{18} + \frac{1}{306}$

Section 6.2

32. Consider a simpler problem. Suppose there are only four players. Visualize this by drawing a square. The four players are represented by the four vertices of the square. The number of matches would be the same as the number of line segments required to connect each vertex with each of the other vertices.

Player A plays B, C, and D. This gives three games.

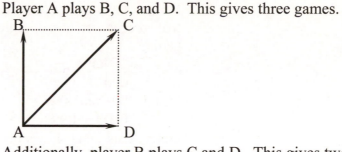

Additionally, player B plays C and D. This gives two more games. Notice that player B already played A.

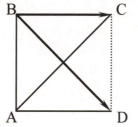

Finally, player C plays D. This gives one more game. Notice that player C already played A and B.

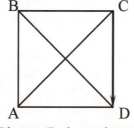

Player D has played everyone at this point. The total number of matches is $3 + 2 + 1 = 6$ matches.

If the tournament begins with eight players, this can be visualized by drawing a regular octagon with vertices labeled A through H. Vertex A can be connected to the 7 other vertices, that is 7 games. Vertex B connects to 6 additional vertices. Vertex C connects to 5 additional vertices; vertex D, 4 additional vertices; vertex E, 3 additional vertices; vertex F, 2 additional vertices; vertex G, 1 additional vertex. The total number of matches is $7 + 6 + 5 + 4 + 3 + 2 + 1 = 28$ matches.

Section 6.2

33. Make a table to help count zeros. First count all the zeros that precede nonzero digits. We'll call these "leading zeros."

Numbers	Number of Leading Zeros
0001 to 0009	$9 \times 3 = 27$
0010 to 0099	$90 \times 2 = 180$
0100 to 0999	$900 \times 1 = 900$

Note: This table shows that there are 9 numbers that have 3 leading zeros, 90 numbers with 2 leading zeros each, and 900 numbers with 1 leading zero each.

Now count all zeros that follow a nonzero digit.

Numbers	Zeros that Follow
0001 to 0009	0
0010 to 0099	$9 \times 1 = 9$
0100 to 0999	$9 \times 2 = 18$
	$81 \times 1 = 81$
	$9 \times 9 = 81$
1000	3

Note: This table shows how many zeros follow nonzero digits and where they come from. Clearly there are no such zeros in the list of numbers from 0001 to 0009. Each of the 9 multiples of 10 between 0010 and 0099 contain 1 zero that follows. Of the numbers in the interval 0100 to 0999, there are 9 multiples of 100, each of which contain 2 zeros that follow, 81 multiples of 10 (not multiples of 100) with 1 zero each, and 81 numbers with a zero in the tens digit but no zeros in the ones and hundreds digits. (For example 0101, 0309, 0704, ...) There are 9 for each of the 9 hundreds. Thus accounting for another 81 zeros that follow. Finally, 1000 contains 3 zeros that follow. The total number of leading zeros and the number of zeros that follow:

$27 + 180 + 900 + 9 + 18 + 81 + 81 + 3 = 1299$ zeros.

For each set of one hundred numbers, 0 to 99, 100 to 199, 200 to 299, 300 to 399, 400 to 499, 500 to 599, 600 to 699, 700 to 799, and 800 to 899, the number of nines will be the same. Therefore, we need to count the number of nines used from 0010 to 0099 and multiply by nine. From 0001 to 0099, the numbers requiring a nine are as follows: 0009, 0019, 0029, 0039, 0049, 0059, 0069, 0079, 0089, 0090,

0091, 0092, 0093, 0094, 0095, 0096, 0097, 0098, and 0099. We see 20 nines are used. So from 0001 to 0899, $9(20) = 180$ nines are used. Finally, from 900 to 999, each number begins with a nine, so in addition to the 20 nines we already know about, there are 100 more nines. Therefore, the total number of nines used when writing the numbers 0001 to 1000 is $180 + 120 = 300$.

Section 6.3

25. For each equation $ax = b$ notice the solution is of the form $x = \dfrac{b}{a}$.

(a) $31x = 15$ has solution $x = \dfrac{15}{31}$. To check this solution

verify $31 \cdot \dfrac{15}{31} = \dfrac{31}{1} \cdot \dfrac{15}{31} = \dfrac{465}{31} = \dfrac{15 \cdot 31}{1 \cdot 31} = 15.$

(b) $67x = 56$ has solution $x = \dfrac{56}{67}$. To check this solution

verify $67 \cdot \dfrac{56}{67} = \dfrac{67}{1} \cdot \dfrac{56}{67} = \dfrac{3752}{67} = \dfrac{56 \cdot 67}{1 \cdot 67} = 56.$

(c) $102x = 231$ has solution $x = \dfrac{231}{102}$.

To check this solution verify

$102 \cdot \dfrac{231}{102} = \dfrac{102}{1} \cdot \dfrac{231}{102} = \dfrac{23562}{102} = \dfrac{231 \cdot 102}{1 \cdot 102} = 231.$

Section 6.3

26. (a) To find a fraction between $\dfrac{7}{8}$ and $\dfrac{8}{9}$ find the average.

$\dfrac{1}{2}\left(\dfrac{7}{8} + \dfrac{8}{9}\right) = \dfrac{1}{2}\left(\dfrac{7 \cdot 9}{8 \cdot 9} + \dfrac{8 \cdot 8}{9 \cdot 8}\right) = \dfrac{1}{2}\left(\dfrac{127}{72}\right) = \dfrac{127}{144}.$ Thus,

$\dfrac{127}{144}$ is between $\dfrac{7}{8}$ and $\dfrac{8}{9}$.

(b) To find a fraction between $\dfrac{7}{12}$ and $\dfrac{11}{16}$ find the average.

$$\frac{1}{2}\left(\frac{7}{12}+\frac{11}{16}\right)=\frac{1}{2}\left(\frac{7\cdot 4}{12\cdot 4}+\frac{11\cdot 3}{16\cdot 3}\right)=\frac{1}{2}\left(\frac{61}{48}\right)=\frac{61}{96}.\quad\text{Thus,}$$

$\dfrac{61}{96}$ is between $\dfrac{7}{12}$ and $\dfrac{11}{16}$

Section 6.3

27. Suppose that each load required 2 cups of detergent. In that case, to find the number of loads that could be done, divide the number of cups in the box by 2. Since in the problem there are 40 cups in the box, and each load requires $1\dfrac{1}{4}$ cups, divide the total number of cups in the box by $1\dfrac{1}{4}$ to obtain $40\div 1\dfrac{1}{4}=40\div\dfrac{5}{4}=40\times\dfrac{4}{5}=32.$
     Therefore, you can do 32 loads.

Section 6.3

28. Use a variable. Let x represent the amount of oil being refined in the United States in April of 2007. Since we know $\dfrac{250}{999}$ of the oil refined in the United States was produced in the United States, and the United States produced 4,201,000 barrels per day in April of 2007, we can set up an equation.

$$\frac{250}{999}x=4,201,000$$
$$250x=4,196,799,000$$
$$x=16,787,196$$

Therefore, approximately 16,787,000 barrels per day of oil were refined in the United States in April of 2007.

Section 6.3

29. Let x represent the total number of students enrolled. Since all but $\dfrac{1}{16}$ of the students enrolled participated, we know

$\dfrac{15}{16}$ of the students enrolled in the school participated in the activities. So, we have the following:

$$\frac{15}{16}x = 405$$

$$15x = 16(405)$$

$$15x = 6480$$

$$x = 432.$$

Therefore, 432 students attend the school.

Section 6.3

30. (a) Try a simpler problem. Suppose that the directions recommended mixing 2 ounces of the concentrate with 1 gallon of the water. To find out how many gallons of mixture can be made from the bottle of concentrate, we need to figure out how many 2-ounce portions there are in the 32-ounce bottle of concentrate.

Divide: $\dfrac{32 \text{ ounces}}{2 \text{ ounces per portion}} = 16$ portions

Therefore, since there are 16 portions, and each portion mixes with 1 gallon of water, we see that approximately 16 gallons of mixture can be made.

For portions of $2\frac{1}{2}$ ounces of concentrate, divide again to find out how many gallons of mixture can be made.

$$\frac{32 \text{ ounces}}{2\frac{1}{2} \text{ ounces per portion}} = 12\frac{4}{5} = 12.8 \text{ portions.}$$

Therefore, approximately 13 gallons of mixture can be made.

(b) For portions of $1\frac{3}{4}$ ounces of concentrate, we can make

$$\frac{32 \text{ ounces}}{1\frac{3}{4} \text{ ounces per portion}} = 18\frac{2}{7} \approx 18.3 \text{ portions.}$$

Therefore approximately 18.3 gallons can be made or about $18.3 - 12.8 = 5.5$ more gallons.

Section 6.3

31. Let x represent the number of employees originally enrolled in a fitness program. By March 2nd, four-fifths of them or $\frac{4}{5}x$ were still participating. By May 2nd, $\frac{5}{6}$ of those who were participating on March 2nd were still participating, that is $\frac{5}{6}\left(\frac{4}{5}x\right) = \frac{2}{3}x$. By July 2nd, $\frac{9}{10}$ of those who were participating on May 2nd were still participating, or $\frac{9}{10}\left(\frac{2}{3}x\right) = \frac{3}{5}x$. Since 36 of the original participants were still active on July 2nd, we know the following:

$$\frac{3}{5}x = 36$$

$$3x = 5(36)$$

$$3x = 180$$

$$x = 60.$$

Therefore, 60 employees were originally enrolled.

Section 6.3

32. We will assume that Tammy walks at a constant speed. Tammy passes the grocery store at 7:40 and the bicycle shop at 7:45. In 5 minutes she walks $\frac{1}{2} - \frac{1}{3} = \frac{1}{6}$ of the distance to school. At 7:45 when she passes the bicycle shop, she still has $\frac{1}{2}$ the distance to go. Since $\frac{1}{2} = \left(\frac{1}{6}\right) \times 3$, it takes $5 \times 3 = 15$ minutes for the second half of the trip. Tammy arrives at school at 8:00 a.m.

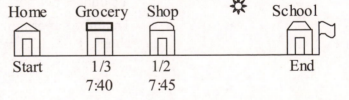

Section 6.3

33. (a) If the recipe is doubled, then the amount of flour required is doubled. The recipe calls for $1\frac{1}{4}$ cups of flour. Double the recipe calls for twice as much flour.

$$2 \times 1\frac{1}{4} = 2 \times \frac{5}{4} = \frac{10}{4} = \frac{5}{2} = 2\frac{1}{2} \text{ cups of flour.}$$

(b) If the recipe is cut in half, then the amount of flour in the recipe is reduced by $\frac{1}{2}$ of the original amount.

$$\frac{1}{2} \times 1\frac{1}{4} = \frac{1}{2} \times \frac{5}{4} = \frac{5}{8} \text{ cups of flour.}$$

(c) Notice that one recipe makes 3 dozen cookies. One recipe = 3 dozen, so $\frac{1}{3}$ recipe = 1 dozen. To make 5 dozen cookies, then, you need $\frac{5}{3}$ of a recipe since

$$5(1 \text{ dozen}) = 5\left(\frac{1}{3} \text{ recipe}\right) = \frac{5}{3} \text{ recipe.} \text{ If you want to}$$

make $\frac{5}{3}$ of a recipe, then the amount of flour required for one recipe should be multiplied by $\frac{5}{3}$.

$$\frac{5}{3} \times 1\frac{1}{4} = \frac{5}{3} \times \frac{5}{4} = \frac{25}{12} = 2\frac{1}{12} \text{ cups of flour.}$$

Section 6.3

34. Let x represent the total number of games played. Since Gale started in $\frac{3}{8}$ of the games played, she started in $\frac{3}{8}x$ games. Since Sandy started in 1 more game than Gale, she started in $\frac{3}{8}x + 1$ games. Since Ruth started in half as many games as Sandy, she started in

$$\frac{\frac{3}{8}x+1}{2} = \frac{\frac{3x+8}{8}}{2} = \frac{3x+8}{16}$$ games. These pitchers were the only three starters, so the total number of games, x, must equal the sum of the number of games each pitcher started.

$$x = \frac{3}{8}x + \frac{3}{8}x + 1 + \frac{3x+8}{16}$$

$$16x = 6x + 6x + 16 + 3x + 8$$

$$16x = 15x + 24$$

$$x = 24 \text{ games.}$$

Therefore, Gale started $\frac{3}{8}(24) = 9$ games, Sandy started

$9 + 1 = 10$ games, and Ruth started $\frac{10}{2} = 5$ games.

Section 6.3

35. Each year the value of the equipment is $\frac{1}{20}$ less than its value the previous year. Thus, each year it retains $1 - \frac{1}{20} = \frac{19}{20}$ of its value from the previous year.

(a) The office equipment was purchased for $60,000. After one year its value is $\frac{19}{20}(\$60,000) = \$57,000$. After the second year, the value of the office equipment is $\frac{19}{20}(\$57,000) = \$54,150$.

(b) Continue calculating the values after successive years.

Year	Value (in dollars)
1	$\frac{19}{20}(60,000) = 57,000$
2	$\frac{19}{20}(57,000) = 54,150$
3	$\frac{19}{20}(54,150) = 51,442.50$

$$4 \quad \left| \quad \frac{19}{20}(51{,}442.50) = 48{,}870.38 \right.$$

$$5 \quad \left| \quad \frac{19}{20}(48{,}870.38) = 46{,}426.86 \right.$$

$$6 \quad \left| \quad \frac{19}{20}(46{,}426.86) = 44{,}105.51 \right.$$

$$7 \quad \left| \quad \frac{19}{20}(44{,}105.51) = 41{,}900.24 \right.$$

$$8 \quad \left| \quad \frac{19}{20}(41{,}900.24) = 39{,}805.23 \right.$$

At the end of the 8th year, the piece of equipment will have a value less than \$40,000.

Section 6.3

36. Let n and m be the two counting numbers. Set up two equations from the information given. Consider n. One more than the number itself is $n + 1$. So $\dfrac{n}{n+1} = \dfrac{1}{5}$. Now consider m. One-fifth of this number itself is $\dfrac{1}{5}m = \dfrac{m}{5}$.

    So $\dfrac{m}{m+1} = \dfrac{m}{5}$. We want the product of the two numbers, n and m, so we will solve for n and m in the equations. Consider that $\dfrac{n}{n+1} = \dfrac{1}{5}$. Cross multiplying gives $5n = n + 1$. So, $4n = 1$ and $n = \dfrac{1}{4}$. Now consider $\dfrac{m}{m+1} = \dfrac{m}{5}$. Because these two fractions are equal and their numerators are the same, their denominators must also be equal. Thus, $m + 1 = 5$, so $m = 4$. Therefore, the product of the two numbers is $m \times n = 4 \times \dfrac{1}{4} = 1$.

Section 6.3

37. (a) Multiply the denominator by 5: $\dfrac{11}{16} \div 5 = \dfrac{11}{16 \times 5} = \dfrac{11}{80}$.

    (b) Yes. $\dfrac{a}{b} \div n = \dfrac{a}{b} \div \dfrac{n}{1} = \dfrac{a}{b} \times \dfrac{1}{n} = \dfrac{a}{b \times n}$.

    (c) Consider $5\dfrac{3}{8} \div 2$. Since 5 is not an even number, we can make this problem simpler by borrowing 1 from 5. Then we divide the whole number in half and multiply the denominator of the fraction by 2. We have

    $$5\dfrac{3}{8} = 4 + 1\dfrac{3}{8} = 4\dfrac{11}{8}, \quad \text{so} \quad 5\dfrac{3}{8} \div 2 = 4\dfrac{11}{8} \div 2 = 2\dfrac{11}{16}.$$

    Consider $10\dfrac{9}{16} \div 2$. Since dividing by 2 is the same as multiplying by $\dfrac{1}{2}$, we can calculate this quotient quickly by dividing 10 in half and multiplying the denominator of the fraction by 2: $10\dfrac{9}{16} \div 2 = 5\dfrac{9}{32}$.

Section 6.3

38. (a) Sam finds the least common denominator first. When he multiplies the fractions, he forgets to multiply the denominators. In the given problem, Sam would write

    $$\dfrac{3}{4} \times \dfrac{1}{6} = \dfrac{9}{12} \times \dfrac{2}{12} = \dfrac{18}{12} = \dfrac{3}{2} = 1\dfrac{1}{2}.$$

    Sandy finds the reciprocal of the second fraction before multiplying. Sandy would write

    $$\dfrac{5}{6} \times \dfrac{3}{8} = \dfrac{5}{6} \times \dfrac{8}{3} = \dfrac{40}{18} = \dfrac{20}{9} = 2\dfrac{2}{9}.$$

    (b) Sam is confusing multiplication with addition. Sandy is confusing multiplication with division.

Section 6.3

39. Let x represent the number of apples in the store. Then we have $\frac{1}{4}x + \frac{1}{5}x + \frac{1}{6}x = 37$. The least common multiple of 4, 5, and 6 is 60. So we can write the following:

$$\frac{15x}{60} + \frac{12x}{60} + \frac{10x}{60} = 37$$

$$\frac{37x}{60} = 37$$

$$x = 60.$$

There were 60 apples in the store.

Section 6.3

40. Define two variables. Let s represent my son's current age and m represent my current age. Seven years ago my son was one-third my age at the time, so $s - 7 = \frac{1}{3}(m - 7)$. Seven years from now he will be one-half my age at that time, so $s + 7 = \frac{1}{2}(m + 7)$. We find my son's age by solving the following equations:

$$s - 7 = \frac{1}{3}(m - 7) \qquad s + 7 = \frac{1}{2}(m + 7)$$

$$3s - 21 = m - 7 \qquad 2s + 14 = m + 7$$

$$3s - 14 = m \qquad 2s + 7 = m$$

By substituting for m,

$$3s - 14 = 2s + 7$$

$$s = 21$$

My son is 21 years old.

Section 6.3

41. Access the eManipulative, *Dividing Fractions*. Try several examples. Adjust the step size to be $\frac{1}{5}$. Create a bar that represents 1 whole and two bars that represent $\frac{3}{5}$. When

dividing 1 whole by $\frac{3}{5}$, notice that there is one group of $\frac{3}{5}$ and a part of a group of $\frac{3}{5}$ leftover. Concentrate on the divisions of $\frac{1}{5}$. There are two parts leftover of the three parts needed to create another group of $\frac{3}{5}$. Thus, there is two-thirds of a group of three-fifths leftover.

SOLUTIONS - PART A PROBLEMS

Chapter 7: Decimals, Ratio, Proportion, and Percent

Section 7.1

18. To be an additive magic square, the three rows, the three columns, and the two diagonals must add up to the same number. The sum of all the numbers is 10.48 + 15.72 + ... + 47.16 + 52.4 = 282.96. Since, for example, each of the three rows must add up to the same number, each row must add up to 282.96 ÷ 3 = 94.32. Guess and test to find sets of three numbers that add up to 94.32. A solution is shown next.

26.2	20.96	47.16
52.4	31.44	10.48
15.72	41.92	36.68

Section 7.1

19. Determine the total wages lost during the strike. In 22 days, if Kathy worked 6-hour days at $9.74 per hour, then she lost

$$\left(\frac{9.74 \text{ dollars}}{1 \text{ hour}}\right)\left(\frac{6 \text{ hours}}{1 \text{ day}}\right)(22 \text{ days}) = \$1285.68.$$

In the new contract, Kathy must make up $1285.68 in 240 days, working six hours per day. That means she is working a total of (6)(240) = 1440 hours in one year. Let x represent the amount of increase in her hourly wage. Since she must make $1285.68 from the increase in her pay during the regular work year, $1440x = 1285.68$, and $x \approx 0.8928$ dollars. Therefore she must receive at least 90¢ more per hour to make up for the lost wages.

Section 7.1

20. Convert each decimal to a fraction.

$$0.6 + 0.783 + 0.29 = \frac{6}{10} + \frac{783}{1000} + \frac{29}{100}$$

Because each denominator is a power of ten, the least common multiple of all the denominators is always the largest denominator. Thus, the common denominator is always one of the existing denominators. It is easier to determine and create the common denominator of a collection of fractions whose denominators are all powers of ten than it is for a collection of fractions whose denominators are not all powers of ten.

$$\frac{6}{10} + \frac{783}{1000} + \frac{29}{100} = \frac{6 \cdot 100}{10 \cdot 100} + \frac{783}{1000} + \frac{29 \cdot 10}{100 \cdot 10}$$

$$= \frac{600}{1000} + \frac{783}{1000} + \frac{290}{1000}$$

$$= \frac{1673}{1000}$$

$$= 1.673$$

Section 7.2

15. Recall that Rate × Time = Distance. Since we know the distance in meters and the rate in meters per light year, we can find the time in light years.

$$T = \frac{D}{R} = \frac{1.5 \times 10^{19} \text{ meters}}{9.46 \times 10^{15} \frac{\text{meters}}{\text{light year}}} \approx 1585.6 \text{ light years.}$$

Therefore, the distance from Earth to Deneb is approximately 1600 light years.

Section 7.2

16. The decimal expansion is nonterminating. If the fraction $\frac{a}{b}$ is in simplest form, then $\frac{a}{b}$ has a repeating decimal that does not terminate if, and only if, b has a prime factor other than 2 or 5. Since 151 is prime, the fraction is in simplest form, and the denominator does not contain 2 or 5 as a

factor (it does not end in 0 or 5 and is not even), the fraction is nonterminating.

Section 7.2

17. For the decimal expansion of a fraction to terminate, the prime factors of the denominator must be only 2s and/or 5s. Make a list of such fractions and find a relationship between the fraction and the number of places in the terminating decimal.

Fraction	Decimal Expansion
$\dfrac{1}{2} = \dfrac{1}{2^1}$	0.5
$\dfrac{1}{4} = \dfrac{1}{2^2}$	0.25
$\dfrac{1}{8} = \dfrac{1}{2^3}$	0.125
$\dfrac{1}{16} = \dfrac{1}{2^4}$	0.0625

Notice that the number of places in the decimal expansion is the same as the exponent in the denominator of the fraction. So we can now write examples of the desired fractions. (Note: Other answers are possible.)

(a) $\dfrac{1}{8} = 0.125$

(b) $\dfrac{1}{16} = 0.0625$

(c) $\dfrac{1}{390,625} = \dfrac{1}{5^8} = 0.00000256$

(d) $\dfrac{1}{131,072} = \dfrac{1}{2^{17}} = 0.00000762939453125$

Section 7.2

18. When mentally converting decimals into fractions, $\dfrac{1}{9}$ can be substituted for the decimal $0.\overline{1}$ since they are equal.

(a) $0.\overline{3} = 3(0.\overline{1}) = 3\left(\dfrac{1}{9}\right) = \dfrac{3}{9} = \dfrac{1}{3}$

(b) $0.\overline{5} = 5(0.\overline{1}) = 5\left(\dfrac{1}{9}\right) = \dfrac{5}{9}$

(c) $0.\overline{7} = 7(0.\overline{1}) = 7\left(\dfrac{1}{9}\right) = \dfrac{7}{9}$

(d) $2.\overline{8} = 2 + 8(0.\overline{1}) = 2 + 8\left(\dfrac{1}{9}\right) = 2\dfrac{8}{9}$

(e) $5.\overline{9} = 5 + 9(0.\overline{1}) = 5 + 9\left(\dfrac{1}{9}\right) = 5 + 1 = 6$

Section 7.2

19. When mentally converting decimals into fractions, $\dfrac{1}{99}$ can be substituted for the decimal $0.\overline{01}$ since they are equal.

(a) $0.\overline{03} = 3(0.\overline{01}) = 3\left(\dfrac{1}{99}\right) = \dfrac{3}{99} = \dfrac{1}{33}$

(b) $0.\overline{05} = 5(0.\overline{01}) = 5\left(\dfrac{1}{99}\right) = \dfrac{5}{99}$

(c) $0.\overline{07} = 7(0.\overline{01}) = 7\left(\dfrac{1}{99}\right) = \dfrac{7}{99}$

(d) $0.\overline{37} = 37(0.\overline{01}) = 37\left(\dfrac{1}{99}\right) = \dfrac{37}{99}$

(e) $0.\overline{64} = 64(0.\overline{01}) = 64\left(\dfrac{1}{99}\right) = \dfrac{64}{99}$

(f) $5.\overline{97} = 5 + 97(0.\overline{01}) = 5 + 97\left(\dfrac{1}{99}\right) = 5\dfrac{97}{99}$

Section 7.2

20. When mentally converting decimals into fractions, $\dfrac{1}{999}$ can be substituted for the decimal $0.\overline{001}$ since they are equal.

(a) $0.\overline{003} = 3(0.\overline{001}) = 3\left(\dfrac{1}{999}\right) = \dfrac{3}{999} = \dfrac{1}{333}$

(b) $0.\overline{005} = 5(0.\overline{001}) = 5\left(\dfrac{1}{999}\right) = \dfrac{5}{999}$

(c) $0.\overline{007} = 7(0.\overline{001}) = 7\left(\dfrac{1}{999}\right) = \dfrac{7}{999}$

(d) $0.\overline{019} = 19(0.\overline{001}) = 19\left(\dfrac{1}{999}\right) = \dfrac{19}{999}$

(e) $0.\overline{827} = 827(0.\overline{001}) = 827\left(\dfrac{1}{999}\right) = \dfrac{827}{999}$

(f) $3.\overline{217} = 3 + 217(0.\overline{001}) = 3 + 217\left(\dfrac{1}{999}\right) = 3\dfrac{217}{999}$

Section 7.2

21. (a) The number of digits in the pattern of the repeating decimal is the same as the number of 9s in the denominator of the fraction.

   (i) $0.\overline{23} = \dfrac{23}{99}$ (Two digits in the pattern.)

   (ii) $0.\overline{010} = \dfrac{10}{999}$

   (iii) $0.\overline{769} = \dfrac{769}{999}$

   (iv) $0.\overline{9} = \dfrac{9}{9} = 1$

   (v) $0.\overline{57} = \dfrac{57}{99} = \dfrac{19}{33}$

   (vi) $0.\overline{1827} = \dfrac{1827}{9999} = \dfrac{203}{1111}$

   (b) See the verifications below.

   (i) Let $n = 0.\overline{23}$. Then, $100n = 23.\overline{23}$.

$$100n = 23.\overline{23}$$
$$-n = -0.\overline{23}$$
$$99n = 23$$
$$n = \frac{23}{99}$$

(ii)   Let $n = 0.\overline{010}$. Then, $1000n = 10.\overline{010}$.

$$1000n = 10.\overline{010}$$
$$-n = -0.\overline{010}$$
$$999n = 10$$
$$n = \frac{10}{999}$$

(iii)   Let $n = 0.\overline{769}$. Then, $1000n = 769.\overline{769}$.

$$1000n = 769.\overline{769}$$
$$-n = -\ 0.\overline{769}$$
$$999n = 769$$
$$n = \frac{769}{999}$$

(iv)   Let $n = 0.\overline{9}$. Then, $10n = 9.\overline{9}$.

$$10n = \ 9.\overline{9}$$
$$-n = -0.\overline{9}$$
$$9n = \ 9$$
$$n = \ 1$$

(v)   Let $n = 0.\overline{57}$. Then, $100n = 57.\overline{57}$.

$$100n = 57.\overline{57}$$

$$\underline{-n = -0.\overline{57}}$$

$$99n = 57$$

$$n = \frac{57}{99} = \frac{19}{33}$$

(vi) Let $n = 0.\overline{1827}$. Then, $10,000n = 1827.\overline{1827}$.

$$10,000n = 1827.\overline{1827}$$

$$\underline{-n = -0.\overline{1827}}$$

$$9999n = 1827$$

$$n = \frac{1827}{9999} = \frac{203}{1111}$$

Section 7.2

22. (a) Recall the pattern we discovered from earlier problems:

$$0.\overline{1} = \frac{1}{9}, \ 0.\overline{01} = \frac{1}{99}, \ 0.\overline{001} = \frac{1}{999}, \ \text{and} \ 0.\overline{0001} = \frac{1}{9999}.$$

If we want to continue this pattern with 4 zeros in the repetend, then there must be five 9s in the denominator of the fraction. That is, $0.\overline{00001} = \frac{1}{99999}$. This is one example of a fraction with a five-digit repetend.

(b) From earlier problems, any number of the form $0.\overline{abcde}$, where a, b, c, d, and e are not all the same can be written as $\frac{x}{99999}$ where $1 \le x \le 99998$, and the digits of x are not all the same. Notice why the digits cannot all be the same. If a, b, c, d, and e all were equal to the digit a, then we would have $0.\overline{abcde} = 0.\overline{aaaaa} = 0.\overline{a}$, which has a single-digit repetend.

Section 7.2

23. $\dfrac{1}{13} = 0.\overline{076923}$. Notice that the decimal representation has a six-digit repetend. Make a table.

Position	1	2	3	4	5	6	7	8	9	10	11	12...
Digit	0	7	6	9	2	3	0	7	6	9	2	3...

Every six digits, the number 3 occurs. This means that 3 is in any position that is a multiple of 6: 6, 12, 18, ...

(a) The 11th digit is a 2 as the table shows.
(b) Since $5 \times 6 = 30$, the 30th digit is 3. Therefore, the 33rd digit is a 6.
(c) Since $455 \times 6 = 2730$, the 2730th digit is a 3. Therefore, the 2731st digit is a 0.
(d) Since $1{,}833{,}333 \times 6 = 10{,}999{,}998$, the 10,999,998th digit is a 3. Therefore, the 11,000,000th digit is a 7.

Section 7.2

24. Consider $\dfrac{1}{13}$ and $\dfrac{10}{13}$. $\dfrac{1}{13} = 0.\overline{076923}$ and $\dfrac{10}{13} = 0.\overline{769230}$.

If we multiply the decimal expansion of $\dfrac{1}{13}$ by 10, then the decimal point is shifted one place to the right. If we ignore the first digit to the right of the decimal point in the expansion of $\dfrac{1}{13}$, then the expansions are the same.

Consider $\dfrac{1}{71} = 0.014084507...$ and $\dfrac{29}{71} = 0.408450704....$

Since $\dfrac{100}{71} = 1\dfrac{29}{71}$, we know that if we disregard the first two digits to the right of the decimal point in the decimal expansion of $\dfrac{1}{71}$, then the decimal expansions of $\dfrac{1}{71}$ and $\dfrac{29}{71}$ are the same.

Section 7.2

25. On an inexpensive, four-function calculator, the number of digits in the numerator and denominator would exceed the display capabilities of the calculator. An error symbol would be displayed if you tried to multiply out the entire numerator or denominator. The calculator can handle smaller calculations, however. Since multiplication and division can be done in any order, calculate the value by alternately dividing and multiplying. $364 \div 365 \times 363 \div 365 \times 362 \div 365 \times 361 \div 365 \times 360 \div 365 \times 359 \div 365 \approx 0.943764297$. (Note: The number of decimal places displayed by your calculator may differ.)

Section 7.2

26. Let x represent the amount of money Gary had before cashing the check. Gary bought the following:

Items	Cost
2 magazines	$2(\$1.95) = \$3.90$
1 book	$5.95
1 tape	$5.98
Total Cost	$15.83

After cashing the check, Gary had $x + 29.35$ dollars. He spent $15.83 and had $21.45 left.

$$x + 29.35 - 15.83 = 21.45$$

$$x + 13.52 = 21.45$$

$$x = 7.93$$

Gary had $7.93 before cashing the check.

Section 7.2

27. Let x represent the original value of the car. After one year has passed, the car is worth $0.8x$. After two years have passed, the car is worth $0.8(0.8x) = 0.64x$. After three years have passed, the car is worth $0.8(0.64x) = 0.512x$. If the car is worth $16,000 after 3 years have passed, then we know the following:

$$\$16,000 = 0.512x$$

$$\$16,000 \div 0.512 = x$$

$$\$31,250 = x$$

Therefore, the original value of the car was $31,250.

Section 7.2

28. A call costs 0.11 dollars per minute. Convert the length of time for the phone call to minutes.

    1 hour and 21 minutes = 60 minutes and 21 minutes

    $$= 81 \text{ minutes}$$

    Now determine the cost of the call.

    (81 minutes)(0.11 dollars per minute) = 8.91 dollars.

    Therefore, the call will cost $8.91.

Section 7.2

29. We assume that at the beginning of the trip, when the odometer read 32,576.7 miles, the gas tank was full. Also, at the end of the trip, when the odometer read 35,701.2 miles, the gas tank was full. To find the miles per gallon averaged over the whole trip, divide the total distance traveled in miles by the total number of gallons used.

    Total distance = 35,701.2 − 32,576.7 = 3124.5 miles

    Total gallons = (282.18 dollars) ÷ (2.89 dollars per gallon)

    $$\approx 97.64 \text{ gallons}$$

    Therefore, they averaged $\dfrac{3124.5}{97.64} \approx 32$ miles per gallon.

Section 7.2

30. In 2007, 121 Japanese yen would be received in exchange for 1 U. S. dollar. 121 yen ÷ 1 dollar = 121 yen per dollar. To find how many dollars would be received in exchange for 10,000 yen, we need to know the exchange rate in terms of "dollars per yen". 1 dollar ÷ 121 yen ≈ 0.00826446 dollars per yen. In 2007, in exchange for 1 yen, about 0.00826446 dollars would be received. In exchange for 10,000 yen, we would receive 10,000(0.00826446) ≈ 82.64 dollars.

Section 7.2

31. Convert each dimension to centimeters. Since there are 2.54 centimeters per inch, multiply.

    (8 inches) (2.54 cm per inch) = 20.32 centimeters.

    (10 inches) (2.54 cm per inch) = 25.40 centimeters.

    Therefore, the text book measures 20.32 cm by 25.40 cm.

Section 7.2

32. In 2007, a book costs $89. Each year the value increases so, in any year, the value of the book can be expressed in the following way:

    Current value = value last year + 0.03(value last year)
    Current value = 1.03(value last year)

    Construct a table and calculate the value for each year up to 2011.

Year	Value (in dollars)
2007	89
2008	1.03(89)
2009	1.03(1.03(89))
2010	1.03(1.03(1.03(89)))
2011	1.03(1.03(1.03(1.03(89))))

    In the year 2011, you would expect the book to cost $1.03(1.03(1.03(1.03(89)))) = (1.03)^4(89) \approx 100.17$, or approximately $100.00.

Section 7.2

33. To compare the capacity of each engine, consider the number of liters per cylinder. In each case **divide** the number of liters by the number of cylinders. A 2.4-liter, 4-cylinder engine has $\dfrac{2.4 \text{ liters}}{4 \text{ cylinders}} = 0.6$ liters per cylinder.

    A 3.5-liter, V-6 engine has $\dfrac{3.5 \text{ liters}}{6 \text{ cylinders}} = 0.58\overline{3}$ liters per cylinder. A 4.9-liter, V-8 engine has $\dfrac{4.9 \text{ liters}}{8 \text{ cylinders}} = 0.6125$ liters per cylinder. A 6.8-liter, V-10 engine has $\dfrac{6.8 \text{ liters}}{10 \text{ cylinders}} = 0.68$ liters per cylinder.

Section 7.2

34. Draw a grid and use the Guess and Test strategy. By making 14 moves, the penny and the dime will be exchanged. Consider the original configuration below. Each nickel is numbered so moves can be identified. Moves are numbered as follows:

P	N_2	D
N_1		N_3

Original

P	N_2	D
	N_1	N_3

Move 1

	N_2	D
P	N_1	N_3

Move 2

N_2		D
P	N_1	N_3

Move 3

N_2	D	
P	N_1	N_3

Move 4

N_2	D	N_3
P	N_1	

Move 5

N_2	D	N_3
P		N_1

Move 6

N_2	D	N_3
	P	N_1

Move 7

	D	N_3
N_2	P	N_1

Move 8

D		N_3
N_2	P	N_1

Move 9

D	P	N_3
N_2		N_1

Move 10

D	P	N_3
N_2	N_1	

Move 11

D	P	
N_2	N_1	N_3

Move 12

D		P
N_2	N_1	N_3

Move 13

D	N_1	P
N_2		N_3

Move 14

Notice if the only coins in the grid were the penny and the dime, it would take a minimum of 6 moves to exchange their places. With the nickels in place, additional moves are required. Before the penny or dime can move, another coin must move, so each of the 6 moves requires another coin to be moved out of the way bringing the minimum moves up to 12. Before the penny can move into the corner an additional nickel must move, and once the dime and penny are in position, one more nickel must move so that the lower, middle space is open. The minimum number of moves is 14.

Section 7.3

12. Grape juice is made from water mixed with juice concentrate. In the problem a "part-to-part" comparison is given: 1 part concentrate to 3 parts water. Since we want to know how much grape juice can be made from 10 ounces of concentrate, we need to set up a proportion using the ratio of concentrate to grape juice. We know that 1 part concentrate + 3 parts water = 4 parts grape juice.

$$\frac{1 \text{ part (concentrate)}}{4 \text{ parts (juice)}} = \frac{10 \text{ ounces (concentrate)}}{x \text{ ounces (juice)}}$$

Cross multiplying gives $x = 4 \times 10$, so $x = 40$ ounces. Therefore, 40 ounces of grape juice can be made.

Section 7.3

13. Set up a proportion using the ratio comparing acres to days.

$$\frac{\frac{1}{2} \text{ acre}}{3 \text{ days}} = \frac{2\frac{3}{4} \text{ acres}}{x \text{ days}}$$

$$\frac{1}{2}x = 3\left(2\frac{3}{4}\right) \qquad \text{Cross multiplying}$$

$$\frac{1}{2}x = 3\left(\frac{11}{4}\right)$$

$$\frac{1}{2}x = \frac{33}{4}$$

$$2x = 33 \qquad \text{Multiplying by 4}$$

$$x = 16\frac{1}{2} \text{ days}$$

It will take $16\frac{1}{2}$ days to clear the entire plot of $2\frac{3}{4}$ acres.

Section 7.3

14. Set up a proportion using ratios comparing peaches to servings.

$$\frac{6 \text{ peaches}}{4 \text{ servings}} = \frac{x \text{ peaches}}{10 \text{ servings}}$$

$$6(10) = 4x$$

$$60 = 4x$$

$$15 = x$$

About 15 peaches would be needed.

Section 7.3

15. Set up a proportion using ratios comparing ounces to weeks. (Note: There are 52 weeks in a year.)

$$\frac{128 \text{ ounces}}{6\frac{1}{2} \text{ weeks}} = \frac{x \text{ ounces}}{52 \text{ weeks}}$$

$$128(52) = 6\frac{1}{2}x$$

$$6656 = 6.5x$$

$$1024 = x$$

Therefore, 1024 ounces of liquid laundry detergent will be needed in one year.

Section 7.3

16. Since he slept 8 hours out of every 24-hour period, he slept $\frac{8}{24} = \frac{1}{3}$ of each day. Therefore, he would have spent $\frac{1}{3}$ of his life of 92 years sleeping. He slept approximately $\frac{1}{3}(92) = 30\frac{2}{3}$ years.

Section 7.3

17. Set up a proportion using ratios comparing weight on earth to weight on the moon.

$$\frac{175 \text{ pounds (on Earth)}}{28 \text{ pounds (on Moon)}} = \frac{30 \text{ pounds (on Earth)}}{x \text{ pounds (on Moon)}}$$

$$175x = 28(30)$$

$$175x = 840$$

$$x = 4.8$$

Therefore, the 30-pound dog would weigh 4.8 pounds on the moon.

Section 7.3

18. Set up a proportion using ratios comparing miles to years.

$$\frac{4460 \text{ miles}}{0.5 \text{ years}} = \frac{x \text{ miles}}{2.75 \text{ years}}$$

$$4460(2.75) = 0.5x$$

$$12,265 = 0.5x$$

$$24,530 = x$$

Your car will have gone 24,530 miles in 2.75 years.

Section 7.3

19. Set up a proportion using ratios comparing altitude in feet to horizontal feet. Notice that the units are inconsistent in the information given. Convert miles to feet using the fact that 1 mile = 5280 feet.

$$\frac{5 \text{ feet (altitude)}}{16.37 \text{ feet (horizontal)}} = \frac{x \text{ feet (altitude)}}{5280 \text{ feet (horizontal)}}$$

$$5(5280) = 16.37x$$

$$26,400 = 16.37x$$

$$1612.71 \approx x$$

She gained approximately 1613 feet in altitude.

Section 7.3

20. The information about the distance the "Spruce Goose" flew is unnecessary to complete this problem. Set up a proportion using ratios comparing length of the plane to wingspan. Be sure to convert all mixed measurements to the same units. Plane length: 218 ft 8 in. = 2624 inches. Plane wingspan: 319 ft 11 in. = 3839 inches.

$$\frac{2624 \text{ inches (plane length)}}{3839 \text{ inches (plane wingspan)}} = \frac{20 \text{ inches (model length)}}{x \text{ inches (model wingspan)}}$$

$$2624x = 3839(20)$$

$$2624x = 76,780$$

$$x \approx 29.26 \text{ inches}$$

Therefore, the wingspan of the model will be approximately 29 inches.

Section 7.3

21. Since the teacher-pupil ratio is 1:35, and the school has 1400 students, set up a proportion to find out how many teachers there are currently.

$$\frac{1 \text{ teacher}}{35 \text{ pupils}} = \frac{x \text{ teachers}}{1400 \text{ pupils}}$$

$$1400 = 35x$$

$$40 = x$$

There are currently 40 teachers.

(a) Set up a similar proportion to find out how many teachers will be needed if we want the teacher-pupil ratio to be 1:20.

$$\frac{1 \text{ teacher}}{20 \text{ pupils}} = \frac{x \text{ teachers}}{1400 \text{ pupils}}$$

$$1400 = 20x$$

$$70 = x$$

70 teachers will be needed, so 30 more teachers will need to be hired.

(b) If the teacher-pupil ratio is 1:35, then from part (a), we know there are 40 teachers. The total cost for teachers is $33,000 \times 40 = \$1,320,000$. The amount spent is $\$1,320,000 \div 1400$ pupils $\approx \$942.86$ per pupil.

(c) If the teacher-pupil ratio is 1:20, then from part (b), we know there are 70 teachers. The total cost for teachers is $33,000 \times 70 = \$2,310,000$. The amount spent is $\$2,310,000 \div 1400$ pupils $= \$1650.00$ per pupil.

Section 7.3

22. (a) Set up a proportion using ratios comparing the distance from Earth to Mars to the distance from Earth to Pluto.

$$\frac{1 \text{ (Earth to Mars)}}{12.37 \text{ (Earth to Pluto)}} = \frac{x \text{ AU (Earth to Mars)}}{30.67 \text{ AU (Earth to Pluto)}}$$

$$30.67 = 12.37x$$

$$2.48 \approx x$$

Mars was about 2.48 AU from Earth.

(b) Set up a proportion using ratios comparing the distance in astronomical units to the distance in miles.

$$\frac{30.67 \text{ AU (Pluto to Earth)}}{2.85231 \times 10^9 \text{ miles (Pluto to Earth)}} = \frac{1 \text{ AU (Earth to Sun)}}{x \text{ miles (Earth to Sun)}}$$

$$30.67x = 2.85231 \times 10^9$$

$$x = 93,000,000$$

The Earth is about 93,000,000 miles from the Sun.

(c) From part (a), we know that Mars was about 2.48 AU from Earth in October 1985. Since we know how miles and AU are related from part (b), we can set up a proportion using ratios comparing the distance in miles to the distance in astronomical units.

$$\frac{93,000,000 \text{ miles}}{1 \text{ AU}} = \frac{x \text{ miles}}{2.48 \text{ AU}}$$

$$93,000,000(2.48) = x$$

$$230,640,000 = x$$

In October 1985, Mars was about 2.31×10^8 miles from Earth.

Section 7.3

23. Set up a proportion in each part.
    (a) We are comparing years to hours in our analogy.

    $$\frac{10^{10} \text{ years}}{24 \text{ hours}} = \frac{x \text{ years}}{1 \text{ hour}}$$

    $$10^{10} = 24x$$

    $$x \approx 416,666,667$$

    One hour corresponds to approximately 416,666,667 years of actual time.
    (b) Since from part (a) we know how one hour is related to actual years, we can set up a proportion using 60 minutes rather than 1 hour.

    $$\frac{416,666,667 \text{ years}}{60 \text{ minutes}} = \frac{x \text{ years}}{1 \text{ minute}}$$

    $$416,666,667 = 60x$$

    $$x \approx 6,944,444$$

    One minute corresponds to approximately 6,944,444 years of actual time.
    (c) Since from part (b) we know how one minute is related to actual years, we can set up a proportion using 60 seconds rather than 1 minute.

    $$\frac{6,944,444 \text{ years}}{60 \text{ seconds}} = \frac{x \text{ years}}{1 \text{ second}}$$

    $$6,944,444 = 60x$$

    $$x \approx 115,741$$

One second corresponds to approximately 115,741 years of actual time.

(d) If Earth was formed approximately 5 billion years ago, then find what length of time this corresponds to in hours. From part (a), we know that 1 hour corresponds to 416,666,667 years.

$$\frac{1 \text{ hour}}{416,666,667 \text{ years}} = \frac{x \text{ hours}}{5,000,000,000 \text{ years}}$$

$$5,000,000,000 = 416,666,667x$$

$$x = 12$$

Since the 24-hour day begins at midnight, the earth was formed at about 12 noon.

(e) From part (c), we know that 1 second corresponds to 115,741 years.

$$\frac{1 \text{ second}}{115,741 \text{ years}} = \frac{x \text{ seconds}}{2,600,000 \text{ years}}$$

$$2,600,000 = 115,741x$$

$$x = 22.5$$

Since the 24-hour day begins at midnight, the creatures who left these remains died close to 24 hours later, at about 22.5 seconds before midnight.

(f) From part (c), we know that 1 second corresponds to 115,741 years.

$$\frac{1 \text{ second}}{115,741 \text{ years}} = \frac{x \text{ seconds}}{10,000 \text{ years}}$$

$$10,000 = 115,741x$$

$$x = 0.0864$$

Thus, the growth of modern civilization began 0.0864 seconds before midnight.

Section 7.3

24. Let d represent the distance to the airport. Recall the relationship: Distance = Rate × Time. Since we want to find the distance and we know the rate, we solve the equation for time so that it can be eliminated: Time = Distance ÷ Rate. If Cary drives at different rates, then his travel times will differ. The time he takes when driving 60

mph, say t_1, is $t_1 = \dfrac{d}{60}$. The time he takes when driving 30 mph, say t_2, is $t_2 = \dfrac{d}{30}$. Notice that there is a two-hour difference in arrival times. Since traveling 30 mph takes 2 hours longer we have $t_2 = t_1 + 2$. Substituting, we get $\dfrac{d}{30} = \dfrac{d}{60} + 2$. Multiplying each term by 60, the least common denominator, yields $2d = d + 120$, so $d = 120$. Thus, the airport was 120 miles away.

Section 7.3

25. Notice that each child had a different number of pennies. Since the ratio of each child's total to the next poorer child's total is a whole number, every child's total must be divisible by each of the poorer children's totals. If all the amounts were added, the poorest child's total could be factored out of the sum. All together they had 2879 cents. Since the poorest child's total can be factored out, we know that (poorest child's total) $\times$? $= 2879$. Notice that 2879 is prime, so $2879 = 1 \times 2879$. Therefore, the poorest child must have only 1 cent.

    The remaining six children must have 2878 cents all together. Once again, each amount is divisible by the second poorest child's total. Since $2878 = 2 \times 1439$ and 1439 is prime, the second poorest child must have 2 cents. Continue in this manner. The remaining five children have 2876 cents. Since $2876 = 4 \times 719$, the third poorest child must have 4 cents. The remaining four children have a total of 2872 cents. Since $2872 = 8 \times 359$, the fourth poorest child must have 8 cents. The 3 remaining children have a total of 2864 cents. Since $2864 = 16 \times 179$, the third richest child has 16 cents. The remaining 2 children have 2848 cents. Since $2848 = 32 \times 89$, the second richest child has 32 cents. There are only 2816 cents left, which belong to the one remaining child. Therefore, the totals for each of the seven children are 1, 2, 4, 8, 16, 32, and 2816 cents.

Section 7.3

26. Eric slumps to 1 hit out of 27 at bats. Overall Eric has a
$\dfrac{31+1}{69+27} = \dfrac{32}{96} = \dfrac{1}{3} \approx 0.333$ batting average.

Morgan slumps to 1 hit out of 9 at bats. Overall Morgan
has a $\dfrac{31+4}{69+36} = \dfrac{35}{105} = \dfrac{1}{3} \approx 0.333$ batting average.

Section 7.3

27. Let x represent the number of pennies the woman has. Notice that x can also represent the number of nickels and the number of dimes since she has an equal number of each coin. When calculating the total value of the coins, be sure that all amounts are expressed in dollars. Use the facts that 1 penny = 0.01 dollar, 1 nickel = 0.05 dollar, and 1 dime = 0.10 dollar. The woman has $0.01x$ dollars in pennies, $0.05x$ dollars in nickels, and $0.10x$ dollars in dimes. Thus, we have the following:

$$0.01x + 0.05x + 0.10x = 12.96$$

$$0.16x = 12.96$$

$$x = 81$$

Therefore, the woman has 81 dimes (and 81 pennies and 81 nickels).

Section 7.3

28. Working backwards, we know the man had no money after he bought the shoes. In order to buy the shoes, he had to have exactly $20, half of which was given to him by his father. Therefore, the man had $10 in his pocket after he bought the slacks. Now in order to buy the slacks *and* have $10 left over, the man must have had $30, half of which was given to him by his father. Therefore, the man had $15 in his pocket after he bought the hat. Finally, in order to buy the hat *and* have $15 left over, the man must have had $35, half of which was given to him by his father. Therefore, the man had $17.50 when he walked into the store.

Another way to solve this problem is to use variables. Let x represent the amount of money the man had when he walked into the store. His father gave him x dollars, and the man bought a \$20 hat. The man had $2x - 20$ dollars after buying the hat. His father gave him $2x - 20$ dollars, and the man bought \$20 slacks. The man had $2x - 20 + 2x - 20 - 20 = 4x - 60$ dollars left after buying the slacks. His father gave him $4x - 60$ dollars, and the man bought \$20 shoes. The man had no money left at this point.

$$4x - 60 + 4x - 60 - 20 = 0$$

$$8x - 140 = 0$$

$$8x = 140$$

$$x = 17.50$$

Therefore, the man had \$17.50 when he walked into the store.

Section 7.3

29. Notice that in order to answer this question, it is necessary to exclude silver dollars or the answer will be infinitely large just by using all silver dollars. If we do not have change for a nickel, we could have at most 4 pennies. If we do not have change for a dime, we could have at most 1 nickel and 4 pennies. If we do not have change for a quarter, we could have at most 1 dime, 1 nickel, and 4 pennies, or 2 dimes and 4 pennies. (Recall that we want the largest sum of money when we are done, so we choose the 2 dimes and 4 pennies option.) If we do not have change for a half-dollar, we could have at most 1 quarter, 4 dimes, and 4 pennies. If we do not have change for a dollar, we could have at most 1 half-dollar, 1 quarter, 4 dimes, and 4 pennies. With this combination, we have 119 cents without being able to give change for a nickel, a dime, a quarter, a half-dollar, or a dollar.

Section 7.3

30. Notice that a single-digit number, 1 to 9, is subtracted during a turn. Consider the winning strategy for a game beginning with 20. If the loser is the one who ends at zero, you want to leave your opponent with 1 after your last turn so that she/he will be forced to subtract 1 and lose. Consider further that if, at the end of a turn, you leave your

opponent with 11, no matter what digit she/he subtracts, you can always subtract enough to leave your opponent with 1, thus forcing her/him to lose. Therefore, for the game beginning at 20, you can always win by going first and subtracting 9. Your opponent will be left with 11. No matter what your opponent subtracts, you can subtract enough to leave her/him with 1, which she/he must subtract, and thus lose. In the game beginning with 100, the first player should always subtract 9, leaving 91. On successive turns, the first player should subtract whatever is necessary to leave 81, 71, 61, 51, 41, 31, 21, 11, and 1, thus forcing the opponent to subtract 1 and lose.

Section 7.3

31. Notice there is a 4-minute difference between the two timers. In order to cook something for exactly 15 minutes, we need to use the 11-minute timer and this 4-minute difference between the timers. Begin both timers at the same time. When the 7-minute timer runs out, begin cooking since there are 4 minutes left on the 11-minute timer. After we have been cooking for 4 minutes, the 11-minute timer will run out. Turn it over and continue cooking until it runs out. If we stop cooking at this point, we will have been cooking for 15 minutes.

Section 7.3

32. Posts: • • • • • • • • • • • •
             1 2 3 4 5 6 7 8 9 10 11 12

The distance from Post 1 to Post 2 is one "post length". Since the runner began at the first post, she traveled only seven post lengths by the time she reached the eighth post. Since we want to know how many seconds it will take to reach the twelfth post, we need to set up a proportion. Notice that by the time she reaches the twelfth post she will have traveled eleven post lengths.

$$\frac{8 \text{ seconds}}{7 \text{ post lengths}} = \frac{x \text{ seconds}}{11 \text{ post lengths}}$$

$$88 = 7x$$

$$12\frac{4}{7} = x$$

It will take $12\frac{4}{7}$ seconds to reach the twelfth post.

Section 7.3

33. Melvina is not on track but she can get back on track by using the scale up/scale down technique. She can scale down 180 miles : 4 hours = 45 miles : 1 hour. Then she can scale up 45 miles : 1 hour = 450 miles : 10 hours. Thus in 10 hours the total distance is 450 miles. Melvina cannot add 450 to her original average of 180 miles in 4 hours.

Section 7.4

14. Access the eManipulative, *Percent Gauge*. We want to find a percent. We are given the other two pieces of information that we need. The "whole" or "total" is the 4200 pound automobile. The "part of the whole" is the 357 pounds of rubber in the automobile. What percent of the whole car's weight is rubber? Set up a proportion by filling in the information for "Part" and "Total".

$$\frac{\text{Part}}{\text{Total}} = \frac{\text{Percent}}{100}$$

$$\frac{357}{4200} = \frac{\text{Percent}}{100}$$

$$\frac{357}{4200}(100) = \text{Percent}$$

$$8.5 = \text{Percent}$$

Thus, only 8.5% of the car's weight is rubber. The rubber weight is only a small percent of the whole car's weight.

Section 7.4

15. Access the eManipulative, *Percent Gauge*. We want to find a part of a whole. We are given the total number of students and a percent. The "whole" or "total" is the class consisting of 2780 students. We know 70% of the whole

class will graduate. The "part of the whole" that we are looking for is the number of students who will graduate. Set up a proportion by filling in the information for "Total" and "Percent".

$$\frac{\text{Part}}{\text{Total}} = \frac{\text{Percent}}{100}$$

$$\frac{\text{Part}}{2780} = \frac{70}{100}$$

$$\text{Part} = \frac{70}{100}(2780)$$

$$\text{Part} = 1946$$

Thus, 1946 students will graduate.

Section 7.4

16. (a) Interest = Principal × Rate is the formula for simple interest. Let p represent the amount of principal. In this case, we know the interest earned and the rate. Convert the rate to a decimal: 4.25% = 0.0425. Therefore, we have $p(0.0425) = 208.76$, and $p = 4912$. The total amount in the account at the end of the year is principal + interest = $4912 + 208.76 = \$5120.76$.

    (b) At the rate of 5.33% which is 0.0533 when we convert to a decimal, the investor would have earned $4912(0.0533) = \$261.81$ in interest. The investor would have earned $\$261.81 - \$208.76 = \$53.05$ more interest at the rate of 5.33%.

Section 7.4

17. Suppose you borrowed $100 by purchasing a vacuum cleaner on credit. You have two options. You can pay the $100 now, or you can wait 15 days and pay a daily interest rate of 0.04839%. How much will you save by paying the loan 15 days before it is due? If you pay now the amount due is $100.00. If you pay in 15 days, the amount due is $p(1 + r)^t$, where p = principal, r = daily interest rate, and t = time in days. Interest is compounded daily for 15 days. Therefore, we have the following:

$$\text{Amount due} = 100(1 + 0.0004839)^{15}$$

$$\approx 100(1.0073)$$

$$\approx 100.73$$

You will save about 73 cents by paying now rather than in 15 days.

Section 7.4

18. They lost 2 out of 35 games, so the fraction of games lost is $\frac{2}{35}$. Since $\frac{2}{35} \approx 0.057$, the percent of games lost is about 5.7%. Together, the percent of games won and the percent of games lost must add to 100%. Therefore, the percent of games won is about $100\% - 5.7\% = 94.3\%$.

Section 7.4

19. The 1997 contributions increased 73% compared to the 1990 contributions. When there is an increase, we must realize that the 1997 contributions were 173% times as large as the 1990 contributions. A 73% **increase** means that 100% of the original value has been maintained and then there was an increase of 73%.

    (a) In 1997, $\$9.9 \times 10^{10}$ was donated to charity. We want to find out how much was donated in 1990. Let c represent the amount donated in 1990. Since the contributions in 1997 increased over those in 1990, the amount donated in 1997 = 1.73×(the amount donated in 1990).

    $$\$9.9 \times 10^{10} = 1.73c$$

    $$\$5.72 \times 10^{10} \approx c$$

    Therefore, the amount donated in 1990 was about $\$5.72 \times 10^{10}$.

    (b) The percent increase is found by calculating the change in value compared to the original value.

$$\text{percent increase} = \frac{3041 - 1958}{1958}(100\%)$$

$$= \frac{1083}{1958}(100\%)$$

$$\approx 0.553(100\%)$$

$$\approx 55.3\%$$

Therefore, the average charitable contribution increased approximately 55.3% from 1990 to 1997.

Section 7.4

20. (a) Notice that each source of energy in the pie graph is given in quadrillion BTUs. Add each amount to find the total amount of energy produced.

$$7.2 + 23.3 + 7.7 + 12.5 + 21.8 = 72.5.$$

Therefore, 72.5 quadrillion BTUs of energy were produced, from all sources, in the United States, in 1999.

(b) To find the percent of the energy produced from each source, divide each source by the total amount of energy produced and multiply by 100%.

$$\text{Renewables: } \frac{7.2}{72.5} \times 100\% \approx 9.9\%$$

$$\text{Coal: } \frac{23.3}{72.5} \times 100\% \approx 32.1\%$$

$$\text{Nuclear: } \frac{7.7}{72.5} \times 100\% \approx 10.6\%$$

$$\text{Crude Oil: } \frac{12.5}{72.5} \times 100\% \approx 17.2\%$$

$$\text{Natural Gas: } \frac{21.8}{72.5} \times 100\% \approx 30.1\%$$

Notice that the percentages do not add to 100% due to rounding.

Section 7.4

21. The price was not consistent with the ad. If the original price was discounted by 15%, then the price should be lowered by ($115)(0.15) = $17.25. Therefore, the new price should be $115.00 − $17.25 = $97.75. The sale price

22. that was offered was $100, which was $15 off the original price. What percent of $115 is this $15? We can now write an equation as shown next where x represents the percent discount.

$$15 = x(115)$$

$$15 \div 115 = x$$

$$0.1304 \approx x$$

The advertised discount was really about 13%.

Section 7.4

22. Since 17% of the selling price is $850, set up an equation to find the selling price. Let x represent the selling price of the car. Then we have the following:

$$0.17x = 850$$

$$x = 850 \div 0.17$$

$$x = 5000$$

Therefore, the car sold for $5000.

Section 7.4

23. Notice a relationship between the following two statements: 20% of 50 is 10, and 10% of 100 is 10. In each case a percent is multiplied by a "whole". If we divide the percent by 2, then we multiply the whole by 2. This can be done mentally.
    (a) Since the percent is divided by 5, multiply 50 by 5. 30% of 50 is 6% of 250.
    (b) Since the percent is divided by 8, multiply 60 by 8. 40% of 60 is 5% of 480.
    (c) Since the whole has been doubled, the percent should be halved. 30% of 80 is 15% of 160.

Section 7.4

24. Let x represent the original price of the car. Since there is an 8% discount, we paid 92% of the original price of the car. We paid $4485.00.

$$\$4485.00 = 92\% \times x$$

$$4485 = 0.92x$$

$$4875 = x$$

The original price of the car was $4875.00.

Section 7.4

25. (a) To find the percent of the surface area of the Earth these continents comprise, consider the ratio that compares the surface areas of these continents to the surface area of the Earth. Multiply that ratio by 100%.

$$\frac{8.5 \times 10^{13}}{5.2 \times 10^{14}} \times 100\% \approx 16.3\%$$

These continents comprise about 16.3% of the Earth's surface area.

(b) Consider the ratio comparing the surface area of the Pacific Ocean to the surface area of the Earth.

$$\frac{1.81 \times 10^{14}}{5.2 \times 10^{14}} \times 100\% \approx 34.8\%$$

The Pacific Ocean covers about 34.8% of the surface area of the Earth.

(c) If oceans cover 70% of the surface area of the Earth, multiply to find how many square meters of the Earth's surface are covered by oceans.

$$(0.70)(5.2 \times 10^{14}) = 3.64 \times 10^{14} \text{ square meters}$$

The Earth is covered by 3.64×10^{14} square meters of ocean.

(d) First we must determine the land mass of the Earth. Since from part (c), the oceans make up 70% of the surface area, we can state that land makes up the other 30% of the surface area. The total surface area of the Earth is $5.2 \times 10^{14} \text{ m}^2$. Thirty percent of the surface area is land.

$$30\% \text{ of } 5.2 \times 10^{14} = (0.30)(5.2 \times 10^{14}) = 1.56 \times 10^{14} \text{ m}^2$$

The percent of the land surface area of the Earth contained in the state of Texas is calculated as follows:

$$\frac{6.92 \times 10^{11}}{1.56 \times 10^{14}} \times 100\% \approx 0.44\%$$

Therefore, Texas contains about 0.44%, or less than 1%, of the total land surface area or land mass of the Earth.

Section 7.4

26. The information provided is not consistent. Let x represent the number of grams of protein recommended. If 3 grams are 4% of the U.S. RDA, then set up a proportion to find out how many grams correspond to 100% U.S. RDA.

$$\frac{3 \text{ grams}}{4\%} = \frac{x \text{ grams}}{100\%}$$

$$300 = 4x$$

$$75 = x$$

Therefore, 75 grams of protein are recommended daily. On the other hand, if 7 grams is 15% of the U.S. RDA, then 100% of the U.S. RDA corresponds to $46\frac{2}{3}$ grams of protein, as shown next.

$$\frac{7 \text{ grams}}{15\% \text{ RDA}} = \frac{x \text{ grams}}{100\% \text{ RDA}}$$

$$700 = 15x$$

$$46\frac{2}{3} = x$$

The U.S. RDA of protein cannot be both 75 grams and about 46.7 grams.

Section 7.4

27. The original inseam is 32 inches. If the inseam is made 10% longer, then it is increased by $32(0.10) = 3.2$ inches. The new inseam is then $32 + 3.2 = 35.2$ inches. The material is expected to shrink by 10%. So, the slacks will shrink by $35.2(0.1) = 3.52$ inches. The final inseam measurement will thus be $35.2 - 3.52 = 31.68$ inches.

Section 7.4

28. Suppose that an item costs $100. If the price is marked up by 10%, then the price is increased by $100(0.10) = \$10$ for a new price of $100 + \$10 = \$110$. Then, if the item is discounted by 10%, the price is decreased by $110(0.10) = \$11$ for a final price of $110 - \$11 = \$99$. On the other hand, if the price of the item is first decreased by 10%, then the price is decreased by $100(0.10) = \$10$ for a new price of $100 - \$10 = \$90$. Then, if the price is marked up by 10%,

then the price is increased by $90(0.10) = \$9$ for a final price of $\$90 + \$9 = \$99$. We see that the final price of $99 is the same either way.

Another way to look at this problem is to use a variable. Let x represent the original price of the item.

Method 1 calls for a 10% markup followed by a 10% discount.

Price after 10% markup: $x + 0.10x = 1.10x$

Price after 10% discount: $1.10x - 1.10x(0.10) = 0.99x$

Method 2 calls for a 10% discount followed by a 10% markup.

Price after 10% discount: $x - 0.10x = 0.90x$

Price after 10% markup: $0.90x + 0.90x(0.10) = 0.99x$

By either method, the final price is 99% of the original price.

Section 7.4

29. Suppose Cathy has 100 baseball cards. Since percent means per hundred, and Joseph has 64% as many cards as Cathy, Joseph has 64 cards. Martin has 50%, or half as many cards as Joseph. Therefore, Martin has $64 \div 2 = 32$ cards. Martin has 32 cards compared to Cathy's 100 cards. Since $32 \div 100 = 32\%$, Martin has 32% as many cards as Cathy.

Section 7.4

30. For a 50-year-old man, first subtract 50 from 220: $220 - 50 = 170$. Now find 70% of this difference: $(0.70)(170) = 119$. Also find 80% of the difference: $(0.80)(170) = 136$. The optimal heart rate for cardiovascular benefits for a 50-year-old man is between 119 and 136 beats per minute.

Section 7.4

31. Let x represent the original number of outputs of audio information provided by the competition. If 6 outputs is 40% more than the competition, then 140% of x should be 6. $1.4x = 6$, so $x \approx 4.2857$ outputs. We have found that the number of outputs of audio information provided by the competition is about 4.2857. However, since outputs of audio information must be whole numbers, the number of

outputs *cannot* be 4.2857. Therefore, 6 is not 40% more than the competition.

Section 7.4

32. Compare these billing rates by supposing the doctor charges you $100. By the first method, 15% would be taken off the bill. 15% of 100 = 0.15(100) = 15, so the bill would be $100 − $15 = $85. By the second method, 10% is taken off first and then 5% is taken off the discounted amount. Ten percent of 100 = (0.10)(100) = 10, for a bill of $100 − $10 = $90. Five percent of 90 = 0.05(90) = 4.5, so the final bill would be $90 − $4.5 = $85.50. You would save money by choosing to have the discounts added, as in the first method.

Section 7.4

33. Let x represent the population of the country at the beginning of 2004. Since the population increased by 4.2% during 2004, there were 104.2% of x, or 1.042x, people at the beginning of 2005. Since the population increased by 2.8% during 2005, there were 102.8% of 1.042x or (1.028)(1.042x) = 1.071176x people at the beginning of 2006. Since the population *decreased* by 2.1% during 2006, there were 97.9% of 1.071176x or (0.979)(1.071176x) ≈ 1.0486813x people at the beginning of beginning of 2007 (or the end of 2006). Therefore, there was an increase of approximately 4.9% over the 3 year period.

Section 7.4

34. You cannot take more than two petals so when it is your turn, you do not want to be left with three petals. If, on your turn, you are faced with three petals, no matter how many you take (one or two), your opponent can take the final one or two petals to win the game.

Similarly, you never want to be left with six petals because no matter what you take (one or two petals), your opponent can take one or two petals to leave you with three petals which is a losing situation for you.

Finally, if you go first when there are nine petals, then you could be forced to lose if your opponent leaves you with six petals and then with three petals on your next turn. The person who begins the game can always be forced to lose. To win, a player should start second and always leave the other player with a multiple of three petals. However, if the player who goes second does not finish a turn by leaving a multiple of three petals, the first player can end up a winner.

Section 7.4

35. Suppose an item was originally priced at $100. By method (i), 20% is deducted first and then a 6% tax is added. Notice that a 20% markdown is the same as paying 80% of the original price. 80% of 100 = 0.80(100) = $80. Adding a 6% tax gives 106% of 80 = 1.06(80) = $84.80. By method (ii), the 6% tax is added first and then 20% is deducted. 106% of 100 = 1.06(100) = $106. Paying 80% of this gives 80% of 106 = 0.80(106) = $84.80. Therefore, the results are the same. To see why this is true, let p represent the original price of the item. The final price by method (i) is found by $p \times 80\% \times 106\%$. The final price by method (ii) is found by $p \times 106\% \times 80\%$. Since multiplication is commutative, both methods yield the same result.

Section 7.4

36. Use the compound interest formula $P\left(1 + \dfrac{r}{n}\right)^{nt}$. Since semiannual compounding means interest is compounded twice a year, $n = 2$. The principal deposited is $12,000, so $P = 12,000$. The annual interest rate is 7%, so $r = 0.07$. The time is 3 years, so $t = 3$.

$$P\left(1+\frac{r}{n}\right)^{nt} = 12,000\left(1+\frac{0.07}{2}\right)^{(2)(3)}$$

$$= 12,000(1.035)^6$$

$$\approx 12,000(1.22925532634)$$

$$\approx 14,751.06$$

Her tax-deferred account will be worth approximately $14,751.06 at the end of 3 years.

Section 7.4

37. Each year she needs to earn 11% more than she did during the previous year. Therefore, one year from now, she needs to earn 111% of her current salary or 1.11(35,000). Two years from now, she needs to earn 111% of her previous year's salary: 1.11(1.11)(35,000) = $(1.11)^2$(35,000). Three years from now, she needs to earn 111% of her previous year's salary; that is, she must earn $(1.11)(1.11)^2$(35000) = $(1.11)^3$(35,000). Four years from now, she needs to earn $(1.11)^4$(35,000). Five years from now, she needs to earn $(1.11)^5$(35,000). Therefore, in order for her to have the same buying power in five years, she must earn $(1.11)^5$(35,000) $\approx$ 58,977.04, or approximately $59,000.

Section 7.4

38. Let x represent the initial investment. At the end of year 1, they will have 8.25% more than the initial investment or 108.25% of the initial investment. (108.25% $x = 1.0825x$.) Each year the amount is 108.25% of the previous year's balance or 1.0825 times as much. After 10 years, this will have been done 10 times, so the amount in the account will be $(1.0825)^{10}x$. Since we want the account to contain $20,000, we must have the following:

$$(1.0825)^{10}x = 20,000$$

$$x = 20,000 \div (1.0825)^{10}$$

$$x \approx 9052.13$$

Therefore, the initial investment must be $9052.13.

Section 7.4

39. The 1982-1984 year was the base year for comparison, so the CPI for it was 100%. In calculating the percent increase from July 2000 to July 2001, we consider the change in value compared to what it was in 2000.

$$\text{Percent Increase} = \frac{\text{CPI for 2001} - \text{CPI for 2000}}{\text{CPI for 2000}} \times 100\%$$

$$= \frac{177.5 - 172.8}{172.8} \times 100\%$$

$$\approx 2.72\%.$$

The increase in the CPI from 2000 to 2001 was approximately 2.72%.

Section 7.4

40. If your income is low, then the percent taken in taxes is low. If your income is high, then the percent taken in taxes is high. Make a table of salaries, taxes, and net earnings, and find the salary that lets you keep the most money.

Salaries (dollars)	Tax (percent)	Tax (dollars)	Net Salary (dollars)
10,000	10	1000	9000
20,000	20	4000	16,000
30,000	30	9000	21,000
40,000	40	16,000	24,000
50,000	50	25,000	25,000
60,000	60	36,000	24,000
70,000	70	49,000	21,000
80,000	80	64,000	16,000
90,000	90	81,000	9000

Notice the symmetry in the net salaries. At $50,000, your net salary is a maximum at $25,000.

Section 7.4

41. The average wage now is $9.99. This is 108% of last year's average wage. Express this situation in words and then translate it into symbols. Let L represent last year's average wage.

$$\text{Current Average Wage} = \left(\begin{array}{c} \text{Percent of Last Year's} \\ \text{Average Wage} \end{array} \right) \left(\begin{array}{c} \text{Last Year's} \\ \text{Average Wage} \end{array} \right)$$

$$9.99 = 108\%(L)$$

$$9.99 = 1.08L$$

$$\frac{9.99}{1.08} = L$$

$$9.25 = L$$

Therefore, the average wage last year was $9.25.

Section 7.4

42. From the problem, we know the year of his birth = 29 × (his age at death), and we know he had to be born before 1949. It would be rare to find a man who lived to be much more than 100 years old. As we systematically guess and check, a reasonable number to start with would be an age which when multiplied by 29 produces a year in the 1800s or the 1900s. Since $63 \times 29 = 1827$, make table of possible ages at death, beginning with age 63, and eliminate unreasonable solutions.

Age at Death	$\times 29$	= Year of Birth	Age in 1949	
63	29	1827	122	Died in 1890
64	29	1856	93	Died in 1920
65	29	1885	64	
66	29	1914	35	
67	29	1943	6	Will die in 2010
68	29	1972	0	Will die in 2040

There is no need to continue checking ages beyond 67 since any number greater than 67 will produce a year greater than 1949 after it is multiplied by 29. In 1949, the man could have been 35 or 64 years old.

Section 7.4

43. Since the area is 72 square feet, and the garden has whole number dimensions, we need to list all possible length × width factor pairs. To find the possible total length of fence needed, we need to find the perimeter of the garden

for each set of dimensions. Recall that Perimeter $= 2 \times$ Length $+ 2 \times$ Width.

Length	Width	Area	Perimeter
1	72	72	146
2	36	72	76
3	24	72	54
4	18	72	44
6	12	72	36
8	9	72	34

Therefore, the possible lengths of fence that could be used are 1, 2, 3, 4, 6, or 8 feet.

Section 7.4

44. Determine the time for a round trip for each of the two days. Recall that Distance $=$ Rate $\times$ Time, so Time $=$ Distance $\div$ Rate.

Today: The sum of the wind speed and the air speed is the ground speed of the plane. Therefore, the ground speed $=$ 50 mph $+$ 150 mph $=$ 200 mph with the wind. In traveling from A to B, he will travel 300 miles at 200 mph so the time required is $\dfrac{300}{200} = 1.5$ hours. On the return trip, his ground speed will be 150 mph $-$ 50 mph $=$ 100 mph. Therefore, in traveling from B to A, he will travel 300 miles at 100 mph. The time required will be $\dfrac{300}{100} = 3$ hours. The total time required for the round trip this morning will be $1.5 + 3 = 4.5$ hours.

Tomorrow: If he waits until tomorrow when there is no wind, he will travel a total distance of 600 miles at 150 mph, so the time required will be $\dfrac{600}{150} = 4$ hours.

Therefore, his travel time will be shorter if he waits until tomorrow when there is no wind.

SOLUTIONS - PART A PROBLEMS

Chapter 8: Integers

Section 8.1

18. Make a table and check the account balance after every transaction. If the balance ever drops below $0, deduct a $10 service charge. Initially Dixie has a balance of $115.

Action	Account Balance
Deposit $384	$115 + $384 = $499
$153 Check	$499 − $153 = $346
$86 Check	$346 − $86 = $260
$196 Check	$260 − $196 = $64
$34 Check	$64 − $34 = $30
$79 Check	$30 − $79 = −$49 Service Charge of $10 $−49 − $10 = $−59
Deposit $123	$−59 + $123 = $64

At the end of the month, Dixie's balance was $64.

Section 8.1

19. (a) The set of integers is closed under subtraction. For the set to be closed under subtraction, we must be able to take any two integers, find their difference, and obtain an integer. As an example, notice that 6 and 8 are integers. Also, $6 - 8 = -2$ and -2 is an integer.

   (b) Integer subtraction is not commutative. We cannot subtract integers in any order and obtain the same result. For example, $2 - 6 = -4$, but $6 - 2 = 4$.

   (c) Integer subtraction is not associative. Consider the following as a counterexample.
$$(10 - 4) - 7 \neq 10 - (4 - 7)$$
$$6 - 7 \neq 10 - (-3)$$
$$-1 \neq 13$$

   (d) Assume that n is the identity element for subtraction. Then it must be true that $a - n = n - a = a$, for any integer a. If $a - n = n - a$, then $a - n = -(a - n)$, but this can only be true when $a - n = 0$. Since $a - n = a$ and $a - n = 0$, it follows that $a = 0$. However, $a - n = n - a = a$ must be true for any a and not just for $a = 0$. Therefore, there is no identity element for integer subtraction.

Section 8.1

20. Suppose the adding-the-opposite approach is true. That is, suppose that $a - b = a + (-b)$. We must show that if $a - b = c$, then $a = b + c$.

Suppose that $a - b = c$.

Then	$a + (-b) = c$	Adding-the-opposite approach
	$a + (-b) + b = c + b$	Add b to both sides
	$a + 0 = c + b$	Additive inverse
	$a = c + b$	Additive identity
	$a = b + c$	Commutative property

Therefore, if $a - b = c$, then $a = b + c$.

Now we must show that if $a = b + c$, then $a - b = c$.
Suppose that $a = b + c$.

Then	$a + (-b) = b + c + (-b)$	Add $(-b)$ to both sides
	$a + (-b) = b + (-b) + c$	Commutative property
	$a + (-b) = 0 + c$	Additive inverse
	$a + (-b) = c$	Identity property
	$a - b = c.$	Adding-the-opposite approach

Therefore, if $a = b + c$, then $a - b = c$.

Therefore, we see that the missing-addend approach is a consequence of the adding-the-opposite approach.

Section 8.1

21. (a) (i) Consider the following examples:
    If $a = 3$ and $b = 11$, then the equation is true.
    $|3 + 11| = |14| = 14$, and

    $|3| + |11| = 3 + 11 = 14$

    Therefore, $|3 + 11| = |3| + |11|$.

    If $a = -13$ and $b = -2$, then the equation is true.
    $|-13 + (-2)| = |-15| = 15$, and

$\left|-13\right|+\left|-2\right|=13+2=15$.

Therefore, $\left|-13+(-2)\right|=\left|-13\right|+\left|-2\right|$.

If $a=-6$ and b $=4$, then the equation is false.

$\left|-6+4\right|=\left|-2\right|=2$, and

$\left|-6\right|+\left|4\right|=6+4=10$.

But, since $2\neq10$, $\left|-6+4\right|\neq\left|-6\right|+\left|4\right|$.

In general, if a and b have the same sign, or if one or both of them are zero, then it is true that $\left|a+b\right|=\left|a\right|+\left|b\right|$.

(ii) Recall the third example from part (i). The numbers in that example have opposite signs. $\left|-6+4\right|=2<10=\left|-6\right|+\left|4\right|$. Notice that when a and b are nonzero and have opposite signs, the quantity $\left|a+b\right|$ is the absolute value of a difference, while the quantity $\left|a\right|+\left|b\right|$ is the sum of two positive numbers. Since adding integers with different signs is like subtracting, in that case, the quantity $\left|a+b\right|$ will always be less than the quantity $\left|a\right|+\left|b\right|$. In general, if a and b are both nonzero and have opposite signs, then $\left|a+b\right|<\left|a\right|+\left|b\right|$.

(iii) The inequality $\left|a+b\right|>\left|a\right|+\left|b\right|$ is never true. Consider the various possibilities for integers a and b. They could have the same signs (positive or negative), different signs, both zero, or one zero. Recall what we did in parts (i) and (ii). If a and b have the same sign or one or both of them are zero, then $\left|a+b\right|=\left|a\right|+\left|b\right|$. If a and b have different signs, then $\left|a+b\right|<\left|a\right|+\left|b\right|$. Since there are no other possibilities for a and b, there is no case where $\left|a+b\right|>\left|a\right|+\left|b\right|$.

(iv) Recall the discussion from part (iii). For any combination of integers a and b, either $\left|a+b\right|=$

$|a| + |b|$ or $|a + b| < |a| + |b|$. Therefore, we have $|a + b| \le |a| + |b|$, and the inequality holds for all integers.

(b) Recall our discussion from part (a) above. The inequality $|a + b| \le |a| + |b|$ will hold for all pairs of integers. Thus, only condition (iv) holds for all pairs of integers.

Section 8.1

22. We need to determine what each row, column, and diagonal will add up to before we can begin placing numbers. In a magic square, each row adds up to the same number. Also, each column and each diagonal add up to the same number. Notice that the total for all three rows is the sum of all the numbers in the three rows. Therefore, the sum for each row, each column, and each diagonal must be $\dfrac{1}{3}$ of the sum of all the numbers. Add up all the numbers and divide by 3:

$10 + 7 + 4 + 1 + (-2) + (-5) + (-8) + (-11) + (-14) = -18$.

Each row, column, and diagonal must add up to $\dfrac{-18}{3} = -6$.

7	-14	1
-8	-2	4
-5	10	-11

Since the middle square contains –2, we need to list all pairs that add up to –4. Each pair will complete one of the diagonals or the row or column that passes through the middle square. Guess and test until each diagonal, each row, and each column add up to the number –6. The pairs that add up to –4 are 10 and –14, 7 and –11, 4 and –8, 1 and –5. One possible solution is shown.

Section 8.1

23. (a) The set A is closed under subtraction. We know that 4 and 9 are elements of A. Recall that we can take any two elements of A, not necessarily different, subtract them and have an element in the set.
    (i)   Since $9 - 4 = 5$, 5 is an element of A.
    (ii) Since $4 - 9 = -5$, –5 is an element of A.
    (iii) Since $4 - 4 = 0$, 0 is an element of A.
    (iv) Since $9 - [(4 - 4) - 4] = 13$, 13 is an element of A.
    (v)   Since $(9 - 4) - 4 = 1$, 1 is an element of A.

(vi) Since $[(9-4)-4]-4=-3$, -3 is an element of A.

(b) Notice from part (a) that 1 and 0 are elements of set A. Using 1 and 0, generate more elements in the set. Note $0-1=-1$, so -1 is in the set. Also, $-1-1=-2$, so -2 is in the set, and $-2-1=-3$, so -3 is in the set. Continuing in this manner will generate all of the negative integers. We can use the negative integers to generate the positive integers. For example, $1-(-1)=2$, $2-(-1)=3$, $3-(-1)=4$, and so on. Since the set contains all of the positive and negative integers, and zero, set A contains all of the integers, and possibly other numbers as well.

(c) Since 8 is a multiple of 4, subtracting 4 repeatedly from 8 generates the elements 4, 0, –4, –8, –12 and so on. Notice that these numbers are all multiples of four. If we subtract –4 repeatedly from 8, we generate the elements 12, 16, 20, and so on. These numbers are also multiples of 4. Therefore, set A will contain all multiples of 4, and possibly other numbers as well.

(d) Notice that in part (a), GCF(4, 9) = 1. In part (b), GCF(4, 8) = 4. In general, if a set contains two numbers whose GCF is different from 1, then the set contains all multiples of that GCF. If a set contains two numbers whose GCF is 1, then the set contains all integers. Try more examples to convince yourself that this is true.

Section 8.1

24. In row three, we can fill in the first two boxes. The first box contains 4 since $-9+13=4$. The second box contains –2 since $13+(-15)=-2$. The sum of the numbers in these two boxes is 2. Therefore, the first box in row two contains a 2. Now since the top box contains –22, and one of the two boxes beneath it contains 2, the other box beneath it must contain the solution to the equation $2+\square=-22$. Therefore, the second box in row two contains –24. Similarly, the third box in row three must contain the

solution to $-2 + \square = -24$, which is -22. The fourth box in row four must contain the solution to the equation $-15 + \square = -22$, which is -7. The solution is shown next.

			-22				
		2		-24			
	4		-2		-22		
-9		13		-15		-7	

Section 8.1

25. Congratulate the student on the technique. It will always work when subtracting integers. Consider a general subtraction problem involving two-digit integers $ab - cd$. In expanded form, this problem can be written as $(10a + b) - (10c + d)$. In the student's algorithm, d is subtracted from b to obtain $b - d$ and then $10c$ is subtracted from $10a$ to obtain $10a - 10c$. These two results are then added, which yields $10a - 10c + b - d$. This result is the same as $(10a + b) - (10c + d) = 10a - 10c + b - d$.

For the given example, we have the following:
$$72 - 38 = (70 + 2) - (30 + 8)$$
$$= (70 - 30) + (2 - 8)$$
$$= 40 + (-6)$$
$$= 34$$

Section 8.1

26. Consider the following figure. Each square has been labeled with a letter.

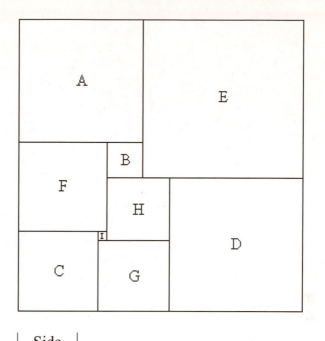

Square	Side Length	Reason
A	14	Given
B	4	Given
C	9	Given
D	15	Given
E	18	Side of A + Side of B = Side of E
F	10	Side of A − Side of B = Side of F
G	8	Side of A + Side of E = 32 Side of G = 32 − Side of C − Side of D
H	7	Side of H = Side of D − Side of G
I	1	Side of I = Side of G − Side of H

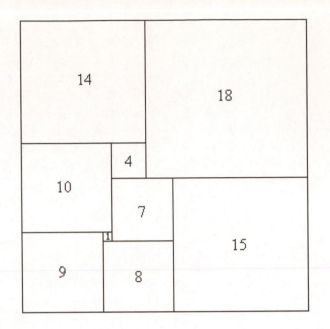

Section 8.1

27. Explore the eManipulative, *Circle 0*. The goal is to place the numbers in the circles so that the sum of the three numbers in each circle is 0. Five of the numbers will be placed for you. Consider the number 0. There are only six options for placing numbers in a circle with 0: 1 and −1, 2 and −2, 3 and −3, 4 and −4, 5 and −5, or 6 and −6.

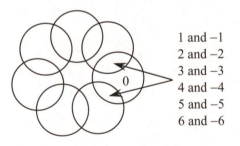

1 and −1
2 and −2
3 and −3
4 and −4
5 and −5
6 and −6

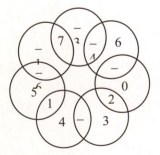

By noting which of these numbers have already been placed in other circles, the list of options will shrink quickly. Notice also that there is no −7, so the sum of the two positive numbers in a circle cannot exceed 6. Use the Systematic Guess and Test strategy. The solution is given at left.

Section 8.1

28. Begin with 3 black chips in the circle. When attempting to subtract 8 chips from 3 chips, notice that there are not enough black chips. In order to complete this subtraction, there must be 8 black chips in the circle. If we insert 5 black chips, then we must also insert 5 red chips. Notice that 5 black and 5 red chips together represent zero. We ensure that there are enough black chips and have not changed the representation of the number 3. Once the 8 black chips are removed only 5 red chips remain. Thus $3 - 8 = -5$.

Section 8.2

24. Consider the first square in the bottom row. Since the number in a square is the product of the two numbers beneath it, we need to solve the equation $\square \times 4 = -20$ to find the missing number. The missing number must be -5. Consider the third square of the bottom row. It must be the solution to $\square \times -5 = -15$. Therefore, the missing number must be 3. Now we can determine the number in the middle box in the third row. Since it is the product of the numbers beneath it, we know that it is 4×3 or 12. At this point, the pyramid of squares is as follows:

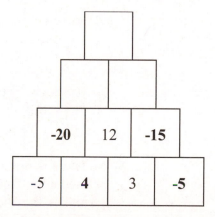

Consider the two empty squares in row two. The first must contain $-20 \times 12 = -240$, and the second one must contain $12 \times -15 = -180$. Finally the top number is $-240 \times -180 = 43,200$. Therefore, the final pyramid of squares is as follows:

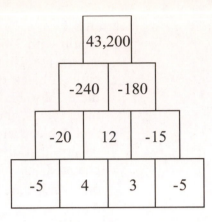

Section 8.2
25. (a) Substitute each of the integers for x in the inequality $3x + 5 < -16$.

$$3(-6) + 5 = -13$$
-13 is not < -16
False when $x = -6$

$$3(-10) + 5 = -25$$
$-25 < -16$
True when $x = -10$

$$3(-8) + 5 = -19$$
$-19 < -16$
True when $x = -8$

$$3(-7) + 5 = -16$$
-16 is not < -16
False when $x = -7$

(b) Solve the inequality for x.
$$3x + 5 < -16$$
$$3x < -21$$
$$x < -7$$

The inequality is true for all values of x less than 7. Therefore, the inequality is true when x is $-8, -9, -10, -11, \dots$. The largest of these integers is -8.

(c) There is not a smallest integer value of x that makes the inequality true. Notice that -8 is the largest integer that makes the inequality true. The inequality is also true for $x = -9$, $x = -10$, $x = -11$, $x = -12$, and so on. Continue substituting smaller and smaller integers for x. The inequality is true for all integers such that $x \leq -8$.

Section 8.2

26. (a) The addition table is shown below.

+	+	−
+	+	?
−	?	−

Positive + Positive = Positive (+ sign in the table).

Negative + Negative = Negative (− sign in the table).

Negative + Positive = Positive or Negative or Zero (thus the ? sign in the table).

(b) (i) The table for subtraction is shown below.

−	+	−
+	?	+
−	−	?

Positive − Positive = Positive or Negative or Zero (thus the ? sign in the table).

Positive − Negative = Positive (+ sign in the table since subtracting a negative is the same as adding a positive.)

Negative −Positive = Negative (− sign in the table since subtracting a positive is the same as adding a negative.)

Negative − Negative = Positive or Negative or Zero (thus the ? sign in the table).

(ii) The table for multiplication is shown below.

×	+	−
+	+	−
−	−	+

Positive × Positive = Positive (+ sign in the table).

Positive × Negative = Negative (– sign in the table. Since a and b are positive, $-b$ is negative. $(a)(-b) = -(ab)$. ab is positive, so $-ab$ is negative.)

Negative × Positive = Negative (– sign in the table).

Negative × Negative = Positive (+ sign in the table. Since a and b are positive, $-a$ and $-b$ are negative. $(-a)(-b) = ab$. ab is positive.)

(iii) The table for division is shown below.

÷	+	–
+	+	–
–	–	+

Positive ÷ Positive = Positive (+ sign in the table).
Positive ÷ Negative = Negative (– sign in the table).
Negative ÷ Positive = Negative (– sign in the table).
Negative ÷ Negative = Positive(+ sign in the table).

Section 8.2

27. (a) (i) If x is a negative integer, then $|x|$ is a positive integer. Thus, for all negative integers x, $|x| > x$.
    (ii) If x is zero or positive, then $|x|$ is zero or positive, respectively. So for all x such that $x \geq 0$, $|x| = x$.
    (iii) If x is a negative integer, then $|x| > x$. If x is zero or a positive integer, then $|x| = x$. Integers can only be negative, positive, or zero, so there is no integer such that $|x| < x$.
    (iv) For any integer x, either $|x| > x$ or $|x| = x$. Since $|x| \geq x$ means $|x| > x$ or $|x| = x$, we know that $|x| \geq x$ holds for any integer.

    (b) Condition (iv), $|x| \geq x$, holds for all integers.

Section 8.2

28. Her reasoning is correct. She will apply the theorem which states "If a is an integer, then $a(-1) = -a$." Let $a = -1$. Because -1 is an integer, we know that $-(-1) = (-1)(-1)$ by the theorem she applied. Since a negative integer

multiplied by a negative integer is a positive integer, we know that $(-1)(-1) = 1$.

Section 8.2

29. Consider debts of $5 and $10. Since it will take more money to pay off the $10 debt, you will be left with *less* money than if you paid off the $5 debt. Alternately, if you put the dollar amounts on the number line, where positive numbers represent assets and negative numbers represent liabilities, then -10 is to the left of -5. Thus, $-10 < -5$.

Section 8.2

−2		
−36	**6**	
3	**−4**	**−18**

30. The product of the numbers in row three is 216, so each row, column, and diagonal must contain integers whose product is 216. In column one there is one square empty. The number in this square must be the solution to the equation $-2 \times \square \times 3 = 216$. The missing integer in column one is $216 \div (-6) = -36$. The middle square must contain the solution to the equation $-2 \times \square \times (-18) = 216$. The missing integer in the middle square is $216 \div 36 = 6$.

In row two, the missing integer must be the solution to the equation $-36 \times 6 \times \square = 216$. Thus, the missing integer is $216 \div (-216) = -1$. The missing integer in column three must be the solution to the equation $\square \times (-1) \times (-18) = 216$. The missing integer is $216 \div 18 = 12$. The missing integer in row one must be the solution to the equation $(-2) \times \square \times 12 = 216$. Therefore, the missing integer is $216 \div (-24) = -9$. The multiplicative magic square is shown at left.

−2	**−9**	**12**
−36	**6**	**−1**
3	**−4**	**−18**

Section 8.2

31. If x and y are positive integers and $x < y$, then we know that $xx < xy$. Thus, $x^2 < yx$, and $yx < yy$, so $yx < y^2$. By the addition approach to less than, $x^2 + c = yx$, for some positive integer c, and $yx + d = y^2$ for some positive integer d. By substitution, $x^2 + c + d = y^2$. Since c and d are positive integers, and the set of integers is closed under addition, $c + d$ is a positive integer. By the addition approach to less than, $x^2 < y^2$.

Section 8.2

32. We must calculate the number of grams in one atom of carbon. That is, we want the number of grams *per* atom. To determine this number, we divide grams by atoms.

$$\frac{12.01 \text{ grams}}{6.022 \times 10^{23} \text{ atoms}} \approx 1.99 \times 10^{-23} \text{ grams per atom}.$$

Therefore, in one atom of carbon, there are 1.99×10^{-23} grams.

Section 8.2

33. (a) The rate of hair growth is 4.3×10^{-9} meters per second. Convert to meters per day.

$$\frac{4.3 \times 10^{-9} \text{ m}}{1 \text{ second}} \times \frac{60 \text{ seconds}}{1 \text{ minute}} \times \frac{60 \text{ minutes}}{1 \text{ hour}} \times \frac{24 \text{ hours}}{1 \text{ day}} = 3.7152 \times 10^{-4} \text{ meters per day}$$

In one month of 30 days, the amount of hair growth would be 30 times as much as for one day.

$$\frac{3.7152 \times 10^{-4} \text{ m}}{1 \text{ day}} \times \frac{30 \text{ days}}{1 \text{ month}} \approx 1.11 \times 10^{-2} \text{ meters per month}$$

(b) Hair grows at a rate of 4.3×10^{-9} meters per second. Let x = the amount of time (in seconds) it takes for hair to grow one meter. Solve the following equation to find the number of seconds it will take for hair to grow one meter.

$$\left(4.3 \times 10^{-9} \frac{\text{meters}}{\text{second}}\right)(x \text{ seconds}) = 1 \text{ meter}$$

$$(4.3 \times 10^{-9})(x) = 1$$

$$x = \frac{1}{4.3 \times 10^{-9}}$$

$$x \approx 2.33 \times 10^{8} \text{ seconds}$$

Convert this to years:

$$\frac{2.33 \times 10^{8} \text{ seconds}}{1} \cdot \frac{1 \text{ hour}}{3600 \text{ seconds}} \cdot \frac{1 \text{ day}}{24 \text{ hours}} \cdot \frac{1 \text{ year}}{365 \text{ days}} \approx 7.4 \text{ years}$$

Therefore, it would take about 7.4 years for hair to grow to one meter in length.

Section 8.2

34. Keeping in mind that the farmer buys only 100 animals and spends only $1000, consider the maximum number of cows, sheep, and rabbits that can be purchased, and make a table. Since cows cost $50 each, the maximum number of cows that can be purchased by the farmer is $1000 ÷ $50 = 20 cows.

Cows	Sheep	Rabbits	Total Cost	Total Number
20	0	0	$1000	20
19	0	100	$1000	119
19	1	80	$1000	100

Continue adjusting the number of cows, sheep, and rabbits. The only other solution occurs when the farmer buys only sheep. Since sheep cost $10 each, the maximum number of sheep that can be purchased is $1000 ÷ $10 = 100 sheep. Therefore, the farmer buys 19 cows, 1 sheep, and 80 rabbits, or the farmer buys 100 sheep.

Section 8.2

35. Try several examples to see that the statement appears to be true. Prove that if x is a whole number, then x^2 is a multiple of 3 or x^2 is one more than a multiple of 3. Suppose that x is a whole number. Then we know that $x = 3n$, $x = 3n + 1$, or $x = 3n + 2$, for some whole number n. (That is, x is a multiple of 3, one more than a multiple of 3, or two more than a multiple of 3. If x is three more than a multiple of 3, then x is back to being a multiple of 3.)
Consider x^2 for each case:
$x^2 = (3n)^2 = 9n^2 = 3(3n^2)$, so x^2 is a multiple of 3.
$x^2 = (3n + 1)^2 = 9n^2 + 6n + 1 = 3(3n^2 + 2n) + 1$, so x^2 is one more than a multiple of 3.
$x^2 = (3n + 2)^2 = 9n^2 + 12n + 4 = 9n^2 + 12n + 3 + 1 = 3(3n^2 + 4n + 1) + 1$, so x^2 is one more than a multiple of 3.
Therefore, if x is a whole number, then x^2 is a multiple of 3, or x^2 is one more than a multiple of 3.

Section 8.2

36. In both weeks, the shopper spent 50¢. Because the price dropped by 10¢ per dozen this week, we have old price per

dozen = (new price + 10) per dozen. Also, we know that the shopper received 5 more apples this week, so we know the number of dozens of apples this week – number of dozens of apples last week = $\frac{5}{12}$ dozen apples. Construct a table and use systematic guess and test.

This Week		Last Week		Dozens This Week – Dozens Last Week
Price per Dozen (cents)	Number of Dozens	Price per Dozen (cents)	Number of Dozens	Difference = $\frac{5}{12}$?
10	5	20	$\frac{5}{2}$	$5 - \frac{5}{2} = \frac{5}{2}$ No
15	$\frac{10}{3}$	25	2	$\frac{10}{3} - 2 = \frac{4}{3}$ No
20	$\frac{5}{2}$	30	$\frac{5}{3}$	$\frac{5}{2} - \frac{5}{3} = \frac{5}{6}$ No
25	2	35	$\frac{10}{7}$	$2 - \frac{10}{7} = \frac{4}{7}$ No
30	$\frac{5}{3}$	40	$\frac{5}{4}$	$\frac{5}{3} - \frac{5}{4} = \frac{5}{12}$ Yes

Therefore, the new price is 30¢ per dozen.

Section 8.2

37. If $ab = 0$ and $b \neq 0$, then $ab = 0 = 0 \cdot b$. Since we assume "If $ac = bc$ and $c \neq 0$, then $a = b$.", we can conclude that $a = 0$. Similarly, if $a \neq 0$, then $ab = 0 = a \cdot 0$, so $b = 0$ by our assumption.

SOLUTIONS - PART A PROBLEMS

Chapter 9: Rational Numbers, Real Numbers, and Algebra

Section 9.1

32. Let n be any nonzero integer. By the definition of equality of rational numbers, to show that two rational numbers are equal, it is necessary to show the "cross products" are equal. Therefore, for $\dfrac{a}{b}$ to be equal to $\dfrac{an}{bn}$, we need to show that $a(bn) = b(an)$.

$$
\begin{aligned}
b(an) &= (ba)n \quad \text{Associativity} \\
&= (ab)n \quad \text{Commutativity} \\
&= a(bn) \quad \text{Associativity}
\end{aligned}
$$

Therefore, since $b(an) = a(bn)$ we know $\dfrac{a}{b} = \dfrac{an}{bn}$.

Section 9.1

33. (a) We need to show that the product of two rational numbers is a rational number. Let $\dfrac{a}{b}$ and $\dfrac{c}{d}$ be rational numbers, where b and d are nonzero integers. By the definition of multiplication of rational numbers, $\dfrac{a}{b} \cdot \dfrac{c}{d} = \dfrac{ac}{bd}$. Since the set of integers is closed under multiplication, ac and bd are integers. Therefore, by the definition of a rational number, $\dfrac{ac}{bd}$ is a rational number.

(b) We need to show that rational numbers can be multiplied in any order. Let $\dfrac{a}{b}$ and $\dfrac{c}{d}$ be rational numbers where b and d are nonzero integers. Then we have the following:

$$\frac{a}{b} \cdot \frac{c}{d} = \frac{ac}{bd} \qquad \text{Multiplication of rational numbers}$$

$$= \frac{ca}{db} \qquad \text{Commutativity for integer multiplication}$$

$$= \frac{c}{d} \cdot \frac{a}{b} \qquad \text{Multiplication of rational numbers}$$

Therefore, $\dfrac{a}{b} \cdot \dfrac{c}{d} = \dfrac{c}{d} \cdot \dfrac{a}{b}$.

(c) We need to show that rational number multiplication is associative. Let $\dfrac{a}{b}$, $\dfrac{c}{d}$, and $\dfrac{e}{f}$ be rational numbers, where b, d, and f are nonzero integers.

$$\left(\frac{a}{b} \cdot \frac{c}{d} \right) \frac{e}{f} = \left(\frac{ac}{bd} \right) \frac{e}{f} \qquad \text{Multiplication of rational numbers}$$

$$= \frac{(ac)e}{(bd)f} \qquad \text{Multiplication of rational numbers}$$

$$= \frac{a(ce)}{b(df)} \qquad \text{Associativity for integer multiplication}$$

$$= \frac{a}{b} \left(\frac{ce}{df} \right) \qquad \text{Multiplication of rational numbers}$$

$$= \frac{a}{b} \left(\frac{c}{d} \cdot \frac{e}{f} \right) \qquad \text{Multiplication of rational numbers}$$

Therefore, $\left(\dfrac{a}{b} \cdot \dfrac{c}{d} \right) \dfrac{e}{f} = \dfrac{a}{b} \left(\dfrac{c}{d} \cdot \dfrac{e}{f} \right)$.

(d) We need to show there exists a rational number so that the product of it and any other rational number is equal to that rational number. Let $\dfrac{a}{b}$ be any rational number where b is a nonzero integer. We know the following:

$$\frac{a}{b} \cdot 1 = \frac{a}{b} \cdot \frac{1}{1}$$

$$= \frac{a \cdot 1}{b \cdot 1} \qquad \text{Multiplication of rational numbers}$$

$$= \frac{a}{b} \qquad \text{Multiplication identity for integers}$$

$$1 \cdot \frac{a}{b} = \frac{1}{1} \cdot \frac{a}{b}$$

$$= \frac{1 \cdot a}{1 \cdot b} \qquad \text{Multiplication of rational numbers}$$

$$= \frac{a}{b} \qquad \text{Multiplicative identity for integers}$$

Therefore, since $\dfrac{a}{b} \cdot 1 = \dfrac{a}{b} = 1 \cdot \dfrac{a}{b}$, 1 is the identity element of rational-number multiplication.

(e) We need to show that for each rational number there exists another rational number, the inverse, so that the product of the rational number and its inverse is the identity element. Let $\dfrac{a}{b}$ be any nonzero rational number. Then $a \neq 0$ and $b \neq 0$.

$$\frac{a}{b} \cdot \frac{b}{a} = \frac{ab}{ba} \qquad \text{Multiplication of rational numbers}$$

$$= \frac{ab}{ab} \qquad \text{Commutativity for integer multiplication}$$

$$= \frac{a}{a} \cdot \frac{b}{b} \qquad \text{Multiplication of rational numbers}$$

$$= 1 \cdot 1 \qquad \text{Since } \frac{m}{m} = 1 \text{ when } m \neq 0$$

$$= 1$$

Therefore, each nonzero rational number $\dfrac{a}{b}$ has a unique inverse, $\dfrac{b}{a}$.

Section 9.1

34. (a) $\dfrac{a}{b} - \dfrac{c}{d} = \dfrac{e}{f}$ if, and only if, $\dfrac{a}{b} = \dfrac{c}{d} + \dfrac{e}{f}$.

(b) $\dfrac{a}{b} - \dfrac{c}{d} = \dfrac{a}{b} + \left(-\dfrac{c}{d}\right)$ by the adding-the-opposite approach. Since $\dfrac{a}{b} - \dfrac{c}{d} = \dfrac{e}{f}$ and $\dfrac{a}{b} - \dfrac{c}{d} = \dfrac{a}{b} + \left(-\dfrac{c}{d}\right)$, we know $\dfrac{a}{b} + \left(-\dfrac{c}{d}\right) = \dfrac{e}{f}$. Adding $\dfrac{c}{d}$ to both sides, we get $\dfrac{a}{b} + \left(-\dfrac{c}{d}\right) + \dfrac{c}{d} = \dfrac{e}{f} + \dfrac{c}{d}$. Thus, $\dfrac{a}{b} = \dfrac{c}{d} + \dfrac{e}{f}$ by the additive inverse and commutative properties. Therefore, we have established that if $\dfrac{a}{b} - \dfrac{c}{d} = \dfrac{e}{f}$, then $\dfrac{a}{b} = \dfrac{c}{d} + \dfrac{e}{f}$.

Now suppose that $\dfrac{c}{d} + \dfrac{e}{f} = \dfrac{a}{b}$. Adding $-\dfrac{c}{d}$ to both sides, we get $-\dfrac{c}{d} + \dfrac{c}{d} + \dfrac{e}{f} = -\dfrac{c}{d} + \dfrac{a}{b}$. By the additive inverse and commutative properties, we know that $\dfrac{e}{f} = \dfrac{a}{b} + \left(-\dfrac{c}{d}\right)$. Also, $\dfrac{e}{f} = \dfrac{a}{b} - \dfrac{c}{d}$ by the adding-the-opposite approach. Therefore, we have established that if $\dfrac{c}{d} + \dfrac{e}{f} = \dfrac{a}{b}$, then $\dfrac{e}{f} = \dfrac{a}{b} - \dfrac{c}{d}$.

By these two parts together, we have verified the missing-addend approach.

(c) Assuming the missing-addend approach holds, we need to show that $\dfrac{a}{b} - \dfrac{c}{d} = \dfrac{a}{b} + \left(-\dfrac{c}{d}\right)$. If $\dfrac{a}{b} - \dfrac{c}{d} = \dfrac{e}{f}$, then $\dfrac{a}{b} = \dfrac{c}{d} + \dfrac{e}{f}$ by the missing-addend approach.

Adding $-\dfrac{c}{d}$ to both sides, we have the following:

$$\frac{a}{b}+\left(-\frac{c}{d}\right)=\frac{c}{d}+\frac{e}{f}+\left(-\frac{c}{d}\right)$$

$$=\frac{c}{d}+\left(-\frac{c}{d}\right)+\frac{e}{f} \quad \text{Commutative Property}$$

$$=\frac{e}{f}$$

Therefore, by substitution, $\dfrac{a}{b}-\dfrac{c}{d}=\dfrac{a}{b}+\left(-\dfrac{c}{d}\right)$.

Section 9.1

35. Let $\dfrac{a}{b}$, $\dfrac{c}{d}$, and $\dfrac{e}{f}$ be rational numbers.

$$\frac{a}{b}\left(\frac{c}{d}+\frac{e}{f}\right)=\frac{a}{b}\left(\frac{cf+de}{df}\right) \qquad \text{Addition of rational numbers}$$

$$=\frac{a(cf+de)}{b(df)} \qquad \text{Multiplication of rational numbers}$$

$$=\frac{a(cf)+a(de)}{b(df)} \qquad \text{Distributive property for integers}$$

$$=\frac{acf+ade}{bdf} \qquad \text{Multiplication of integers}$$

$$=\frac{acf}{bdf}+\frac{ade}{bdf} \qquad \text{Addition of rational numbers}$$

$$=\frac{ac}{bd}\cdot\frac{f}{f}+\frac{ae}{bf}\cdot\frac{d}{d} \qquad \text{Mult. of rational numbers and commutativity}$$

$$=\frac{ac}{bd}+\frac{ae}{bf} \qquad \text{Multiplicative identity for rational numbers}$$

$$=\frac{a}{b}\cdot\frac{c}{d}+\frac{a}{b}\cdot\frac{e}{f} \qquad \text{Multiplication of rational numbers}$$

Section 9.1

36. If $\dfrac{a}{b} < \dfrac{c}{d}$, then there exists some positive rational number

$\dfrac{m}{n}$ so that $\dfrac{a}{b} + \dfrac{m}{n} = \dfrac{c}{d}$. For the nonzero rational number

$\dfrac{e}{f}$, $\dfrac{a}{b} + \dfrac{m}{n} + \dfrac{e}{f} = \dfrac{c}{d} + \dfrac{e}{f}$. Then $\dfrac{a}{b} + \dfrac{e}{f} + \dfrac{m}{n} = \dfrac{c}{d} + \dfrac{e}{f}$ by

the commutative property for rational-number addition.

Thus, $\dfrac{a}{b} + \dfrac{e}{f} < \dfrac{c}{d} + \dfrac{e}{f}$ by the additive approach to less

than. Therefore, if $\dfrac{a}{b} < \dfrac{c}{d}$ then $\dfrac{a}{b} + \dfrac{e}{f} < \dfrac{c}{d} + \dfrac{e}{f}$.

Section 9.1

37. Prove that $-\left(-\dfrac{a}{b}\right) = \dfrac{a}{b}$ using additive cancellation. To

show this property, we need to find a rational number $\dfrac{e}{f}$

such that $-\left(-\dfrac{a}{b}\right) + \dfrac{e}{f} = \dfrac{a}{b} + \dfrac{e}{f}$. Then, by the additive

cancellation property, $-\left(-\dfrac{a}{b}\right)$ will equal $\dfrac{a}{b}$. Let

$\dfrac{e}{f} = \dfrac{-a}{b}$, which is equivalent to $-\dfrac{a}{b}$. We must show that

$-\left(-\dfrac{a}{b}\right) + \dfrac{-a}{b} = \dfrac{a}{b} + \dfrac{-a}{b}$.

Because addition of rational numbers is commutative, we

have $-\left(-\dfrac{a}{b}\right) + \dfrac{-a}{b} = \dfrac{-a}{b} + -\left(-\dfrac{a}{b}\right)$. By the additive

inverse property, $\dfrac{-a}{b} + -\left(-\dfrac{a}{b}\right) = 0$. Also by the additive

inverse property, $\dfrac{a}{b} + \dfrac{-a}{b} = 0$. Therefore, we have

$$-\left(-\frac{a}{b}\right)+\frac{-a}{b}=0=\frac{a}{b}+\frac{-a}{b}, \text{ and thus, } -\left(-\frac{a}{b}\right)=\frac{a}{b} \text{ by}$$

the additive cancellation property.

Section 9.1

38. We will use each timer twice. Begin the timers at the same time. As soon as the 5-minute timer goes off, restart it. Wait for the 8-minute timer to go off and immediately restart it also. When the 5-minute timer rings for the second time, there will be exactly 6 minutes left on the other timer. Begin measuring the 6 minutes when the 5-minute timer rings for the second time and end when the 8-minute timer rings for the second time.

```
8-minute timer  - - - - - - - -|- - - - - - - -|
5-minute timer  - - - - -|- - - - -| 6 min  |
                       begin     end
```

Section 9.2

26. Use indirect reasoning. Suppose that there is a rational number $\frac{a}{b}$ such that $\frac{a}{b}=\sqrt{3}$. Then squaring both sides yields $\left(\frac{a}{b}\right)^2=3$. So $\frac{a^2}{b^2}=3$, and $a^2=3b^2$. By the Fundamental Theorem of Arithmetic, we know that every whole number has a unique prime factorization. Since perfect squares have an even number of prime factors, a^2 and b^2 have an even number of prime factors. Notice, however, that since 3 is prime, $3b^2$ must have an odd number of prime factors. Since a whole number cannot have an even number *and* an odd number of prime factors, $\sqrt{3}$ must not be rational.

Section 9.2

27. Suppose there is a rational number $\frac{a}{b}$ such that $\frac{a}{b}=\sqrt{9}$.

Squaring both sides yields $\left(\frac{a}{b}\right)^2=9$. Then $\frac{a^2}{b^2}=9$ and $a^2=9b^2$. By the Fundamental Theorem of Arithmetic, a^2

and $9b^2$ must have the same prime factorization. We know a^2 and b^2 have an even number of prime factors since they are both perfect squares.

No contradiction arises now, however, since $9 = 3^2$ and $3^2b^2 = (3b)^2$, which also has an even number of prime factors. Therefore, there is not necessarily a contradiction when trying to show $\sqrt{9}$ is irrational in this way.

Section 9.2

28. Suppose there is a rational number $\dfrac{a}{b}$ such that $\dfrac{a}{b} = \sqrt[3]{2}$.

    Cubing both sides yields $\left(\dfrac{a}{b}\right)^3 = 2$. Then $\dfrac{a^3}{b^3} = 2$ and

    $a^3 = 2b^3$. By the Fundamental Theorem of Arithmetic, the prime factorization of a^3 and $2b^3$ must be the same. Note that each prime factor in the prime factorization of a perfect cube has an exponent that is a multiple of 3. Thus the exponent on 2 in the prime factorization of $a^3 = 2b^3$ is a multiple of 3. However, when $2b^3$ is written in its prime factorization, the exponent on the 2 will be one more than a multiple of 3. Since the exponent on the 2 is not the same in the prime factorizations of a^3 and $2b^3$, there is a contradiction. Therefore, $\sqrt[3]{2}$ is irrational.

Section 9.2

29. (a) Suppose there exists a rational number $\dfrac{a}{b}$ so that

    $\dfrac{a}{b} = 5\sqrt{3}$. Multiplying both sides by the rational

    number $\dfrac{1}{5}$ yields $\dfrac{a}{5b} = \sqrt{3}$. Since the set of rational

    numbers is closed under multiplication, $\dfrac{a}{5b}$ is a rational

    number. However, we know $\sqrt{3}$ is irrational. Therefore, since a number cannot be both rational *and* irrational, we have a contradiction. Therefore, $5\sqrt{3}$ is irrational.

(b) Suppose m is an irrational number and n is a nonzero rational number. We need to show nm is also irrational. Suppose there is a rational number $\dfrac{a}{b}$ so that $\dfrac{a}{b} = nm$. Multiplying both sides by the rational number $\dfrac{1}{n}$ yields $\dfrac{a}{nb} = m$. Since the set of rational numbers is closed under multiplication, $\dfrac{a}{nb}$ is rational. However, we have assumed that m is irrational. Since $\dfrac{a}{nb}$ cannot be both rational and irrational, we have a contradiction. Therefore, the product of any nonzero rational number with an irrational number is an irrational number.

Section 9.2

30. (a) Suppose there is a rational number $\dfrac{a}{b}$ such that $\dfrac{a}{b} = 1 + \sqrt{3}$. Subtracting 1 from both sides yields $\dfrac{a}{b} - 1 = \sqrt{3}$. Since $\dfrac{a}{b}$ and 1 are rational numbers, $\dfrac{a}{b} - 1$ is a rational number by the closure property. However, we know $\sqrt{3}$ is irrational. Since a number cannot be both rational and irrational, we have a contradiction. Therefore, $1 + \sqrt{3}$ is irrational.

(b) Let m and n where $n \neq 0$ be rational numbers. Suppose there is a rational number $\dfrac{a}{b}$ such that $\dfrac{a}{b} = m + n\sqrt{3}$. Subtracting m from both sides yields $\dfrac{a}{b} - m = n\sqrt{3}$. Since $\dfrac{a}{b}$ and m are rational numbers,

$\dfrac{a}{b} - m = \dfrac{a - bm}{b}$ is rational by the closure property.

Multiplying both sides by $\dfrac{1}{n}$ yields $\dfrac{a - bm}{bn} = \sqrt{3}$.

Since $\dfrac{1}{n}$ is rational, $\dfrac{a - bm}{bn}$ is rational. However, we know that $\sqrt{3}$ is irrational. Therefore, we have a contradiction, so $m + n\sqrt{3}$ must have been irrational.

Section 9.2

31. (a) $6\sqrt{2}$ is irrational since we proved that $\sqrt{2}$ is irrational. We also proved that the product of a rational and an irrational number is irrational in problem 29(b).

   (b) $2 + \sqrt{3}$ is irrational since we proved that any number of the form $m + n\sqrt{3}$ is irrational for rational numbers m and n from problem 30(b). (Here $m = 2$ and $n = 1$.)

   (c) $5 + 2\sqrt{3}$ is irrational since we proved that any number of the form $m + n\sqrt{3}$ is irrational for rational numbers m and n from problem 30(b). (Here $m = 5$ and $n = 2$.)

Section 9.2

32. If the student checks other examples, he will notice that $\sqrt{a} + \sqrt{b} = \sqrt{a + b}$ only when a or b or both are zero. For example, let $a = 36$ and $b = 64$. See if the equation is true.

$$\sqrt{36} + \sqrt{64} \overset{?}{=} \sqrt{36 + 64}$$

$$6 + 8 \overset{?}{=} 10$$

$$14 \neq 10$$

As another example, let $a = 49$ and $b = 0$.

$$\sqrt{49} + \sqrt{0} \overset{?}{=} \sqrt{49 + 0}$$

$$7 + 0 \overset{?}{=} 7$$

$$7 \neq 7$$

Therefore, $\sqrt{a} + \sqrt{b} \neq \sqrt{a + b}$, except when $a = 0$, $b = 0$, or both a and b are zero.

Section 9.2

33. In this section, $\sqrt{a}$ was defined only when $a \geq 0$. Therefore, the rule $\sqrt{a} \cdot \sqrt{b} = \sqrt{ab}$ is only true when $a \geq 0$ and $b \geq 0$. It is not true that $\sqrt{-1} \cdot \sqrt{-1} = \sqrt{(-1)(-1)}$, which is what led to the contradictory statement $-1 = 1$.

Section 9.2

34. Consider multiples of the Pythagorean triple (3, 4, 5). One multiple is (6, 8, 10). This is a Pythagorean triple since $6^2 + 8^2 = 36 + 64 = 100 = 10^2$. Also (9, 12, 15) is a Pythagorean triple since $9^2 + 12^2 = 225 = 15^2$. It is true that $(3n, 4n, 5n)$ is a Pythagorean triple for any counting number n since $(3n)^2 + (4n)^2 = 9n^2 + 16n^2 = 25n^2 = (5n)^2$. Since there are infinitely many counting numbers, there are infinitely many nonzero, whole-number Pythagorean triples. These, however, are not the only Pythagorean triples. Others include (5, 12, 13) and (7, 24, 25) and whole number multiples of these.

Section 9.2

35. When generating other primitive triples, choose a value for u and then carefully consider the restrictions to find v.

Let $u = 2$. Choose v such that v is odd, $v < 2$, and v and 2 are relatively prime. Since u and v must also be whole numbers, the only choice for v is 1. Therefore, we have $a = 2(2)(1) = 4$, $b = 2^2 - 1^2 = 4 - 1 = 3$, and $c = 2^2 + 1^2 = 4 + 1 = 5$.

Let $u = 3$. Choose v such that v is even, $v < 3$, and v and 3 are relatively prime. The only choice for v is 2. Therefore, $a = 2(3)(2) = 12$, $b = 3^2 - 2^2 = 9 - 4 = 5$, and $c = 3^2 + 2^2 = 9 + 4 = 13$.

Let $u = 8$. Choose v such that v is odd, $v < 8$ and v and 8 are relatively prime. v could be 7, 5, 3, or 1.

If $v = 7$, then $a = 2(8)(7) = 112$, $b = 8^2 - 7^2 = 15$, and $c = 8^2 + 7^2 = 113$.

If $v = 5$, then $a = 2(8)(5) = 80$, $b = 8^2 - 5^2 = 39$, and $c = 8^2 + 5^2 = 89$.

If $v = 3$, then $a = 2(8)(3) = 48$, $b = 8^2 - 3^2 = 55$, and $c = 8^2 + 3^2 = 73$.

If $v = 1$, then $a = 2(8)(1) = 16$, $b = 8^2 - 1^2 = 63$, and $c = 8^2 + 1^2 = 65$.

Therefore, five primitive triples are $(5, 12, 13)$, $(15, 112, 113)$, $(39, 80, 89)$, $(48, 55, 73)$, and $(16, 63, 65)$.

Section 9.2

36. Let x represent the smallest of the three consecutive integers. Then x, $x + 1$, and $x + 2$ are the three consecutive integers. Since adding two of them and dividing by the third is the same as the smallest of the three integers, we can set up three equations and solve to obtain all possible solutions.

Case 1: Add the two smallest integers, x and $x + 1$.

$$\frac{x + x + 1}{x + 2} = x$$

$$\frac{2x + 1}{x + 2} = x$$

$$2x + 1 = x^2 + 2x$$

$$0 = x^2 - 1$$

$$0 = (x - 1)(x + 1)$$

$$x = 1 \text{ or } x = -1$$

Two possible sets of numbers that satisfy the restrictions are 1, 2, 3 and −1, 0, 1.

Case 2: Add the smallest and largest integers, x and $x + 2$.

$$\frac{x + x + 2}{x + 1} = x$$

$$\frac{2x + 2}{x + 1} = x$$

$$2x + 2 = x^2 + x$$

$$0 = x^2 - x - 2$$

$$0 = (x - 2)(x + 1)$$

$$x = 2 \text{ or } x = -1$$

Only one additional solution is found: 2, 3, 4, since we cannot divide by 0.

Case 3: Add the two largest integers, $x + 1$ and $x + 2$.

$$\frac{x+1+x+2}{x} = x$$

$$\frac{2x+3}{x} = x$$

$$2x + 3 = x^2$$

$$0 = x^2 - 2x - 3$$

$$0 = (x-3)(x+1)$$

$$x = 3 \text{ or } x = -1$$

Only one additional solution is found: 3, 4, 5.
Therefore, the solutions are (–1, 0, 1); (1, 2, 3); (2, 3, 4); or (3, 4, 5).

Section 9.2

37. Consider the various forms the rational number and its reciprocal can take. There are three cases to consider.

   Case 1: Suppose the rational number and its reciprocal are both integers. We know the sum of two integers is an integer by the closure property of integer addition. The only integers whose reciprocals are also integers are 1 and –1.

   Case 2: Suppose the rational number is an integer, n, and its reciprocal is a fraction, $\frac{1}{n}$, where $n \neq 1$ and $n \neq -1$. We know the sum of an integer and a non-integer fraction is never an integer.

   Case 3: Suppose $\frac{a}{b}$ is the rational number in lowest terms (a and b are nonzero and have no common factors). The reciprocal of $\frac{a}{b}$ is $\frac{b}{a}$. Let's suppose $\frac{a}{b} + \frac{b}{a}$ is an integer, m. Then we have the following:

   $$\frac{a}{b} + \frac{b}{a} = \frac{a^2 + b^2}{ab} = m \text{ and } abm = a^2 + b^2.$$

Since $a \mid (a^2 + b^2)$ and $a \mid a^2$, we know that $a \mid (a^2 + b^2 - a^2)$ so $a \mid b^2$. This is impossible since a and b have no common factors other than 1. Therefore, the sum of a rational number (of this form) and its reciprocal cannot be an integer.

Therefore, there are only two rational numbers, namely 1 and -1, which, when added to their reciprocals, yield integers.

Section 9.2

38. Consider the diagram .

$$\underline{\hspace{1cm}x\hspace{1cm}} \qquad \underline{\hspace{1cm}y\hspace{1cm}}$$

Let x and y be the lengths of the original pieces of wire. Cut the wire with length y at a point that is m units from the end. The two pieces have lengths $y - m$ and m.

$$\underline{\hspace{1cm}x\hspace{1cm}} \qquad \underline{\hspace{0.6cm}y-m\hspace{0.6cm}}\;\underline{\hspace{0.8cm}m\hspace{0.8cm}}$$

If m is the average of the lengths of the other two pieces, then the sum of the lengths of the other two pieces divided by 2 is equal to length m.

$$\frac{x+y-m}{2} = m$$

$$x+y-m = 2m$$

$$x+y = 3m$$

$$\frac{x+y}{3} = m$$

The cut should be made at point m, one-third of the way along the wire when they are placed end to end. Since the longer wire is at least $\dfrac{x+y}{3}$ in length, cut the piece of length m from it. Therefore, it is possible to cut one of two wires in such a way that one of the three pieces is the average of the lengths of the other two.

Section 9.2

39. Carefully consider what is revealed by each sentence. First we learn the names of four men and four occupations. Then we learn how the occupations compare in terms of salary. Because the druggist earns exactly twice as much as the grocer, we know the druggist earns more than the grocer. Similarly, the architect earns more than the druggist, and the banker earns more than the architect. Therefore, listing the occupations in decreasing order of income, we have the following arrangement: banker, architect, druggist, then grocer. If we can also arrange the men in order of income, then we can match each man with his occupation. Since Mr. Smith earns exactly $3776 more than Mr. Milne, we know that he earns more than Mr. Milne. With only four positions to choose from, Mr. Smith's and Mr. Milne's occupations must be separated by two positions, separated by one position, or adjacent.

Case 1: If Mr. Smith and Mr. Milne's positions are separated by two places, then Mr. Smith earns eight times as much as Mr. Milne. Let x represent Mr. Milne's salary. Then $8x$ represents Mr. Smith's salary. We know the following:

$$\text{Mr. Milne's salary} + 3776 = \text{Mr. Smith's salary}$$

$$x + 3776 = 8x$$

$$3776 = 7x$$

But 3776 is not divisible by 7, which means that Mr. Smith cannot earn **exactly** $3776 more than Mr. Milne. Thus, in the order of occupations, Mr. Smith and Mr. Milne must not be separated by two positions.

Case 2: If Mr. Smith and Mr. Milne's positions are separated by one position, then Mr. Smith will earn four times as much as Mr. Milne. This yields the following equation:

$$x + 3776 = 4x$$
$$3776 = 3x$$

But 3776 is not divisible by 3, which means that Mr. Smith cannot earn **exactly** $3776 more than Mr. Milne. Thus, in the order of occupations, Mr. Smith and Mr. Milne must not be separated by one position. Therefore, we know that

Mr. Smith's and Mr. Milne's positions must be adjacent, with Mr. Smith earning the greater salary.

Now consider Mr. Carter and Mr. Farrell. Because Mr. Carter is older than anyone who earns more than Mr. Farrell, we can conclude that Mr. Carter does **not** make more money than Mr. Farrell (since Mr. Carter cannot be older than himself). Notice also that Mr. Farrell does not make twice as much as Mr. Carter. Now we know that not only does Mr. Farrell make more than Mr. Carter, but their occupations are not adjacent to each other in the lineup.
In summary, we know:
  (1) Mr. Farrell earns more than Mr. Carter.
  (2) Mr. Farrell and Mr. Carter are not adjacent.
  (3) Mr. Smith earns more than Mr. Milne.
  (4) Mr. Smith and Mr. Milne are adjacent.
Thus, we conclude that Mr. Farrell is the banker, Mr. Smith is the architect, Mr. Milne is the druggist, and Mr. Carter is the grocer.

Section 9.2

40. Let x and y represent the ages of the two people and suppose that $y > x$. Because one person multiplied the ages, we know that $xy = 1280$. Because the other person subtracted the ages, we know that $y - x = 44$. Make a list of all pairs of whole numbers whose product is 1280. From this list find the pair whose difference is 44.

Pairs (x, y)	Difference $(y - x)$
1, 1280	1279
2, 640	638
4, 320	316
5, 256	251
8, 160	152
10, 128	118
16, 80	64
20, 64	44
32, 40	8

From our table, we see that the only pair of ages that satisfies the requirements is 20 and 64.

Section 9.3

16. For fraction equality to be an equivalence relation, it must be reflexive, symmetric and transitive. Fraction equality is reflexive because every fraction is equivalent to itself: $\frac{a}{b} = \frac{a}{b}$ since $ab = ba$ where $b \neq 0$. Fraction equality is symmetric because if $\frac{a}{b} = \frac{c}{d}$, then $ad = bc$ where $d \neq 0$ and $b \neq 0$. By the commutative property of multiplication we know $cb = da$, so $\frac{c}{d} = \frac{a}{b}$. Fraction equality is transitive since, if we assume $\frac{a}{b} = \frac{c}{d}$ and $\frac{c}{d} = \frac{e}{f}$, where b, d and $f \neq 0$, then $ad = bc$ and $cf = de$. Therefore we know that $f = \frac{de}{c}$ and $af = a\frac{de}{c} = \frac{ade}{c} = \frac{bce}{c} = be$. The equivalence class that contains $\frac{1}{2}$ is the set described by $\left\{ \frac{a}{2a} \text{ where } a \neq 0 \right\}$. The set looks like $\left\{ \frac{1}{2}, \frac{2}{4}, \frac{3}{6}, \frac{4}{8}, \frac{5}{10}, \ldots \right\}$.

Section 9.3

17. (a) In each case, replace n with the number in parentheses.
$$f(0) = \frac{9}{5}(0) + 32 = 32$$

$$f(100) = \frac{9}{5}(100) + 32 = 180 + 32 = 212$$

$$f(50) = \frac{9}{5}(50) + 32 = 90 + 32 = 122$$

$$f(-40) = \frac{9}{5}(-40) + 32 = -72 + 32 = -40$$

(b) In each case, replace m with the number in parentheses.

$$g(32) = \frac{5}{9}(32 - 32) = \frac{5}{9}(0) = 0$$

$$g(212) = \frac{5}{9}(212 - 32) = \frac{5}{9}(180) = 100$$

$$g(104) = \frac{5}{9}(104 - 32) = \frac{5}{9}(72) = 40$$

$$g(-40) = \frac{5}{9}(-40 - 32) = \frac{5}{9}(-72) = -40$$

(c) If degrees Celsius = degrees Fahrenheit, then $f(n) = n$ and $g(m) = m$. Notice from part (a) that $f(-40) = -40$ and from part (b) that $g(-40) = -40$. Therefore, $-40°C = -40°F$.

Section 9.3

18. Create a table and study the sequence of numbers. Notice that there is a common difference of 8 between consecutive terms.

Term	Number
1	21
2	$29 = 21 + 1(8)$
3	$37 = 21 + 2(8)$
4	$45 = 21 + 3(8)$
$\vdots$	$\vdots$
n	$21 + (n - 1)(8)$

Notice that each term is made up of the sum of 21 and a certain number of 8s. The number of 8s in the sum is always 1 less than the term number. The 458th number is $21 + (458 - 1)(8) = 21 + 457(8) = 3677$.

Section 9.3

19. (a) Since there is a $35 per month charge, after x months, it would cost $35x$ dollars. However, there is also an initiation fee of $85. Thus, the total cost for x months is $C(x) = 35x + 85$.

(b) $C(18) = 35(18) + 85 = 630 + 85 = 715$. Thus, the total amount spent by a member after 18 months is $715.

(c) We want to find x when $C(x) > 1000$. If $C(x) > 1000$, then $35x + 85 > 1000$. We must solve for x, as shown next.

$$35x > 1000 - 85$$

$$35x > 915$$

$$x > 26.14$$

Since $C(26) = 35(26) + 85 = 995$ and $C(27) = 35(27) + 85 = 1030$, we see at 27 months the cost first exceeds $1000.

Section 9.3

20. A geometric sequence is of the form ar^{n-1} where r is the common ratio.

(a) Since the second term is 1200, $1200 = ar^{2-1} = ar$. Since the fifth term is 150, $150 = ar^{5-1} = ar^4$. Now we have two equations and two unknowns.

$1200 = ar$ Solve for a.

$\dfrac{1200}{r} = a$ Substitute into $150 = ar^4$.

$150 = \dfrac{(1200)}{r}r^4$ Simplify.

$\dfrac{150}{1200} = r^3$ Divide both sides by 1200.

$\dfrac{1}{8} = r^3$ Therefore, $r = \dfrac{1}{2}$.

(b) To find the first six terms of the sequence, we must find a. Use $r = \dfrac{1}{2}$ and $1200 = ar$ from part (a). Since

$1200 = a\left(\dfrac{1}{2}\right)$, we see $2400 = a$.

Term	Number
1	$2400\left(\dfrac{1}{2}\right)^{1-1} = 2400\left(\dfrac{1}{2}\right)^{0} = 2400$
2	$2400\left(\dfrac{1}{2}\right)^{2-1} = 2400\left(\dfrac{1}{2}\right)^{1} = 1200$
3	$2400\left(\dfrac{1}{2}\right)^{3-1} = 2400\left(\dfrac{1}{2}\right)^{2} = 2400\left(\dfrac{1}{4}\right) = 600$
4	$2400\left(\dfrac{1}{2}\right)^{4-1} = 2400\left(\dfrac{1}{2}\right)^{3} = 2400\left(\dfrac{1}{8}\right) = 300$
5	$2400\left(\dfrac{1}{2}\right)^{5-1} = 2400\left(\dfrac{1}{2}\right)^{4} = 2400\left(\dfrac{1}{16}\right) = 150$
6	$2400\left(\dfrac{1}{2}\right)^{6-1} = 2400\left(\dfrac{1}{2}\right)^{5} = 2400\left(\dfrac{1}{32}\right) = 75$

Therefore, the first six terms are 2400, 1200, 600, 300, 150, and 75.

Section 9.3

21. (a) Count the number of toothpicks in each figure.

n	$T(n)$
1	4
2	12
3	20
4	28
5	36
6	44
7	52
8	60

(b) Notice the numbers have a common difference of 8 between consecutive terms. This sequence is arithmetic. Let $a = 4$ and $d = 8$.

(c) In an arithmetic sequence, $T(n) = a + (n-1)d$. Thus, $T(n) = 4 + (n-1)8$ or $T(n) = 4 + 8n - 8 = 8n - 4$.

(d) $T(20) = 8(20) - 4 = 160 - 4 = 156$.

$T(150) = 8(150) - 4 = 1200 - 4 = 1196$.

(e) The domain is the set of values for n. Therefore, the domain is the set $\{1, 2, 3, 4, \ldots\}$ and the range is the set $\{4, 12, 20, 28, \ldots\}$.

Section 9.3

22. (a) Count the number of toothpicks in each figure.

n	$T(n)$
1	3
2	9
3	18
4	30
5	45
6	63
7	84
8	108

(b) There is neither a common ratio nor a common difference between consecutive terms, so this is neither a geometric nor an arithmetic sequence.

(c) Notice that the number of upright triangles in the nth figure is the sum of the first n counting numbers or $\frac{n(n+1)}{2}$ triangles. Since there are 3 toothpicks in each triangle, we can say $T(n) = \frac{3n(n+1)}{2}$.

(d) $T(15) = \frac{3(15)(15+1)}{2} = \frac{3(15)(16)}{2} = 3(15)(8) = 360.$

$T(100) = \frac{3(100)(100+1)}{2} = \frac{3(100)(101)}{2} = 3(50)(101).$

$= 15{,}150.$

(e) The domain is $\{1, 2, 3, 4, \ldots\}$.
The range is $\{3, 9, 18, 30, \ldots\}$.

Section 9.3

23. (a) See the table below.

n = Number of Years	Annual Interest Earned	Value of Account
0	0	100
1	5	105
2	5	110
3	5	115
4	5	120
5	5	125

6	5	130
7	5	135
8	5	140
9	5	145
10	5	150

(b) Since the difference between consecutive terms is 5 dollars, the sequence is arithmetic, with $a = 100$ and $d = 5$. (Note: In the text, terms are usually numbered beginning with 1. Here we begin numbering with 0. Therefore, the formula for the arithmetic sequence is $A(n) = a + n\,d$.) For this sequence, $A(n) = 100 + 5n$.

Section 9.3

24. (a) See the following table.

n = Number of Years	Annual Interest Earned	Value of Account
0	0	100.00
1	$(0.05)(100.00) = 5.00$	105.00
2	$(0.05)(105.00) = 5.25$	110.25
3	$(0.05)(110.25) = 5.51$	115.76
4	$(0.05)(115.76) = 5.79$	121.55
5	$(0.05)(121.55) = 6.08$	127.63
6	$(0.05)(127.63) = 6.38$	134.01
7	$(0.05)(134.01) = 6.70$	140.71
8	$(0.05)(140.71) = 7.04$	147.75
9	$(0.05)(147.75) = 7.39$	155.13
10	$(0.05)(155.13) = 7.76$	162.89

(b) Since the value of the account in any one year is 1.05 times the value of the account in the previous year, the sequence for the value of the account is geometric, with $a = 100$ and $r = 1.05$. So $A(n) = ar^n$, or $A(n) = 100(1.05)^n$. (Notice that we began numbering terms in the sequence with zero, so the general geometric formula changed to ar^n.)

(c) The value of the account after 10 years using simple interest is $150 (from problem 23) and the value in the account after 10 years using compound interest is $162.89. You earn $162.89 − $150.00 = $12.89 more when compounding.

Section 9.3

25.   To find her height, replace t with 1, 2, and 3.

$$h(1) = -16(1)^2 + 64(1)$$
$$= -16 + 64$$
$$= 48 \text{ feet.}$$

$$h(2) = -16(2)^2 + 64(2)$$
$$= -16(4) + 128$$
$$= -64 + 128$$
$$= 64 \text{ feet.}$$

$$h(3) = -16(3)^2 + 64(3)$$
$$= -16(9) + 192$$
$$= -144 + 192$$
$$= 48 \text{ feet.}$$

To determine how many seconds of flight she has, we need to determine t when $h(t) = 0$ since, at a height of 0 feet, she is either starting or finishing her trip.

$$0 = -16t^2 + 64t$$
$$0 = -16t(t - 4)$$
$$t = 0 \ \text{ or } \ t = 4.$$

Therefore, after 4 seconds she hits the ground. Her flight was 4 seconds long.

Section 9.3

26.   Consider a simpler problem such as determining a 3-digit number in base ten. Each of the 3-digits would require at most 9 questions for a maximum total of $3 \times 9 = 27$ questions needed to determine the number. On the other hand, if the 3-digit number was written in a smaller base, such as base four, each digit would require at most 3 questions. Since the largest 3-digit number, 999, is between $4^4 = 256$ and $4^5 = 1024$, the converted number in base four would contain at most 5 digits. Therefore, at most $3 \times 5 = 15$ questions would be needed. We see fewer questions are needed when we use a smaller base. In the original problem, we would have the person convert the number to base two. Since the largest 7-digit number,

9,999,999, is between $2^{23} = 8,388,608$ and $2^{24} = 16,777,216$, the base two number will have at most 24 digits. At most $1 \times 24 = 24$ questions would be needed to determine the number. (The base ten phone number would require at most $7 \times 9 = 63$ questions.) Once the number is determined, convert back to base ten.

Section 9.3

27. (a) Consider consecutive terms. Notice $12 - 7 = 5$, $17 - 12 = 5$, $22 - 17 = 5$, and $27 - 22 = 5$. The common difference is 5. The nth term can be found as $7 + (n - 1)5$. If $n = 200$, then the 200th term is $7 + (200 - 1)5 = 1002$. Thus, the sequence is arithmetic, the common difference is 5, and the 200th term is 1002.

(b) Consider consecutive terms. Notice, $\dfrac{28}{14} = 2$, $\dfrac{56}{28} = 2$, and $\dfrac{112}{56} = 2$. The common ratio is 2. The nth term can be found as $14(2)^{n-1}$. If $n = 200$, then the 200th term is $14(2)^{200-1} = 14(2)^{199}$. Thus, the sequence is geometric, the common ratio is 2, and the 200th term is $14(2)^{199}$.

(c) Consider consecutive terms. Notice $14 - 4 = 10$, $24 - 14 = 10$, $34 - 24 = 10$, and $44 - 34 = 10$. The common difference is 10. The nth term can be found as $4 + (n - 1)10$. If $n = 200$, then the 200th term is $4 + (200 - 1)10 = 1994$. Thus, the sequence is arithmetic, the common difference is 10, and the 200th term is 1994.

(d) By subtracting consecutive terms, you can see there is no common difference. By dividing consecutive terms, you can see there is no common ratio. Thus, this sequence is neither arithmetic nor geometric.

Section 9.3

28. Consider consecutive terms. Notice $4 - 1 = 3$, $7 - 4 = 3$, $10 - 7 = 3$, and $13 - 10 = 3$. The common difference is 3. The nth term can be found as $1 + (n - 1)3$. We would like to know which term in the sequence generates the value

682, so call 682 the *n*th term. Then, $682 = 1 + (n - 1)3$. Now, solve for *n*.

$$682 = 1 + (n-1)3$$

$$681 = (n-1)3$$

$$\frac{681}{3} + 1 = n$$

$$228 = n$$

Thus, 682 is the 228th term.

Section 9.3

29. Access the eManipulative, *Function Machine*. The function machine will use an unknown function to take an input and create an output. You will be given several numbers to put into the function machine. Click on each and drag them to the function machine. The inputs and outputs will be placed into the table for you. Study the table to determine the rule used by the function machine. When you think you have the rule figured out, use the rule to fill in the output values for the remaining input values in the table. If the output values turn blue when you press the enter button, then you know you have used the correct rule.

Section 9.4

17. (a) In each case, use the graph to locate the *y*-coordinate paired with the given *x*-coordinate.
    (i) $f(1) = 3$.
    (ii) $f(-1) = -4$.
    (iii) $f(4.5) = 0$.

    (b) The domain is the set of *x*-coordinates included in the graph. This would include all of the real numbers from −3 to 6. Thus, the domain is represented by $\{x | -3 \le x \le 6\}$. The range is the set of *y*-coordinates included in the graph. Thus, the range is represented by $\{y | -4 \le y \le 3\}$.

    (c) To determine all *x*-coordinates that have 2 as the *y*-coordinate, draw a horizontal line through the *y*-value 2 and note the horizontal line intersects the graph in three places. The *x*-coordinates of these are 0, 2, and 5. Thus $f(0) = f(2) = f(5) = 0$.

Section 9.4

18. (a) Using the formula, replace h with the given value.

$$d(4) = 1.2\sqrt{4} = 1.2(2) = 2.4 \text{ miles}$$

$$d(5.5) = 1.2\sqrt{5.5} \approx 1.2(2.345) = 2.814 \text{ miles}$$

Using the graph, draw a vertical line through the given h-value to the graph. From there draw a horizontal line to the y-axis. Notice the points of intersection on the y-axis correspond to the values found by using the formula.

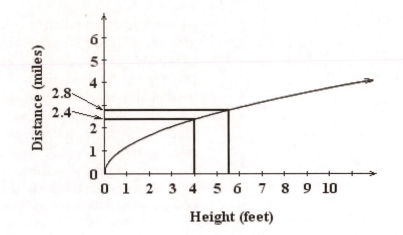

(b) Convert inches to feet before using the formula. A child with eyes at 3 feet 3 inches from the ground eyes that are at a height of 3.25 feet from the ground. Using the formula, replace h with 3.25.

$$d(3.25) = 1.2\sqrt{3.25} \approx 1.2(1.80) \approx 2.16 \text{ miles}$$

The child can see 2.16 miles.

(c) The domain is the set of h-coordinates included in the graph. This would include all of the numbers greater than or equal to 0. Thus, the domain is the set of all nonnegative real numbers. The range is the set of nonnegative real numbers up to the farthest distance a person can see.

Section 9.4

19. (a) The graphs of the functions r and R are sketched next on the same set of axes.

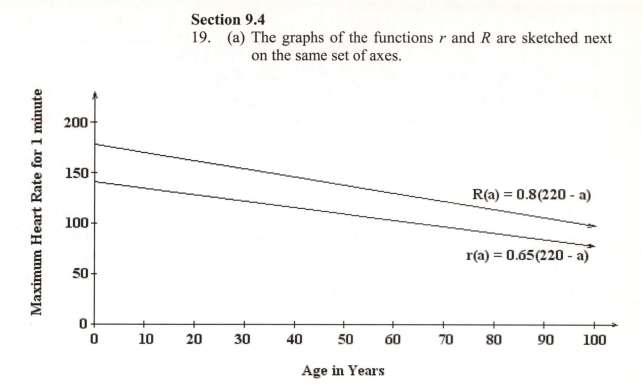

(b) A woman who is 30 years old should have a minimum heart rate of $r(30) = 0.65(220 - 30) = 123.5$ beats in one minute and a maximum heart rate of $R(30) = 0.8(220 - 30) = 152$ beats in one minute.

(c) As age increases, the recommended heart rates decrease. Notice how the graphs each slant downward as age increases.

Section 9.4

20. (a) The length of the shadow varies as time passes. It is not the case that the changing time varies as the length of the shadow passes. Therefore, L depends on n. The graph appears to be exponential when compared to the basic function types in this section.

(b) To approximate the function value for each of the given hours past noon, construct a vertical line through the x-axis point of interest and note where it intersects the graph. Through that intersection point, construct a horizontal line and note where it intersects the y-axis. The y-axis intersection point is the function value.

$$L(5) = 150$$

$$L(8) = 1100$$

$$L(2.5) = 50$$

(c) To find the point on the x-axis that corresponds to a shadow of 100 meters, construct a horizontal line through the y-axis at the given shadow length and note where it intersects the graph. Through that intersection point, construct a vertical line and note where it intersects the x-axis. This point on the x-axis corresponds to the given shadow length. After $4\frac{1}{2}$ hours, the shadow is 100 meters long. After 6 hours, the shadow is 200 meters long.

(d) The graph stops at $n = 8$ since that is approximately when sundown occurs.

Section 9.4

21. (a) Use a graphics calculator, if available, to sketch the graph of the function $s(t) = -16t^2 + 70t + 55$ over the interval $0 \le t \le 5$.

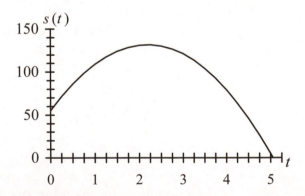

(b) Consider the graph from part (a). Construct a horizontal line through the s-axis at $s(t) = 90$. Notice where this line intersects the graph. Construct a vertical line through each of these intersection points to the t-axis.

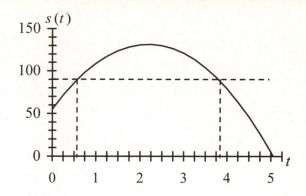

Estimate these values for t. They appear to be at approximately $t = 0.5$ and about $t = 3.75$. (Alternatively, use a graphics calculator to "trace" the graph, and identify the times when the ball is about 90 feet above the ground.) Using algebra, we see the following:

$$90 = -16t^2 + 70t + 55$$

$$0 = -16t^2 + 70t - 35$$

$$t = \frac{-b \pm \sqrt{b^2 - 4ac}}{2a}$$

$$t = \frac{-70 \pm \sqrt{(70)^2 - 4(-16)(-35)}}{2(-16)}$$

$$t = \frac{-70 \pm \sqrt{2660}}{-32}$$

$$t \approx 0.58 \quad \text{or} \quad t \approx 3.8$$

Thus the ball is at a height of 90 feet above the ground at about 0.58 seconds and again at about 3.8 seconds after its release.

(c) The ball hits the ground when $s(t) = 0$. We can solve the equation $0 = -16t^2 + 70t + 55$, or we can "trace" the function on the calculator. Solving, we obtain:

$$0 = -16t^2 + 70t + 55$$

$$t = \frac{-70 \pm \sqrt{70^2 - 4(-16)(55)}}{2(-16)}$$

$$t = \frac{-70 \pm \sqrt{8420}}{-32}$$

$$t \approx 5.055 \text{ or } t \approx -0.68$$

Since t is measuring time, we can ignore the negative solution. Therefore, the ball hits the ground after about 5.1 seconds.

(d) The ball reaches its maximum height when it is at the vertex point of the parabolic height curve. Recall that the x-coordinate of the vertex of a parabola can be found by using the formula $\dfrac{-b}{2a}$.

$$\frac{-b}{2a} = \frac{-70}{2(-16)} = \frac{-70}{-32} = 2.1875$$

Therefore, the ball reaches its maximum height after 2.1875 seconds, at which time its height is $-16(2.1875)^2 + 70(2.1875) + 55 \approx 131.6$ feet.

Section 9.4

22. (a) Use a graphics calculator to sketch the graph of the function $P(t) = 5.284e^{0.0139t}$.

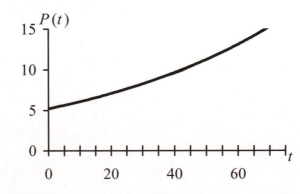

In 1990, when $t = 0$, $P(0) \approx 5.284$. This is the P-intercept.

(b) Since t represents the number of years since 1990, the value of t in 2006 is 16. The population of the world in 2006 can be estimated, by using the function as follows:

$$P(16) = 5.284e^{0.0139(16)}$$

$$\approx 5.284(1.249071)$$

$$\approx 6.6 \text{ billion people}$$

(c) Use your graphing calculator to trace the graph until you locate the point with a y-coordinate value of 8. Alternatively, you can locate 8 on the vertical axis of your graph, and then construct a horizontal line through 8. At the point where this line intersects the graph, construct a vertical line, and note where it intersects the t-axis. This value is about 29.8. Approximately 29.8 years after 1990, in the year 2020, the world will reach a population of 8 billion people.

(d) To estimate the current doubling time, choose any point on the graph. Find the point on the graph where the value of P is twice as large. For example, when $t = 0$, there were about $5.284e^{0.0139(0)} = 5.284$ billion people in the world. We need to find t when the population is $2(5.284) = 10.568$ billion. This occurs when t is about 50. Therefore, the current doubling time is approximately 50 years.

Section 9.4

23. The speed of the cyclist will remain about the same until she gets to the base of the hill. As she begins up the hill, her speed slows (the graph of the function decreases) since it is more difficult to pedal up a hill. At the top of the hill, her speed will stop decreasing (the graph bottoms out). As she begins cycling down the other side, the speed will increase (the graph increases) and will continue to increase so that she will be moving faster than before she started up the hill. Once she reaches the bottom of the hill, her speed gradually decreases (the graph decreases) until she resumes traveling at a constant rate on the flat part of the route (the graph is constant as before). Therefore, graph (a) is the best choice.

Section 9.4

24. Notice that there is a weight restriction for the elevator and that one person must be in the elevator to operate it. The person who weighs 210 pounds must always ride alone, so that person cannot go first. We send the people who weigh 130 pounds and 160 pounds up first. One of these people must ride the elevator back down. It does not matter who comes down, but suppose it is the 130-pound person. Both the 130-pound person and the 210-pound person cannot ride up at the same time. The 210-pound person goes up next, sending the 160-pound person back down. This allows the 160-pound and 130-pound people to both ride back up to the top floor.

Section 9.4

25. Access the dynamic spread sheet, *Cubic*. Change the values of the coefficients of y_1 so that $a = c = d = 1$. Try different values for b. For example, start by letting $b = 2, 3, 4, 5,$ or 6. Note what happens to the graph. Then try letting $b = -2, -3, -4, -5,$ or -6. Note what happens to the graph. For $b > 1$ and larger, the graph increasingly shows a lump like an upside down parabolic curve forming along the x-axis. For $b < -1$ and smaller, the graph increasingly shows a lump like an upright parabolic curve forming along the x-axis.

SOLUTIONS - PART A PROBLEMS

Chapter 10: Statistics

Section 10.1

18. Access the eManipulative, *Histogram*. Enter the 30 data values into the data column. Move the slider labeled "Cell width" to the left and to the right. Notice, the cell width can take on values as low as 1.83 to as high as 44, in this case.

    (a) As the cell width gets smaller, the number of bars increases. The data values do not change, but the number of intervals increases, so the number of bars must increase.

    (b) When the cell width gets smaller, gaps will appear when no data values fall into a particular interval.

Section 10.1

19. (a) We are comparing the projected enrollment (in thousands) of public and private schools in the United States in 2015. A double-bar graph will nicely demonstrate this comparison because for each type of school, the bars which represent the projected enrollment in public and private schools will be side-by-side.

    (b)

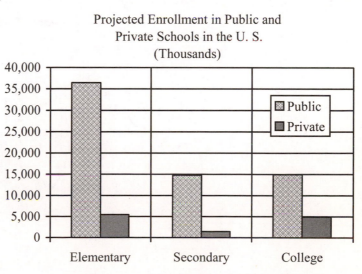

Projected Enrollment in Public and Private Schools in the U. S. (Thousands)

Section 10.1

20. (a) In the table, the federal budget revenue for 2007 is divided into parts. In displaying the data, we would like to see how each part compares to the whole budget. A circle graph would allow us to see the relative size of each revenue source. Notice also that dollar amounts are not given, just percentages. Circle graphs generally show relative amounts and not necessarily absolute amounts.

(b) A breakdown, by percentages, of the federal budget revenue is as follows:

Individual Income Taxes	45.3%
Social Insurance Receipts	33.9%
Corporate Taxes	14.4%
Excise Taxes	2.5%
Estate and Gift Taxes	3.9%

When constructing the circle graph, recall that the central angle for each sector is found by multiplying the percent by 360°. Round the values to the nearest degree.

Individual Income Taxes:	$(0.453)(360°) =$	$163°$
Social Insurance Receipts:	$(0.339)(360°) =$	$122°$
Corporate Taxes:	$(0.144)(360°) =$	$52°$
Excise Taxes:	$(0.025)(360°) =$	$9°$
Estate and Gift Taxes:	$(0.039)(360°) =$	$14°$

The corresponding circle graph is given next.

Federal Budget Revenue
2007

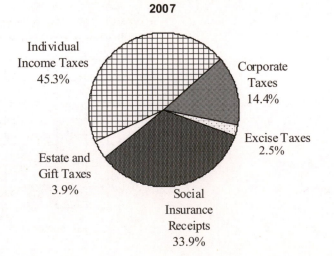

Individual Income Taxes 45.3%

Corporate Taxes 14.4%

Excise Taxes 2.5%

Estate and Gift Taxes 3.9%

Social Insurance Receipts 33.9%

Section 10.1

21. (a) For each year, the data represents the average cost of tuition and fees for public and private U.S. colleges. Notice that many consecutive years are given, so the graph chosen should show any time trends in the data. Line graphs are useful for plotting data over a period of time to indicate trends. A line graph for each school will show the time trends and give a visual comparison at the same time.

    (b) A line graph of the data is given next.

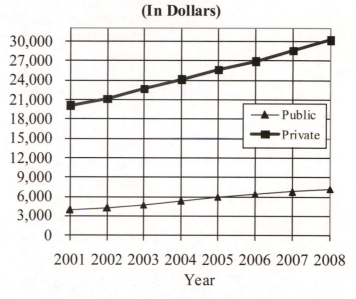

U.S. College Tuition and Fees (In Dollars)

    (c) Notice that the slope of the line graph of the private college is generally steeper, so over the eight-year period, private school costs increased at a greater rate. Confirm this by calculating the rate of increase.

$$\text{Rate of increase} = \frac{\text{change in cost}}{\text{change in years}} = \frac{\text{change in cost}}{8 \text{ years}}$$

    Calculate the rate of increase for public colleges and for private colleges. Compare these rates to determine whether public or private colleges experienced a greater rate of increase in costs.

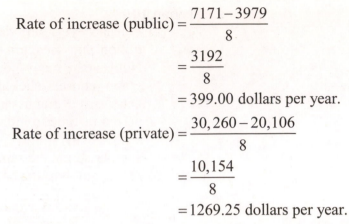

$$\text{Rate of increase (public)} = \frac{7171 - 3979}{8}$$

$$= \frac{3192}{8}$$

$$= 399.00 \text{ dollars per year.}$$

$$\text{Rate of increase (private)} = \frac{30,260 - 20,106}{8}$$

$$= \frac{10,154}{8}$$

$$= 1269.25 \text{ dollars per year.}$$

Therefore, we see that private colleges experienced a greater rate of increase in costs over the eight-year period.

Section 10.1

22. (a) The table lists the percent of persons in each category who participated in television viewing or newspaper reading in the week prior to the survey in the spring of 2007. A graph should demonstrate how the groups compare to each other and allow for a quick assessment of the total percents for each group. A multiple-bar graph would be appropriate.

(b) A bar graph of the data is shown.

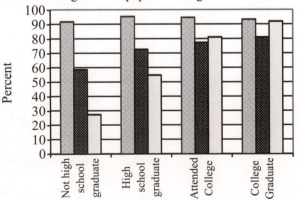

Percent of Persons Participating in Television Viewing, Newspaper Reading, or Accessing the Internet in the Spring of 2007

Section 10.1

23. (a) A line graph is appropriate for showing trends over time. The data given shows an increasing trend in cellular telephone subscribers from 2000 to 2007. A line graph would demonstrate this nicely.

    (b) A line graph of the data is shown next.

Cell Phone Subscribers

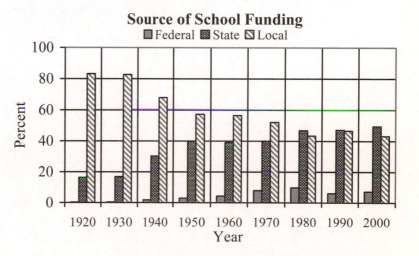

Section 10.1

24. (a) The data given are revenues from three sources over a period of 80 years. We are interested in the trends over time and how the relationship between revenue sources changed over time. A multiple-line graph or a multiple-bar graph will show this relationship.

    (b) A multiple-bar graph of the data is shown next.

Source of School Funding
■ Federal ▨ State ▨ Local

(c) Funds from federal sources increased steadily until sometime during the 1980s then they decreased. State funding nearly doubled by 1940 then increased in small increments. After providing over 80% of the school funding, local sources decreased steadily, eventually providing less than 50% of the funds.

Section 10.1

25. (a) A scatterplot of the data is shown.

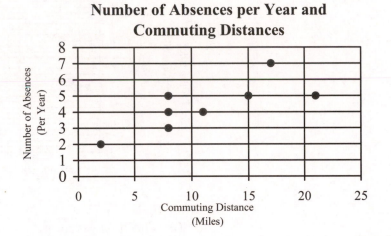

(b) Notice the regression line sketched next does not pass through any of the original data points exactly. To find the equation of the line it is necessary to estimate two points which lie on the line. From the two points, the equation of the line can be calculated. Your line and equation may be different.

**Number of Absences per Year and
Commuting Distances**

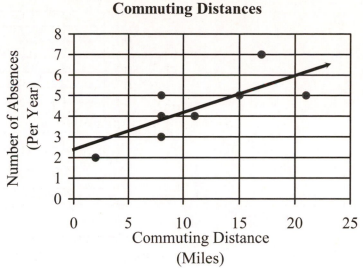

Two points on the line: (5, 3.25) and (20, 6)

$$m = \text{slope} = \frac{6 - 3.25}{20 - 5} = \frac{2.75}{15} \approx 0.183.$$

$$y = mx + b$$

$$y = 0.183x + b$$

$$6 = 0.183(20) + b$$

$$2.34 = b$$

Regression Equation: $y = 0.183x + 2.34$

(c) An employee with a commute of 15 miles is predicted to have $y = 0.183(15) + 2.34 = 5.085$ or about 5 absences per year.

Section 10.1

26. To make a prediction, construct a scatter plot and estimate the regression line. Construct a scatter plot with the median weekly salary for men on the *x*-axis and the median weekly salary for women on the *y*-axis.

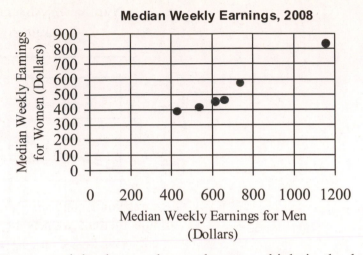

Use a straightedge to draw what you think is the best-fitting line. Your line may not pass through any of the points, or it may pass through several of the points.

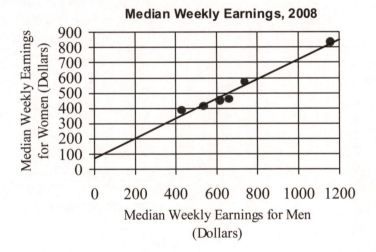

To make a prediction about the median weekly salary for a woman if the median weekly salary for a man is $800, you can estimate from the graph. It appears to be about $600. Alternately, you can determine the equation of your line and use it to predict the median weekly salary for a woman if the median salary for a man is $800. There are many lines which would do a reasonable job modeling the trend in the data. Many solutions are possible. The regression line shown appears to pass through one of the original points. To create the line equation use the points (537, 418) and (200, 200), as read from the graph.

$$m = \text{slope} = \frac{418 - 200}{537 - 200} = \frac{218}{337} \approx 0.65$$

$$y = mx + b$$

$$y = \frac{218}{337}x + b$$

$$200 = \frac{218}{337}(200) + b$$

$$71 \approx b$$

Regression Equation: $y \approx 0.65x + 71$

If the median weekly salary for a man is \$800, then the median weekly salary for a woman would be approximately $y = 0.65(800) + 71 \approx \$591$.

Section 10.2

15. (a) The revenue of Company *B* is twice the revenue of Company *A*. The area of the circle representing Company *B*s revenue must be twice the area of the circle representing Company *A*s revenue. The radius of the circle for Company *A* is 1 inch so the area of the circle is $\pi r^2 = \pi(1)^2 = \pi$ square inches.

It follows that the area of Company *B*s circle must be 2π square inches. Since the formula for the area of a circle is πr^2 and Company *B*s circle must have area 2π, we know that $\pi r^2 = 2\pi$. Solve for *r*. $r^2 = 2$, so $r = \sqrt{2}$. The radius of the circle for Company *B* should be $\sqrt{2}$ inches.

(b) The volume of Company *A*s sphere would be $\frac{4}{3}\pi r^3 = \frac{4}{3}\pi(1)^3 = \frac{4}{3}\pi$ cubic inches. The volume of Company *B*s sphere must be twice that of Company *A* or $2\left(\frac{4}{3}\pi\right) = \frac{8}{3}\pi$ cubic inches. Since the formula for the volume of a sphere is $\frac{4}{3}\pi r^3$ and the volume of

Company *B*s sphere is $\frac{8}{3}\pi$, we know $\frac{4}{3}\pi r^3 = \frac{8}{3}\pi$.

Solve for *r*.

$$4\pi r^3 = 8\pi$$
$$r^3 = 2$$
$$r = \sqrt[3]{2}$$

Therefore, the radius of the sphere for Company *B* should be $\sqrt[3]{2}$ inches.

Section 10.2

16. By cropping the graph, the increase can appear more dramatic.

Aluminum Imports

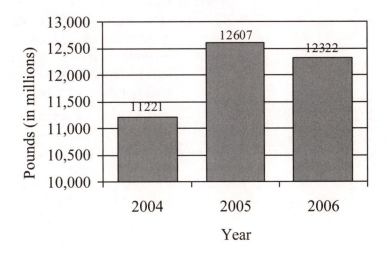

Section 10.2

17. Changes will appear more dramatic if the vertical scale begins at 6000 rather than at 0.

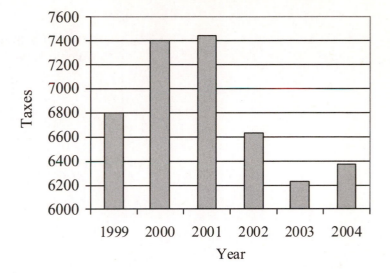

Federal Tax Burden per Capita

Section 10.2

18. Changes will appear more less dramatic if the vertical axis begins at 0 and extends beyond the largest data value.

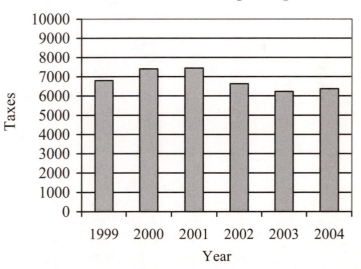

Federal Tax Burden per Capita

Section 10.2

19. Extending the scale of the vertical axis will make changes appear less dramatic.

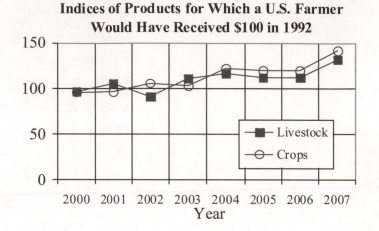

Indices of Products for Which a U.S. Farmer Would Have Received $100 in 1992

Section 10.2

20. The population is the entire group of fish in the lake. There are 500 fish in the sample. Bias in this case could occur for a variety of reasons. If fish tend to swim in schools in the same general areas, then sampling in the same area where the fish were tagged could lead to an underestimate of the number of fish in the lake. More tagged fish would be caught again making the population appear smaller. On the other hand, if fish have any memory of being caught and tagged, then sampling in the same area could cause an overestimate of the number of fish. Fewer of the tagged fish would be caught again making it appear that the population is larger than it really is.

Section 10.2

21. The population is not clear in this case. It could be the set of all doctors in a certain state or certain country. The population could be the entire collection of doctors in the world. This company samples 20 doctors. Bias can show up in the way these 20 doctors are chosen. These 20 doctors in the sample could all hold stock in the drug company. The company could sample only local doctors or ones involved in a certain specialty which would make

them more likely to favor the drug. It also sounds like they may try to resample until they get the result they want.

Section 10.3

19. From the given information, we know the mean is 169 points and one observation is 150. The 31st percentile z-score is -0.496. Use the definition of the z-score, insert the values you know, and solve for the standard deviation.

$$z = \frac{x - \bar{x}}{s}$$

$$-0.496 = \frac{150 - 169}{s}$$

$$-0.496s = -19$$

$$s = \frac{-19}{-0.496}$$

$$s \approx 38.3$$

Thus, the standard deviation is about 38.3 pounds.

Section 10.3

20. Vince's 2009 ACT reading score was below 33% of all of the scores, so he was in the $100 - 33 = $ 67th percentile. According to Table 10.17, the z-score corresponding to the 67th percentile is 0.44. The mean and standard deviation for all ACT reading scores in 2009 was 21.4 and 6.2, respectively.

$$z = \frac{x - \bar{x}}{s}$$

$$0.44 = \frac{x - 21.4}{6.2}$$

$$6.2(0.44) = x - 21.4$$

$$2.728 + 21.4 = x$$

$$24.138 = x$$

Thus, Vince's score was about 24.

Section 10.3

21. Access the Chapter 10 dynamic spreadsheet, *Standard Deviation*. The spreadsheet contains tables that correspond to two different data sets. To change a data value or input a

new data value in a table, click on the cell and type a new value. The summary statistics, including the standard deviations as well as means, medians, and modes, are displayed below the tables. Input a set of data for Data Set 1. Try manipulating the values from Data Set 1 to create Data Set 2 in order to achieve a new data set with a standard deviation that is twice as large as the first data set. For example, what happens if you add 5 to each values of Data Set 1 to create Data Set 2? What happens if you multiply each value in Data Set 1 by the same value to create Data Set 2? Continue exploring until you have created the required two data sets.

Section 10.3

22. Out of a possible 40 points, the class average (mean) was 27.5. The average is found by adding up the total points for all girls and all boys and dividing by the number of students. There are 19 girls and 11 boys for a total of 30 students.

$$\frac{\text{Total Score for Girls} + \text{Total Score for Boys}}{30} = 27.5.$$

Since the total score for girls is 532 we can substitute that value into the equation.

$$\frac{532 + \text{Total Score for Boys}}{30} = 27.5$$

$$532 + \text{Total Score for Boys} = 825$$

$$\text{Total Score for Boys} = 293.$$

Notice that 40 is the total number of points possible on the test and is unnecessary information.

Section 10.3

23. Recall how the average score was found. After the scores are totaled, the total is divided by 100. Two more students take the test. The new average is found by adding the two new scores to the original total and dividing by 102.

$$\text{Original Average} = \frac{\text{Total of 100 Scores}}{100} = 77.1$$

$$\text{Total of 100 Scores} = 7710$$

$$\text{New Average} = \frac{\text{Total of 100 Scores} + \text{Two New Scores}}{102}$$

$$= \frac{7710 + 125}{102}$$

$$= \frac{7835}{102}$$

$$\approx 76.81.$$

Therefore, the new average is about 76.81.

Section 10.3

24. The mean score of 41.6 was found by dividing the sum of the math scores by 35. Set up an equation and solve for the unknown value.

$$\frac{\text{Sum of Scores}}{35} = 41.6$$

Sum of Scores $= (41.6)(35) = 1456$

Notice that the information about the standard deviation is unnecessary.

Section 10.3

25. We want to find Lora's place relative to the rest of the class. We need to find on which test she has the better z-score. On test 1, the mean score was 81, and the standard deviation was 6.137. Her z-score for test 1 is calculated as

$$z = \frac{\text{Lora's score} - \text{mean score}}{\text{standard deviation}} \quad \text{so,} \quad z = \frac{85 - 81}{6.137} \approx 0.65.$$

On test 2, the mean score was 80.33, and the standard deviation was 13.732. Thus, Lora's z-score for test 2 is

$$z = \frac{89 - 80.33}{13.732} \approx 0.63.$$ Since her z-score was higher on

test 1, and a positive z-score is a score above the mean, Lora did better relative to the rest of the class on test 1.

Section 10.3

26. The statistic that represents the most frequently purchased shoe size would be most helpful when the manager is ordering shoes to replace her stock. Therefore, the manager should calculate the mode.

Section 10.3

27. (a) Two normal distributions with different variances will have different spreads. Both distributions will still be bell shaped. If they have the same means, then they will be centered at the same place. The distribution with the smaller variance will have data that is more concentrated around the mean forcing it to have a higher "peak".

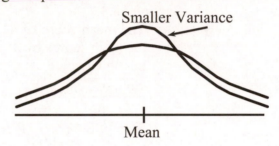

(b) Two normal distributions with different means will be centered in different places. Since the variances are the same, the shape will be the same. The distribution with the larger mean will be shifted to the right.

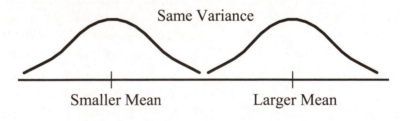

Section 10.3

28. Recall that the z-score of a number indicates how many standard deviations the number is away from the mean.

(a) The z-score for Smithville's average score is

$$z = \frac{\text{Smithville average} - \text{national average}}{\text{standard deviation}}$$

$$z = \frac{69.2 - 60.3}{7.82}$$

$$z \approx 1.14$$

(b) The z-score for Miss Brown's class average score is

$$z = \frac{\text{Miss Brown's class average} - \text{national average}}{\text{standard deviation}}$$

$$z = \frac{75.9 - 60.3}{7.82}$$

$$z \approx 1.99$$

(c) The distribution of scores is normal. The z-score for Miss Brown's class is approximately $z = 2$. In the standard normal distribution, we know that about 95% of the data falls between $z = -2$ and $z = 2$. Therefore about 47.5% of data falls between $z = 0$ and $z = 2$. Since 50% of the data falls below $z = 0$, $50\% + 47.5\% = 97.5\%$ of students in the country scored below Miss Brown's class average.

SOLUTIONS - PART A PROBLEMS

Chapter 11: Probability

Section 11.1

22. (a) Use ordered pairs to represent the outcomes. The first number in the ordered pair represents the number of spots on the first die. The second number represents the number of spots on the second die. The sum for each pair is indicated.

$(1,1) = 2$ $(1,2) = 3$ $(1,3) = 4$ $(1,4) = 5$ $(1,5) = 6$ $(1,6) = 7$
$(2,1) = 3$ $(2,2) = 4$ $(2,3) = 5$ $(2,4) = 6$ $(2,5) = 7$ $(2,6) = 8$
$(3,1) = 4$ $(3,2) = 5$ $(3,3) = 6$ $(3,4) = 7$ $(3,5) = 8$ $(3,6) = 9$
$(4,1) = 5$ $(4,2) = 6$ $(4,3) = 7$ $(4,4) = 8$ $(4,5) = 9$ $(4,6) = 10$
$(5,1) = 6$ $(5,2) = 7$ $(5,3) = 8$ $(5,4) = 9$ $(5,5) = 10$ $(5,6) = 11$
$(6,1) = 7$ $(6,2) = 8$ $(6,3) = 9$ $(6,4) = 10$ $(6,5) = 11$ $(6,6) = 12$

Sum	2	3	4	5	6	7	8	9	10	11	12
Ways	1	2	3	4	5	6	5	4	3	2	1

(b) A: The sum is prime. The prime numbers up to 12 are 2, 3, 5, 7, and 11 and these are all mutually exclusive outcomes for possible sums when rolling two dice. $P(A) = P(2) + P(3) + P(5) + P(7) + P(11)$. Notice that there are 36 possible sums, so, for example, since there are 2 ways to obtain a sum of 3, the probability of obtaining a 3 is 2/36. Therefore,

$$P(A) = \frac{1}{36} + \frac{2}{36} + \frac{4}{36} + \frac{6}{36} + \frac{2}{36} = \frac{15}{36} = \frac{5}{12}.$$

B: The sum is a divisor of 12. The divisors of 12 are 1, 2, 3, 4, 6, and 12. Of these, the only ones that are a possible sum of two dice are 2, 3, 4, 6, and 12 and these are all mutually exclusive outcomes for possible sums when rolling two dice. Thus,

$$P(B) = P(2) + P(3) + P(4) + P(6) + P(12)$$
$$= \frac{1}{36} + \frac{2}{36} + \frac{3}{36} + \frac{5}{36} + \frac{1}{36} = \frac{12}{36} = \frac{1}{3}.$$

C: The sum is a power of 2. The powers of 2 that are also possible sums are 2, 4, and 8. Thus, $P(C) = P(2) + P(4) + P(8) = \dfrac{1}{36} + \dfrac{3}{36} + \dfrac{5}{36} = \dfrac{9}{36} = \dfrac{1}{4}$.

D: The sum is greater than 3. There are many sums greater than 3. It may be easier to consider the complement of event D, or $\overline{D}$. This would be the event of a sum less than or equal to 3. So, $\overline{D} = \{\text{sum} \le 3\}$, and $P(\overline{D}) = P(2) + P(3) = \dfrac{1}{36} + \dfrac{2}{36} = \dfrac{3}{36} = \dfrac{1}{12}$.

Since $P(D) = 1 - P(\overline{D})$, $P(D) = 1 - \dfrac{1}{12} = \dfrac{11}{12}$.

Therefore, the probability of obtaining a sum greater than 3 is $\dfrac{11}{12}$.

Section 11.1

23. (a) $m(S) = 100$ miles, the distance from Albany to Binghamton, as indicated in the diagram.

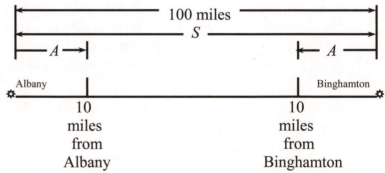

(b) Because event A involves the part of the road that is 10 miles from either city, $m(A) = 20$ miles.

(c) $P(A) = \dfrac{m(A)}{m(S)} = \dfrac{20}{100} = \dfrac{1}{5}$

Section 11.1

24. Refer to problem 23. The probability that the dart hits the bull's-eye is determined by comparing the area of the bull's-eye to the area of the entire dart board. A is the event the dart hits the bull's-eye. $m(A) = \pi(1)^2 = \pi$ square

units. S is the sample space, so S is the whole dart board. The radius of the dart board is 4 units, so $m(S) = \pi(4)^2 = 16\pi$ square units. Therefore, $P(A) = \dfrac{m(A)}{m(S)} = \dfrac{\pi}{16\pi} = \dfrac{1}{16}$.

The probability that the dart hits the bull's-eye is $\dfrac{1}{16}$.

Section 11.2

14. The digits are 0, 1, 2, 3, 4, 5, 6, 7, 8, and 9.

(a) A digit can be repeated, so there are 10 possible choices for each numeral in the code. Hence, there are $10 \times 10 = 100$ possible two-digit code numbers.

(b) There is a restriction on the first digit in the code. The digit 0 cannot be used, so there are only 9 possible choices. Because there are no restrictions on the other two digits, they each can be chosen in 10 ways. Thus, there are $9 \times 10 \times 10 = 900$ possible such 3-digit identification code numbers.

(c) Notice that no digit can be repeated. There are 10 choices for the first numeral. The second numeral cannot be a repeat of the first, so there are only 9 choices for it. The third numeral can be any one of only 8 numerals since it cannot be a repeat of either of the first two. Finally, there are only 7 possible choices for the fourth numeral, since 3 digits have already been used. Therefore there are $10 \times 9 \times 8 \times 7 = 5040$ possible bicycle lock numbers.

(d) The only restriction is that the first digit cannot be zero. Consequently, the first digit can be any one of 9 numerals. There are no restrictions on the rest of the digits, so there are 10 choices for each of the four remaining digits. Therefore we see that there are $9 \times 10 \times 10 \times 10 \times 10 = 90{,}000$ possible five-digit zip code numbers.

Section 11.2

15. (a) There are 3 finishing places to fill. The first finishing place can be filled in 8 ways since there are 8 horses. Once a horse has finished in a certain spot, he cannot finish in another spot, so repetition is not allowed. The

second finishing place can be filled in 7 ways. The third finishing place can be filled in 6 ways. Hence, there are $8 \times 7 \times 6 = 336$ finishing orders.

(b) We are still considering 3 finishing places. This time, however, there are only 3 horses to consider. Therefore, there are $3 \times 2 \times 1 = 6$ finishing orders.

(c) Determining the probability that these three particular horses are the top finishers involves comparing the number of ways Lucky One, Lucky Two, and Lucky Three can finish in the top three places to the number of ways that the top three places can be determined in an eight-horse race. Compare part (b) to part (a).

$P(A) = \dfrac{6}{336} = \dfrac{1}{56}$, so the probability that these three

horses are the top finishers in the race is $\dfrac{1}{56}$.

Section 11.2

16. (a) There are eight possible orders of boys, B, and girls, G.

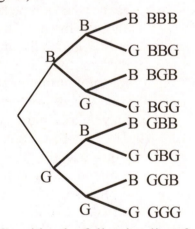

(b) Consider the following list of outcomes:
All girls, 1: GGG
Two girls, one boy, 3: BGG, GBG, GGB
One girl, two boys, 3: BBG, BGB, GBB
No girls, 1: BBB

(c) This result is the same as the third row of Pascal's Triangle, if we look at the number of outcomes for just the girls (or boys).

	All Girls	Two Girls	One Girl	No Girls
	1	3	3	1

Section 11.2

17. (a) The number of ways to hit the target when shooting four times should be the 4th row of Pascal's Triangle.

Number of Hits	4	3	2	1	0
Number of Ways	1	4	6	4	1
Probability	$\frac{1}{16}$	$\frac{4}{16}$	$\frac{6}{16}$	$\frac{4}{16}$	$\frac{1}{16}$

Each trial will result in a hit or miss (2 outcomes). Therefore, there are $2 \times 2 \times 2 \times 2 = 16$ possible sequences of hits or misses when shooting four times.

(b) Compare the probability for 3 hits out of 3 shots with the probability for 3 hits and 1 miss out of 4 shots.

$$P(3 \text{ hits}) = \frac{1}{8} \quad \text{(from the table in the book)}$$

$$P(3 \text{ hits and 1 miss}) = \frac{4}{16} = \frac{1}{4} \quad \text{(from our table)}$$

Thus, it is twice as likely that you will get 3 hits and 1 miss in 4 shots as 3 hits out of 3 shots.

Section 11.2

18. (a) No matter how many games are won or lost, the probability that either team wins any game is still $\frac{1}{2}$.

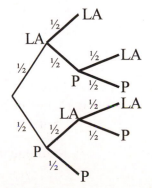

(b) Find the probability that Los Angeles wins in two straight games. We will denote the probability of this event as $P(LL)$. Each game is independent of every other game, so we multiply probabilities to get $P(LL) = \dfrac{1}{2} \times \dfrac{1}{2} = \dfrac{1}{4}$. If Portland wins the series after losing the first game, then Portland wins the final two games. So, $P(LPP) = \dfrac{1}{2} \times \dfrac{1}{2} \times \dfrac{1}{2} = \dfrac{1}{8}$.

(c) (i) There are two ways for Los Angeles to win in a 3 game series: *LPL* or *PLL*. We know that $P(LPL) = \dfrac{1}{8}$ and $P(PLL) = \dfrac{1}{8}$. Since Los Angeles can win the series if either event occurs, and the events are mutually exclusive, we can add.

$$P(LPL \text{ or } PLL) = P(LPL) + P(PLL) = \dfrac{1}{8} + \dfrac{1}{8} = \dfrac{1}{4}$$

(ii) In this best two out of three series, there are three ways for Portland to win: *LPP*, *PLP*, or *PP*. Since the events are mutually exclusive, we add probabilities.

$P(\text{Portland Wins}) = P(LPP) + P(PLP) + P(PP)$

$$= \dfrac{1}{8} + \dfrac{1}{8} + \dfrac{1}{4}$$

$$= \dfrac{1}{2}$$

(iii) There are four ways for the series to require three games to decide a winner: *LPL*, *LPP*, *PLL*, or *PLP*. We add the probabilities.

$$P(3 \text{ Games are Required}) = \dfrac{1}{8} + \dfrac{1}{8} + \dfrac{1}{8} + \dfrac{1}{8} = \dfrac{1}{2}$$

Section 11.2

19. (a) The probability that Los Angeles or Portland wins a game is 1. The probability Los Angeles wins an individual game is $\dfrac{3}{5}$. The probability that Portland wins an individual game is $1 - \dfrac{3}{5} = \dfrac{2}{5}$.

(b) The probability tree diagram is given next.

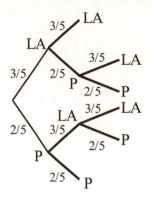

(c) The probability that Portland wins the series in two games involves the outcome PP. $\mathrm{P}(PP) = \dfrac{2}{5} \times \dfrac{2}{5} = \dfrac{4}{25}$.

(d) The probability that Los Angeles wins the series after losing the second game involves the outcome LPL. We have $P(LPL) = \dfrac{3}{5} \times \dfrac{2}{5} \times \dfrac{3}{5} = \dfrac{18}{125}$.

(e) The probability that the series goes for three games involves four outcomes. Since there are two outcomes that correspond to the event not happening, consider the probability of the complement of the event, that is, the probability that the series ends in 2 games. The complement involves outcomes LL and PP.

$$P(LL \text{ or } PP) = P(LL) + P(PP)$$

$$= \frac{3}{5} \times \frac{3}{5} + \frac{2}{5} \times \frac{2}{5}$$

$$= \frac{9}{25} + \frac{4}{25}$$

$$= \frac{13}{25}$$

Therefore, the probability that the series goes for 3 games = 1 – the probability that the series goes for 2 games = $1 - \dfrac{13}{25} = \dfrac{12}{25}$.

(f) The probability that Los Angeles wins the series involves the outcomes *LL*, *LPL*, and *PLL*.

$P(\text{Los Angeles Wins}) = P(LL \text{ or } LPL \text{ or } PLL)$

$$= P(LL) + P(LPL) + P(PLL)$$

$$= \frac{3}{5} \times \frac{3}{5} + \frac{3}{5} \times \frac{2}{5} \times \frac{3}{5} + \frac{2}{5} \times \frac{3}{5} \times \frac{3}{5}$$

$$= \frac{9}{25} + \frac{18}{125} + \frac{18}{125}$$

$$= \frac{81}{125}$$

Section 11.2

20. (a) Since the probability that team A wins any game is $\frac{2}{3}$, label each branch of the path $\frac{2}{3}$. The probability that team A wins the series in 3 games is $P(AAA) = \frac{2}{3} \times \frac{2}{3} \times \frac{2}{3} = \frac{8}{27}$.

(b) If team A wins with probability $\frac{2}{3}$, then team B wins with probability $1 - \frac{2}{3} = \frac{1}{3}$. Consider the following portions of the probability tree:

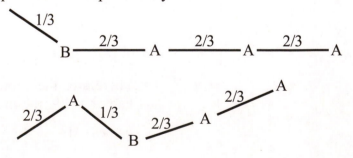

$$P(BAAA) = \frac{1}{3} \times \frac{2}{3} \times \frac{2}{3} \times \frac{2}{3} = \frac{8}{81}$$

$$P(ABAA) = \frac{2}{3} \times \frac{1}{3} \times \frac{2}{3} \times \frac{2}{3} = \frac{8}{81}$$

The probability of each event is $\frac{8}{81}$, so it does not matter which of the first three games team A loses. On each path, the same probabilities are rearranged. The probability that team A wins the series in four games is

$$P(BAAA \text{ or } ABAA \text{ or } AABA) = 3 \times \frac{8}{81} = \frac{8}{27}.$$ We do

not need to compute $P(AAAB)$ since the fourth game would not be played.

(c) There are six ways for team A to win in a five-game series: *AABBA*, *ABABA*, *BAABA*, *ABBAA*, *BABAA*, and *BBAAA*. Notice that it will not matter which two of the first four games team A loses. Since the probabilities are the same (just rearranged), we need to calculate only one of these probabilities:

$$P(AABBA) = \frac{2}{3} \times \frac{2}{3} \times \frac{1}{3} \times \frac{1}{3} \times \frac{2}{3} = \frac{8}{243}.$$

Therefore, the probability that team A wins the series in five games is $6 \times \frac{8}{243} = \frac{48}{243} = \frac{16}{81}$.

(d) The probability that team A wins the series corresponds to the sum: probability that team A wins in 3 games + probability that team A wins in 4 games + probability that team A wins in 5 games. Therefore, from parts (a), (b), and (c) we know that

$$P(A \text{ wins}) = \frac{8}{27} + \frac{8}{27} + \frac{16}{81} = \frac{64}{81}.$$ The probability that

team B wins is the complementary event. So, we know

that $P(B \text{ wins}) = 1 - \frac{64}{81} = \frac{17}{81}.$

Section 11.2

21. (a) The tree diagram is given next:

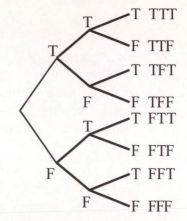

- T TTT
- F TTF
- T TFT
- F TFF
- T FTT
- F FTF
- T FFT
- F FFF

(b) There are 3 questions with 2 choices each. Thus, there are $2 \times 2 \times 2 = 8$ outcomes. There are 8 possible outcomes that correspond to the number of end branches in the tree diagram.

(c) Each sequence of answers is different, so only one can be correct.

(d) From part (b) and part (c), we know the probability of guessing all the correct answers is $\frac{1}{8}$.

Section 11.2

22. (a) The tree diagram will have two stages corresponding to the two sock selections. Each time you reach into the drawer, there are three possible colors that could be drawn. Since there are two of each color, the probability of getting any one color (blue, brown, or black) is $\frac{2}{6}$ or $\frac{1}{3}$. Once a sock is selected, the possibilities change for the next selection since fewer socks are in the drawer. For example, suppose that you select a blue sock first. On the second draw, there are two black and two brown socks, but one blue sock. Therefore, on the second draw, the probability of obtaining a black sock is $\frac{2}{5}$, a brown $\frac{2}{5}$, and a blue $\frac{1}{5}$. The tree diagram is at left.

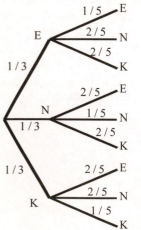

(b) The sample space is the set {*EE, EN, EK, NE, NN, NK, KE, KN, KK*}.

(c) A matched pair means two of the same color sock. Three outcomes correspond to the event that you get a matched pair: {*EE, NN, KK*}.

(d) The probability of getting a matched pair is calculated as follows:

$$P(EE \text{ or } NN \text{ or } KK) = P(EE) + P(NN) + P(KK)$$

$$= \frac{1}{3} \times \frac{1}{5} + \frac{1}{3} \times \frac{1}{5} + \frac{1}{3} \times \frac{1}{5}$$

$$= \frac{1}{15} + \frac{1}{15} + \frac{1}{15}$$

$$= \frac{1}{5}.$$

(e) The probability of getting a matched blue pair, *EE*, is

$$P(EE) = \frac{1}{3} \times \frac{1}{5} = \frac{1}{15}.$$

Section 11.2

23. Since there are three different colors, in the worst case you could draw one of each color before obtaining a matched pair. The fourth draw will always match one of the socks you already have. Therefore, the minimum number of socks you need to take to be sure you have a matched pair is four.

Section 11.2

24. Since there are three puppies, each of which can be male or female, the only possibilities for the sexes of the puppies are *MMM, MMF, MFM, FMM, MFF, FMF, FFM,* and *FFF*. Therefore, there are eight elements in the sample space. Seven of the eight elements contain at least one male puppy, therefore the probability that the pet store has a male puppy is $\frac{7}{8}$.

Section 11.2

25. In box 1, there are 10 balls: 4 white and 6 black. The probability of choosing a white ball is $\dfrac{4}{10}$, and the probability of choosing a black ball is $\dfrac{6}{10}$. If we pick a white ball and place it in box 2, then we will have increased the total number of balls to 11. In box 2 then, there would be 8 white balls and 3 black balls. Therefore, the probability of choosing a white ball is $\dfrac{8}{11}$; of choosing a black ball, $\dfrac{3}{11}$. If, on the other hand, a black ball is chosen from box 1 and placed in box 2, then the number of balls still increases to 11, but the number of white balls remains 7, and the number of black balls increases to 4. In this case, the probability of choosing a white ball from box 2 is $\dfrac{7}{11}$; of choosing a black ball, $\dfrac{4}{11}$.

A white ball can be chosen from the second box in two ways: (1) choose a black ball from box 1 and choose a white ball from box 2 *or* (2) choose a white ball from box 1 and choose a white ball from box 2. Therefore, the probability of choosing a white ball from box 2 is

$$\frac{6}{10}\cdot\frac{7}{11}+\frac{4}{10}\cdot\frac{8}{11}=\frac{42}{110}+\frac{32}{110}=\frac{74}{110}=\frac{37}{55}\approx 0.673.$$

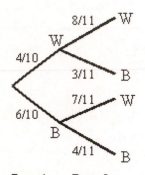

Section 11.2

26. (a) Make a table listing the number of equilateral triangles of all sizes for a $2 \times 2 \times 2$, $3 \times 3 \times 3$, $4 \times 4 \times 4$, and $5 \times 5 \times 5$ equilateral triangle. Make a note of which triangles are pointing up and which are pointing down in the figure. Look for a pattern, which will help you generate the total number of triangles for a $6 \times 6 \times 6$ equilateral triangle.

Large Equilateral Triangle	Possible Sizes of Equilateral Triangles	Number of Triangles Pointing Up	Number of Triangles Pointing Down	Total Number of Equilateral Triangles
$2 \times 2 \times 2$	$1 \times 1 \times 1$	$1 + 2 = 3$	1	
	$2 \times 2 \times 2$	1	0	
				5
$3 \times 3 \times 3$	$1 \times 1 \times 1$	$1 + 2 + 3 = 6$	$1 + 2 = 3$	
	$2 \times 2 \times 2$	$1 + 2 = 3$	0	
	$3 \times 3 \times 3$	1	0	
				13
$4 \times 4 \times 4$	$1 \times 1 \times 1$	$1 + 2 + 3 + 4 = 10$	$1 + 2 + 3 = 6$	
	$2 \times 2 \times 2$	$1 + 2 + 3 = 6$	1	
	$3 \times 3 \times 3$	$1 + 2 = 3$	0	
	$4 \times 4 \times 4$	1	0	
				27
$5 \times 5 \times 5$	$1 \times 1 \times 1$	$1 + 2 + 3 + 4 + 5 = 15$	$1 + 2 + 3 + 4 = 10$	
	$2 \times 2 \times 2$	$1 + 2 + 3 + 4 = 10$	$1 + 2 = 3$	
	$3 \times 3 \times 3$	$1 + 2 + 3 = 6$	0	
	$4 \times 4 \times 4$	$1 + 2 = 3$	0	
	$5 \times 5 \times 5$	1	0	
				48

At this point, recall the triangular numbers (discussed in Chapter 1). They are: 1, 3, 6, 10, 15, 21, 28, ... Notice a pattern in the table. The number of equilateral triangles of all sizes pointing up in an $n \times n \times n$ equilateral triangle is the sum of the first n triangular numbers. The number of equilateral triangles of all sizes pointing down in an $n \times n \times n$ equilateral triangle depends upon whether n is even or odd. For example, if n is even, then the number of triangles is the sum of every other triangular number beginning with 1 and ending with the $n - 1$st triangular number. Therefore, for a $6 \times 6 \times 6$ equilateral triangle, the number of triangles pointing up is $1 + 3 + 6 + 10 + 15 + 21 = 56$. The number of triangles pointing down is $1 + 6 + 15 = 22$. The total number of equilateral triangles of all sizes is $56 + 22 = 78$.

(b) Assuming our observations hold for $n > 5$, for an $8 \times 8 \times 8$ equilateral triangle, the number of triangles pointing up is $1 + 3 + 6 + 10 + 15 + 21 + 28 + 36 = 120$. The number of triangles pointing down is $1 + 6 + 15 + 28 = 50$. The total number of equilateral triangles of all sizes in an $8 \times 8 \times 8$ equilateral triangle is $120 + 50 = 170$.

Section 11.3

15. (a) We would like to show $_{n+1}C_r = {_n}C_{r-1} + {_n}C_r$. Start on the right-hand side of the equation and rewrite the expression using the definition of a combination. Use properties of factorials and add fractions to show the equation is true.

$$_nC_{r-1} + {_n}C_r$$

$$= \frac{n!}{(n-r+1)!(r-1)!} + \frac{n!}{(n-r)!r!}$$

$$= \frac{n!}{(n-r+1)(n-r)!(r-1)!} + \frac{n!}{(n-r)!r(r-1)!}$$

$$= \frac{r \cdot n!}{r(n-r+1)(n-r)!(r-1)!} + \frac{(n-r+1)n!}{r(n-r+1)(n-r)!(r-1)!}$$

$$= \frac{r \cdot n! + (n-r+1)n!}{r(n-r+1)(n-r)!(r-1)!}$$

$$= \frac{(r+n-r+1)n!}{r(n-r+1)(n-r)!(r-1)!}$$

$$= \frac{(n+1)n!}{(n-r+1)(n-r)!r(r-1)!}$$

$$= \frac{(n+1)!}{(n-r+1)!r!}$$

$$= {_{n+1}}C_r$$

(b) Each entry, other than the 1s, are formed by adding the two entries above it. The result from part (a), shows how two entries add to form the entry below them.

Section 11.3

16. (a) There are nine positions to fill. A single letter can be placed in any of the nine positions. Once it is placed, the next letter can be placed in any of eight positions, and so on. Therefore, there are 9! way to place the three letters. Because each letter is used three times, we must remove duplicate orders. Each letter is used three times, so for any given order, we have counted 3! arrangements for each letter that all look the same. Divide away the duplicate arrangements. Thus, there are $\dfrac{9!}{3!3!3!} = \dfrac{362,880}{216} = 1680$ nine-letter ID numbers that can be generated.

    (b) If GHS must start the ID number, then there are six spots to fill with the other letters. This can be done in 6! ways. Divide out the duplicates numbers, so the number of nine-letter ID numbers that start with GHS is $\dfrac{6!}{2!2!2!} = \dfrac{720}{8} = 90$. The probability that a random ID number starts with GHS is $\dfrac{90}{1680} = \dfrac{3}{56}$.

Section 11.3

17. Assume that letters and numbers can be repeated.

    (a) Think of the license plates as having six blanks, the first three for letters and the last three for digits. For each blank involving letters, there are 26 choices. For each blank involving digits, there are 10 choices. Thus there are $\underline{26} \times \underline{26} \times \underline{26} \times \underline{10} \times \underline{10} \times \underline{10} = 26^3 10^3$ combinations of license plates with Edwardo's initials. How many of these will have Edwardo's initials, EAM, in any order? By the fundamental counting property there are $3 \times 2 \times 1 = 6$ ways to fill up the letter positions of the license plates. Therefore, there are $3 \times 2 \times 1 \times 10 \times 10 \times 10 = 6 \cdot 10^3$ license plates with Edwardo's initials. The probability a license will have his initials is $\dfrac{6 \cdot 10^3}{26^3 10^3} = \dfrac{6}{26^3} \approx 0.00034$.

(b) If he wants the license plate to have his initials in the correct order, there are $1 \times 1 \times 1 \times 10 \times 10 \times 10 = 1 \cdot 10^3$ of these license plates. The probability of this occurring is $\dfrac{1 \cdot 10^3}{26^3 10^3} = \dfrac{1}{26^3} \approx 0.000056896$.

Section 11.3

18. Since there are four digits to try, think of the problem as four blanks to fill: __ __ __ __. The first digit could be any of the four. The second could be any of the remaining three. The third could be either of the remaining two. The fourth would be the last remaining digit. There are at most $\underline{4} \times \underline{3} \times \underline{2} \times \underline{1} = 24$ combinations he must try.

Section 11.3

19. (a) Since $\quad {}_m P_n = \dfrac{m!}{(m-n)!} \quad$ and $\quad {}_{10} C_7 = \dfrac{10!}{(10-7)! \times 7!} \quad$ set up an equation and solve.

$$ {}_m P_n = {}_{10} C_7 $$

$$ \frac{m!}{(m-n)!} = \frac{10!}{3! \times 7!} = \frac{10 \times 9 \times 8}{3 \times 2 \times 1} = 120 $$

$$ \frac{m!}{(m-n)!} = m(m-1)(m-2)\cdots(m-n+1) = 120. $$

Notice the factorization of 120 above. For the value of m to be as small as possible, the smallest factor, $(m-n+1)$, must be 1. If $m-n+1 = 1$ then $m = n$. So, $\dfrac{m!}{(m-n)!} = \dfrac{m!}{(m-m)!} = \dfrac{m!}{0!} = \dfrac{m!}{1} = 120$ and $m = 5 = n$.

(b) Consider the following equation:

$$ {}_m C_n = {}_{15} P_2 $$

$$ \frac{m!}{n!(m-n)!} = \frac{15!}{(15-2)!} $$

$$ \frac{m!}{n!(m-n)!} = 210 $$

Remember that the entries in Pascal's triangle are the values of $_mC_n$. Construct Pascal's triangle and locate the value 210.

$$
\begin{array}{ccccccccccc}
& & & & & 1 & & & & & \\
& & & & 1 & & 1 & & & & \\
& & & 1 & & 2 & & 1 & & & \\
& & 1 & & 3 & & 3 & & 1 & & \\
& 1 & & 4 & & 6 & & 4 & & 1 & \\
1 & & 5 & & 10 & & 10 & & 5 & & 1 \\
\end{array}
$$

```
                    1
                 1     1
              1     2     1
           1     3     3     1
        1     4     6     4     1
     1     5    10    10     5     1
  1     6    15    20    15     6     1
1     7    21    35    35    21     7     1
  1  8   28   56   70   56   28  8     1
    1  9  36   84  126  126  84  36  9    1
     1  10  45  120  210
     n=0  n=1  n=2  n=3  n=4
```

If the rows are counted beginning at zero, then the value 210 occurs in row 10 so $m = 10$ and $n = 4$. Therefore, $210 = {}_{10}C_4$.

Section 11.3

20. (a) Since five numbers are picked without regard to order, find the number of combinations when choosing 5 numbers from the set of 36 numbers. The number of ways the five winning numbers can be picked is as follows.

$$
{}_{36}C_5 = \frac{36!}{31! \times 5!}
$$

$$
= \frac{36 \times 35 \times 34 \times 33 \times 32 \times 31!}{31! \times 5 \times 4 \times 3 \times 2 \times 1}
$$

$$
= 376,992
$$

(b) For picking six numbers without regard to order, find the combination ${}_{36}C_6 = \dfrac{36!}{30! \times 6!} = 1,947,792.$

Section 11.3

21. (a) There are 10 seats available and 10 passengers. Each passenger will get a seat. The first passenger can fill any of the 10 empty seats. The second passenger can fill any of the 9 remaining seats, etc. This is a

permutation of 10 passengers chosen to fill 10 seats. The number of ways to do that is calculated as follows.

$$_{10}P_{10} = \frac{10!}{(10-10)!} = \frac{10!}{0!} = \frac{10!}{1} = 3,628,800$$

There are $10! = 3,628,800$ ways to seat 10 passengers.

(b) With 10 seats available and only 9 passengers, one seat will be left empty. The first passenger can fill any of the 10 empty seats. The second passenger can fill any of the 9 remaining seats. Continue this pattern until all of the passengers are seated. There are $10 \times 9 \times 8 \times 7 \times 6 \times 5 \times 4 \times 3 \times 2$ ways to seat the passengers. Notice that this is the permutation $_{10}P_9$.

$$_{10}P_9 = \frac{10!}{(10-9)!}$$

$$= 10 \times 9 \times 8 \times 7 \times 6 \times 5 \times 4 \times 3 \times 2$$

$$= 3,628,800$$

There are $10! = 3,628,800$ ways to seat 9 passengers.

(c) Again there are 10 seats, but this time, only 8 passengers. Two seats will be left empty. The first passenger can fill any of the 10 empty seats. The second passenger can fill any of the 9 remaining seats. Continue until all passengers are seated. Notice then that the number of ways of seating 8 passengers in 10 seats is the permutation $_{10}P_8$.

$$_{10}P_8 = \frac{10!}{(10-8)!}$$

$$= \frac{10!}{2!}$$

$$= 10 \times 9 \times 8 \times 7 \times 6 \times 5 \times 4 \times 3$$

$$= 1,814,400$$

Alternately, 8 passengers can pick from 10 seats to occupy in $_{10}C_8$ ways. For each of these choices, the 8 seats can be filled in $8!$ ways, so the total number of ways to seat 8 passengers in 10 seats is

$$_{10}C_8 \cdot 8! = \frac{10!}{2!8!} \cdot 8! = \frac{10!}{2!} = 1,814,400 \, .$$

There are $1,814,400$ ways to seat 8 passengers.

(d) Placing 5 passengers in the 10 seats requires the permutation $_{10}P_5$.

$$_{10}P_5 = \frac{10!}{(10-5)!}$$

$$= \frac{10!}{5!}$$

$$= 10 \times 9 \times 8 \times 7 \times 6$$

$$= 30,240$$

Alternately, 5 passengers can pick from 10 seats to occupy in $_{10}C_5$ ways. For each of these choices, the 5 seats can be filled in 5! ways, so the total number of ways to seat 5 passengers in 10 seats is $_{10}C_5 \cdot 5! = \frac{10!}{5!5!} \cdot 5! = \frac{10!}{5!} = 30,240.$

(e) For r passengers where $0 \le r \le 10$, the number of ways to seat r passengers in 10 seats is the permutation $_{10}P_r$ which is equal to $_{10}C_r \cdot r!$.

Section 11.3

22. (a) The chips are numbered and not replaced once they are drawn from the hat. On the first draw, any of the ten chips can be chosen. On the second draw, there are only nine left to select from, etc. This is a permutation of 10 objects chosen from 10 objects.

$$_{10}P_{10} = \frac{10!}{(10-10)!}$$

$$= \frac{10!}{0!}$$

$$= 10!$$

$$= 3,628,800$$

Therefore, there are 10! = 3,628,800 possible sequences.

(b) There are no longer ten options on the first selection. Chip number 5 must be selected first. There are $_1P_1 \cdot _9P_9 = 1 \times 9 \times 8 \times 7 \times 6 \times 5 \times 4 \times 3 \times 2 \times 1 = 9! = 362,880$ sequences with chip 5 as the first selection.

(c) Out of the numbers 1 through 10, five are odd. Thus, there are five options for the first selection. There are $_5P_1 \cdot _9P_9 = 5 \times 9 \times 8 \times 7 \times 6 \times 5 \times 4 \times 3 \times 2 \times 1 = 5 \cdot 9! = 1,814,400$ such sequences.

(d) Since there are five odd numbers and five even numbers, the first position and last position each have 5 options. Each of the remaining middle positions can be filled in turn with the 8 remaining chips. There are $_5P_1 \cdot _8P_8 \cdot _5P_1 = 5 \times 8 \times 7 \times 6 \times 5 \times 4 \times 3 \times 2 \times 1 \times 5 = 25 \cdot 8! = 1,008,000$ possible sequences.

Section 11.3

23. (a) Each letter is different, so no repetition is allowed. The number of five letter "words" is the number of permutations of 5 distinct letters taken altogether which is $5! = 120$.

(b) The first letter must be "P". The remaining letters can be arranged in 4! ways. Therefore, there are $1 \times 4! = 1 \times 4 \times 3 \times 2 \times 1 = 24$ "words".

(c) There are two consonants so either one could be the first letter. Once the first letter is chosen from the 2 consonants, the remaining letters can be arranged in 4! ways. Thus, there are $2 \times 4! = 2 \times 4 \times 3 \times 2 \times 1 = 48$ "words".

(d) There are two consonants and three vowels. Once the first letter is chosen from the set of consonants, and the last letter is chosen from the set of vowels, the remaining letters can be arranged in 3! ways. There are $2 \times 3! \times 3 = 2 \times 3 \times 2 \times 1 \times 3 = 36$ "words".

Section 11.3

24. (a) When calculating combinations of 5 objects or 15 objects from 20 objects, there is a complementary relationship to notice. $20 - 15 = 5$ and $20 - 5 = 15$. Without calculating the total number of combinations, we note:

$$_{20}C_5 = \frac{20!}{5!(20-5)!} = \frac{20!}{5!15!}$$

$$= \frac{20!}{15!5!} = \frac{20!}{15!(20-15)!} = {}_{20}C_{15}$$

(b)

$$_nC_r = \frac{n!}{r!(n-r)!}$$

$$= \frac{n!}{(n-r)!r!} = \frac{n!}{(n-r)!(n-(n-r))!} = {}_nC_{n-r}$$

(c) Notice ${}_{50}C_{43} = {}_{50}C_{50-43} = {}_{50}C_7$ since from part (b) we found $_nC_r = {}_nC_{n-r}$. Thus, $_{50}C_{43} = 99{,}884{,}400$.

Section 11.3

25. Refer to the Initial Problem in Chapter 1 for the figures.
    (a) There are nine spots to fill so there are $9! = 362{,}880$ possible arrangements. Notice that these are not all possible solutions.
    (b) There are three corners which can be filled in $3 \times 2 \times 1$ ways. The remaining spots can then be filled in $6 \times 5 \times 4 \times 3 \times 2 \times 1$ ways. With 1, 2 and 3 in the corners, there are $3 \times 2 \times 1 \times 6 \times 5 \times 4 \times 3 \times 2 \times 1 = 3!6! = 4320$ arrangements.
    (c) There are two, two-digit sums of 14: $6 + 8$ and $9 + 5$.
    (d) Once the corner spots are filled, the digits 9 and 5 can be placed in two ways. The other pairs of digits between the corners also can be placed two ways. There are $2 \times 2 \times 2 = 8$ solutions with the numbers 5 and 9 in the 1–2 row.
    (e) There are two solutions to the puzzle. For each of these solutions, the corners can be filled in 3! ways. Between the corners, the three pairs of digits have $2 \times 2 \times 2 = 8$ arrangements. There are $2(3!\times8) = 96$ possible arrangements.

Section 11.3

26. (a) Order is not important so use combinations. Choose four students from the group of 15.

$$_{15}C_4 = \frac{15!}{4! \times 11!} = 1365$$

Thus, there are 1365 different ways.

(b) Since Glenn is in the group for sure, calculate how many ways there are to choose the remaining 3 students from 14.

$$_{14}C_3 = \frac{14!}{3! \times 11!} = 364 \text{ ways}$$

The probability that Glenn is in the group is $\frac{364}{1365} \approx 0.267$.

(c) Since Glenn and Mickey are in the group for sure, calculate how many ways there are to choose the remaining 2 students from 13.

$$_{13}C_2 = \frac{13!}{2! \times 11!} = 78 \text{ ways}$$

The probability that Glenn and Mickey are in the group is $\frac{78}{1365} \approx 0.057$.

Section 11.3

27. Order is not important in a hand of cards, so use combinations.

(a) In the five card hand, if four are aces, then only one more card is needed out of the remaining 48 cards. Notice choosing four aces from the set of 4 aces can be done in $_4C_4 = 1$ way. The probability the hand contains four aces is calculated as follows:

$$\frac{_4C_4 \cdot {_{48}C_1}}{_{52}C_5} = \frac{48}{_{52}C_5} = \frac{48}{2,598,960} \approx 0.000\,018\,469.$$

(b) Out of 4 kings, 3 can be chosen in $_4C_3$ ways. Out of 4 queens, 2 can be chosen in $_4C_2$ ways. The probability the hand contains 3 kings and 2 queens is calculated as follows:

$$\frac{_4C_3 \cdot {_4C_2}}{_{52}C_5} = \frac{4 \cdot 6}{_{52}C_5} = \frac{24}{_{52}C_5} = \frac{24}{2,598,960} \approx 0.000\,009\,234.$$

(c) Out of 13 diamonds, 5 can be chosen in $_{13}C_5$ ways. All cards are accounted for, so no more are needed. The probability the hand contains 5 diamonds is calculated as follows:

$$\frac{_{13}C_5}{_{52}C_5} = \frac{1287}{2,598,960} \approx 0.000\,495\,198.$$

(d) Each of the cards chosen is one choice out of 4 possible choices. The probability the hand contains an ace, king, queen, jack and ten is calculated as follows:

$$\frac{_4C_1 \cdot {}_4C_1 \cdot {}_4C_1 \cdot {}_4C_1 \cdot {}_4C_1}{_{52}C_5} = \frac{4 \cdot 4 \cdot 4 \cdot 4 \cdot 4}{_{52}C_5}$$

$$= \frac{4^5}{_{52}C_5}$$

$$= \frac{1024}{2,598,960}$$

$$\approx 0.000\,394\,004.$$

Section 11.3

28. (a) Order is not important. The five people can be chosen in $_{20}C_5 = 15,504$ ways.

   (b) Three people have been exposed. The number of ways of choosing 1 of those 3 people is $_3C_1$. The remaining 4 people must be chosen from the 17 nonexposed people. Thus, the probability of selecting exactly one person who has been exposed is calculated as follows:

   $$\frac{_3C_1 \cdot {}_{17}C_4}{_{20}C_5} = \frac{3 \cdot {}_{17}C_4}{_{20}C_5} = \frac{3 \cdot 2380}{15,504} \approx 0.46.$$

   (c) Add the probability that one person was exposed and the probability that two people were exposed. The probability that one was exposed is $\dfrac{_3C_1 \cdot {}_{17}C_4}{_{20}C_5} \approx 0.46$.

   The probability that two people were exposed is $\dfrac{_3C_2 \cdot {}_{17}C_3}{_{20}C_5} \approx 0.13$. Therefore, the probability that one person or two people were exposed is approximately $0.46 + 0.13 = 0.59$ or $\dfrac{_3C_1 \cdot {}_{17}C_4 + {}_3C_2 \cdot {}_{17}C_3}{_{20}C_5}$.

Section 11.4

22. (a) To find P(A), multiply probabilities along the branches of the tree diagram and then add.

$$P(A) = P(a) + P(b) + P(c)$$

$$= \frac{1}{3} \cdot \frac{1}{4} + \frac{1}{3} \cdot \frac{3}{4} + \frac{2}{3} \cdot \frac{2}{5}$$

$$= \frac{1}{12} + \frac{1}{4} + \frac{4}{15}$$

$$= \frac{5}{60} + \frac{15}{60} + \frac{16}{60}$$

$$= \frac{36}{60}$$

$$P(A) = \frac{3}{5}$$

(b) To find P(B), multiply probabilities along the branches of the tree diagram and then add.

$$P(B) = P(b) + P(c) + P(d)$$

$$= \frac{1}{3} \cdot \frac{3}{4} + \frac{2}{3} \cdot \frac{2}{5} + \frac{2}{3} \cdot \frac{3}{5}$$

$$= \frac{1}{4} + \frac{4}{15} + \frac{6}{15}$$

$$= \frac{15}{60} + \frac{16}{60} + \frac{24}{60}$$

$$= \frac{55}{60}$$

$$P(B) = \frac{11}{12}$$

(c) Event $A \cap B = \{b, c\}$. To find $P(A \cap B)$, multiply probabilities along the branches of the tree diagram and then add.

$$P(A \cap B) = \frac{1}{3} \cdot \frac{3}{4} + \frac{2}{3} \cdot \frac{2}{5} = \frac{1}{4} + \frac{4}{15} = \frac{15}{60} + \frac{16}{60} = \frac{31}{60}$$

(d) Recall that $P(A \cup B) = P(A) + P(B) - P(A \cap B)$.

$$P(A \cup B) = P(A) + P(B) - P(A \cap B)$$

$$= \frac{3}{5} + \frac{11}{12} - \frac{31}{60}$$

$$= \frac{36}{60} + \frac{55}{60} - \frac{31}{60}$$

$$= \frac{60}{60}$$

$$P(A \cup B) = 1$$

Alternatively, notice that $A \cup B = \{a, b, c, d\} = S$ and $P(S) = 1$.

(e) $P(A|B) = \dfrac{P(A \cap B)}{P(B)} = \dfrac{\dfrac{31}{60}}{\dfrac{11}{12}} = \dfrac{31}{60} \cdot \dfrac{12}{11} = \dfrac{31}{55}$

(f) $P(B|A) = \dfrac{P(A \cap B)}{P(A)} = \dfrac{\dfrac{31}{60}}{\dfrac{3}{5}} = \dfrac{31}{60} \cdot \dfrac{5}{3} = \dfrac{31}{36}$

Section 11.4

23. (a) There are a total of 15 students in class 1, and 105 students won awards, so the probability a student chosen at random from the award winners is in class 1 is $\dfrac{15}{105} = \dfrac{1}{7}$.

   (b) There are a total of $20 + 19 + 21 = 60$ students in classes 4, 5, and 6, and 105 students won awards, so the probability a student chosen at random from the award winners is in class 4, 5, or 6 is $\dfrac{60}{105} = \dfrac{4}{7}$.

   (c) A total of 61 students won math awards out of the 105 students, so the probability a student chosen at random from the award winners won a math award is $\dfrac{61}{105}$.

   (d) There are a total of 53 girls out of 105 students, so the probability a student chosen at random from the award winners is a girl is $\dfrac{53}{105}$.

(e) There are a total of 29 boys who won a math award out of 105 students, so the probability a student chosen at random from the award winners is a boy who won an award is $\dfrac{29}{105}$.

(f) If we let M be the event that a student won a math award and $C1$ be the event the student is in class 1, then we must find $P(M\,|\,C1)$.

$$P(M|C1) = \frac{P(M \cap C1)}{P(C1)}$$

$$= \frac{7}{15}$$

Thus, the probability the student won a math award given that he or she is in class 1 is $\dfrac{7}{15}$.

(g) If we let M be the event that a student won a math award and C be the event the student is in class 1, 2, or 3, then we must find $P(M\,|\,C)$.

$$P(M|C) = \frac{P(M \cap C)}{P(C)}$$

$$= \frac{24}{45}$$

Thus, the probability the student won a math award given that he or she is in class 1, 2, or 3 is $\dfrac{24}{45}$.

(h) If we let G be the event that a student is a girl and M be the event the student won a math award, then we must find $P(G\,|\,M)$.

$$P(G|M) = \frac{P(G \cap M)}{P(M)}$$

$$= \frac{32}{61}$$

Thus, the probability the student is a girl given that he or she won a math award is $\dfrac{32}{61}$.

(i) If we let G be the event that a student is a girl and M be the event the student won a math award, then we must find $P(M\,|\,G)$.

$$P(M|G) = \frac{P(M \cap G)}{P(G)}$$

$$= \frac{32}{53}$$

Thus, the probability the student won a math award given that she is a girl is $\frac{32}{53}$.

Section 11.4

24. (a) When the teams are closely matched, it is not likely that one team will "run away" with the series. The prospects for a long series would increase when the teams are closely matched, so the statement does not make sense. You should disagree with the statement.

    (b) Construct a tree diagram. If the probability that the American League team wins any game is p, then the probability that the National League team wins any game is $1 - p = q$. The tree diagram will have four stages corresponding to each game. Consider the event $AAAA$. We see that $P(AAAA) = P$(American League wins in 4 games) $= p \times p \times p \times p = p^4$.

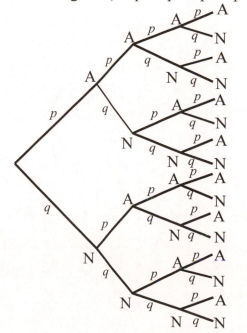

(c) Consider the diagram from part (b). Consider event *NNNN*. We see that $P(NNNN)$ = P(National League team wins in 4 games) $= q \times q \times q \times q = q^4$.

(d) For the series to end in four games, either the American League team would have to win in four games or the National League team would have to win in four games. These are mutually exclusive events. The probability that the series ends in four games is the sum of the probability that the American League team wins in four games plus the probability that the National League team wins in four games $= p^4 + q^4$.

(e) Given the odds in favor of an event, recall how the probability is calculated. If the odds in favor of an event are $a:b$, then the probability of the event occurring is $\dfrac{a}{a+b}$.

Odds Favoring American League	1:1	2:1	3:1	3:2
p	$\dfrac{1}{1+1} = \dfrac{1}{2}$	$\dfrac{2}{2+1} = \dfrac{2}{3}$	$\dfrac{3}{3+1} = \dfrac{3}{4}$	$\dfrac{3}{3+2} = \dfrac{3}{5}$
$q = 1-p$	$1 - \dfrac{1}{2} = \dfrac{1}{2}$	$1 - \dfrac{2}{3} = \dfrac{1}{3}$	$1 - \dfrac{3}{4} = \dfrac{1}{4}$	$1 - \dfrac{3}{5} = \dfrac{2}{5}$
P(American win in 4)	$\left(\dfrac{1}{2}\right)^4 = \dfrac{1}{16}$	$\left(\dfrac{2}{3}\right)^4 = \dfrac{16}{81}$	$\left(\dfrac{3}{4}\right)^4 = \dfrac{81}{256}$	$\left(\dfrac{3}{5}\right)^4 = \dfrac{81}{625}$
P(National win in 4)	$\left(\dfrac{1}{2}\right)^4 = \dfrac{1}{16}$	$\left(\dfrac{1}{3}\right)^4 = \dfrac{1}{81}$	$\left(\dfrac{1}{4}\right)^4 = \dfrac{1}{256}$	$\left(\dfrac{2}{5}\right)^4 = \dfrac{16}{625}$
P(4-game series)	$\dfrac{1}{16} + \dfrac{1}{16} = \dfrac{1}{8}$	$\dfrac{16}{81} + \dfrac{1}{81} = \dfrac{17}{81}$	$\dfrac{81}{256} + \dfrac{1}{256} = \dfrac{41}{128}$	$\dfrac{81}{65} + \dfrac{16}{625} = \dfrac{97}{625}$

(f) When the teams are evenly matched (as with 1:1 odds), the probability of the series ending in four games is small (0.125) compared to when the teams are not evenly matched.

Section 11.4

25. (a) Assuming independence of games, each of the four ways the American League can win in five games is a combination of four wins and one loss. Therefore, when calculating the probability for any of the four events, there would be a product of 4 ps (wins) and 1 q (loss). The probability of each of the events is p^4q, so the probability that the American League wins in five games is $4p^4q$.

(b) The four ways for the National League to win the series in five games are *ANNNN*, *NANNN*, *NNANN*, and *NNNAN*. The probability of each event is found by multiplying 4 qs (for 4 National League wins) and 1 p (for 1 National League loss). Thus, the probability of each event is q^4p, so the probability that the National League wins in five games is $4q^4p$.

(c) Since the events are mutually exclusive, we add their probabilities. The probability the series will end after five games is $4p^4q + 4q^4p$.

Section 11.4

26. (a) Since there are ten ways the American League can win a six-game world series and each of these ways involves four wins and two losses, the probability calculation for each of the ten ways is the same. The probability of a win is $P(A) = p$, so $P(N) = q$. The probability that the American League wins a six-game series is $10p^4q^2$.

(b) Similarly, the probability that the National League wins a six-game series is $10\,p^2q^4$.

(c) Since these events are mutually exclusive, the probability that the series will end at six games is the sum of the probability that the American League wins in six games and the probability that the National League wins in six games: $10p^4q^2 + 10\,p^2q^4$.

Section 11.4

27. These probabilities follow the same pattern as in problems 25 and 26.

    (a) The probability that the American League wins in 7 games is $20p^4q^3$.

    (b) The probability that the National League wins in 7 games is $20\, p^3q^4$.

    (c) The probability that the World Series goes all 7 games is $20p^4q^3 + 20\, p^3q^4$.

Section 11.4

28. (a) Consider our work from problems 24 through 27.

x=Number of Games	4	5	6	7
P(American wins)	p^4	$4p^4q$	$10p^4q^2$	$20p^4q^3$
P(National wins)	q^4	$4pq^4$	$10\,p^2q^4$	$20\,p^3q^4p^3$
P(x games in series)	$p^4 + q^4$	$4p^4q + 4pq^4$	$10p^4q^2 + 10\,p^2q^4$	$20p^4q^3 + 20p^3q^4$

(b) The odds favoring the American League are 1:1, so

$$p = \frac{1}{1+1} = \frac{1}{2}, \text{ so } q = 1 - \frac{1}{2} = \frac{1}{2}.$$ Consider the row labeled P(x games in series).

x = Number of Games	$P(x)$
4	$\left(\frac{1}{2}\right)^4 + \left(\frac{1}{2}\right)^4 = \frac{1}{8}$
5	$4\left(\frac{1}{2}\right)^4\left(\frac{1}{2}\right) + 4\left(\frac{1}{2}\right)\left(\frac{1}{2}\right)^4 = \frac{1}{4}$
6	$10\left(\frac{1}{2}\right)^4\left(\frac{1}{2}\right)^2 + 10\left(\frac{1}{2}\right)^2\left(\frac{1}{2}\right)^4 = \frac{5}{16}$
7	$20\left(\frac{1}{2}\right)^4\left(\frac{1}{2}\right)^3 + 20\left(\frac{1}{2}\right)^3\left(\frac{1}{2}\right)^4 = \frac{5}{16}$

(c) Let v_i = number of games and p_i = the probability that the series ends in v_i games, for $i = 4, 5, 6, 7, \ldots$ Then the expected value is calculated as follows:

$$v_4 p_4 + v_5 p_5 + v_6 p_6 + v_7 p_7 = 4 \times \frac{1}{8} + 5 \times \frac{1}{4} + 6 \times \frac{5}{16} + 7 \times \frac{5}{16}$$

$$\approx 5.8 \text{ games.}$$

Therefore, we expect the length of the series to be approximately 6 games.

Section 11.4

29. Access the eManipulative, *Simulation*. Because the snack company has put five different toys in the snack boxes, and the same number of each toy has been used, each toy has the same probability of being selected.

   (a) In the activity, *Simulation*, click on the numbers 1, 2, 3, 4 and 5. These will represent the five different toys. Clicking on the numbers will place them in the box. Click "Start" and let the computer draw numbers until all five numbers have been drawn. Record the number of draws and clear the results. Repeat the simulation. The problem suggests that we run at least 100 trials. With the results of 100 trials, the number of boxes of snacks we would expect to buy before we have all five toys can be approximated by the average (mean) of the number of draws. While each person who runs 100 trials will have a different mean, one set of 100 trials yielded a mean of 10.88 boxes. In other words, you would expect to have to buy approximately 11 boxes to collect all five toys.

   (b) Consider the number of draws required to select all five numbers for 30 trials: 7, 13, 8, 11, 10, 9, 8, 14, 7, 14, 12, 8, 19, 7, 10, 16, 14, 6, 18, 8, 10, 9, 15, 10, 7, 14, 9, 11, 17, 14. The mean number of draws is $\frac{335}{30} \approx 11.17$. From this simulation, we would conclude that we would expect to buy approximately 11.17 boxes of snacks to collect all five toys.

Section 11.4

30. Eight points are evenly spaced around a circle as shown to the left. Select one point and notice that you can connect it to each of the seven remaining points, for a total of 7 segments.

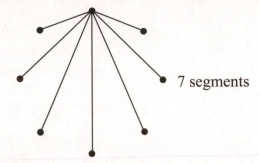

7 segments

Select another point. Notice it has already been connected to one point, so there are 6 points left to connect. Connect these for an additional 6 segments.

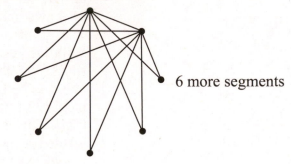

6 more segments

Continue in this manner and there will be $7 + 6 + 5 + 4 + 3 + 2 + 1 = 28$ segments.

Alternately, recall that any two points determine a segment and conversely, any segment determines two points. The number of ways of selecting 2 points out of 8 is $_8C_2 = 28$, so this also enumerates the total number of segments.

SOLUTIONS - PART A PROBLEMS

Chapter 12: Geometric Shapes

Section 12.1

12. (a) To change from A to B, the diagonal of the square has been constructed between the lower left and the upper right vertices. The figure X is a rectangle, and it belongs with choice (ii) since (ii) is the only rectangle with a diagonal.

(b) To change from A to B, the rhombus was rotated one-half turn. The figure X is a square with a dot in the right-hand triangle formed by the two diagonals. X belongs with choice (i) since it is a square with a dot in the left-hand triangle, which resulted from a rotation of one-half turn.

Section 12.1

13. (a) The unfolded paper will look like the following.

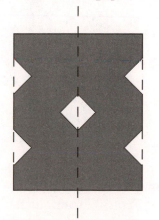

(b) The unfolded paper will look like the following.

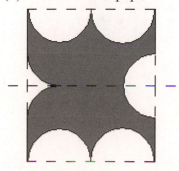

Section 12.1

14. The folded papers are shown next.

    (a)   (b)

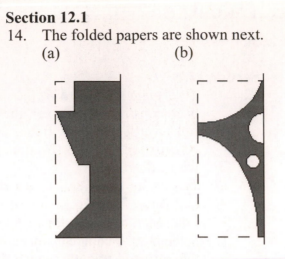

Section 12.1

15. The unfolded paper is shown next.

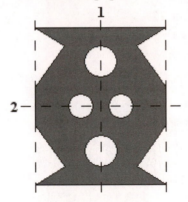

Section 12.1

16. (a) You will unfold the paper in the reverse order of the folds, so you will unfold over line 2 first.

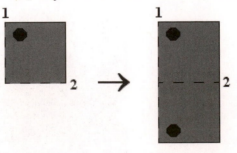

Unfold over line 1 next to reveal the final shape.

(b) There is more than one way to accomplish this task for each figure. Use the figure and sketch a line over which it will be folded. Both halves must fold together so that the holes line up. Using the folded figure, sketch a second line over which to fold so that both halves fold onto each other and the holes line up. Notice that all folds need not be horizontal and vertical.

(i) One possible solution is shown next.

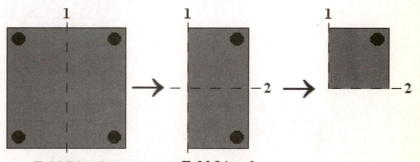

      Fold Line 1   **Fold Line 2**

Thus, fold on the lines indicated and punch a hole as shown in the following figure.

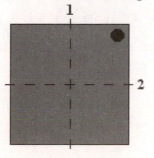

(ii)   One possible solution is shown next.

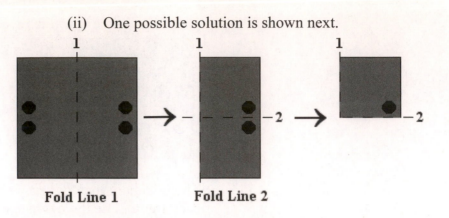

Thus, fold on the lines indicated and punch a hole as shown in the following figure.

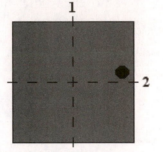

(iii)   One possible solution is shown next.

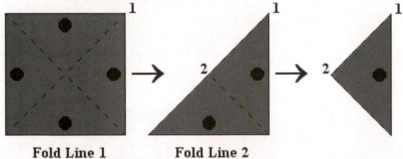

Thus, fold on the lines indicated and punch a hole as shown in the following figure.

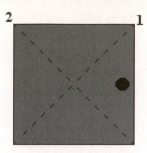

(iv) One possible solution is shown next.

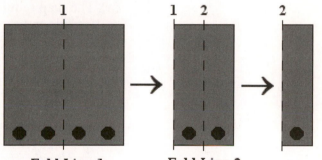

Fold Line 1   Fold Line 2

Thus, fold on the lines indicated and punch a hole as shown in the following figure.

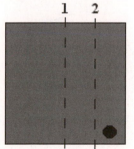

Section 12.1

17. If the arrow *A* were continued downward, it would meet arrow *D*. One way to check this is by folding the paper along arrow *A* and creasing the paper. The crease will extend along arrow *D*. You could also use a ruler.

Section 12.1

18. (a) Both are the same length. Measure to verify.
    (b) Both are the same length. Measure to verify.

Section 12.1

19. For these maps, it may be helpful to number the colors used as the regions are colored. For example, in the solution shown for part (a), we use color number 1 to color the region in the upper left-hand corner. Remember that if two regions touch in **more than one** point, they must be colored differently.
    (a) The map requires three colors.

    (b) The map requires only two colors.

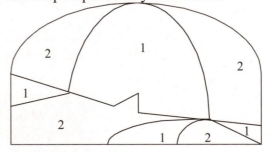

Section 12.1

20. (a) Use a ruler, protractor, or the eManipulative, *Geoboard – Triangular Lattice*, to attempt to draw parallel lines on dot paper. Notice that it can be done by drawing lines along two rows of dots or along any two columns of dots. Notice that other parallel lines can also be drawn. $l_1 \parallel l_2$ and $l_3 \parallel l_4$.

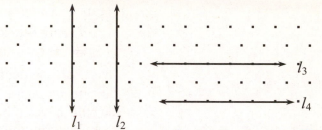

(b) If you attempt to draw perpendicular lines, you will see that by drawing a line along a row (horizontally) and a column (vertically), perpendicular lines result. Notice that other perpendicular lines are possible. In part (a), l_2 is perpendicular to l_3, l_1 is perpendicular to l_3, l_2 is perpendicular to l_4, and l_1 is perpendicular to l_4.

Section 12.1

21. (a) A rhombus is a quadrilateral having all four sides the same length. Notice that in the triangular lattice, the distance from any dot to every adjacent dot is the same. Connecting dots in the following manner forms a rhombus.

(b) Since every rhombus is also a parallelogram, and we can draw a rhombus on a triangular lattice, we can draw a parallelogram on a triangular lattice. A parallelogram that is not a rhombus is shown.

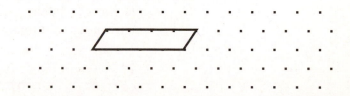

(c) Perpendicular lines can be drawn by constructing lines horizontally and vertically. Let x be the distance between a pair of adjacent dots. Consider any vertical column of dots. The distance between adjacent dots can be determined by the Pythagorean theorem to be $x\sqrt{3}$. Any horizontal segment would have length x, $2x$, $3x$, or some other whole number multiple of x. Any vertical segment would be a multiple of $x\sqrt{3}$. To create a square, the horizontal and vertical segments would have to be the same length. There is no whole number multiple of length x that will equal a whole number multiple of $x\sqrt{3}$. Therefore, a square, which is a quadrilateral with four right angles and equal side lengths, cannot be drawn on the triangular lattice. Similar reasoning holds for perpendicular lines that are not horizontal and vertical.

$$x^2 + b^2 = (2x)^2$$
$$b^2 = 4x^2 - x^2$$
$$b^2 = 3x^2$$
$$b = x\sqrt{3}$$

(d) We can construct a rectangle on a triangular lattice since four equal side lengths are not required. Four right angles are required, so perpendicular lines are needed. The sides of the rectangle can be horizontal and vertical. Choose any two rows and draw horizontal lines through them. Choose any two columns and draw vertical lines through them. The intersection points of the lines form the vertices of a rectangle. Notice that many other solutions are possible.

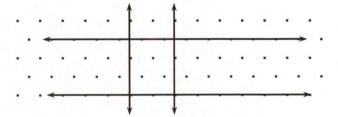

Section 12.1

22. (a) Consider the first two rows of dots. The following three parallelograms can be drawn:

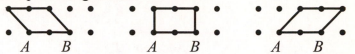

Similar parallelograms can be drawn for each of the other three rows of dots. Therefore, there is a total of (4 rows) × (3 parallelograms) = 12 parallelograms with $\overline{AB}$ as a side.

(b) Because rectangles are parallelograms that also have four right angles, none of the slanted parallelograms found in part (a) are rectangles. Therefore, only parallelograms that use dots directly above or below dots *A* and *B* form rectangles. See the middle figure above. There is only one rectangle formed with each of the other four rows. Therefore, four rectangles can be drawn.

(c) A rhombus has four equal side lengths. Thus, neither row adjacent to side $\overline{AB}$ will produce a rhombus since those rows are less than the length *AB* (2 units) away.

Also, row 5 is more than 2 units from side $\overline{AB}$. Only in row 4 will we find possible vertices for a rhombus. Connect points *A* and *B* to dots directly below them in row 4. Each side will be 2 units in length. This figure is a rhombus.

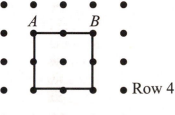

Connecting *A* and *B* to any other dots in row 4 produces a slanted quadrilateral whose side length is $\sqrt{5}$ units. Therefore, no slanted figure will be a rhombus. Only one rhombus can be drawn on the lattice.

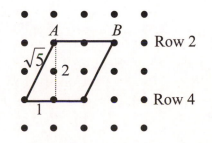

(d) Every square is a rhombus, and we found that there can be at most one rhombus. Because the rhombus in part (c) has four sides of length 2 units and four right angles, it is a square. Therefore, there is one square.

Section 12.1

23. Copy rectangle *ABCD*, including the diagonals. Flip the tracing and place it over the original so that the vertices of the original and the tracing correspond in the following way: *A* to *D*, *B* to *C*, *C* to *B*, and *D* to *A*. Notice that the diagonals are the same length.

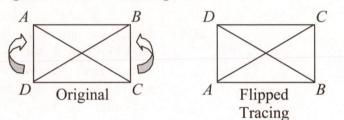

Section 12.2

11. Make several copies of the 3-shape.
    (i) The 3-shape can cover a 3 × 4 rectangle. Many solutions are possible.

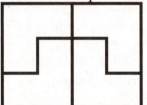

    (ii) The 3-shape cannot cover a 4 × 4 rectangle. A 4 × 4 rectangle contains a total of 16 squares. It is impossible to completely cover 16 squares with a shape containing 3 squares. Five of the 3-shapes could cover a total of 15 squares. Six of the 3-shapes could cover a total of 18 squares.

Section 12.2

12. Construct two copies of each tetromino on graph paper and cut out the pieces. Draw a 5 × 8 rectangle. The pieces fit together as shown in the next figure. Other solutions are possible.

Section 12.2

13. Copy the square. Rotate the figure clockwise about its center. See the figure. By rotating square *ABCD* one-quarter turn, the traced image coincides with the original square. Notice also that the tracing coincides with the original square after a $\frac{1}{2}$ turn and a $\frac{3}{4}$ turn. Therefore, the rotations of symmetry of a square are $\frac{1}{4}$, $\frac{1}{2}$, and $\frac{3}{4}$ of a full turn around the center.

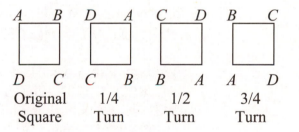

Section 12.2

14. Copy the equilateral triangle. The center of rotation is the intersection of the reflection lines. Label the triangle and rotate it clockwise $\frac{1}{3}$ of a turn until the traced triangle coincides with the original triangle. A $\frac{2}{3}$ turn will also cause the tracing to coincide with the original triangle.

Therefore, the rotations of symmetry of an equilateral triangle are $\frac{1}{3}$ and $\frac{2}{3}$ of a full turn around the center.

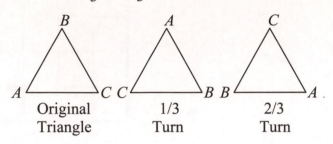

| Original | 1/3 | 2/3 |
| Triangle | Turn | Turn |

Section 12.2

15. Other quadrilaterals including the rhombus, square, and kite have diagonals which bisect opposite angles. Neither the isosceles trapezoid nor the rectangle have such a property. However, their diagonals are congruent.

Section 12.3

13. We know that $m(\angle BFC) = 55°$, and $m(\angle AFD) = 150° = m(\angle AFB) + m(\angle BFC) + m(\angle CFD)$.

By substitution, we have the following:
$$150° = m(\angle AFB) + 55° + m(\angle CFD)$$
$$95° = m(\angle AFB) + m(\angle CFD).$$

We are also given that $m(\angle BFE) = 120°$. Therefore, $m(\angle BFE) = 120° = m(\angle BFC) + m(\angle CFD) + m(\angle DFE)$. We see by substitution, $120° = 55° + m(\angle CFD) + (180° - 150°)$, since $\angle AFD$ and $\angle DFE$ are supplementary. Thus, $35° = m(\angle CFD)$ and $m(\angle AFB) = 95° - 35° = 60°$.

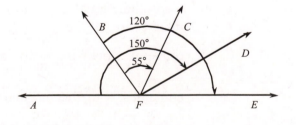

Section 12.3

14. Because the measure of $\angle 1$ is $9°$ less than half the measure of $\angle 2$, $m(\angle 1) = \dfrac{1}{2}m(\angle 2) - 9°$. Because $\angle 1$ and $\angle 2$ are supplementary, we know that $m(\angle 1) + m(\angle 2) = 180°$. By substitution, we have the following:

$$\left(\frac{1}{2}m(\angle 2) - 9°\right) + m(\angle 2) = 180°$$

$$\frac{3}{2}m(\angle 2) = 189°$$

$$m(\angle 2) = 126°$$

$$m(\angle 1) = 180° - 126° = 54°.$$

Therefore, $m(\angle 1) = 54°$ and $m(\angle 2) = 126°$.

Section 12.3

15. We are given that $m(\angle 1) = 80°$. We know the following:

By vertical angles, $m(\angle 11) = 80°$.

By supplementary angles, $m(\angle 2) = 180° - 80° = 100°$.

By supplementary angles, $m(\angle 12) = 180° - 80° = 100°$.

We are given that $m(\angle 4) = 125°$. We know the following:

By vertical angles, $m(\angle 6) = 125°$.

By supplementary angles, $m(\angle 5) = 180° - 125° = 55°$.

By supplementary angles, $m(\angle 7) = 180° - 125° = 55°$.

Because m and l are parallel, $\angle 1$ and $\angle 16$ are corresponding angles. We know the following:

By corresponding angles, $m(\angle 16) = 80°$.

By vertical angles, $m(\angle 18) = 80°$.

By supplementary angles, $m(\angle 17) = 180° - 80° = 100°$.

By supplementary angles, $m(\angle 15) = 180° - 80° = 100°$.

Because *m* and *l* are parallel, $\angle 4$ and $\angle 13$ are corresponding angles. We know the following:

By corresponding angles, $m(\angle 13) = 125°$.

By vertical angles, $m(\angle 19) = 125°$.

By supplementary angles, $m(\angle 14) = 180° - 125° = 55°$.

By supplementary angles, $m(\angle 20) = 180° - 125° = 55°$.

The measures of the angles in any triangle must add up to $180°$, so $m(\angle 10) + m(\angle 11) + m(\angle 14) = 180°$. By substitution, $m(\angle 10) = 180° - 80° - 55° = 45°$. We know the following:

By vertical angles, $m(\angle 8) = 45°$.

By supplementary angles, $m(\angle 9) = 180° - 45° = 135°$.

By supplementary angles, $m(\angle 3) = 180° - 45° = 135°$.

Section 12.3

16. We are given $m(\angle 1) = m(\angle 2)$. By vertical angles, we know $m(\angle 2) = m(\angle 3)$. By substitution, we know $m(\angle 1) = m(\angle 3)$, and thus $\angle 1 \cong \angle 3$. Notice that $\angle 1$ and $\angle 3$ are congruent corresponding angles. Therefore, $l \parallel m$, because corresponding angles are congruent.

Section 12.3

17. (a) Suppose $m(\angle 1) = m(\angle 6)$. We know $m(\angle 4) = m(\angle 6)$ by vertical angles. By substitution, we know $m(\angle 1) = m(\angle 4)$, so $\angle 1 \cong \angle 4$. Notice that $\angle 1$ and $\angle 4$ are corresponding angles. Because corresponding angles are congruent, $l \parallel m$.

   (b) If $l \parallel m$, then $m(\angle 3) = m(\angle 6)$ by corresponding angles. By vertical angles, $m(\angle 1) = m(\angle 3)$. By substitution, we have that $m(\angle 1) = m(\angle 6)$.

   (c) Two lines are parallel if, and only if, at least one pair of alternate exterior angles formed by the intersection of the two lines and the transversal have the same measure.

Section 12.3

18. Notice in the figure that $\angle 2$ and $\angle 3$ are corresponding angles. We know $m(\angle 2) = 90°$, because it is supplementary with a 90° angle, and $m(\angle 3) = 90°$ by vertical angles. Because $m(\angle 2) = 90° = m(\angle 3)$, we see that corresponding angles are congruent. Therefore, by the Corresponding Angles Property, lines $\overleftrightarrow{AB}$ and $\overleftrightarrow{DC}$ are parallel. Notice also that $\angle 1$ and $\angle 3$ are corresponding angles. $m(\angle 1) = 90°$ by supplementary angles. Because $m(\angle 1) = 90° = m(\angle 3)$, we see that corresponding angles are congruent. Therefore, by the Corresponding Angles Property, lines $\overleftrightarrow{AD}$ and $\overleftrightarrow{BC}$ are parallel. Because there are two pairs of opposite sides parallel, the quadrilateral $ABCD$ is a parallelogram.

Section 12.3

19. Notice that each angle measures $90°$. The angle formed by connecting the two endpoints of a semicircle and any point on the perimeter of the semicircle is a $90°$ angle.

Section 12.3

20. Draw pictures and count the number of regions into which the plane is divided by each set of lines. Make a table. Keep in mind that two lines can intersect in at most one point. To maximize the number of regions, each new line should intersect each existing line once. When introducing a third line, be sure to construct it so that it intersects each of the existing lines at different points.

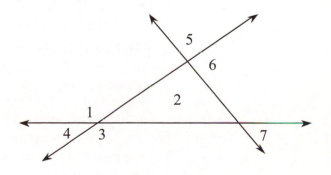

We see that three lines divide the plane into at most seven regions. Consider four lines. To maximize the number of regions, construct the fourth line so that it intersects each of the three existing lines in different places. Avoid previous intersection points.

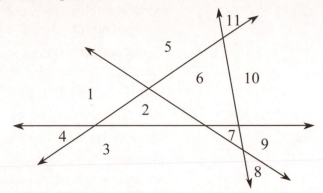

We see that four lines divide the plane into at most eleven regions.

Now consider five lines. Construct the fifth line so that it intersects each of the four existing lines in different places. Avoid all previous intersection points.

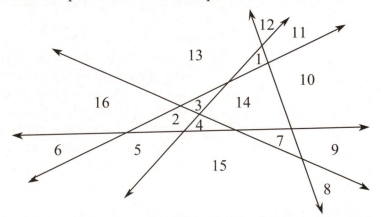

We see that five lines divide the plane into at most sixteen regions. We will summarize our results and look for a pattern in the table shown next.

Number of Lines	Number of Regions
1	$2 = 1 + 1$
2	$4 = 1 + 1 + 2$
3	$7 = 1 + 1 + 2 + 3$
4	$11 = 1 + 1 + 2 + 3 + 4$
5	$16 = 1 + 1 + 2 + 3 + 4 + 5$
$\vdots$	
10	$56 = 1 + 1 + 2 + 3 + 4 + 5 + 6 + 7 + 8 + 9 + 10$
$\vdots$	
n	$1 + 1 + 2 + 3 + 4 + 5 + \ldots + (n-1) + n$ $= 1 + n\text{th triangular number}$ $= 1 + \dfrac{n(n+1)}{2}$

Therefore, we see that the greatest number of regions into which the plane can be divided by n lines is $1 + \dfrac{n(n+1)}{2}$.

Section 12.3

21. Access Geometer's Sketchpad® and follow the instructions in the problem. The angle formed by connecting the endpoints of a radius of a circle with any point on the perimeter of the circle is a 90° angle. This is consistent with the results from problem 19.

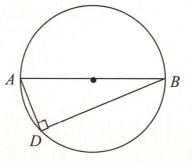

Section 12.3

22. Access the Chapter 12 eManipulative *Geoboard-Square Lattice*.

    (a) An acute triangle has three acute angles and can be drawn on a square lattice as shown next. Many acute triangles are possible.

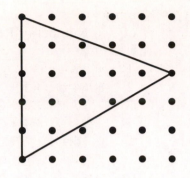

(b) An obtuse triangle has one obtuse angle and can be drawn on a square lattice as shown next. Many obtuse triangles are possible.

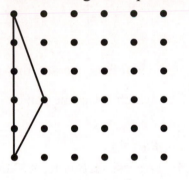

(c) An equilateral triangle has three congruent sides and cannot be drawn on a square lattice.

Section 12.4

22. (a) (i) The figures do not intersect.
(ii) The figures intersect in one point.
(iii) The figures must overlap for them to intersect in two points.
(iv) The figures must overlap as in part (iii). Continue moving the square into the circle until a vertex of the square just touches the inside of the circle. In this way, the figures will intersect in three points.

(b) We have drawn the figures so that they intersect in one, two, or three points. To draw figures that intersect in four points, draw the circle inside the square or draw the square inside the circle.

(i)

(ii)

(iii)

(iv)

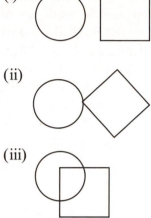

Circle Inside Square
4 Intersection Points

Square Inside Circle
4 Intersection Points

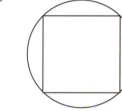

Consider the figure with the square inside the circle. If we reduce the radius of the circle, keeping the centers of both figures the same, eventually the circle will intersect each side of the square twice. This gives eight intersection points, two on each side of the square. There is no way for a circle to intersect the side of a square in more than two points. Therefore, the maximum number of intersection points of a square and a circle is eight.

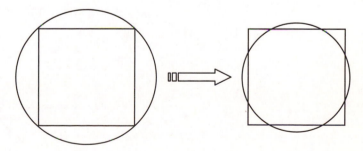

Section 12.4

23. Notice the small white triangle, surrounded by shaded squares, is a right triangle. Consider the areas of the shaded squares. The largest shaded square is made up of four such small triangles. The two smaller shaded squares are each made up of two such small triangles, for a total of four small triangles. If we let a and b represent the lengths of the two short sides of this small, white right triangle, then a^2 and b^2 represent the areas of the small squares. If we let c represent the length of the hypotenuse of the small right triangle, then c^2 represents the area of the large square. Thus, $a^2 + b^2 = c^2$.

Section 12.4

24. $\angle d$: Because the sum of the measures of the angles in a triangle is $180°$, $m(\angle d) = 180° - 110° - 50° = 20°$.

$\angle e$: Because $\angle d$ and $\angle e$ make up one angle in a right triangle, and we know $m(\angle d)$, we know the following:

$$m(\angle e) = 180° - 50° - 90° - m(\angle d)$$

$$= 180° - 50° - 90° - 20°$$

$$= 20°.$$

$\angle c$: Because $\angle c$ is supplementary with a $60°$ angle, we know that $m(\angle c) = 180° - 60° = 120°$.

$\angle g$: Let x be the angle shown below. Because $\angle g$ is congruent, by vertical angles, to $\angle x$ and we know $m(\angle x) = 180° - 90° - 30° = 60°$, $m(\angle g) = 60°$.

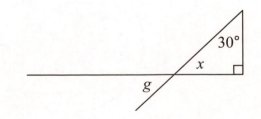

$\angle f$: $m(\angle f) = 180° - 40° - 60° = 80°$.

$\angle a$: Because $\angle a$ is congruent to $\angle y$ (as shown next),
$m(\angle a) = m(\angle y)$.

$$m(\angle a) + m(\angle y) + 40° = 180°$$

$$2m(\angle a) = 140° \quad \text{By substitution}$$

$$m(\angle a) = 70°.$$

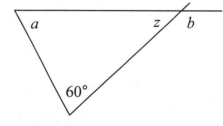

$\angle b$: Notice, in the figure below, $\angle b$ is supplementary to $\angle z$ and we know $m(\angle z) = 180° - 60° - m(\angle a)$, then by substitution we know $m(\angle z) = 180° - 60° - 70° = 50°$. Thus, we have $m(\angle b) = 180° - 50° = 130°$.

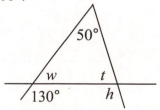

$\angle h$: Because we know $m(\angle b)$, we can find $m(\angle w)$, as labeled below, by supplementary angles. $m(\angle w) = 180° - m(\angle b) = 180° - 130° = 50°$ and $m(\angle t) = 180° - 50° - 50° = 80°$. Because $\angle h$ and $\angle t$ are supplementary angles, we know that $m(\angle h) = 180° - 80° = 100°$.

Section 12.4

25. For each polygon, count the number of vertices, diagonals from each vertex, and total number of diagonals. Sketches of the figures including the diagonals will be helpful.

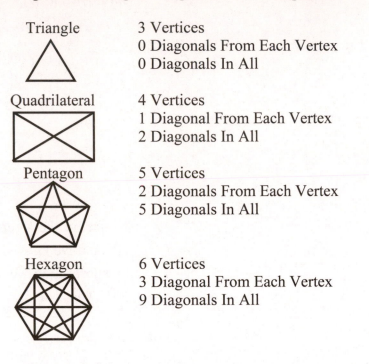

Triangle   3 Vertices
                        0 Diagonals From Each Vertex
                        0 Diagonals In All

Quadrilateral   4 Vertices
                        1 Diagonal From Each Vertex
                        2 Diagonals In All

Pentagon   5 Vertices
                        2 Diagonals From Each Vertex
                        5 Diagonals In All

Hexagon   6 Vertices
                        3 Diagonal From Each Vertex
                        9 Diagonals In All

Fill in the table and look for a pattern or relationship that will allow you to express V, D, and T for an n-gon.

Polygon	V	D	T
Triangle	3	0	0
Quadrilateral	4	1	2
Pentagon	5	2	5
Hexagon	6	3	9

At this point, notice that for each polygon with n sides, there are n vertices. Therefore, $V = n$. For each n-gon, there are $n - 3$ diagonals from each vertex. Therefore, $D = n - 3$. For each n-gon, the total number of diagonals is $T = \dfrac{1}{2}(VD)$ since each diagonal connects two vertices.

We can use these results to find the number of diagonals in other polygons.

Heptagon ($n = 7$) $V = 7$ $D = 7 - 3$ $T = \dfrac{1}{2}(7 \cdot 4) = 14$

Octagon ($n = 8$) $V = 8$ $D = 8 - 3$ $T = \dfrac{1}{2}(8 \cdot 5) = 20$

n-gon ($n = n$) $V = n$ $D = n - 3$ $T = \dfrac{1}{2}n(n - 3)$

Section 12.4

26. Consider a simpler problem. Suppose there were only four people in the room. Let the four people be represented by *A*, *B*, *C*, and *D*. Make a systematic list of all possible handshakes. Keep in mind that a handshake between *A* and *B*, "*AB*", is the same as a handshake between *B* and *A*, "*BA*". Avoid counting handshakes twice.

Handshakes: *AB*
     AC *BC*
     AD *BD* *CD*

When there are four people, there are 6 possible handshakes.

Suppose there are 5 people: *A*, *B*, *C*, *D*, and *E*.

Handshakes: *AB*
     AC *BC*
     AD *BD* *CD*
     AE *BE* *CE* *DE*

When there are 5 people, there are 10 possible handshakes.

Number of People	Number of Handshakes
4	$6 = 1 + 2 + 3$
5	$10 = 1 + 2 + 3 + 4$

Notice a pattern in the number of handshakes. The number of handshakes possible among *n* people is the sum of the first $n - 1$ counting numbers. Therefore, if there are 20 people, the number of handshakes possible is $1 + 2 + 3 + 4 + \ldots + 18 + 19 = \dfrac{19 \times 20}{2} = 190$ handshakes.

Section 12.4

27. The center figure in the star is a regular pentagon. Each vertex angle measures 108° by the Angle Measure Theorem in a regular *n*-gon. By supplementary angles, each base angle in each triangle has measure $180° - 108° = 72°$. Because the sum of the angles in any triangle is 180°, each angle of the star ($\angle A$, $\angle B$, $\angle C$, $\angle D$, and $\angle E$) measures $180° - 72° - 72° = 36°$. Therefore, the sum of the angle measures in the star is $m(\angle A) + m(\angle B) + m(\angle C) + m(\angle D) + m(\angle E) = 5(36°) = 180°$.

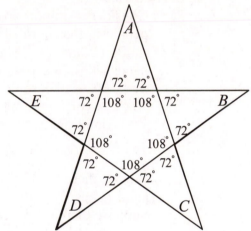

Section 12.4

28. Consider the following portion of the tiling.

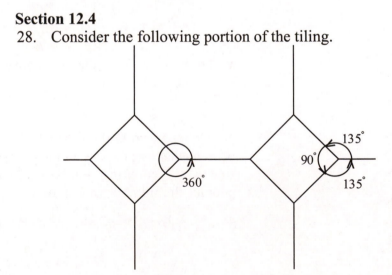

Recall that the number of degrees in a circle is 360. We know that each angle in a square measures 90°. The remaining 270° is divided into two equal angles, each measuring 135°. Therefore, each of the angles that form the octagon measures 135°.

Section 12.4

29. For each pair of polygons, draw pictures and try overlapping and intersecting them in various ways. Try different sizes and positions for each polygon.

(a) A triangle and a square can intersect in at most six points because the square cannot intersect any of the three sides of the triangle in more than two places.

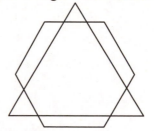

(b) A triangle and a hexagon can intersect in at most six points because the hexagon cannot intersect any of the three sides of the triangle in more than two places.

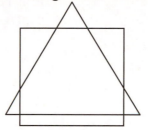

(c) A square and a pentagon can intersect in at most eight points because the pentagon cannot intersect any of the four sides of the square in more than two places.

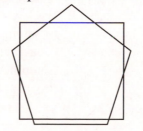

(d) An *n*-gon $(n \geq 2)$ and a *p*-gon can intersect in at most $2n$ points if $n \leq p$ because the *p*-gon cannot intersect any of the *n* sides of the *n*-gon in more than two places. If $n > p$, then the maximum number of points of intersection is $2p$.

Section 12.4

30. Access Geometer's Sketchpad®, construct a five-point star, measure the angles, and add the measures of the angles.
(a) No matter how the vertices are moved, the sum of the measured angles at the points is 180°.
(b) No matter how the vertices are moved, the inside shape is a pentagon. The sum of the interior angles of a pentagon is 540°.

$$m(\angle v) + m(\angle w) + m(\angle x) + m(\angle y) + m(\angle z) = 540°.$$

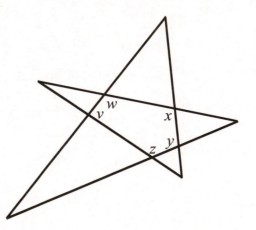

No matter how the vertices are moved, there are five triangles in the figure. The sum of the angles in one triangle is 180°. The sum of the angles in five triangles is $5(180°) = 900°$.

No matter how the vertices are moved, angles from each triangle and interior angles of the pentagon are supplementary.

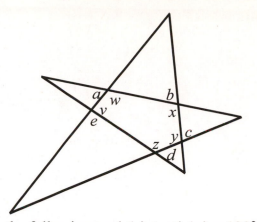

We have the following: $m(\angle a) + m(\angle w) = 180°$
$m(\angle b) + m(\angle x) = 180°$
$m(\angle c) + m(\angle y) = 180°$
$m(\angle d) + m(\angle z) = 180°$
$m(\angle e) + m(\angle v) = 180°$

Adding the five equations, we have the following:

$$m(\angle a) + m(\angle b) + m(\angle c) + m(\angle d) + m(\angle e) +$$
$$m(\angle w) + m(\angle x) + m(\angle y) + m(\angle z) + m(\angle v) = 900°$$

$$m(\angle a) + m(\angle b) + m(\angle c) + m(\angle d) + m(\angle e) +$$
$$\text{(sum of interior angles of a pentagon)} = 900°$$

$$m(\angle a) + m(\angle b) + m(\angle c) + m(\angle d) + m(\angle e) + (540°) = 900°$$

$$m(\angle a) + m(\angle b) + m(\angle c) + m(\angle d) + m(\angle e) = 360°$$

Notice in the figure below that there are five sets of vertical angles. Vertical angles are congruent and are marked with the same letter.

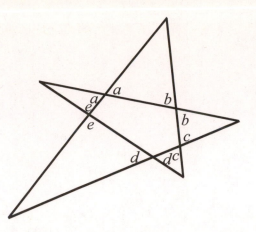

Sum of the angles in five triangles = 900°

Sum of five angles at the points + 2($m\angle$a + $m\angle$b + $m\angle$c + $m\angle$d + $m\angle$e) = 900°

Sum of five angles at the points + 2(360°) = 900°

Sum of five angles at the points + 720° = 900°

Sum of five angles at the points = 180°

No matter how the vertices are moved, the sum of the measured angles at the points is still 180°.

Section 12.4

31. Label the vertices of the hexagon *A* through *F*.

   (a) Consider the center of the hexagon. Draw a rhombus so that two adjacent sides $\overline{AB}$ and $\overline{AF}$ lie on the hexagon, and the opposite vertex is at the center of the hexagon. By connecting the center of the hexagon to vertices *B* and *F*, one rhombus is formed. If you construct the segment that connects the center of the hexagon to vertex *D*, two more rhombuses will be formed.

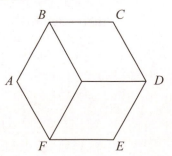

(b) Connect the center of the hexagon to the midpoints of each of the six sides. Six kites will be formed. Notice that the kites are not rhombuses.

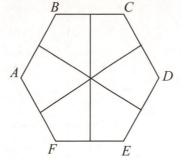

Section 12.5

17. (a) The figure appears to be a cube sitting in a corner. It also appears to be a cube situated on an outer corner of a cube. It changes as you point of focus changes. Try focusing on the white face of the little cube. Then focus on the shaded sides of the small cube.

(b) Imagine a person walking along the steps at the top of the figure. If the person walks clockwise, then the person will appear to be walking downstairs. If the person walks counterclockwise, then the person will appear to be walking upstairs. It is impossible to locate the highest step if we move clockwise. Each corner is higher than the other steps.

Section 12.5

18. Assume there are 9 cubes that form the first layer of the figure. Some cubes are hidden, but we will assume they are there. There are 4 cubes that form the second layer and 1 cube that forms the third layer. Thus, there is a total of 14 cubes in the stack.

Section 12.5

19. Pay close attention to the orientation of the A and F on the original cube. Both are upright. If the original cube is tipped over counterclockwise, so that it sits on the face opposite the F, then the A and F will both be sideways as in options (a) and (c). Tipping the cube in this manner would place the face with the B on it out of view, so option (c) is the correct choice.

Section 12.5

20. (a)   Top   Front   Right side

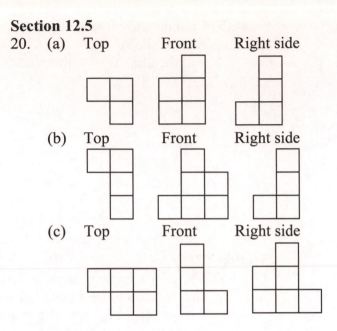

    (b)   Top   Front   Right side

    (c)   Top   Front   Right side

Section 12.5

21. (a) Notice in the front of the shape, there is one cube next two cubes, which is next to three cubes. The base design will have a 1, 2, and 3 in the same row. The only base design that has this is (ii).

    (b) (i)

3	3	3	3
1	2	3	3
1	2	2	3
1	1	1	3

    (ii)

3	2	4	2
3	2	4	2

Section 12.5

22. Make a model and compare each of the choices given to your model. When comparing your cube to the choices, be sure your model has the same orientation. That is, be sure you can see the front, top, and left side.
    (a) The net will fold to become cube (iii).
    (b) The net will fold to become cube (v).

Section 12.5

23. (a) Because there are three sets of opposite faces, there are three planes of symmetry of this type.

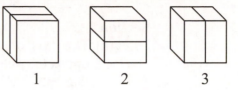

1   2   3

(b)   There are twelve edges on a cube, which means there are six sets of opposite edges. Therefore, there are six planes of symmetry of this type.

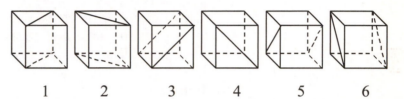

1   2   3   4   5   6

(c) The only planes of symmetry result from cutting the cube midway between opposite faces or from cutting through pairs of opposite edges. Because there are three and six of these types of symmetries, respectively, there are only nine planes of symmetry for a cube.

Section 12.5

24.   The axis of rotation passes through pairs of opposite faces of the cube. Because there are three pairs of opposite faces, there are three axes of symmetry of order four in a cube.

Section 12.5

25.   (a) Three faces of the cube shown in the text meet at one vertex. When the cube is in its original position, one of these faces is showing. (Face E is the one showing in the picture when the cube is in its original position.) As the cube is rotated on the axis, the "original" arrangement appears each time another face rotates into the position that E held. Therefore, since there are three faces that can occupy the position that E held, the order is three.

(b) Because there are eight vertices, there are four sets of opposite pairs. Therefore, there are four axes of symmetry for this cube of order three.

Section 12.5

26. (a) The axis of rotation passes through the midpoints of opposite edges. For any single edge, two faces meet at that edge. When the cube is in its original position, one of these two faces is showing. As the cube is rotated on the axis, it will only return to its original position when the other of the two faces is showing. Therefore, since there are two faces under consideration, the order is two.

    (b) Because there are twelve edges on a cube, there are six pairs of opposite edges. Therefore, there are six possible axes of symmetry of this type.

Section 12.5

27. The center tube for a paper towel roll is a cylinder. Notice there are spiral seam lines on any paper towel roll. Cut along the seam line and unroll the cardboard. The piece of cardboard from which the tube was made is a long parallelogram.

Original Roll   Unrolled

Section 12.5

28. The goal is to use four slices to cut away parts of the cube so that you are left with a regular tetrahedron. This may take some practice.

Regular Tetrahedron   Cube

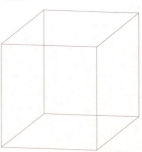

It will help to visualize how a regular tetrahedron would be situated inside a cube. Align each edge of the tetrahedron along the diagonal of a face of the cube. This will enable you to see where to make the cuts.

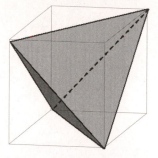

Make four cuts identical to the one shown next so that each of the corners of the cube not touched by a vertex of the tetrahedron are removed.

SOLUTIONS - PART A PROBLEMS

Chapter 13: Measurement

Section 13.1

23. Use dimensional analysis and the facts that 1 gallon of water weighs about 8.3 pounds and that 1 cubic foot of water weighs 62 pounds to convert to gallons.

$$62 \text{ pounds} \times \frac{1 \text{ gallon}}{8.3 \text{ pounds}} = \frac{62}{8.3} \text{ gallons} \approx 7.5 \text{ gallons}.$$

Therefore, there are about 7.5 gallons in one cubic foot of water.

Section 13.1

24. To find the approximate number of red blood cells in the body of an adult male, use the fact that there are about 5.4×10^6 cells per microliter of blood. The 70-kg man has a blood volume of about 5 liters. Recall that there are 1 million microliters (μL) in 1 liter.

$$5 \text{ L} \times \frac{1,000,000 \ \mu\text{L}}{1 \text{ L}} \times \frac{5.4 \times 10^6 \text{ red blood cells}}{1 \ \mu\text{L}} = 2.7 \times 10^{13}.$$

Therefore, there are about 2.7×10^{13} red blood cells in the body of an adult male.

Section 13.1

25. (a) Recall that there are 1000 grams in a kilogram, and there are 10 centimeters in 1 decimeter, so there are 1000 cm³ in 1 dm³.

$$\frac{8.94 \text{ g}}{1 \text{ cm}^3} \times \frac{1000 \text{ cm}^3}{1 \text{ dm}^3} \times \frac{1 \text{ kg}}{1000 \text{ g}} = 8.94 \frac{\text{kg}}{\text{dm}^3}.$$

The density of copper is 8.94 kg/dm³.

(b) Since density $= \dfrac{\text{mass}}{\text{volume}}$, the wood has a density of $\dfrac{2.85 \text{ kg}}{4100 \text{ cm}^3}$. Convert to $\dfrac{\text{grams}}{\text{cm}^3}$ using dimensional analysis.

$$\frac{2.85 \text{ kg}}{4100 \text{ cm}^3} \times \frac{1000 \text{ g}}{1 \text{ kg}} \approx 0.695 \frac{\text{g}}{\text{cm}^3}.$$

Therefore, the density of oak is about $0.695 \dfrac{\text{g}}{\text{cm}^3}$.

(c) Recall that 16 ounces = 1 pound, 2.2 pounds = 1 kilogram, 1 kilogram = 1000 grams, and 2.54 centimeters = 1 inch. Thus, $(2.54 \text{ centimeters})^3 = (1 \text{ inch})^3$, so $16.387 \text{ cm}^3 \approx 1 \text{ in}^3$.

$$\dfrac{45 \text{ oz}}{10 \text{ in}^3} \times \dfrac{1 \text{ lb}}{16 \text{ oz}} \times \dfrac{1 \text{ kg}}{2.2 \text{ lb}} \times \dfrac{1000 \text{ g}}{1 \text{ kg}} \times \dfrac{1 \text{ in}^3}{16.387 \text{ cm}^3} \approx 7.8 \dfrac{\text{g}}{\text{cm}^3}.$$

Therefore, the density of iron is about $7.8 \dfrac{\text{g}}{\text{cm}^3}$.

Section 13.1

26. The English system is not portable since it cannot be reproduced without reference to a prototype. The natural English units were standardized so that the foot was defined by a prototype metal bar. Because of this, the foot cannot be reproduced anywhere that there is no prototype available. In the English system, there are not simple (decimal) ratios among units of the same type. This means it is not easily convertible. The natural progression of units in the English system is inches, feet, yards, and miles. There are 12 inches in 1 foot, 3 feet in 1 yard, and 1760 yards in 1 mile. There is no direct interrelatedness in the English system. Conversions would be relatively simple if cubic inches, quarts, and pounds were related because they are basic units of length, volume, and weight.

Section 13.1

27. (a) We would like to convert miles per second to miles per year using conversion ratios.

$$\dfrac{186{,}282 \text{ miles}}{1 \text{ second}} \times \dfrac{60 \text{ seconds}}{1 \text{ minute}} \times \dfrac{60 \text{ minutes}}{1 \text{ hour}} \times \dfrac{24 \text{ hours}}{1 \text{ day}} \times \dfrac{365 \text{ days}}{1 \text{ year}} \approx 5.8746 \times 10^{12} \dfrac{\text{miles}}{\text{year}}.$$

Therefore, the distance that light travels in one year is approximately 5.8746×10^{12} miles.

(b) Since 1 light year $\approx 5.8746 \times 10^{12}$ miles, and the star in Andromeda is 76 light years away, the light will travel

$$76 \text{ light years} \times \dfrac{5.8746 \times 10^{12} \text{ miles}}{1 \text{ light year}} \approx 4.4647 \times 10^{14} \text{ miles}.$$

(c) Since we know 1 light year $\approx 5.8746 \times 10^{12}$ miles, we will use this conversion ratio to convert 480,000,000 miles to years.

$$480,000,000 \text{ miles} \times \frac{1 \text{ year}}{5.8746 \times 10^{12} \text{ miles}} \times \frac{365 \text{ days}}{1 \text{ year}} \times \frac{24 \text{ hours}}{1 \text{ day}} \times \frac{60 \text{ minutes}}{1 \text{ hour}}$$

$$\approx 42.9456 \text{ minutes.}$$

Therefore, it takes approximately 43 minutes for the light to travel from the sun to Jupiter.

Section 13.1

28. If you are a passenger in a train moving 50 mph, and you observe a train traveling in the opposite direction at 50 mph, it will seem as though the train is passing you by at 100 mph. We need to determine how far a train traveling at 100 mph would go in 5 seconds. If we convert the speed to feet per second, we can determine how far the train travels in feet.

$$\frac{100 \text{ miles}}{1 \text{ hour}} \times \frac{5280 \text{ feet}}{1 \text{ mile}} \times \frac{1 \text{ hour}}{3600 \text{ seconds}} = 146\frac{2}{3} \frac{\text{feet}}{\text{second}}.$$

Since rate × time = distance, we know that the length of the train is $146\frac{2}{3} \frac{\text{feet}}{\text{second}} \times 5 \text{ seconds} = 733\frac{1}{3} \text{ feet.}$

Section 13.1

29. (a) To determine the number of cubic inches of water, we need to convert 1 acre of ground into square inches.

$$1 \text{ acre} = 43,560 \text{ ft}^2 \times \frac{144 \text{ in}^2}{1 \text{ ft}^2} = 6,272,640 \text{ in}^2.$$

Since 1 inch of rain fell, the number of cubic inches is 6,272,640 in^2 × 1 in = 6,272,640 in^3. To determine what this volume is in cubic feet, use the fact that 1 acre = 43,560 ft^2. We know that 1 inch = $\frac{1}{12}$ foot, so

1 inch of rain covering 1 acre = 43,560 ft^2 × $\frac{1}{12}$ ft = 3630 ft^3.

(b) One cubic foot of water weighs approximately 62 pounds. Use this fact to convert the weight of 3630 cubic feet of water into pounds. From part (a), we know that one inch of rain covering one acre of ground has a volume of 3630 ft^3. Thus, the water weight is calculated as follows:

$$3630\,\text{ft}^3 \times \frac{62\,\text{pounds}}{1\,\text{ft}^3} = 225{,}060\,\text{pounds}.$$

Therefore, the water weighs 225,060 pounds.

(c) One gallon of water weighs approximately 8.3 pounds. From part (b), we know that 225,060 pounds of water fell. $225{,}060\ \text{pounds} \times \dfrac{1\,\text{gallon}}{8.3\,\text{pounds}} \approx 27{,}116$ gallons.

Therefore, approximately 27,116 gallons of water fell.

Section 13.1

30. (a) If the ruler had marks at only 1, 4, and 6, then it would look like the ruler below. (Note: 8 is automatically marked.)

To measure a length of
1, use the distance from the left end to 1.
2, use the distance from 4 to 6.
3, use the distance from 1 to 4.
4, use the distance from the left end to 4.
5, use the distance from 1 to 6.
6. use the distance from the left end to 6.
7, use the distance from 1 to 8.
8, use the distance from the left end to 8.

(b) To measure a length of 1, we could have a mark one unit from either end. Place a mark one unit from the left end. Notice that we can measure a length of 1, a length of 8 (by using the distance from 1 to 9) and a length of 9 (by using the whole ruler). To measure a length of 2, place a mark three units from the left. Notice that we can measure a length of 2 (by using the distance from 1 to 3), a length of 3 (by using the distance from the left end to 3), and a length of 6 (by using the distance from 3 to 9). Placing a mark five units from the left allows us to measure a length of 4 (by using 1 to 5) and a length of 5 (by using the left end to 5). Finally, to measure a length of 7, place a mark seven units from the left.

| 1 | 3 | 5 | 7 | 9 |

Our solution is one of several possible solutions which use the minimum of 4 marks. There are others, such as placing marks at 1, 2, 3, and 5; placing marks at 1, 3, 5, and 8; or placing marks at 1, 4, 6, and 7.

(c) On a 10-unit ruler, place a mark 1 unit from the left. This will allow us to measure lengths of 1, 9, and 10. If a mark is placed 3 units from the left, then we will be able to measure lengths of 2, 3, and 7. If we place a mark 6 units from the left, then we will be able to measure lengths of 4, 5, and 6. A mark placed 8 units from the left will allow us to measure a length of 8.

| 1 | 3 | 6 | 8 | 10 |

Another solution using the minimum of four marks has marks at 1, 4, 6, and 8.

Section 13.1

31. (a) Together they cut 48 ft^3 in 1 hour. There are $4 \times 4 \times 8 = 128$ ft^3 in a cord of wood. Using conversion ratios, we can convert from 48 ft^3 per hour to dollars per day.

$$\frac{48\,\text{ft}^3}{1\,\text{hour}} \times \frac{8\,\text{hours}}{1\,\text{day}} \times \frac{1\,\text{cord}}{128\,\text{ft}^3} \times \frac{\$100}{1\,\text{cord}} = \$300 \text{ per day}.$$

(b) If they split the money evenly, the son would earn $150 for 8 hours of work or $\dfrac{\$150}{8\,\text{hours}} = \$18.75$ per hour.

(c) In one day they cut $\dfrac{48\,\text{ft}^3}{1\,\text{hour}} \times \dfrac{8\,\text{hours}}{1\,\text{day}} = \dfrac{384\,\text{ft}^3}{1\,\text{day}}$. Since the truck can hold 100 ft^3 per trip, it would take 4 trips to deliver all the wood cut in a day. Notice that 3 truck loads are full, and the last truck carries only 84 ft^3.

(d) Since the truck holds 100 ft^3 of wood, and they sell it for $85, we can convert from dollars per cubic foot to dollars per cord.

$$\frac{\$85}{100 \text{ ft}^3} \times \frac{128 \text{ ft}^3}{1 \text{ cord}} = \$108.80 \text{ per cord.}$$

Section 13.1

32. Let d represent the distance from the bottom of the hill to the summit. Since distance = rate × time, we know that $t = \dfrac{d}{r}$. The time uphill = $\dfrac{d}{2}$. The time downhill = $\dfrac{d}{6}$. The total time for the entire trip is $\dfrac{d}{2} + \dfrac{d}{6} = \dfrac{2d}{3}$. The total distance for the entire trip is $2d$. Therefore, the rate for the entire trip is given by the following fraction:

$$\frac{\text{distance for the entire trip}}{\text{time for the entire trip}} = \frac{2d}{\frac{2d}{3}} = 3 \frac{\text{km}}{\text{hour}}.$$

Thus, the average speed for the trip is $3 \dfrac{\text{km}}{\text{hour}}$.

Section 13.1

33. Use the technique of dimensional analysis.

$$\frac{1,000,000,000 \text{ people}}{1} \times \frac{1 \text{ row}}{4 \text{ people}} \times \frac{1 \text{ minute}}{25 \text{ rows}} = \frac{1,000,000,000 \text{ minutes}}{100}$$

$$= 10,000,000 \text{ minutes.}$$

Convert this period of time to years.

$$\frac{10,000,000 \text{ minutes}}{1} \times \frac{1 \text{ hour}}{60 \text{ minutes}} \times \frac{1 \text{ day}}{24 \text{ hours}} \times \frac{1 \text{ year}}{365 \text{ days}} \approx 19 \text{ years.}$$

Section 13.1

34. Use dimensional analysis to determine the height of a stack of 80 billion hamburgers in miles.

$$\frac{80,000,000,000 \text{ hamburgers}}{1} \times \frac{0.5 \text{ inch}}{1 \text{ hamburger}} \times \frac{1 \text{ foot}}{12 \text{ inches}} \times \frac{1 \text{ mile}}{5280 \text{ feet}} \approx 631,313 \text{ miles.}$$

To find the percent of the distance to the moon that is the height of a stack of 80 billion hamburgers, form the ratio comparing the height of the stack of hamburgers to the distance to the moon. Then make it a percent by multiplying by 100.

$$\frac{631,313}{240,000} \times 100 \approx 263\%.$$

Therefore, the height of a stack of 80 billion hamburgers is about 263% of the distance from the earth to the moon.

Section 13.2

27. Notice, in the following picture, that the wall of the building, the ground, and the ladder form a right triangle, since the ground and the wall of the building are perpendicular. By the Pythagorean theorem, we know $15^2 + 20^2 = x^2$, so $625 = x^2$, and $25 = x$. Therefore, the ladder is 25 feet long.

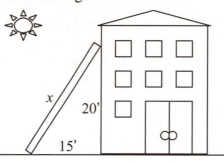

Section 13.2

28. Recall that the area of a rectangle is length × width. Area = $x \times y$. Since 96 meters of fencing are used, we know that $2x + y = 96$. Make a table of whole-number values of x and y that satisfy $2x + y = 96$ and compare areas.

x	y	$2x + y$	$A = x \times y$
1	94	96	94
2	92	96	184
3	90	96	270
4	88	96	352
5	86	96	430
6	84	96	504
7	82	96	574
8	80	96	640
9	78	96	702
10	76	96	760
11	74	96	814
12	72	96	864

13	70	96	910
14	68	96	952
15	66	96	990
16	64	96	1024
17	62	96	1054
18	60	96	1080
19	58	96	1102
20	56	96	1120
21	54	96	1134
22	52	96	1144
23	50	96	1150
24	48	96	1152
25	46	96	1150

Notice that areas increase until the width is exactly half as big as the length. After that point, the areas decrease. Therefore, the whole-number dimensions that yield the largest area are $x = 24$ m and $y = 48$ m.

Section 13.2

29. Consider a picture, as shown. Since the plane has a wingspan of 7.1 feet, it will have to be carried diagonally through the door, which is only $6\frac{1}{2}$ feet tall. Let the diagonal of the door have length c. Notice that the diagonal is the hypotenuse of a right triangle with legs 3 feet and $6\frac{1}{2}$ feet. By the Pythagorean theorem $3^2 + (6.5)^2 = c^2$, so $9 + 42.25 = 51.25 = c^2$. Therefore, $c \approx 7.159$ feet. He should just be able to get the plane through the door.

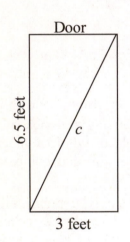

Section 13.2

30. The area of the large figure is the area of a square with side length c. Area $= c^2$. Consider one of the right triangles. The legs of the triangle are a and b, so the area is $\frac{1}{2}ba$.

Four right triangles have an area of $4\left(\frac{1}{2}ba\right) = 2ba$. The small square has side lengths $b - a$, so its area is $(b - a)^2$. The sum of the areas of the four triangles and the small square is equal to the area of the large square figure. So we have the following:

$$c^2 = 4\left(\frac{1}{2}ab\right) + (b-a)^2$$

$$c^2 = 2ab + b^2 - 2ab + a^2$$

$$c^2 = a^2 + b^2.$$

BEHOLD!

Section 13.2

31. In the diagram, let m represent the length of $\overline{AB}$ and n represent the length of $\overline{AC}$.

    (a) By the Pythagorean theorem, we know $l^2 + w^2 = m^2$.

    Therefore, $m = \sqrt{l^2 + w^2}$.

    (b) Notice that $\triangle ABC$ is a right triangle with sides m and h and hypotenuse n. By the Pythagorean theorem, $m^2 + h^2 = n^2$. Therefore, $n = \sqrt{m^2 + h^2}$. From part (a) since $l^2 + w^2 = m^2$, $n = \sqrt{l^2 + w^2 + h^2}$.

    (c) A rectangular box that has a width (w) of 40 cm, length (l) of 60 cm, and height (h) of 20 cm, has the length of the longest diagonal given by $n = \sqrt{l^2 + w^2 + h^2}$ from part (b). Therefore, the longest diagonal has a length of $\sqrt{60^2 + 40^2 + 20^2} = \sqrt{5600} \approx 74.8$ cm.

Section 13.2

32. An old trunk can be considered a rectangular prism with length 30 inches, width 16 inches, and height 12 inches. From problem 31 we know the length of the longest diagonal is found as follows:

    $$\sqrt{l^2 + w^2 + h^2} = \sqrt{30^2 + 16^2 + 12^2} = \sqrt{1300} \approx 36.06 \text{ in.}$$

    (a) A telescope measuring 40 inches would *not* fit diagonally into the trunk.

    (b) A baseball bat measuring 34 inches would fit diagonally into the trunk.

    (c) A tennis racket measuring 32 inches would fit diagonally into the trunk. Therefore, Jason could store the baseball bat and the tennis racket in the trunk.

Section 13.2

33. (a) Without using Pick's Theorem, we could try to divide the polygonal region into polygons whose areas we can calculate. Notice, however, that the region outside the polygon can be divided into triangles and a rectangle. The area of the polygonal region is equal to the area of the square lattice minus the area outside the polygonal region.

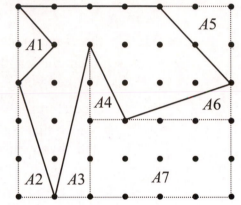

Areas:

Square Lattice: $A = 5 \times 6 = 30$

Triangle 1: $A1 = \dfrac{1}{2}(2)(1) = 1$

Triangle 2: $A2 = \dfrac{1}{2}(1)(3) = \dfrac{3}{2}$

Triangle 3: $A3 = \dfrac{1}{2}(1)(4) = 2$

Triangle 4: $A4 = \dfrac{1}{2}(1)(2) = 1$

Triangle 5: $A5 = \dfrac{1}{2}(2)(2) = 2$

Triangle 6: $A6 = \dfrac{1}{2}(3)(1) = \dfrac{3}{2}$

Rectangle: $A7 = 4 \times 2 = 8$

The area of the region outside the polygon =
$1 + \dfrac{3}{2} + 2 + 1 + 2 + \dfrac{3}{2} + 8 = 17$. Therefore, the area of the polygonal region $= 30 - 17 = 13$ square units.

(b) Using Pick's Theorem, $A = \left(\dfrac{b}{2} + i - 1\right)$, find b and i in each case.

(i) b = the number of dots on the border. $b = 14$. i = number of dots on the inside. $i = 0$.

$$A = \left(\dfrac{b}{2} + i - 1\right) = \dfrac{14}{2} + 0 - 1 = 7 - 1 = 6 \text{ square units.}$$

(ii) b = the number of dots on the border. $b = 35$. i = the number of dots on the inside. $i = 68$.

$$A = \left(\dfrac{b}{2} + i - 1\right) = \dfrac{35}{2} + 68 - 1 = 84.5 \text{ square units.}$$

Section 13.2

34. Let w represent the width of the rectangle. The length is $w + 3$ since the length is 3 cm more than its width. Since the area of a rectangle is length × width, we know the following:

$$40 = (w + 3)w$$
$$0 = w^2 + 3w - 40$$
$$0 = (w - 5)(w + 8)$$
$$w = 5 \text{ or } w = -8$$

Since width cannot be negative we eliminate $w = -8$. Therefore, the width is 5 cm and the length is $5 + 3 = 8$ cm.

Section 13.2

35. Access the eManipulative, *Geoboard*. Consider a 5×5 node section of the geoboard. Use trial and error to place bands as you attempt to create an equilateral triangle. Consider any triangle with one side horizontal. Let the horizontal distance between two adjacent dots be 1 unit. In an equilateral triangle, all three sides must be the same length. If the horizontal side has length 1, then the other two sides must each have length 1 also. Notice, however, that the only other dots that are 1 unit away lie directly above, directly below, or along the same line as the

endpoints of the original side. Since the dots directly above or directly below form right angles when connected to the horizontal base, and since a triangle cannot be constructed from three collinear points, no equilateral triangle can be constructed having a horizontal side.

(A similar argument holds for a triangle having a vertical side.) If we are to construct an equilateral triangle on the square lattice, then it must have no sides horizontal or vertical. Try all possibilities using the geoboard. It is often possible to create two sides that are the same length but the third side never is the same length. Therefore, no equilateral triangle can be constructed on the square lattice.

Section 13.2

36. Check to see if the Pythagorean theorem holds for each set of lengths. If it does not hold, then the triangle is either acute or obtuse. Consider an equilateral triangle which has three $60°$ angles. It is also called an acute triangle. Suppose its sides were each of length 4; that is, let $a = 4$, $b = 4$, and $c = 4$. Then $a^2 + b^2 = 4^2 + 4^2 = 16 + 16 = 32$, and $c^2 = 4^2 = 16$. Therefore, for an acute triangle, $a^2 + b^2 > c^2$. For an obtuse triangle, then, $a^2 + b^2 < c^2$, where c is the length of the longest side.

    (a) $a^2 + b^2 = 54^2 + 70^2 = 2916 + 4900 = 7816 < 8100 = 90^2 = c^2$. The triangle is obtuse.

    (b) $a^2 + b^2 = 16^2 + 63^2 = 256 + 3969 = 4225 = 65^2 = c^2$. The triangle is a right triangle.

    (c) $a^2 + b^2 = 24^2 + 48^2 = 576 + 2304 = 2880 > 2704 = 52^2 = c^2$. The triangle is acute.

    (d) $a^2 + b^2 = 27^2 + 36^2 = 729 + 1296 = 2025 = 45^2 = c^2$. The triangle is a right triangle.

    (e) $a^2 + b^2 = 46^2 + 48^2 = 2116 + 2304 = 4420 > 2500 = 50^2 = c^2$. The triangle is acute.

    (f) $a^2 + b^2 = 9^2 + 40^2 = 81 + 1600 = 1681 < 2116 = 46^2 = c^2$. The triangle is obtuse.

Section 13.2

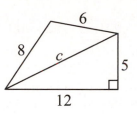

37. Recall that Hero's formula tells us how to find the area of a triangle if we know the lengths of three sides. We want to build a right triangle in the given quadrilateral so we can apply Hero's formula. Construct the diagonal from the lower left vertex to the upper right vertex. Since a right triangle is formed, by the Pythagorean Theorem, the diagonal has length $c = \sqrt{a^2 + b^2} = \sqrt{5^2 + 12^2} = 13$. Now we have two triangles, and we know all the side lengths. Find the area of each triangle and add to find the area of the quadrilateral.

Hero's formula:

Area $= \sqrt{s(s-a)(s-b)(s-c)}$, where a, b, and c are the lengths of the sides and $s = \dfrac{a+b+c}{2}$.

For the right triangle, $s = \dfrac{5+12+13}{2} = 15$.

$$\text{Area of the right triangle} = \sqrt{15(15-5)(15-12)(15-13)}$$
$$= \sqrt{15(10)(3)(2)}$$
$$= 30 \text{ square units}$$

For the other triangle, $s = \dfrac{6+8+13}{2} = 13.5$.

$$\text{Area of the other triangle} = \sqrt{13.5(13.5-8)(13.5-6)(13.5-13)}$$
$$= \sqrt{13.5(5.5)(7.5)(0.5)}$$
$$\approx 16.7 \text{ square units}$$

Area of quadrilateral $\approx 30 + 16.7 = 46.7$ square units.

Section 13.2

38. (a) In the diagram, since there are parallel lines cut by a transversal, the measure of the indicated angle is $7.5°$ by the Alternate Interior Angles Congruence Property.

(b) Set up a proportion using the ratios of arc length to central angle:

$$\frac{500 \text{ miles}}{7.5^\circ} = \frac{\text{circumference (in miles)}}{360^\circ}$$

$$24{,}000 \text{ miles} = c.$$

(c) Eratosthenes was off by only $24{,}901.55 - 24{,}000 = 901.55$ miles.

Section 13.2

39. The diameter of the hole is also the diagonal of the square plug. Recall that a square has equal side lengths. Let x represent the length of the side of the square. Since the square has all right angles, we can find x using the Pythagorean theorem.

$$x^2 + x^2 = (3.16)^2$$

$$2x^2 = 9.9856$$

$$x^2 = 4.9928$$

$$x \approx 2.23 \text{ cm.}$$

Therefore, the square must have a side length of about 2.23 cm.

Section 13.2

40. Let the point O be the center of the circle. Since the segments $\overline{OA}$ and $\overline{AB}$ are perpendicular, right angles are formed. Length $\overline{AB}$ is 1 unit. Let x represent the length of $\overline{OA}$. By the Pythagorean theorem, the length of $\overline{OB}$ can be calculated as follows: length of $\overline{OB} = \sqrt{x^2 + 1^2} = \sqrt{x^2 + 1}.$

Therefore, the radius of the outer circle is $\sqrt{x^2 + 1}$, and the radius of the inner circle is x. If we calculate the area of the large circle and subtract the area of the small circle, we will be left with the area in between. Recall that the area of a circle $= \pi r^2$.

Area of large circle $= \pi \left(\sqrt{x^2 + 1} \right)^2 = \pi(x^2 + 1) = \pi x^2 + \pi.$

Area of small circle $= \pi(x^2) = \pi x^2.$
Area in between $= \pi x^2 + \pi - \pi x^2 = \pi$ square units.

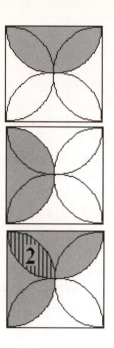

Section 13.2

41. Recall that the area of a circle is πr^2. It follows that the area of a semicircle is $\dfrac{\pi r^2}{2}$. Calculate the area of each semicircle. Notice that the radius of each semicircle is 4 units. The area of the upper semicircle shown is $\dfrac{\pi(4)^2}{2} = \dfrac{16\pi}{2} = 8\pi$ square units. The area of the left hand semicircle shown is $\dfrac{\pi(4)^2}{2} = \dfrac{16\pi}{2} = 8\pi$ square units.

Notice that the highlighted "petal" is included in both calculations and has been counted twice. The other two semicircles will each be 8π square units in area. If we shade the appropriate regions, we will see that the area of each of the petals will be counted twice. Therefore, the area of the petal can be found by finding the area of the four semicircles and subtracting the area of the square.

Area of petals = area of four semicircles − area of square

$$= 8\pi + 8\pi + 8\pi + 8\pi - 64$$

$$= 32\pi - 64 \text{ square units.}$$

Section 13.2

42. (a) The field measures $(100)(100) = 10{,}000$ m². The diameter of the circle is 100 m so the radius is 50 m. The area of irrigation is $\pi(50)^2 = 2500\pi$ m². The percent irrigated is $\dfrac{2500\pi}{10{,}000} \approx 0.785 = 78.5\%$.

(b) Since the field measures 100 m on a side, and two circles span a side, the diameter of each circle is 50 m. The radius of each circle is 25 m, and the area of each is $\pi(25)^2 = 625\pi$ m². The total area of irrigation is $4(625\pi \text{ m}^2) = 2500\pi$ m². The percent irrigated is $\dfrac{2500\pi}{10{,}000} = \dfrac{\pi}{4} \approx 0.785 = 78.5\%$.

(c) Both systems will irrigate the same amount of land.

(d) Since they both irrigate the same amount, it is unnecessary to use more sprinklers with a smaller radius.

Section 13.2

43. Let x represent the width (radius) of the innermost ring. The radius of the inner shaded region is $3x$. The outer shaded ring is formed by taking the whole region, which has a radius of $5x$, and removing the inner 4 rings, which have a combined radius of $4x$. Recall, the area of a circle is πr^2. Area of inner shaded region: $\pi(3x)^2 = 9x^2\pi$. Area of outer shaded ring: $\pi(5x)^2 - \pi(4x)^2 = 25x^2\pi - 16x^2\pi = 9x^2\pi$. The areas are the same.

Section 13.2

44. Because the price per square centimeter is the same for both pizzas, the size of the pizza does not matter. Neither pizza is a better buy. They are the same.

Section 13.2

45. Find the area of each triangle by constructing the perpendicular height. The height can be found by using the Pythagorean theorem. Then the area can be calculated. Notice that both of the triangles are isosceles.

Triangle 1:

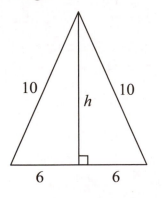

$$h^2 + 6^2 = 10^2$$

$$h^2 = 100 - 36$$

$$h = \sqrt{64}$$

$$h = 8$$

$$\text{Area} = \frac{1}{2}bh$$

$$\text{Area} = \frac{1}{2}(12)(8)$$

$$\text{Area} = 48 \text{ square units}$$

Triangle 2:

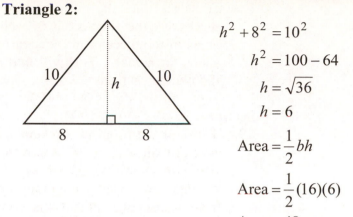

$$h^2 + 8^2 = 10^2$$

$$h^2 = 100 - 64$$

$$h = \sqrt{36}$$

$$h = 6$$

$$\text{Area} = \frac{1}{2}bh$$

$$\text{Area} = \frac{1}{2}(16)(6)$$

$$\text{Area} = 48 \text{ square units}$$

Therefore, both triangles have the same area.

Section 13.2

46. (a) Use dimensional analysis. Be careful when using square units. Note that a pizza with a diameter of 14 inches has a 7-inch radius.

$$\frac{250{,}000{,}000 \text{ Americans}}{1} \times \frac{0.25 \text{ pizza}}{1 \text{ American}} \times \frac{49\pi \text{ in}^2}{1 \text{ pizza}} \times \frac{1 \text{ ft}^2}{12^2 \text{ in}^2} \times \frac{1 \text{ mi}^2}{5280^2 \text{ ft}^2} \times \frac{640 \text{ acres}}{1 \text{ mi}^2}$$

$$\approx 1533.82 \text{ acres.}$$

Therefore, Americans eat about 1534 acres of pizza per week.

(b) Because a 14-inch diameter pizza costs $8.00, we know that a pizza costs 8 dollars per 49π square inches. Use dimensional analysis to determine the cost of one acre of pizza.

$$\frac{8 \text{ dollars}}{49\pi \text{ in}^2} \times \frac{12^2 \text{ in}^2}{1 \text{ ft}^2} \times \frac{5280^2 \text{ ft}^2}{1 \text{ mi}^2} \times \frac{1 \text{ mi}^2}{640 \text{ acres}} \approx \frac{325{,}982.58 \text{ dollars}}{\text{acre}}.$$

Therefore, the pizza costs $325,982.58 per acre.

Section 13.2

47. Access the Chapter 13 eManipulative, *Pythagorean Theorem*. Notice the sides of a right triangle and a square are labeled. Use the right triangles and square(s) given below each white filled shape to fill in the shape completely. You may need to rotate some pieces. To rotate a piece, use the pointer to point to a corner. A black circle will appear over the corner. You can click the black

circle and turn the piece. Once you fill in a shape with pieces, use the dimensions of each of the pieces to show the areas of the pieces and the area of the original white-filled shape are equal. You will end up with the Pythagorean theorem in each case.

Section 13.3

13. Think of the room as a rectangular box. We know that a liter of paint covers 20 square meters of surface area. We need to determine the areas of the four walls and the ceiling. Two walls have dimensions 3 meters by 7 meters. Two walls have dimensions 3 meters by 4 meters. The ceiling has dimensions 4 meters by 7 meters.

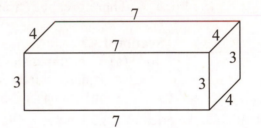

$$\begin{aligned}
\text{Area to be painted} &= \text{Area of walls} + \text{Area of ceiling} \\
&= [2(3)(7) + 2(3)(4)] + (4)(7) \\
&= 42 + 24 + 28 \\
&= 94
\end{aligned}$$

Thus, the area to be painted is 94 square meters. Use dimensional analysis to determine the number of liters of paint needed.

$$\frac{94 \, \text{m}^2}{1} \times \frac{1 \, \text{liter}}{20 \, \text{m}^2} = 4.7 \, \text{liters}.$$

Therefore, 5 liters of paint should be purchased.

Section 13.3

14. Since the scale is 5 cm = 3 m, square both sides to find the scale for area: 25 cm² = 9 m². Use dimensional analysis to find the area of the exposed surfaces of the building in square meters. We can use the surface area of the model to determine the surface area of the building.

$$27,900 \, \text{cm}^2 \times \frac{9 \, \text{m}^2}{25 \, \text{cm}^2} = 10,044 \, \text{m}^2$$

Therefore, the area of the exposed surface of the building is 10,044 m².

Section 13.3

15. (a) Any right rectangular prism has a surface area found by calculating $2lw + 2wh + 2lh$. Use systematic guess and test to find arrangements of 36 cubes that yield the required surface area, 96 square units.

Length	Width	Height	Surface Area
36	1	1	$72 + 2 + 72 = 146$
18	2	1	$72 + 4 + 36 = 112$
12	3	1	$72 + 6 + 24 = 102$
9	4	1	$72 + 8 + 18 = 98$
6	6	1	$72 + 12 + 12 = 96$

The arrangement that yields a surface area of 96 square units is a right rectangular prism with dimensions 6 by 6 by 1 unit.

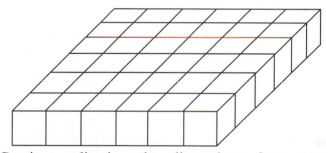

(b) Continue adjusting the dimensions from part (a). Notice that we cannot, however, adjust only length and width. Consider a height of 2 cubes.

Length	Width	Height	Surface Area
9	2	2	$36 + 8 + 36 = 80$

The required arrangement has dimensions 9 by 2 by 2.

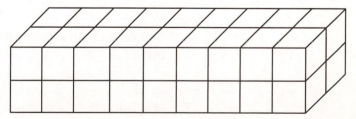

(c) Notice that as we increase the height and bring the length and width closer in dimension, we decrease the surface area.

Length	Width	Height	Surface Area
6	3	2	36 + 12 + 24 = 72
4	3	3	24 + 18 + 24 = 66

Since there are no other unique dimension combinations, the dimensions 3 × 4 × 3 give the smallest surface area of 66 square units.

(d) Notice that when the values of the length, width, and height are very different, the surface area was larger. When the values for length, width, and height are very similar, the surface area is smaller. From part (a), we see that when the difference in dimensions is the most extreme, (36 × 1 × 1), the largest surface area of 146 square units was obtained.

Section 13.3

16. Consider a box. Let l = length, w = width, and h = height. The new box will have dimensions $2l$, $2w$, and $2h$. Calculate the surface area for each box and compare.

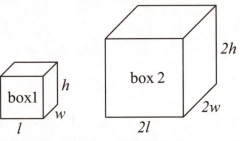

Each box has six sides. The surface area is the sum of the areas of the six sides.

Surface Area for box 1 = $2(lw) + 2(wh) + 2(lh)$

Surface Area for box 2 = $2(2l)(2w) + 2(2w)(2h) + 2(2l)(2h)$
$$= 8(lw) + 8(wh) + 8(lh)$$
$$= 4[2(lw) + 2(wh) + 2(lh)]$$
$$= 4(\text{Surface Area for box 1})$$

Notice that box 2 requires 4 times as much cardboard as box 1.

Section 13.3

17. (a) Since the Earth has a diameter of 12,760 kilometers, it has a radius of 12,760 ÷ 2 = 6380 kilometers.

    (b) Recall the formula for the surface area of a sphere:

$S = 4\pi r^2$. Therefore, the surface area of the Earth is
$4\pi(6380)^2 = 4\pi(40{,}704{,}400) \approx 5.12 \times 10^8 \text{ km}^2$.

(c) Since land area is 135,781,867 km², the percent of the Earth's surface that is land can be found as follows:

$$\frac{\text{land area}}{\text{total surface area}} \times 100\% \approx \frac{135{,}781{,}867}{5.2 \times 10^8} \times 100\%$$

$$\approx 26.1\%.$$

Therefore, about 26.1% of the Earth's surface is land.

Section 13.3

18. Recall that the surface area of a sphere is $4\pi r^2$ where r is the radius. Consider sphere 1 with radius r. If the radius is cut in half, the radius for sphere 2 will be $\dfrac{r}{2}$.

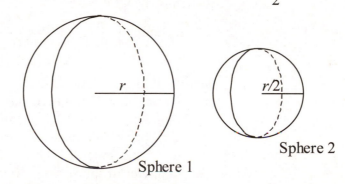

Surface area (sphere 1) = $4\pi r^2$.

Surface area (sphere 2) = $4\pi\left(\dfrac{r}{2}\right)^2 = 4\pi\dfrac{r^2}{4} = \pi r^2$.

Therefore, when the radius of a sphere is reduced by half, the surface area is one-fourth as large.

Section 13.3

19. A square is rolled up to form a cylinder, as shown in the figure on the next page. The surface area can be found by adding the lateral surface (the original square) and the circular bases.

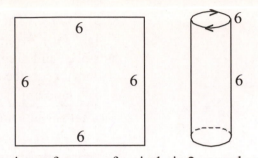

Since the circumference of a circle is $2\pi r$, and each circular base has a circumference of length 6 cm, $6 = 2\pi r$, so $r = \dfrac{6}{2\pi} = \dfrac{3}{\pi}$ cm. The area of each of the circular bases is

$$\pi r^2 = \pi\left(\dfrac{3}{\pi}\right)^2 = \dfrac{9}{\pi} \text{ cm}^2.$$ The total surface area of the

cylinder is $\dfrac{9}{\pi} + \dfrac{9}{\pi} + 36 = \left(\dfrac{18}{\pi} + 36\right) \text{cm}^2$.

Section 13.3

20. Notice that the sphere has a diameter of 10 units, so its radius is 5 units. The smallest cylinder that would contain the sphere would be such that the top, bottom, and sides touch the sphere. The height of the cylinder would be the diameter of the sphere, 10 units. The radius of the base of the cylinder would be the radius of the sphere, 5 units. Therefore, the surface area of the smallest cylinder that contains the sphere is $2\pi r^2 + 2\pi rh = 2\pi(5)^2 + 2\pi(5)(10) = 50\pi + 100\pi = 150\pi$ square units.

Section 13.4

12. Since they are stacks of unit cubes, each cube has a volume of 1 cubic unit. Therefore, the volume of each stack is the total number of cubes in the stack. When calculating the surface area for each stack, consider each of the six sides carefully. It may be helpful to sketch each of the side views. We will denote the sides as "Top", "Bottom", "Front", "Back", Right" , and "Left". (Note: If you have a difficult time visualizing each side, try using dice to build each stack.)

(a) The volume is the number of cubes: $3 + 4 + 2 + 1 + 1 + 3 = 14$ cubic units. Consider the following sketches when finding the surface area.

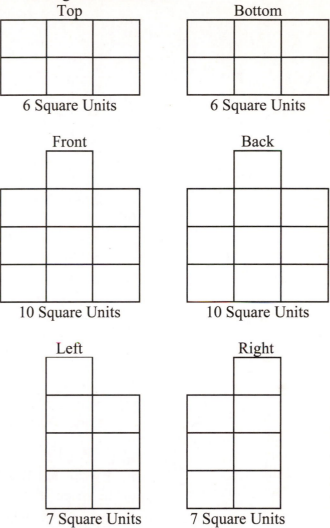

The surface area is the sum of the areas of the sides. Surface area $= 6 + 6 + 10 + 10 + 7 + 7 = 46$ square units. Notice that the top and bottom views have the same area. The front and back views have the same area, and the right and left views have the same area. When calculating surface area, we need only find the areas of the top, front, and left side and multiply by two.

(b) The volume is 1 + 4 + 2 = 7 cubic units. For surface area, consider the top, front, and left side views.

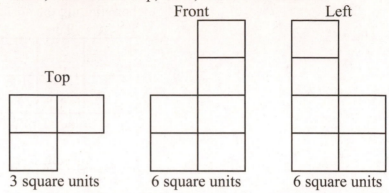

Top

Front

Left

3 square units   6 square units   6 square units

Surface area = 2(3 + 6 + 6) = 2(15) = 30 square units.

(c) The volume is 3 + 3 + 3 + 1 + 2 + 3 + 1 + 2 + 3 = 21 cubic units. For surface area, consider the top, front, and left side views.

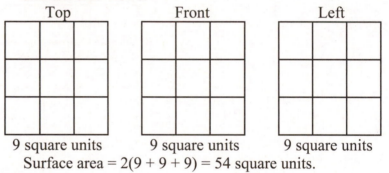

Top   Front   Left

9 square units   9 square units   9 square units

Surface area = 2(9 + 9 + 9) = 54 square units.

Section 13.4

13. Each shape has a "cut" made in it. We will find the volume of the shape without the "cut", then subtract the volume of the "cut" to find the volume of the shape.

(a) Without the "cut", the figure is a rectangular prism with length = 9 inches, width = 8 inches, and height = 8 inches. Since the volume of a rectangular prism is length × width × height, the volume without the "cut" is 9 × 8 × 8 = 576 cubic inches. The "cut" is a triangular prism with an equilateral triangular base which has side lengths of 3 inches each. Since the volume of a prism is the product of the area of the base and the height, we need to find the area of the base. The area of a

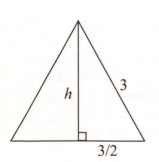

triangle is $\frac{1}{2}bh$. Find h by using the Pythagorean theorem.

$$h = \sqrt{3^2 - \left(\frac{3}{2}\right)^2} = \frac{3\sqrt{3}}{2}$$

Area $= \frac{1}{2}(3)\left(\frac{3\sqrt{3}}{2}\right) = 9\frac{\sqrt{3}}{4}$ square inches

Triangular Prism Volume $= \left(\frac{9\sqrt{3}}{4}\right)(8) = 18\sqrt{3}$ in^3

Therefore, the volume of the figure = volume without the "cut" – volume of "cut". Volume $= 576 - 18\sqrt{3} \approx$ 545 cubic inches.

(b) Without the "cut", the figure is a hemisphere with radius 4.5 inches (diameter 9 inches). The "cut" is a hemisphere with radius 3.5 inches. Find the volume of each hemisphere, and then subtract to find the volume of the figure. (Note: The volume of a sphere is $\frac{4}{3}\pi r^3$, so the volume of a hemisphere is $\frac{2}{3}\pi r^3$.) The volume of the larger hemisphere is $\frac{2}{3}\pi r^3 = \frac{2}{3}\pi(4.5)^3 \approx 60.75\pi$ in^3. The volume of the smaller hemisphere is $\frac{2}{3}\pi r^3 = \frac{2}{3}\pi(3.5)^3 \approx 28.58\pi$ in^3.

Thus, the volume of the figure is approximately $60.75\pi - 28.58\pi \approx 101$ cubic inches.

Section 13.4

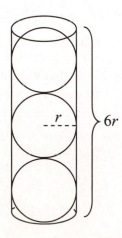

14. Suppose that the tennis balls touch the sides, the top, and the bottom of the can. Let r represent the radius of a tennis ball.

(a) The circumference of the can is $2\pi r$. The height is $6r$.
Since $2\pi > 6$, circumference is greater than height.

(b) The percent of the can occupied by air outside the balls can be calculated as follows:

$$\frac{\text{Volume of the can} - \text{Volume of 3 balls}}{\text{Volume of can}} \times 100\%.$$

Volume of the can $= \pi r^2 h = \pi (3.5)^2 (21) = 257.25\pi$ cm³

Volume of 3 balls $= 3(\text{volume of 1 ball})$

$$= 3\left(\frac{4}{3}\pi r^3\right)$$

$$= 4\pi(3.5)^3$$

$$= 171.5\pi \text{ cm}^3$$

The percent occupied by air can be found as follows:

$$\frac{257.25\pi - 171.5\pi}{257.25\pi} \times 100\% = \frac{85.75\pi}{257.25\pi} \times 100\% = 33.\overline{3}\%$$

Section 13.4

15. Draw a picture for each problem.

    (a) The bases of the prism are equilateral triangles.

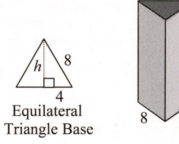

Equilateral Triangle Base

Volume = area of triangular base × height of prism. The altitude of triangle is given by $h = \sqrt{8^2 - 4^2} = 4\sqrt{3}$ units. The area of each triangular base is $\frac{1}{2}bh = \frac{1}{2}(8)(4\sqrt{3}) = 16\sqrt{3}$ square units. The height of the prism is 10 units. Therefore, the volume is $16\sqrt{3} \times 10 = 160\sqrt{3}$ cubic units.

(b) The bases of the prism are trapezoids.

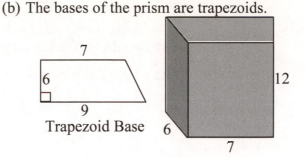

Trapezoid Base

Volume = area of trapezoidal base × height of prism. We know that the area of the trapezoid base is $\frac{1}{2}(b_1 + b_2)h = \frac{1}{2}(7+9)(6) = 48$ square units. The height of the prism is 12 units. Therefore, the volume of the prism is $(48)(12) = 576$ cubic units.

(c) The bases of the prism are right triangles.

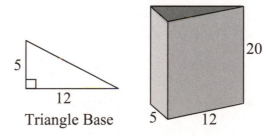

Triangle Base

Volume = area of triangular base × height of prism. The area of the right triangle $= \frac{1}{2}bh = \frac{1}{2}(12)(5) = 30$ square units. The height of the prism is 20 units. Therefore, the volume of the prism is $(30)(20) = 600$ cubic units.

Section 13.4

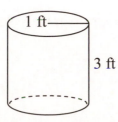

16. Find the volume of the cylinder that has a diameter of 2 feet (radius 1 foot) and that has a height of 3 feet.
Volume $= \pi r^2 h = \pi(1)^2(3) = 3\pi$ cubic feet.

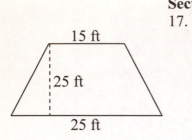

15 ft

25 ft

25 ft

Cross Section of Wall

Section 13.4

17. Think of the Great Wall as a prism. The volume of a prism is the area of the base × height. The base is a trapezoid. The "height" is the length of the wall, which is 1500 miles.

The area of the trapezoidal base $= \frac{1}{2}(15+25)(25) = 500$ square feet. The height of the prism $= 1500$ miles $\times \frac{5280 \text{ feet}}{1 \text{ mile}} = 7,920,000$ feet. Therefore, the volume of the wall is $(500)(7,920,000) = 3,960,000,000$ cubic feet. Recall that 3 feet = 1 yard, so 27 cubic feet = 1 cubic yard.

$3,960,000,000 \text{ ft}^3 \times \frac{1 \text{ yd}^3}{27 \text{ ft}^3} \approx 1.47 \times 10^8 \text{ yd}^3$. Therefore, about 1.47×10^8 cubic yards of material make up the Great Wall of China.

Section 13.4

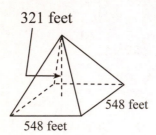

321 feet

548 feet

548 feet

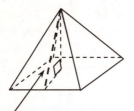

Slant Height

18. (a) The volume of a pyramid is $\frac{1}{3}$(area of base)(height).

The base is a square with side lengths 548 feet. The area of the square $= 548^2 = 300,304$ square feet. Therefore, the volume of the pyramid $= \frac{1}{3}(300,304)(321) = 32,132,528 \text{ ft}^3$, or approximately $32,100,000 \text{ ft}^3$.

(b) The lateral surface area excludes the base and is $\frac{1}{2}$(perimeter)(slant height). The perimeter is $(4)(548) = 2192$ feet. By the Pythagorean theorem, we calculate the slant height to be $\sqrt{(321)^2 + (274)^2} \approx 422.04$ feet. The lateral surface area is calculated as $\frac{1}{2}(2192)(422.04) \approx 462,555$ or approximately 463,000 square feet.

Section 13.4

19. (a) Think of the pipe as a right circular cylinder. The volume of water in the pipe can be calculated by using the formula for the volume of a cylinder. Notice that the radius measures 4 inches. For consistency, convert all dimensions to yards.

$$\text{Radius} = \frac{4 \text{ inches}}{1} \times \frac{1 \text{ yd}}{36 \text{ in}} = \frac{1}{9} \text{ yd}$$

Now calculate the volume of the cylindrical pipe.

$$\text{Volume of the cylinder} = \pi r^2 h$$

$$= \pi \left(\frac{1}{9}\right)^2 (100)$$

$$\approx 1.23\pi$$

$$\approx 3.88 \text{ yd}^3$$

Therefore, the volume of the pipe is approximately 3.88 cubic yards.

(b) Notice that the radius measure 4 centimeters. Convert all dimensions to meters.

$$\text{Radius} = \frac{4 \text{ cm}}{1} \times \frac{1 \text{ m}}{100 \text{ cm}} = 0.04 \text{ m}$$

Now calculate the volume of the pipe.

$$\text{Volume of the cylinder} = \pi r^2 h$$

$$= \pi (0.04)^2 (100)$$

$$= 0.16\pi$$

$$\approx 0.50 \text{ m}^3$$

Therefore, the volume of the pipe is approximately 0.50 cubic meters.

(c) The computation in part (b) is easier because the metric conversions are simpler.

Section 13.4

20. Since the scale is 5 cm = 3 m, cube both sides to find the scale for volume: $125 \text{ cm}^3 = 27 \text{ m}^3$. Use dimensional analysis to find the volume of the finished structure in cubic

meters. $396{,}000 \text{ cm}^3 \times \dfrac{27 \text{ m}^3}{125 \text{ cm}^3} = 85{,}536 \text{ m}^3$. The volume of the finished structure is 85,536 m³.

Section 13.4

21. (a) First find the volume of the spherical tank. If the diameter is 60 feet, then the radius is 30 feet. The volume of a sphere is $\dfrac{4}{3}\pi r^3$. Volume $= \dfrac{4}{3}\pi(30)^3 = 36{,}000\pi \text{ ft}^3$. The formula for the volume of a right circular cylinder is $\pi r^2 h$. We want the volume of the cylinder to be the same as the volume of the spherical tank, $36{,}000\pi \text{ ft}^3$, and we know the radius of the cylinder is 30 feet.

$$\pi(30)^2 h = 36{,}000\pi$$

$$900\pi h = 36{,}000\pi$$

$$h = 40 \text{ feet}$$

   (b) Each tank has a volume of $36{,}000\pi$ cubic feet. Use dimensional analysis to change cubic feet to gallons.

$$36{,}000\pi \text{ cubic feet} \times \dfrac{7.5 \text{ gallons}}{1 \text{ cubic foot}} \approx 848{,}000 \text{ gallons}$$

   (c) The formula for the surface area of a sphere is $4\pi r^2$. Since the radius of the sphere is 30 feet, the surface area is $4\pi(30)^2 = 3600\pi$ square feet. The formula for the surface area of a cylinder is $2\pi r^2 + 2\pi rh$. Since the radius of the cylinder is 30 feet and the height is 40 feet, the surface area is $2\pi(30)^2 + 2\pi(30)(40) = 1800\pi + 2400\pi = 4200\pi$ square feet. Therefore, the sphere will require less material in its construction.

Section 13.4

22. Calculate the volume of the sculpture in cubic centimeters, keeping in mind that the sphere and the square prism are both hollow. They each have a thickness of 2 mm, or 0.2 cm. Consider each piece separately.

Sphere: Since the outer radius is 18 cm, and the sphere is 0.2 cm thick, the inner radius is 17.8 cm. The volume of metal can be found by calculating the volume of a sphere with radius 18 cm and subtracting the volume of a sphere with radius 17.8 cm. The volume of the spherical portion of the sculpture is calculated as follows:

$$\text{Volume of Sphere} = \frac{4}{3}\pi(18)^3 - \frac{4}{3}\pi(17.8)^3$$

$$\approx 7776\pi - 7519.7\pi$$

$$\approx 256.3\pi$$

$$\approx 805.29 \text{ cm}^3$$

<u>Prism</u>: Since the outside dimensions are 40 cm by 40 cm by 1 m (100 cm) and it is 0.2 cm thick, the inside dimensions are 39.6 cm by 39.6 cm by 99.6 cm. The volume of the metal can be found by calculating the volume of the prism with the "outside" dimensions and subtracting the volume of the prism with the "inside" dimensions.

$$\text{Volume of Prism} = (40)(40)(100) - (39.6)(39.6)(99.6)$$

$$= 160,000 - 156,188.736$$

$$\approx 3811.26 \text{ cm}^3$$

The total volume of the metal in the sculpture is (805.29 + 3811.26) cm$^3 \approx$ 4616.55 cm^3. Since the density of iron is $7.87\dfrac{\text{g}}{\text{cm}^3}$, we can find the weight by multiplying the volume by the density of iron. The weight of the sculpture is calculated as follows:

$$\text{Weight} = 4616.56 \text{ cm}^3 \times \frac{7.87 \text{ g}}{\text{cm}^3} \times \frac{1 \text{ kg}}{1000\text{g}} \approx 36.3 \text{ kg}$$

The sculpture weighs approximately 36.3 kilograms.

Section 13.4

23. (a) The volume of the rock is equal to the volume of the water it displaces in the aquarium.

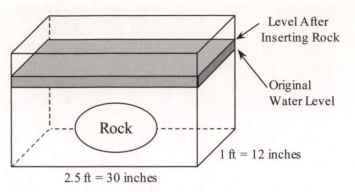

2.5 ft = 30 inches

Volume of the shaded region = volume of the rock. The volume of the water = $(30)(12)\left(\dfrac{1}{4}\right)$ = 90 cubic inches. Therefore, the volume of the rock is 90 cubic inches.

(b) From part (a) we know that a $\dfrac{1}{4}$-inch height of water in the aquarium has a volume of 90 cubic inches, so a $\dfrac{1}{2}$-inch height of water will have a volume that is twice as large, or 180 cubic inches. The volume of the 200 marbles = 200(volume of 1 marble). Since the diameter of each marble is 1.5 cm and the radius of each is 0.75 cm, the volume of 1 marble is $\dfrac{4}{3}\pi(0.75)^3 \approx 1.77\,\text{cm}^3$.

Therefore, the volume of 200 marbles is $200(1.77) \approx 353.4$ cm^3. Since 2.54 cm = 1 inch, we know that 16.387 cm$^3 \approx 1$ in^3.

$$353.4\ \text{cm}^3 \times \frac{1\ \text{in}^3}{16.387\ \text{cm}^3} \approx 21.6\ \text{in}^3$$

Therefore, the 21.6 cubic inches of volume occupied by the marbles is far less than the 180 cubic inches needed to overflow the tank. The tank will not overflow.

Section 13.4

24. (a) A cube is one example of a square prism. If the length of the side of the cube is s, then the volume is s^3. If all the dimensions are doubled, then the volume becomes $(2s)^3 = 8s^3$. The volume is increased by a factor of 8.

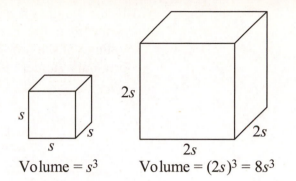

Volume = s^3 Volume = $(2s)^3 = 8s^3$

(b) Refer to the diagram in part (a). The surface area for the original cube is 6(area of one side) = $6s^2$ square units. The surface area for the new cube is 6(area of one side) = $6(2s)^2 = 6(4s^2) = 24s^2$ square units. The surface area is increased by a factor of 4.

Section 13.4

25.   (a) The volume of a circular cylinder is $\pi r^2 h$.

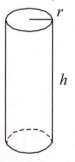

If the radius is doubled and the height remains the same, then the new volume is $\pi(2r)^2 h = \pi\, 4r^2 h = 4\pi r^2 h$. The volume of the new cylinder is increased by a factor of 4 compared to the original cylinder.

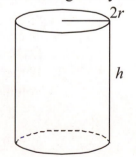

(b) If the height is doubled and the radius remains the same, then the new volume is $\pi r^2(2h) = 2\pi r^2 h$. The volume of the new cylinder is double the volume of the original cylinder. See the following figure.

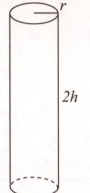

Section 13.4

26. The arrangement of pipes which fill the pool the fastest will be the one with the largest combined opening (area).
   (i) Three pipes, each with a diameter of 9 cm or a radius of 4.5 cm, have an area of 3(area of one pipe) = $3(\pi r^2) = 3\pi(4.5)^2 = 60.75\pi$ cm².
   (ii) Two pipes, each with a diameter of 12 cm or a radius of 6 cm, have a combined area of 2(area of one pipe) = $2(\pi r^2) = 2\pi(6)^2 = 72\pi$ cm².
   (iii) One pipe, with a diameter of 16 cm or a radius of 8 cm, has an area $= 1(\pi r^2) = 1\pi(8)^2 = 64\pi$ cm².
   The two 12-cm diameter pipes will fill the pool the fastest.

Section 13.4

27. The volume of a cube is s^3, where s represents the edge length.
   (a) The volume of a cube with edges of length 2 meters is $(2)^3 = 8$ m³.
   (b) If the volume of a cube is 16 m³, which is twice the volume of the cube in part (a), then $16 = s^3$, so $s = 2\sqrt[3]{2}$. The length of an edge is $2\sqrt[3]{2}$ m.

Section 13.4

28. To determine the percent difference, we need to find the area of the circles with diameters 6 inches (radius 3 inches) and 8 inches (radius 4 inches).

Area of the larger circle $= \pi(4)^2$ in^2 $= 16\pi$ in^2

Area of smaller circle $= \pi(3)^2$ in^2 $= 9\pi$ in^2

$$\text{Percent difference} = \frac{\text{difference in area}}{\text{smaller area}} \times 100\%$$

$$= \frac{16\pi - 9\pi}{9\pi} \times 100\%$$

$$= \frac{7\pi}{9\pi} \times 100\%$$

$$\approx 78\%$$

The area of the larger circle is approximately 78% greater than the area of the smaller circle. Therefore, the amount of dirt removed by the larger digger is 78% greater than the amount of dirt removed by the small digger.

Section 13.4

29. The water tank has a diameter of 10 feet (radius 5 feet) and a height of 15 feet. The volume of a cone is $\frac{1}{3}\pi r^2 h$. The volume of the original tank is $\frac{1}{3}\pi(5)^2(15) = 125\pi$ ft^3. The new tank will have the same height but will have half the capacity (volume). The volume of the new tank will be $\frac{1}{2}(125\pi) = 62.5\pi$ ft^3. Since $V = \frac{1}{3}\pi r^2 h$, $V = 62.5\pi$, and $h = 15$, we can solve for r.

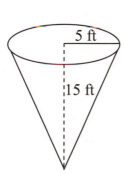

5 ft

15 ft

$$62.5\pi = \frac{1}{3}\pi r^2(15) \quad \text{so,} \quad r = \sqrt{\frac{3(62.5\pi)}{15\pi}} = \frac{5}{\sqrt{2}} = \frac{5\sqrt{2}}{2} \text{ ft.}$$

Therefore, the diameter of the smaller tank is $5\sqrt{2}$ feet or approximately 7.07 feet.

Section 13.4

30. We need to find the height, h, of the cylinder and the slant height, l, of the cone. The formula for the volume of a cylinder is $V_{\text{cylinder}} = \pi r^2 h$. We know the radius, r, is

1 unit. We need to know the volume before the height can be determined. Since the volume of each solid is the same, find the volume of the sphere using $V_{\text{sphere}} = \dfrac{4}{3}\pi r^3$.

Because $r = 1$, we have $V_{\text{sphere}} = \dfrac{4}{3}\pi(1)^3 = \dfrac{4}{3}\pi$.

Therefore, the volume of each solid is $\dfrac{4}{3}\pi$ cubic units.

First we find the height of the cylinder.

$$V_{\text{cylinder}} = \pi r^2 h$$

$$\frac{4}{3}\pi = \pi(1)^2 h$$

$$\frac{4}{3} = h$$

Thus, the height of the cylinder is $\dfrac{4}{3}$ units.

Now we can find the slant height of the cone. To find the slant height of the cone, we will need to use the height and radius of the cone plus the Pythagorean theorem. First find the height of the cone using the given information.

$$V_{\text{cone}} = \frac{1}{3}\pi r^2 h$$

$$\frac{4}{3}\pi = \frac{1}{3}\pi(1)^2 h$$

$$4 = h$$

The height of the cone is 4 units. Now the slant height of the cone can be found by using the Pythagorean theorem.

$$r^2 + h^2 = l^2$$

$$\sqrt{r^2 + h^2} = l$$

$$\sqrt{(1)^2 + (4)^2} = l$$

$$\sqrt{17} = l$$

Therefore, the slant height of the cone is $\sqrt{17}$ units.

Section 13.4

31. One board foot = (1 ft)(1 ft)(1 inch). Thus, the volume of a board foot is calculated as follows:

$$l \times w \times h = (1 \text{ ft}) \times (1 \text{ ft}) \times (\frac{1}{12} \text{ ft})$$

$$= \frac{1}{12} \text{ ft}^3$$

$$= 0.08\overline{3} \text{ ft}^3$$

Therefore, since 1 board foot $= \frac{1}{12}$ ft^3, 1 ft^3 = 12 board feet.

(a) A two by four measures $1\frac{1}{2}$" by $3\frac{1}{2}$". If it is 6 feet long (72 inches), then its volume is $(1.5)(3.5)(72) = 378$ in^3, and 378 in$^3 \times \dfrac{1 \text{ ft}^3}{1728 \text{ in}^3} = 0.21875$ ft^3. There are 0.21875 ft$^3 \times \dfrac{12 \text{ board feet}}{1 \text{ ft}^3} = 2.625$ board feet in this piece of lumber.

(b) A two by eight measures $1\frac{1}{2}$" by $7\frac{1}{2}$". If it is 10 feet long (120 inches), then its volume is $(1.5)(7.5)(120) = 1350$ in^3, and 1350 in$^3 \times \dfrac{1 \text{ ft}^3}{1728 \text{ in}^3} = 0.78125$ ft^3. There are 0.78125 ft$^3 \times \dfrac{12 \text{ board feet}}{1 \text{ ft}^3} = 9.375$ board feet in this piece of lumber.

(c) Plywood is sold in exact dimensions, so the number of board feet can be calculated directly. A 4-foot by 8-foot by $\frac{3}{4}$-inch sheet has a volume of $(4)(8)\left(\dfrac{3}{4}\right) = 24$ board feet.

(d) A 4-foot by 6-foot by $\frac{5}{8}$- inch sheet of plywood has a volume of $(4)(6)\left(\dfrac{5}{8}\right) = 15$ board feet.

Section 13.4

32. Use blocks of equal size or dice to help you visualize the arrangements. In arranging the cubes as required you may need to apply the guess and test strategy a considerable number of times.

(a) Each of the following arrangements of 10 cubes has a surface area of 34 square units. There are many other arrangements possible.

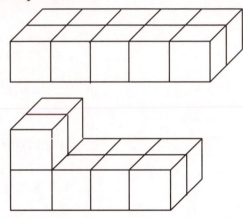

(b) The greatest possible surface area will minimize the number of faces touching each other. Arrange all of the cubes in a row. The surface area is 42 square units.

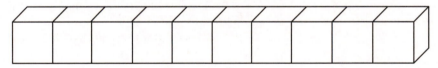

(c) The least possible surface area will maximize the number of faces touching each other. We want to crowd the cubes together and on top of each other in a larger cube formation or an arrangement as close to cubical as possible in this case. The surface area for the following arrangement is 30 square units.

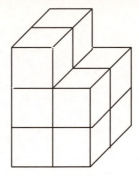

(d) Once again, to obtain the greatest possible surface area, lay each set of cubes in a row. For 27 cubes, the greatest surface area is 110 square units. For 64 cubes, the greatest surface area is 258 square units. To obtain the least possible surface area, form the set of 27 cubes into a $3 \times 3 \times 3$ cube with a surface area of 54 square units. Form the 64 cubes into a $4 \times 4 \times 4$ cube with a surface area of 96 square units.

(e) For any given number of cubes, the greatest surface area is obtained by forming one line of cubes.

(f) For any given number of cubes, the least surface area is obtained by stacking them to form an arrangement that approximates a large cube as closely as possible and is a perfect cube when there are n^3 cubes.

(g) Desert animals are long and thin so the area over which heat is lost is maximized. Furry animals curl up in a ball to minimize their surface area, thus reducing heat loss.

SOLUTIONS - PART A PROBLEMS

Chapter 14: Geometry Using Triangle Congruence and Similarity

Section 14.1

9. (a) For the given triangles, there are two pair of sides marked congruent as well as the included angle. Thus, the SAS congruence property can be used.

   (b) For the given triangle, there are two pair of sides marked congruent, but the included angle is not marked congruent. Thus, the SAS congruence property cannot be used. Because only one pair of angles is marked congruent the ASA congruence property cannot be used. The third pair of sides is not marked congruent so the SSS congruence property cannot be used.

   (c) For the given triangles, there are two pair of sides marked congruent. The included angles for both triangles are marked as right angles, so they are congruent. Thus, the SAS congruence property can be used.

Section 14.1

10. (a) Triangle ABC is isosceles so m$\angle C$ = 70° and m$\angle A$ = 40°. Thus, $\triangle ABC \cong \triangle DEF$ by SAS.

   (b) In $\triangle RST$, m$\angle T$ = 50°. In $\triangle UVW$, m$\angle V$ = 50° also. However, there is no SAS or ASA correspondence so the triangles are not congruent.

   (c) Both triangles are equilateral because all angles measure 60°. They also each have one side marked as 7 units long. Thus, $\triangle JKL \cong \triangle XYZ$ by ASA.

Section 14.1

11. (a) Both pairs of legs are marked congruent. For both triangles, the included angle is a right angle. Thus the SAS congruence property holds for this pair of right triangles.

   (b) The right angles are congruent. Another pair of angles is marked congruent as well as the included sides of both triangles. Thus, the ASA congruence property holds for this pair of right triangles.

   (c) The hypotenuse of each triangle is marked congruent as well as one acute angle in each triangle. Both triangles contain a right angle so the remaining angles must also be congruent. Thus, the ASA congruence property holds for this pair of right triangles.

Section 14.1

12. (a) $\angle A \cong \angle D$ since they both measure 30°. $\overline{AB} \cong \overline{DE}$ and $\overline{BC} \cong \overline{EF}$.

(b) No, the triangles do not appear to be congruent.

(c) Triangles cannot be shown to be congruent by a SSA property. When two pairs of corresponding sides are congruent, but not the included angle, there is the potential for two very different triangles to be formed.

Section 14.1

13. $\overline{BC}$ is longer than $\overline{YZ}$. The 70° angle opens wider than a 40° angle so the side directly across from the 70° angle must be longer.

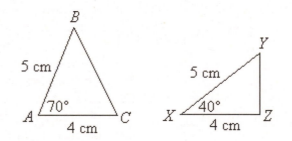

Section 14.1

14. (a) Since, after marking off $\overline{AB}$, Ken walked the same distance to C, $\overline{AB} \cong \overline{AC}$. Both $\angle TAB$ and $\angle DCB$ are right angles and therefore congruent. From where Ken stands at point D, Betty is lined up with the tree. Therefore, the points D, B, and T are collinear. By vertical angles, $\angle TBA \cong \angle DBC$.

(b) $\triangle ABT \cong \triangle CBD$ by ASA.

(c) Since the triangles are congruent and side $\overline{CD}$ of $\triangle CBD$ corresponds to side $\overline{AT}$ of $\triangle ABT$, $\overline{CD} \cong \overline{AT}$.

Ken and Betty can find the length of $\overline{CD}$, so they will know the width of the river.

Section 14.1

15. (a) We can draw two noncongruent triangles that have three pairs of corresponding parts congruent. Consider two different equilateral triangles.

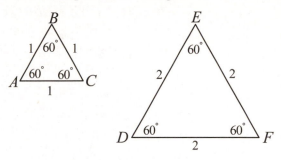

All pairs of corresponding angles of the two triangles are congruent, but the triangles are not congruent.

(b) It is impossible to draw two noncongruent triangles that have four pairs of corresponding parts congruent. Consider all possible situations:

(i)   If three pairs of corresponding sides and one pair of corresponding angles is congruent, then the triangles will be congruent by SSS.

(ii) If two pairs of corresponding sides and two pairs of corresponding angles are congruent, then the triangles will be congruent by ASA since the third pair of angles is forced to also be congruent.

(iii) If one pair of corresponding sides and three pairs of corresponding angles are congruent, then the triangles will be congruent by ASA.

(c) It is impossible to draw two noncongruent triangles with five pairs of corresponding parts congruent. Consider all cases:

(i) If three pairs of corresponding sides and two pairs of corresponding angles are congruent, then the triangles are congruent by SSS or ASA.

(ii) If two pairs of corresponding sides and three pairs of corresponding angles are congruent, then the triangles will be congruent by ASA.

(d) It is impossible to draw two noncongruent triangles with six pairs of corresponding parts congruent. If all three corresponding angles are congruent and all three corresponding sides are congruent, then the triangles are congruent by SSS, ASA, or SAS.

Section 14.1

16. (a) $\triangle XYZ \cong \triangle BCD$ by SAS since $\overline{BC} \cong \overline{XY}$, $\angle C \cong \angle Y$, and $\overline{CD} \cong \overline{YZ}$.

    (b) We are given that $\angle ABC \cong \angle WXY$. Since $\triangle XYZ \cong \triangle BCD$, $\angle 2 \cong \angle 6$ by corresponding parts.
    $m(\angle ABC) = m(\angle 1) + m(\angle 2)$ and
    $m(\angle WXY) = m(\angle 5) + m(\angle 6)$
    $m(\angle 1) + m(\angle 2) = m(\angle 5) + m(\angle 6)$ ($\angle ABC \cong \angle WXY$)
    $m(\angle 1) + m(\angle 6) = m(\angle 5) + m(\angle 6)$ (by substitution)
    $m(\angle 1) \cong m(\angle 5)$ (by subtraction)
    So, $\angle 1 \cong \angle 5$.

    (c) Since $\triangle XYZ \cong \triangle BCD$, we know $\overline{BD} \cong \overline{XZ}$. Therefore, $\triangle ABD \cong \triangle WXZ$ by SAS. ($\overline{AB} \cong \overline{WX}$, $\angle 1 \cong \angle 5$, and $\overline{BD} \cong \overline{XZ}$.) Other corresponding parts that are congruent are $\overline{AD}$ and $\overline{WZ}$, and $\angle BAD \cong \angle XWZ$.

    (d) Since $\triangle ABD \cong \triangle WXZ$, $\angle 3 \cong \angle 7$ by corresponding parts. Since $\triangle BCD \cong \triangle XYZ$, $\angle 4 \cong \angle 8$ by corresponding parts. Therefore, since $m(\angle ADC) = m(\angle 3) + m(\angle 4)$ and $m(\angle WZY) = m(\angle 7) + m(\angle 8)$, by substitution we have $m(\angle ADC) = m(\angle 7) + m(\angle 8)$. Thus, $\angle ADC \cong \angle WZY$.

    (e) All corresponding parts of quadrilaterals $ABCD$ and $WXYZ$ have been shown to be congruent. Therefore, $ABCD \cong WXYZ$.

Section 14.1

17. Suppose $\angle D$ and $\angle E$ are supplementary and congruent. Let $m(\angle D) = x$. Then $m(\angle E) = x$. Since the angles are supplementary, $m(\angle D) + m(\angle E) = 180^\circ$. By substitution, $x + x = 180^\circ$, or $2x = 180^\circ$, so $x = 90^\circ$. Therefore, $m(\angle D) = 90^\circ$ and $m(\angle E) = 90^\circ$.

Section 14.1

18. (a) and (b)

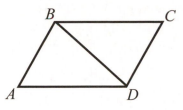

From Example 14.3, we know that in parallelogram *ABCD* with diagonal $\overline{DB}$, $\triangle ABD \cong \triangle CDB$. By corresponding parts, $\overline{AB} \cong \overline{CD}$, $\overline{BC} \cong \overline{DA}$, $\overline{BD} \cong \overline{DB}$, $\angle ABD \cong \angle CDB$, $\angle ADB \cong \angle CBD$, and $\angle A \cong \angle C$. Notice that $m(\angle B) = m(\angle ABD) + m(\angle CBD)$, and $m(\angle D) = m(\angle CDB) + m(\angle ADB)$. So we have the following:

$m(\angle B) = m(\angle ABD) + m(\angle CBD)$
$\qquad = m(\angle CDB) + m(\angle CBD) \text{ (by } \angle ABD \cong \angle CDB\text{)}$
$\qquad = m(\angle CDB) + m(\angle ADB) \text{ (by } \angle ADB \cong \angle CBD\text{)}$
$m(\angle B) = m(\angle D)$

Therefore, $\angle B \cong \angle D$.

Section 14.1

19. Access the Chapter 14 eManipulative, *Congruence*.

(a) Click on the SAS option. Each blue segment or angle given is equal in length to a red segment or angle. Move the blue segments and angle so they form a triangle. Do the same with the red segments and angle. Position one triangle on top of the other to determine if they are congruent. The two triangles will always be congruent because of the SAS Congruence Property.

(b) Click on the SSA option. Rearrange the sides and angles to create two triangles. Notice that sometimes you create congruent triangles and sometimes you do not. There is no guarantee that you will end up with congruent triangles in this situation. The following figures demonstrate this.

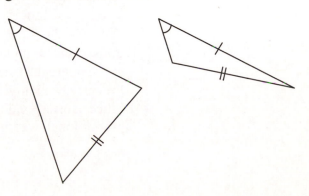

Section 14.2

10. (a) Line l_1 contains $\overline{AD}$ and is parallel to line l_2 which contains $\overline{BE}$, so $\overline{AD} \parallel \overline{BE}$. Transversal m contains $\overline{AB}$ and is parallel to transversal n which contains $\overline{DE}$, so $\overline{AB} \parallel \overline{DE}$. Therefore, quadrilateral $ABED$ is a parallelogram because it has two pairs of opposite sides parallel. Similarly, using lines l_2 and l_3, $\overline{BE} \parallel \overline{CF}$ and $\overline{BC} \parallel \overline{EF}$, so quadrilateral $BCFE$ is a parallelogram.

(b) Since $ABED$ is a parallelogram such that $\overline{AB}$ and $\overline{DE}$ are opposite sides, we know $AB = DE$ since opposite sides of a parallelogram are congruent. Similarly, since $BCFE$ is a parallelogram, we know that $BC = EF$.

(c) Complete the proportion by identifying the corresponding parts of parallelograms $ABED$ and $BCFE$. $\overline{AB}$ and $\overline{BC}$ are corresponding parts, and $\overline{DE}$ and $\overline{EF}$ are corresponding parts. Therefore, $\dfrac{AB}{BC} = \dfrac{DE}{EF}$.

(d) Since $\dfrac{AB}{BC} = \dfrac{DE}{EF}$, we see that lines l_1, l_2, and l_3 have intercepted proportional segments on transversals m and n.

Section 14.2

11. (a) Consider the following triangles: ΔPAD, ΔPBE, and ΔPCF. We know $\angle APD \cong \angle BPE \cong \angle CPF$ since the transversals that form the angles for each triangle intersect at P. We also know $\angle PAD \cong \angle PBE \cong \angle PCF$ since these angles are corresponding angles formed when parallel lines l_1, l_2, and l_3, respectively, are cut by transversal m, and we know that corresponding angles are congruent. Therefore, by the AA Similarity Property, we know that $\Delta PAD \sim \Delta PBE \sim \Delta PCF$.

(b) Since corresponding parts of similar triangles are proportional, we know the following:

$$\frac{a}{a+b} = \frac{x}{x+y}$$

$$a(x+y) = x(a+b)$$

$$ax + ay = ax + bx$$

$$ay = bx$$

(c) Since corresponding parts of similar triangles are proportional, we know the following:

$$\frac{a}{a+b+c} = \frac{x}{x+y+z}$$

$$a(x+y+z) = x(a+b+c)$$

$$ax + ay + az = ax + bx + cx$$

$$ay + az = bx + cx$$

(d) From part (b), we know $ay = bx$, and from part (c), we know $ay + az = bx + cx$. Therefore, we can substitute bx for ay.

$$bx + az = bx + cx$$

$$az = cx$$

(e) From part (b), we know that $ay = bx$. From part (d), we know $az = cx$. Therefore, $\frac{bx}{cx} = \frac{ay}{az}$ and simplifying gives $\frac{b}{c} = \frac{y}{z}$.

(f) From part (b), we know $\frac{a}{b} = \frac{x}{y}$ since $ay = bx$. From part (d), we know $\frac{a}{c} = \frac{x}{z}$ since $az = cx$. From part (e), we know $\frac{b}{c} = \frac{y}{z}$. Therefore parallel lines l_1, l_2, and l_3 have intercepted proportional segments on transversals m and n.

Section 14.2

12. (a) Consider parallel lines l_1, l_2, and l_3: $\frac{AB}{BC} = \frac{EF}{FG} = \frac{KJ}{JG}$.

(b) Consider parallel lines l_2, l_3, and l_4: $\frac{FG}{GH} = \frac{BC}{CD} = \frac{JG}{GI}$.

(c) Consider parallel lines l_1, l_2, l_3, and l_4:
$$\frac{IJ}{JK} = \frac{DB}{BA} = \frac{HF}{FE}.$$

Section 14.2

13. Assume that the tree and the pole are on level ground and create right angles with the ground. The rays of light that strike the tree and pole are parallel. Consider the following diagram.

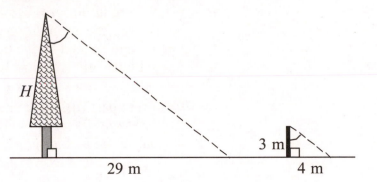

Notice that the right triangles formed are similar by the AA Similarity Property. Therefore, corresponding sides of the triangles are proportional. Set up a proportion and solve it.

$$\frac{H}{3 \text{ m}} = \frac{29 \text{ m}}{4 \text{ m}}$$

$$4H = 87 \text{ m}$$

$$H = 21.75 \text{ m}$$

Therefore, the height of the tree is approximately 22 meters.

Section 14.2

14. (a) Assume that the ground is level and that the tree and the person each form a right angle with the ground. We know then that $m(\angle ABC) = 90° = m(\angle EDC)$, so we have $\angle ABC \cong \angle EDC$. Because the person sees the top of the tree when looking in the mirror, the angle from the mirror to the top of the tree must be the same as the angle from the mirror to the top of the person. (That is, the angle of incidence is congruent to the angle of reflection.) Therefore, $\angle ACB \cong \angle ECD$. By the AA Similarity Property, $\triangle ABC \cong \triangle EDC$.

(b) Set up a proportion to find the height, AB, of the tree.

$$\frac{AB}{ED} = \frac{BC}{DC}$$

$$\frac{AB}{1.5} = \frac{18}{1}$$

$$AB = 27 \text{ m}$$

Therefore, the tree is 27 meters tall.

Section 14.2

15. (a) Notice, in our problem, that the triangle formed by the person, the ground, and the shadow is similar to the triangle formed by the tree, the ground, and the shadow. Set up a proportion to find the length of the shadow of the tree.

$$\frac{\text{Height of person}}{\text{Height of tree}} = \frac{\text{Length of person's shadow}}{\text{Length of tree's shadow}}$$

Let x represent the length of the tree's shadow.

$$\frac{6}{100} = \frac{9}{x}$$

$$6x = 900$$

$$x = 150 \text{ feet}$$

Therefore, the tree casts a shadow 150 feet in length.

(b) Consider how this situation creates similar triangles in the following diagram.

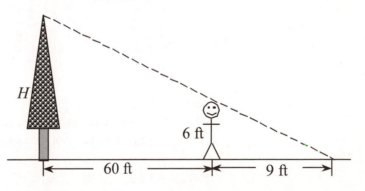

$$\frac{H}{6} = \frac{60+9}{9}$$

$$\frac{H}{6} = \frac{69}{9}$$

$$9H = 414$$

$$H = 46 \text{ feet}$$

Therefore, the tree is 46 feet tall.

Section 14.2

16. (a) Set up a proportion using ratios that compare thumb height to distance from the projector.

$$\frac{\text{Thumb length (actual)}}{\text{Thumb to screen distance}} = \frac{\text{Thumb length (on screen)}}{\text{Projector to screen distance}}$$

$$\frac{2 \text{ inches}}{5 \text{ feet}} = \frac{x \text{ inches}}{24 \text{ feet}}$$

$$2(24) = 5x$$

$$48 = 5x$$

$$9.6 = x$$

Therefore, the thumb appears to be 9.6 inches tall on the screen.

(b) Change the measurement in the proportion from part (a) to reflect the change in the distance from the projector.

$$\frac{2 \text{ inches}}{10 \text{ feet}} = \frac{x \text{ inches}}{24 \text{ feet}}$$

$$2(24) = 10x$$

$$48 = 10x$$

$$4.8 = x$$

Therefore, the thumb appears to be 4.8 inches tall on the screen, or half as tall as before.

Section 14.2

17. Consider the diagram shown below.

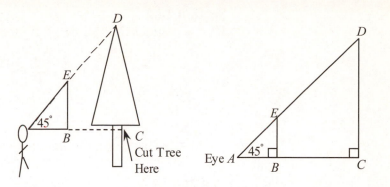

$\triangle ABE$ is a right isosceles triangle. Notice that $m(\angle ABE) = 90°$, $m(\angle EAB) = 45°$ and $m(\angle BEA) = 45°$. Consider $\triangle ACD$. In $\triangle ACD$, $m(\angle ACD) = 90°$ assuming the tree is vertical and is growing on level ground. We know $m(\angle DAC) = 45°$ since the top of the tree is exactly in line with the hypotenuse of $\triangle ABE$. We also know $m(\angle CDA) = 45°$ since the sum of the angles in any triangle is 180°. Therefore, $\triangle ABE \sim \triangle ACD$ by the AA Similarity Property. Hence, $\triangle ACD$ is also a right isosceles triangle. The height, *CD*, above the cut line is the same length as *AC*, the distance from where you stand to the tree. The tip of the top of the tree will land where you are standing.

Section 14.2

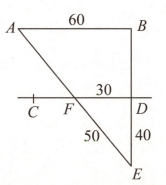

18. Since $\overline{AB} \parallel \overline{CD}$ and $\overline{AE}$ and $\overline{EB}$ are transversals, $\angle BAE \cong \angle DFE$, and $\angle ABE \cong \angle FDE$ by corresponding parts. Therefore, $\triangle EBA \sim \triangle EDF$. Since all angles are congruent (Note: $\angle E \cong \angle E$), corresponding parts are proportional.

$$\frac{DE}{FD} = \frac{BE}{AB}$$

$$\frac{40}{30} = \frac{40 + BD}{60}$$

$$\frac{2400}{30} = 40 + BD$$

$$80 - 40 = BD$$

$$40 = BD$$

Therefore, the canyon is 40 meters wide.

Section 14.2

19. Consider the following figures.

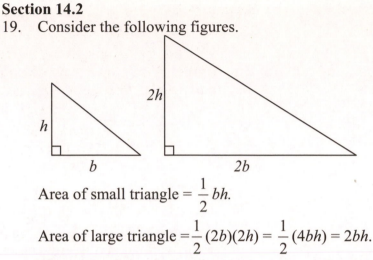

Area of small triangle $= \dfrac{1}{2}bh$.

Area of large triangle $= \dfrac{1}{2}(2b)(2h) = \dfrac{1}{2}(4bh) = 2bh$.

The area of the large triangle is 4 times the area of the small triangle.

Section 14.2

20. (1) $\Delta ACB \sim \Delta CDB$ since corresponding angles are congruent. $m(\angle ACB) = 90° = m(\angle CDB)$, and $\angle CBA \cong \angle DBC$, since they are the same angle. Therefore, since two pairs of corresponding angles are congruent, the third pair is also congruent.

(2) Also, $\Delta ACB \sim \Delta ADC$ since corresponding angles are congruent. $m(\angle ACB) = 90° = m(\angle ADC)$. $\angle BAC \cong \angle CAD$ since they are the same angle. Therefore, since two pairs of corresponding angles are congruent, the third pair is also congruent.

(3) Therefore, $\Delta CDB \sim \Delta ADC$ since both of them are similar to ΔACB. Corresponding sides of similar triangles are proportional.

$$\frac{AD}{DC} = \frac{CD}{DB}$$

$$\frac{a}{x} = \frac{x}{1}$$

$$a = x^2$$

$$\sqrt{a} = x$$

Section 14.2

21. We are given that $\overline{DE} \parallel \overline{AB}$, and we can think of segments $\overline{AC}$ and $\overline{BC}$ as transversals. From problem 11, we know parallel lines intercept proportional segments on all transversals. Therefore, we have the following:

$$\frac{CD}{DA} = \frac{CE}{EB}$$

$$\frac{9}{3} = \frac{CE}{2}$$

$$18 = 3CE$$

$$6 = CE$$

$CB = CE + EB = 6 + 2 = 8$ and $CA = CD + DA = 9 + 3 = 12$. By the Pythagorean theorem, $12^2 + 8^2 = (AB)^2$, or $208 = (AB)^2$, so $\sqrt{208} = 4\sqrt{13} = AB$.

Section 14.2

22. Consider the following diagram. Notice that there are three right triangles: $\triangle ABC$, $\triangle ADB$, and $\triangle BDC$.

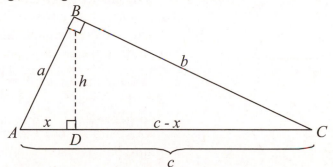

$\angle ABC \cong \angle BDC \cong \angle ADB$, since they are all right angles.

$\angle ACB \cong \angle BCD$, since they are the same angle.

$\angle CAB \cong \angle BAD$, since they are the same angle.

By the AA Similarity Property, we know that $\triangle ABC \sim \triangle BDC$ and $\triangle ABC \sim \triangle ADB$, so all three triangles are similar. Therefore, we know that side lengths are proportional.

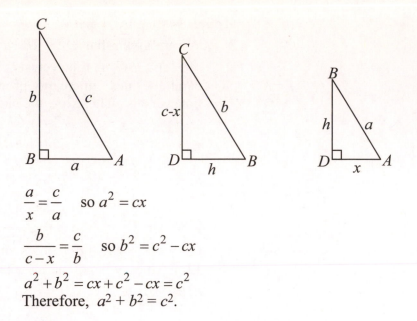

$$\frac{a}{x} = \frac{c}{a} \quad \text{so } a^2 = cx$$

$$\frac{b}{c-x} = \frac{c}{b} \quad \text{so } b^2 = c^2 - cx$$

$$a^2 + b^2 = cx + c^2 - cx = c^2$$

Therefore, $a^2 + b^2 = c^2$.

Section 14.2

23. (a) The initial Koch curve is a three-pointed star. If each side has length 1 unit, then the perimeter is 3 units.

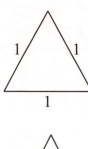

(b) The second curve is a six-pointed star. Since each side of the original three-pointed star has the middle third replaced with an equilateral triangle, the side lengths must each be $\frac{1}{3}$ unit. Therefore, the perimeter of the curve is $\frac{1}{3}$(the number of flat sides) = $\frac{1}{3}(12) = 4$ units.

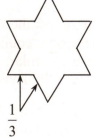

(c) In the third curve, each flat side will be $\frac{1}{3}$ as large as each flat side in the second curve. Therefore, each flat side in the third curve will have a length of $\frac{1}{3}\left(\frac{1}{3}\right) = \frac{1}{9}$ unit. The perimeter of the third curve is $\frac{1}{9}$(the number of flat sides) = $\frac{1}{9}(48) = 5\frac{1}{3}$ units.

(d) To find the perimeter of the nth curve, make a table. In the construction of each curve, every line segment from the previous curve is replaced with four shorter segments. Each of these segments is one-third as long as the line segment from the previous curve.

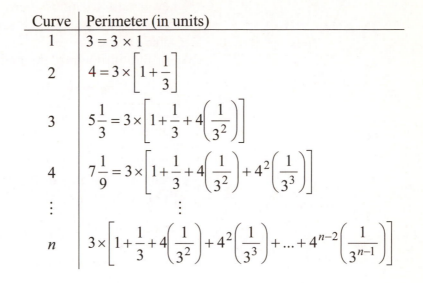

Curve	Perimeter (in units)
1	$3 = 3 \times 1$
2	$4 = 3 \times \left[1 + \dfrac{1}{3} \right]$
3	$5\dfrac{1}{3} = 3 \times \left[1 + \dfrac{1}{3} + 4 \left(\dfrac{1}{3^2} \right) \right]$
4	$7\dfrac{1}{9} = 3 \times \left[1 + \dfrac{1}{3} + 4 \left(\dfrac{1}{3^2} \right) + 4^2 \left(\dfrac{1}{3^3} \right) \right]$
⋮	⋮
n	$3 \times \left[1 + \dfrac{1}{3} + 4 \left(\dfrac{1}{3^2} \right) + 4^2 \left(\dfrac{1}{3^3} \right) + \dots + 4^{n-2} \left(\dfrac{1}{3^{n-1}} \right) \right]$

Section 14.2

24. (a) Consider the original curve and the second curve. Notice that the dotted length in the second curve is $\dfrac{1}{3}$ of the length of the side of the original curve. Recall that the area of a triangle is $\dfrac{1}{2}$(base)(height) $= \dfrac{1}{2}bh$. Notice that the original

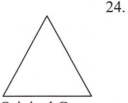

Original Curve

Second Curve

curve and the small triangle formed by the dotted line in the second curve are both equilateral triangles. Therefore, they are similar, and corresponding parts are proportional. We know that the base of the small triangle is $\dfrac{1}{3}$ of the base of the original curve. The height of the small triangle is $\dfrac{1}{3}$ of the height of the original curve. Therefore,

the area of the small triangle is calculated as follows:

$$\frac{1}{2}\left(\frac{1}{3}b \right)\left(\frac{1}{3}h \right) = \frac{1}{3^2}\left(\frac{1}{2}bh \right) = \frac{1}{9}(\text{original curve area})$$

Since the original curve has an area of 9 square units, each small triangle has an area of 1 square unit. Three new small triangles were added to form the second curve, so the area of the second curve is $9 + 3(1) = 12$ square units.

(b) For the third curve, the area of each new small triangle is $\dfrac{1}{9}$ of the area of a small triangle from the second curve, or $\dfrac{1}{9}(1) = \dfrac{1}{9}$ square unit. Since 12 new triangles were added to form the third curve, the area of the third curve is the area of the second curve plus the areas of the 12 new triangles.

$$\text{Area} = 12 + 12\left(\frac{1}{9}\right) = 12 + \frac{4}{3} = 13\frac{1}{3} \text{ square units}$$

(c) For the fourth curve, the area of each new small triangle is $\dfrac{1}{9}$ of the area of a small triangle from the third curve, or $\dfrac{1}{9}\left(\dfrac{1}{9}\right) = \dfrac{1}{81}$ square units. Since there are $4 \times 12 = 48$ new triangles in the fourth curve, the area of the fourth curve $= 13\dfrac{1}{3} + 48\left(\dfrac{1}{81}\right) = 13\dfrac{1}{3} + \dfrac{16}{27} = 13\dfrac{25}{27}$ square units.

(d) To find the area of the nth curve, make a table. In the construction of each curve, four smaller triangles are added on to each section of the figure. The area of each of the smaller triangles is $\dfrac{1}{3^2}$ or $\dfrac{1}{9}$ as large as the area of a small triangle from the previous curve.

Curve	Area (in square units)
1	$9 = 3 \times 3$
2	$12 = 3 \times [3 + 1]$
3	$13\dfrac{1}{3} = 3 \times \left[3 + 1 + 4\left(\dfrac{1}{3^2}\right)\right]$

4	$13\frac{25}{27} = 3 \times \left[3 + 1 + 4\left(\frac{1}{3^2}\right) + 4^2\left(\frac{1}{3^4}\right) \right]$
5	$14\frac{46}{243} = 3 \times \left[3 + 1 + 4\left(\frac{1}{3^2}\right) + 4^2\left(\frac{1}{3^4}\right) + 4^3\left(\frac{1}{3^6}\right) \right]$
$\vdots$	$\vdots$
n	$3 \times \left[3 + 1 + 4\left(\frac{1}{3^2}\right) + 4^2\left(\frac{1}{3^4}\right) + \ldots + 4^{n-2}\left(\frac{1}{3^{2n-4}}\right) \right]$

Section 14.3

10. There are several different ways these constructions can be carried out.

    (a) A 90° angle can be constructed in several ways. One way would be to follow the *Construct a Perpendicular Bisector* construction.

    (b) To create a 45° angle, use the right angle from part (a) and follow the *Bisect an Angle* construction.

    (c) A 270° angle can be constructed by constructing perpendicular lines. Follow the *Construct a Perpendicular Line Through a Point on a Line* construction and then follow the *Bisect an Angle* construction to obtain the 135° angle.

    (d) A 67.5° angle can be constructed by following the *Bisect an Angle* construction on the 135° angle from part (c).

Section 14.3

11. Follow the *Construct a Perpendicular Bisector* construction to locate the midpoint of each of the three sides of the triangle. Use a straightedge to connect each midpoint to the opposite vertex. Notice all three medians intersect in a single point as shown.

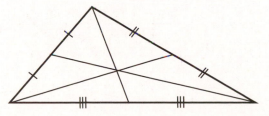

Section 14.3

12. Use the *Construct a Perpendicular Line to a Given Line Through a Point Not on the Line* construction. For each altitude use the vertex as the point not on the line and construct a perpendicular segment to side opposite the vertex. Notice all three altitudes intersect in a single point as shown.

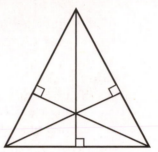

Section 14.3

13. (a) Use a compass and straightedge and the Construct a Perpendicular Bisector construction to construct a right angle. Using a convenient length as 1 unit, mark off 3 units along one side of the right angle and 4 units along the other. According to the Pythagorean theorem, the hypotenuse should be 5 units long, since $3^2 + 4^2 = 9 + 16 = 25 = 5^2$. Use your compass to mark off 5 units along the hypotenuse to check.

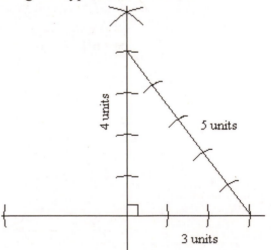

(b) This time the hypotenuse should be 13 units long since $5^2 + 12^2 = 25 + 144 = 169 = 13^2$. Use your compass to mark off 13 units along the hypotenuse to check.

(c) The other leg should 15 units long. Let b represent the length of the other leg, then by the Pythagorean theorem, we know $8^2 + b^2 = 17^2$. Thus, $b = \sqrt{17^2 - 8^2} = \sqrt{289 - 64} = \sqrt{225} = 15$. Use your compass to mark off 15 units along the other leg to check.

Section 14.3

14. (a) Construct a segment and use the compass to mark a length $3a$ units long. Construct two more segments, one $3b$ units long, and the other $3c$ units long.

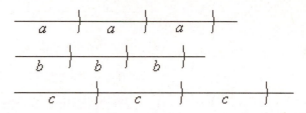

The endpoints of the segment with length $3c$ form two of the three vertices of the triangle. Label them P and Q. From point P, swing an arc with radius $3b$. From point Q, swing an arc with radius $3a$ that intersects the first arc in point R. Draw the sides to complete the $\triangle PQR$.

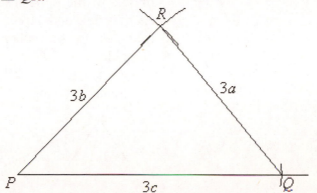

(b) Using a protractor, we can verify that the measures of $\angle P$, $\angle Q$, and $\angle R$ are equal to the measures of $\angle A$, $\angle B$, and $\angle C$, respectively.

(c) $\triangle ABC \sim \triangle PQR$ since corresponding angles are congruent and sides are proportional by construction.

(d) This construction verifies the SSS similarity property.

Section 14.3

15. Use the Copy an Angle construction to copy $\angle A$. Label the copy $\angle P$. Pick a convenient point along one side of $\angle P$ as the vertex of the triangle and copy $\angle B$. Label this angle as $\angle Q$. The intersection of the two extended sides is point R.

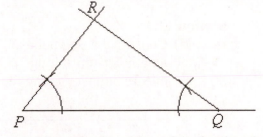

(a) Measure the sides of each triangle. Compare ratios of corresponding sides. Notice $\dfrac{PQ}{AB} = \dfrac{PR}{AC} = \dfrac{QR}{BC}$.

(b) Corresponding angles are congruent by construction and corresponding sides are proportional, so $\triangle ABC \sim \triangle PQR$.

(c) This construction verifies the AA similarity property.

Section 14.3

16. The medians of a triangle extend from each vertex to the middle of the opposite side. Angle bisectors extend from each vertex and bisect the angle. Draw several types of triangles to see when the median and angle bisector coincide.

Scalene Triangle

The median and angle bisector do not coincide in a scalene triangle.

Angle Bisector   Median

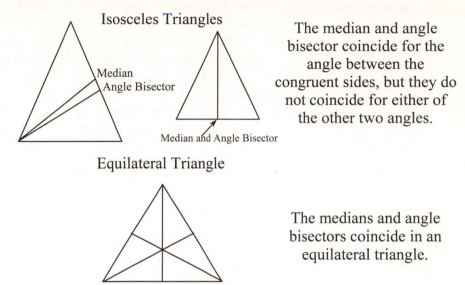

Isosceles Triangles

Median
Angle Bisector

Median and Angle Bisector

The median and angle bisector coincide for the angle between the congruent sides, but they do not coincide for either of the other two angles.

Equilateral Triangle

The medians and angle bisectors coincide in an equilateral triangle.

Each Median is an Angle Bisector

All medians and angle bisectors coincide in equilateral triangles, and in isosceles triangles, one median coincides with one angle bisector for the angle between the congruent sides.

Section 14.3

17. Access Geometer's Sketchpad® and construct a triangle, ΔABC, including all three angle bisectors and all three medians. Remember that a median of a triangle is a segment joining a vertex and the midpoint of the opposite side. After the constructions are completed, move the vertices and determine what types of triangle have exactly one median that coincides with an angle bisector. In an isosceles triangle, that is not equilateral, the angle formed by the congruent sides will have its median coincide with the angle bisector. In an equilateral triangle, all three angle bisectors coincide with medians.

Section 14.3
18. Draw several types of triangles, constructing the medians and the perpendicular bisectors in each of them.

Scalene Triangle

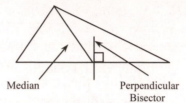

Median   Perpendicular
Bisector

The median and perpendicular bisector do not coincide in a scalene triangle.

Isosceles Triangle

Median and Perpendicular Bisector

Perpendicular Bisector

Median

The median and perpendicular bisector coincide for the angle between congruent sides, but they do not coincide for either of the other two angles.

Equilateral Triangle

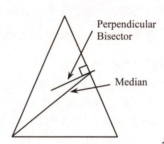

Each Median is a Perpendicular Bisector

The medians and perpendicular bisectors coincide in an equilateral triangle.

All medians and perpendicular bisectors coincide in equilateral triangles, and in isosceles triangles, one median coincides with one perpendicular bisector for the angle between the congruent sides.

Section 14.3

19. Access Geometer's Sketchpad® and construct a triangle, $\triangle ABC$, with all three perpendicular bisectors and all three medians. Remember that a median of a triangle is a segment joining a vertex and the midpoint of the opposite side. After the constructions are completed, move the vertices and determine what type of triangle(s) have exactly one median that coincides with a perpendicular bisector. In an isosceles triangle, that is not equilateral, the angle formed by the congruent sides, will have its median coincide with the perpendicular bisector. In an equilateral triangle, all three perpendicular bisectors will coincide with the medians.

Section 14.3

20. (a) In the first two steps of the construction, we marked off arcs of radius r from A to B and labeled the points of intersection P and Q. $\triangle APQ$ and $\triangle BPQ$ are formed by drawing segments. The distances from A to P and from B to P are both r. Therefore, $\overline{AP} \cong \overline{BP}$ by construction. Similarly, $\overline{AQ} \cong \overline{PQ}$ by construction. Since $\overline{PQ} \cong \overline{PQ}$, we know $\triangle APQ \cong \triangle BPQ$ by SSS.

(b) From (a), we know $\overline{AP} \cong \overline{BP}$. Since $\triangle APQ \cong \triangle BPQ$, we know $\angle APR \cong \angle BPR$ by corresponding parts. $\overline{PR} \cong \overline{PR}$ since every segment is congruent to itself. Therefore, $\triangle APR \cong \triangle BPR$ by SAS.

(c) A, R, and B are collinear. $\angle PRB$ and $\angle PRA$ are supplementary so $m(\angle PRB) + m(\angle PRA) = 180°$. Since $\triangle APR \cong \triangle BPR$, we know $\angle PRB \cong \angle PRA$ by corresponding parts. Therefore, by substitution, $m(\angle PRB) + m(\angle PRB) = 180°$. So $m(\angle PRB) = 90°$ and $m(\angle PRA) = 90°$. We conclude $\overline{PR}$ is perpendicular to $\overline{AB}$.

(d) Since $\triangle APR \cong \triangle BPR$, we know corresponding parts are congruent. Therefore, $\overline{AR} \cong \overline{BR}$. Since $\overline{PQ}$ passes through point R, $\overline{PQ}$ bisects $\overline{AB}$.

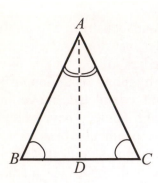

Section 14.3

21. Consider $\triangle ABC$ with equal base angles. Construct the bisector of $\angle A$. Label the intersection of the angle bisector and $\overline{BC}$ point D. By the definition of angle bisector, $\angle BAD \cong \angle CAD$. We know $\overline{AD} \cong \overline{AD}$, and $\angle ABD \cong \angle ACD$, so by AAS, $\triangle BAD \cong \triangle CAD$. Therefore, since corresponding parts of congruent triangles are congruent, $\overline{AB} \cong \overline{AC}$, and $\triangle ABC$ is isosceles.

Section 14.4

12. (a) Follow the *Equilateral Triangle* construction to create a 60° angle. Bisect the 60° angle to create a 30° angle. Bisect the 30° angle to create a 15° angle.

    (b) Use the *Copy an Angle* construction to copy a 60° angle and a 15° angle from part (a) so that they share a side.

    (c) Create a 90° angle by following the *Construct a Perpendicular Bisector* construction. Use the Copy an Angle construction to copy a 15° angle from part (a) so that the 90° angle and the 15° angle share a side.

Section 14.4

13. Use the Construct a Perpendicular Bisector construction to create a 90° angle and bisect $\overline{AB}$. From B, swing an arc with radius $2a$ so that it intersects the other leg of the right angle. This creates a 60° angle. [Notice that if we would swing an arc with radius $2a$ from point A, it would intersect the first arc. The point of intersection of the arcs together with points A and B would create the vertices of an equilateral triangle, which has 60° angles.] The remaining angle of the triangle must measure 30°. Notice the hypotenuse has a length that is twice as long as the shorter leg. This relationship will always be true for any 30°-60°-90° triangle.

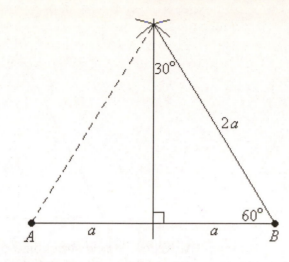

Section 14.4

14. Follow the instructions in part (i.) through (v.) to construct a golden rectangle. The figure for one such construction is given in the problem. Yours will be similar. Very carefully measure the length and width of your golden rectangle to the nearest tenth of a millimeter and calculate $\dfrac{\text{length}}{\text{width}}$. You should observe $\dfrac{\text{length}}{\text{width}} \approx 1.618$. The golden ratio is $\dfrac{1+\sqrt{5}}{2}$ which can be approximated by 1.618.

Section 14.4

15. (a) Draw an acute triangle. Recall that the circumcenter of a triangle must be a point on each of the perpendicular bisectors of the sides. Construct each perpendicular bisector, as shown in the next figure. Point D is the circumcenter.

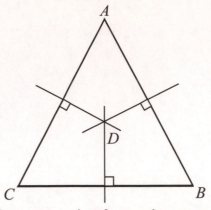

(b) Repeat the construction for another acute triangle.

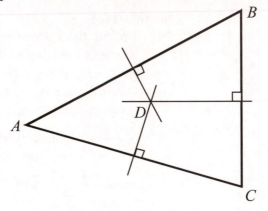

(c) The circumcenter appears to lie inside an acute triangle.

Section 14.4

16. (a) Draw an obtuse triangle. Construct the perpendicular bisector of each side, as shown in the next figure. Point *D* is the circumcenter.

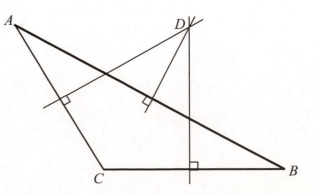

(b) Repeat the construction with a different obtuse triangle.

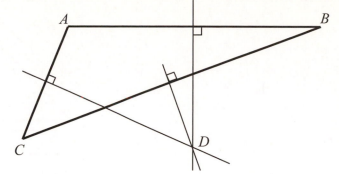

(c) The circumcenter appears to lie outside an obtuse triangle.

Section 14.4

17. (a) Use your ruler to measure the length of each side of $\Delta C_1 C_2 C_3$. Notice that they have equal measures. Use your protractor to measure each angle. Notice that they all measure 60°. Therefore, $\Delta C_1 C_2 C_3$ is equilateral.

(b) Repeat the construction using a right triangle and an obtuse triangle. In each case, $\Delta C_1 C_2 C_3$ is equilateral.

(c) $\Delta C_1 C_2 C_3$ formed in this manner is always an equilateral triangle. (Napoleon's theorem)

Section 14.4

18. **Case 1:** $a > 1$

Let $\overline{AD}$ be a line segment of length a. Let C be any point not on $\overline{AD}$ such that $AC = 1$. Let E be the point on $\overline{AD}$ such that $AE = 1$. Connect points C and D. Construct a line, m, through point E so that m is parallel to $\overline{CD}$. Let B be the point of intersection of m and $\overline{AC}$. We know $\angle AEB \cong \angle ADC$. Since $\angle BAE \cong \angle CAD$, we know that $\Delta ACD \sim \Delta ABE$ by the AA Similarity Property. Let $x = AB$. Using similar triangles $\dfrac{x}{1} = \dfrac{1}{a}$, so $x = \dfrac{1}{a}$.

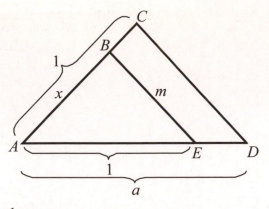

Case 2: $a < 1$

Construct a line segment, $\overline{AE}$, of length 1. Let $\overline{AD}$ be a line segment of length a on the line segment $\overline{AE}$. Let C be any point not on $\overline{AD}$ such that $AC = 1$. Connect points C and D. Construct a line, m, through point E so that m is parallel to $\overline{CD}$. Let B be the point of intersection of m and $\overleftrightarrow{AC}$. We know that $\angle AEB \cong \angle ADC$. Since $\angle BAE \cong \angle CAD$, we know that $\triangle ACD \sim \triangle ABE$ by the AA Similarity Property. Let $x = AB$. Then, using similar triangles, we have $\dfrac{x}{1} = \dfrac{1}{a}$, so $x = \dfrac{1}{a}$.

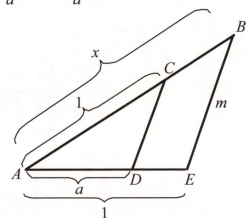

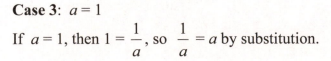

Case 3: $a = 1$

If $a = 1$, then $1 = \dfrac{1}{a}$, so $\dfrac{1}{a} = a$ by substitution.

Section 14.4

19. (a) We want to construct the geometric mean of 2 = a and
1 = b. Choose a length to represent a length of 1 unit.
Draw a line segment of length greater than 3 and label
one endpoint A. Place a compass at A and mark off a
length of 1. Label this point B.

Place a compass at B and mark off a length of 1.
Label this point C.

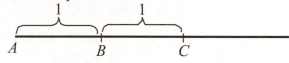

Then we have AC = 2 and BC = 1. Place a compass at
B and mark off a length of 2. Label this point D.

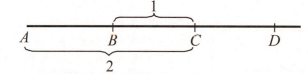

With the compass open to a length of 2, construct arcs
from points A and D. Label the intersection of these
arcs point E. Construct $\overline{EA}$, $\overline{EB}$, $\overline{EC}$, and $\overline{ED}$. The
length of $\overline{EB}$ is x. Since x is the geometric mean of
2 = a and 1 = b and we know $\dfrac{a}{x} = \dfrac{x}{b}$. If we substitute,

then we have $\dfrac{2}{x} = \dfrac{x}{1}$ so $2 = x^2$ and $x = \sqrt{2}$.

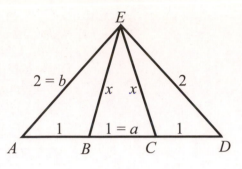

(b) By construction, $\overline{AC} \cong \overline{AE}$ so $\triangle AEC$ is isosceles. Also, $\overline{EB} \cong \overline{EC}$, so $\triangle EBC$ is isosceles. Therefore, we have $\angle EBC \cong \angle ECB$ and $\angle ACE \cong \angle AEC$. Now notice that $\angle ECB \cong \angle ACE$ since they are the same angle (just renamed). We see that $\triangle EBC$ and $\triangle AEC$ share the same base angle. Therefore, $\triangle EBC \sim \triangle AEC$ by the AA Similarity Property. Corresponding sides are proportional so $\dfrac{BC}{EB} = \dfrac{EC}{AE}$ or $\dfrac{a}{x} = \dfrac{x}{b}$.

Section 14.4

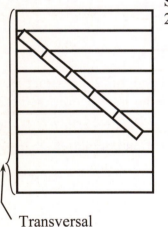

Transversal

20. Consider the edge of the lined paper. Let it be a transversal. The parallel lines on the page intercept congruent segments on the transversal. Place the plastic strip on the page so that the two corners of one edge lie exactly on lines five apart. This edge of the plastic strip can be thought of as another transversal. Mark five line segments on the plastic strip perpendicular to the length of the strip. Since parallel lines intercept proportional segments on all transversals, the line segments on the plastic strip are proportional to the line segments formed by the parallel lines on the paper. Since the line segments on the plastic strip are proportional to congruent segments, they are congruent.

Section 14.5

1. (a) $\angle CAD \cong \angle BAD$, since $\overline{AD}$ bisects $\angle CAB$. $\overline{AC} \cong \overline{AB}$ because $\triangle CAB$ is isosceles.
   (b) $\angle B \cong \angle C$, since angles opposite congruent sides of isosceles triangles are congruent.
   (c) ASA

(d) Corresponding parts of congruent triangles are congruent.

(e) Since $\angle ADC \cong \angle ADB$ and $\angle ADC$ and $\angle ADB$ are supplementary, the angles are right angles. Therefore, $\overline{AD}$ is perpendicular to $\overline{BC}$.

(f) From (c), $\triangle ACD \cong \triangle ABD$. Thus, $\overline{CD} \cong \overline{BD}$, since corresponding parts of congruent triangles are congruent. We know $\overline{AD}$ is perpendicular to $\overline{BC}$. Thus, $\overline{AD}$ is the perpendicular bisector of $\overline{BC}$.

Section 14.5

2. $\overline{AB} \cong \overline{CB}$ and $\overline{AD} \cong \overline{CD}$ since all sides of a rhombus are congruent. Also, $\overline{BD} \cong \overline{BD}$ because every segment is congruent to itself. Thus, $\triangle ABD \cong \triangle CBD$ by SSS. Now $\angle ABE \cong \angle CBE$ because they are corresponding parts, and $\overline{BE} \cong \overline{BE}$, since every segment is congruent to itself. Therefore, $\triangle ABE \cong \triangle CBE$ by SAS. $\angle AEB \cong \angle CEB$, since they are corresponding parts of congruent triangles. $m(\angle AEB) = 90° = m(\angle CEB)$ as the angles are both supplementary and congruent. Therefore, $\overline{AC}$ is perpendicular to $\overline{DB}$.

Section 14.5

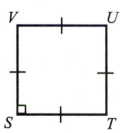

3. Consider quadrilateral $STUV$. $STUV$ is a rhombus, which has four sides of equal length, and $\angle S$ is a right angle. Since every rhombus is a parallelogram, rhombus $STUV$ is a parallelogram with four congruent sides. Since opposite angles in a parallelogram are congruent, $\angle S \cong \angle U$. Therefore, $\angle U$ is a right angle. We also know that adjacent angles are supplementary in a parallelogram, so $\angle S$ and $\angle T$ are supplementary.

$$m(\angle S) + m(\angle T) = 180°$$
$$90° + m(\angle T) = 180°$$
$$m(\angle T) = 90°$$

Therefore, $\angle T$ is a right angle. Similarly, since $\angle U$ and $\angle V$ are supplementary and $\angle U$ is a right angle, $\angle V$ is a right angle. Quadrilateral $STUV$ has four congruent sides and four right angles. Thus, $STUV$ is a square.

Section 14.5

4.	Since quadrilateral *ABCD* is a parallelogram, we know that $\overline{AB} \parallel \overline{CD}$. Think of $\overline{BD}$ and $\overline{AC}$ as transversals. Because alternate interior angles are congruent, we know that $\angle EBA \cong \angle EDC$ and $\angle EAB \cong \angle ECD$. We also know that $AB \cong CD$, since opposite sides of a parallelogram are congruent. By the ASA Congruence Property, we know that $\triangle EAB \cong \triangle ECD$. Corresponding parts of congruent triangles are congruent, and, consequently, $\overline{AE} \cong \overline{CE}$ and $\overline{BE} \cong \overline{DE}$. Therefore, the diagonals of a parallelogram bisect each other.

Section 14.5

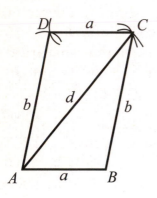

5.	Since the diagonal of a parallelogram divides the parallelogram into two congruent triangles, we will begin by constructing one triangle composed of the diagonal and the given side lengths. Construct one side of the triangle using length *a*. Label the endpoints as points *A* and *B*. Open the compass to length *d*. Place the compass at *A* and construct an arc of radius *d*. Open the compass to length *b*. Place the compass at point *B* and construct an arc of radius *b*. Label the point of intersection of the arcs as point *C*. Draw $\triangle ABC$. Using the SSS Congruence Property, we will complete the parallelogram. Open the compass to length *a*. Place the compass at point *C* and construct an arc of radius *a*. Open the compass to length *b*. Place the compass at point *A* and construct an arc of radius *b*. Label the point of intersection of the arcs as *D*. Draw $\triangle ADC$. *ABCD* is the desired parallelogram.

Section 14.5

6.	Consider quadrilateral *STUV* such that *STUV* is a rhombus and the diagonals are congruent. Remember, every rhombus is a parallelogram. We know $\overline{ST} \cong \overline{ST}$, $\overline{SV} \cong \overline{TU}$, and we assumed $\overline{SU} \cong \overline{TV}$. By the SSS Congruence Property, $\triangle STV \cong \triangle TSU$. Since corresponding parts of congruent triangles are congruent, $\angle STU \cong \angle TSV$. $\angle STU$ and $\angle TSV$ are also supplementary, since consecutive angles in a parallelogram are supplementary. Since $\angle STU$

and ∠*TSV* are both congruent and supplementary, they are both right angles. Recall that we proved previously that consecutive angles of a parallelogram are supplementary. Therefore, ∠*TSV* and ∠*SVU* are supplementary, and ∠*UTS* and ∠*VUT* are supplementary. This forces ∠*SVU* and ∠*VUT* to both be right angles, since ∠*TSV* and ∠*UTS* are right angles. Because each angle in *STUV* is a right angle, and all sides are congruent, *STUV* is a square.

Section 14.5

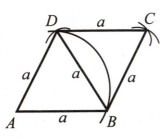

7. The diagonal of a rhombus divides the rhombus into two congruent triangles, and when the diagonal is the same length as the sides, the triangles are equilateral. To construct the required rhombus, we will construct two equilateral triangles. Pick a point and label it *A*. Place the compass at *A* and construct an arc of radius *a*. Pick a point on the arc and label it *B*. Place the compass at *B* and construct an arc of radius *a*. Label the intersection of the arcs *D*. Construct △*ABD*. To complete the rhombus, construct arcs of radius *a* from points *B* and *D*. Label the intersection of these arcs as point *C*. Construct △*BCD*. Quadrilateral *ABCD* has four sides of length *a*, and diagonal $\overline{BD}$ has length *a*. Therefore, *ABCD* is the desired rhombus.

Section 14.5

8. Consider an isosceles trapezoid *ABCD*.

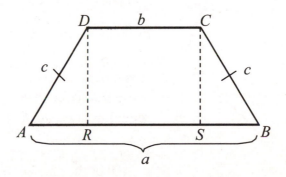

Draw the perpendicular heights from points *D* and *C*. Label the points of intersection with the base as *R* and *S*. Since *AR* + *RS* + *SB* = *a* and *RS* = *b*, we know

$AR + SB = a - b$. Since $\overline{AR} \cong \overline{SB}$, $AR = \dfrac{a-b}{2}$ and $SB = \dfrac{a-b}{2}$. Knowing this, to construct such a trapezoid $ABCD$ we need to find the length $\dfrac{a-b}{2}$ to find points R and S on $\overline{AB}$. At points R and S we will construct perpendicular segments to intersect arcs of radius c from points A and B.

Step 1: Find length $\dfrac{a-b}{2}$.

Construct a segment of length a. Mark off length b.

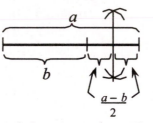

Bisect the remaining segment. The original segment has been divided into three smaller segments of length b, $\dfrac{a-b}{2}$, and $\dfrac{a-b}{2}$.

Step 2: Construct the trapezoid.

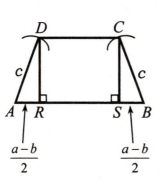

Construct the base $\overline{AB}$ to have length a. Place the compass at A and construct an arc of radius $\dfrac{a-b}{2}$. Label the intersection on $\overline{AB}$ as point R. Place the compass at point B and construct an arc of radius $\dfrac{a-b}{2}$. Label the intersection on $\overline{AB}$ as point S. Construct perpendicular segments at points R and S.

Place the compass at point A, and construct an arc of radius c. Label the intersection of the arc and the perpendicular segment as point D. Place the compass at point B and construct an arc of radius c. Label the intersection of the arc and the perpendicular segment as point C. Construct segments $\overline{AD}$, $\overline{DC}$, and $\overline{CB}$.

Quadrilateral $ABCD$ is the desired isosceles trapezoid.

Section 14.5

9. In $\triangle ADC$ and $\triangle ACB$, since AC is the geometric mean of AD and AB, we know $\dfrac{AD}{AC} = \dfrac{AC}{AB}$. $\angle A \cong \angle A$ since every angle is congruent to itself. Therefore, $\triangle ADC \sim \triangle ACB$ by the SAS Similarity Property. Corresponding angles in similar triangles are congruent, so $\angle ADC \cong \angle ACB$. Since $\angle ADC$ is a right angle, $\angle ACB$ is a right angle, and thus $\triangle ABC$ is a right triangle.

Section 14.5

10. (a) Recall that all rectangles have four right angles. This means that adjacent sides are perpendicular. Since each side of the midquad is parallel to a diagonal of the quadrilateral, the diagonals of the quadrilateral must be perpendicular in order for the midquad to be a rectangle. Therefore, $M_1 M_2 M_3 M_4$ will be a rectangle when diagonals $\overline{PR}$ and $\overline{QS}$ are perpendicular.

    (b) Recall that all four sides of a rhombus have the same length. Because each side of the midquad is half the length of the diagonal, the diagonals must be equal in length in order for the midquad to be a rhombus. Therefore, $M_1 M_2 M_3 M_4$ will be a rhombus when $\overline{PR} \cong \overline{QS}$.

    (c) To be a square, a quadrilateral must have four right angles, as in part (a), and four sides of equal lengths as in part (b). Therefore, $M_1 M_2 M_3 M_4$ will be a square if $\overline{PR}$ and $\overline{QS}$ are perpendicular and congruent.

Section 14.5

11. (a) Since $\angle A \cong \angle A$ and $\angle ADC \cong \angle ACB$, we know $\triangle ADC \sim \triangle ACB$ by the AA Similarity Property.

    (b) Since $\angle B \cong \angle B$ and $\angle BDC \cong \angle BCA$, we know $\triangle BDC \cong \triangle BCA$ by the AA similarity property.

(c) Since $a^2 = xy + y^2$ and $b^2 = x^2 + xy$, we have the following:

$$a^2 + b^2 = xy + y^2 + xy + x^2$$
$$= x^2 + 2xy + y^2$$
$$= (x + y)(x + y)$$
$$= (x + y)^2$$
$$a^2 + b^2 = c^2$$

Therefore, $a^2 + b^2 = c^2$, and the Pythagorean theorem is proved.

Section 14.5

12. (a) Notice that in kite $ABCD$, $\overline{AB} \cong \overline{AD}$ and $\overline{BC} \cong \overline{DC}$ by the definition of a kite, which states that two pairs of adjacent sides are congruent. Because $\overline{AC} \cong \overline{AC}$, we see that $\triangle ABC \cong \triangle ADC$ by SSS.

We know that corresponding parts of congruent triangles are congruent, so we have $\angle DAC \cong \angle BAC$. Because $\overline{AE} \cong \overline{AE}$, we have $\triangle AED \cong \triangle AEB$ by SAS. Notice that $m(\angle AED) + m(\angle AEB) = 180°$. Because $\angle AEB \cong \angle AED$ by corresponding parts, we know that $m(\angle AED) = 90° = m(\angle AEB)$. Therefore, $\overline{AC} \perp \overline{DB}$, and the diagonals of kite $ABCD$ are perpendicular.

(b) Notice that the kite can be thought of as two triangles: $\triangle ABD$ and $\triangle CBD$. The formula for the area of a triangle is $\frac{1}{2}$(base)(height).

Area of $\triangle ABD = \frac{1}{2}(BD)(AE)$

Area of $\triangle CBD = \frac{1}{2}(BD)(CE)$

Area of kite $= \frac{1}{2}(BD)(AE) + \frac{1}{2}(BD)(CE)$

$$= \frac{1}{2}(BD)(AE + CE)$$

$$\text{Area of kite} = \frac{1}{2}(BD)(AC)$$

Section 14.5

13. We are given that $\triangle ABC$ and $\triangle A'B'C'$ have three pairs of corresponding sides congruent. However, we cannot use the SSS Congruence Property to conclude that the triangles are congruent. We must show congruence in another way.

    Construct $\triangle ABD$ so that $\angle BAD \cong \angle B'A'C'$ and $AD = A'C'$. We know then that $\triangle BAD \cong \triangle B'A'C'$ by SAS. By congruence of corresponding parts, we know $\overline{BD} \cong \overline{B'C'}$. Also, $\overline{BD} \cong \overline{B'C'} \cong \overline{BC}$ by our initial assumption. Now $\triangle ACD$ and $\triangle BCD$ are both isosceles, so their base angles are congruent: $\angle ACD \cong \angle ADC$ and $\angle BCD \cong \angle BDC$. By addition we know $\angle ACB = \angle ACD + \angle BCD$ and $\angle ADB = \angle ADC + \angle BDC$. Substituting, we have $\angle ACB = \angle ADC + \angle BDC$. Therefore, $\angle ADB \cong \angle ACB$ and $\triangle BAD \cong \triangle BAC$ by SAS. Finally, $\triangle B'A'C' \cong \triangle BAC$, since both triangles are congruent to $\triangle BAD$.

Section 14.5

14. We are given that $\angle A \cong \angle A'$. If $\frac{AC}{AB} = \frac{A'C'}{A'B'}$, then $\triangle ABC \sim \triangle A'B'C'$ by the SAS Similarity Property. If $\frac{AC}{AB} \neq \frac{A'C'}{A'B'}$, then point D' can be found on $\overline{A'C'}$ such that $\frac{AC}{AB} = \frac{A'D'}{A'B'}$.

    Therefore, since $\angle A \cong \angle A'$, we know $\triangle ABC \sim \triangle A'B'D'$ by the SAS Similarity Property.

    Similar triangles have congruent corresponding angles. Therefore, $\angle ABC \cong \angle A'B'D'$. However, we also know that $\angle ABC \cong \angle A'B'C'$, but $\angle A'B'C'$ and $\angle A'B'D'$ are not the same angle. Since an angle cannot be congruent to two angles of different measures, we have a contradiction.

Therefore, $\dfrac{AC}{AB} = \dfrac{A'C'}{A'B'}$ and $\triangle ABC \sim \triangle A'B'C'$ by the SAS Similarity Property.

Section 14.5

15. (a) We want to show that $\triangle ABD \cong \triangle FBC$ and $\triangle ACE \cong \triangle KCB$.

   $\overline{AB} \cong \overline{FB}$ and $\overline{BC} \cong \overline{BD}$ by the definition of a square.

   $m(\angle FBC) = m(\angle FBA) + m(\angle ABC)$ by angle addition.

   $m(\angle ABD) = m(\angle CBD) + m(\angle ABC)$ by angle addition.

   $m(\angle FBA) = 90°$ and $m(\angle CBD) = 90°$ by the definition of a square.

   Therefore, $\angle FBC \cong \angle ABD$ by substitution.

   So, $\triangle ABD \cong \triangle FBC$ by SAS.

   Similarly, $\triangle ACE \cong \triangle KCB$.

   (b) Use $\overline{BD}$ as a base in $\triangle ABD$, and use $\overline{CE}$ as the base in $\triangle ACE$. Notice that $\overline{CE} \cong \overline{BD}$.

   Height of $\triangle ABD$ + height of $\triangle ACE = BC$.

Area of $\triangle ABD = \dfrac{1}{2}$ (base)(height) $= \dfrac{1}{2}(BD)$(height of $\triangle ABD$).

Area of $\triangle ACE = \dfrac{1}{2}$ (base)(height) $= \dfrac{1}{2}(BD)$(height of $\triangle ACE$), since $\overline{CE} \cong \overline{BD}$.

Area of $\triangle ABD$ + Area of $\triangle ACE = \dfrac{1}{2}(BD)$(height of $\triangle ABD$ + height of $\triangle ACE$)

$$= \dfrac{1}{2}(BD)(BC)$$

$$= \dfrac{1}{2}(\text{Area of square } BCED).$$

(c) Area of $\triangle FBC = \dfrac{1}{2}$ (base)(height)

$$= \dfrac{1}{2}(FB)(BA)$$

$$= \dfrac{1}{2}(\text{Area of square } ABFG).$$

Area of $\triangle KCB = \dfrac{1}{2}$ (base)(height)

$$= \frac{1}{2}(KC)(AC)$$

$$= \frac{1}{2}(\text{Area of square } ACKH).$$

(d) From part (c), we see that the area of square *ABFG* is twice the area of $\triangle FBC$, and the area of square *ACKH* is twice the area of $\triangle KCB$.

Area of square *ABFG* + Area of square *ACKH*

$= 2(\text{Area of } \triangle FBC) + 2(\text{Area of } \triangle KCB)$

$= 2(\text{Area of } \triangle ABD) + 2(\text{Area of } \triangle ACE)$ by part (a)

$= 2(\text{Area of } \triangle ABD + \text{Area of } \triangle ACE)$

$= 2\left(\frac{1}{2} \text{Area of square BCED}\right)$ by part (b)

$= \text{Area of square } BCED$

(e) The Pythagorean theorem states that the sum of the areas of the squares on the legs of a right triangle is equal to the area of the square on the hypotenuse.

Section 14.5

16. Access the Chapter 14 Geometer's Sketchpad® activity, *Midquad*. A quadrilateral and its midquad are given. The area of the quadrilateral and the area of its midquad are both displayed. You are able to click and drag vertices to change the shape of the original quadrilateral. Notice how the areas change as you change the quadrilateral's shape. As you explore, notice there is a special relationship between the areas of the quadrilateral and its midquad. The area of any quadrilateral is twice the area of its midquad. Alternately, the area of a midquad is one half the area of the original quadrilateral.

SOLUTIONS - PART A PROBLEMS

Chapter 15: Geometry Using Coordinates

Section 15.1

15. (a) A rectangle is a quadrilateral with four right angles. Calculate the slopes of $\overline{AB}$, $\overline{BC}$, $\overline{CD}$, and $\overline{AD}$.

Slope of $\overline{AB}$ is $\dfrac{3-7}{15-5} = \dfrac{-4}{10} = \dfrac{-2}{5}$.

Slope of $\overline{BC}$ is $\dfrac{-2-3}{13-15} = \dfrac{-5}{-2} = \dfrac{5}{2}$.

Slope of $\overline{CD}$ is $\dfrac{-2-2}{13-3} = \dfrac{-4}{10} = \dfrac{-2}{5}$.

Slope of $\overline{AD}$ is $\dfrac{7-2}{5-3} = \dfrac{5}{2}$.

Thus, $\overline{AB} \perp \overline{AD}$, $\overline{AB} \perp \overline{BC}$, $\overline{BC} \perp \overline{CD}$, and $\overline{AD} \perp \overline{CD}$.

(b) Use the distance formula to calculate the lengths BD and AC.

$$AC = \sqrt{(5-13)^2 + (7-(-2))^2} = \sqrt{145}$$

$$BD = \sqrt{(15-3)^2 + (3-2)^2} = \sqrt{145}$$

Thus, $AC = BD$.

(c) It appears that both pairs are congruent. To be sure find the midpoint of $\overline{AC}$ and the midpoint of $\overline{DB}$ and see if the ordered pairs are the same.

Midpoint of $\overline{AC} = \left(\dfrac{5+13}{2}, \dfrac{7-2}{2}\right) = (9, 2.5)$.

Midpoint of $\overline{DB} = \left(\dfrac{3+15}{2}, \dfrac{2+3}{2}\right) = (9, 2.5)$.

Thus $\overline{AE} \cong \overline{CE}$ and $\overline{BE} \cong \overline{DE}$, where E is the point $(9, 2.5)$.

(d) The slope of $\overline{AC} = \dfrac{-2-7}{13-5} = \dfrac{-9}{8}$.

The slope of $\overline{BD} = \dfrac{3-2}{15-3} = \dfrac{1}{12}$.

The product of the slopes is $\dfrac{-9}{8} \cdot \dfrac{1}{12} = \dfrac{-3}{32}$, which is not

-1, so the segments are not perpendicular.

(e) In a rectangle, diagonals are congruent and they bisect each other, however, they are not necessarily perpendicular.

Section 15.1

16. Access the eManipulative *Coordinate Geoboard*.
   (a) Systematically create all possible parallelograms.
      (1, 5), (3, 5); (2, 5), (4, 5); (3, 5), (5, 5);
      (1, 3), (3, 3); (2, 3), (4, 3); (3, 3), (5, 3);
      (1, 2), (3, 2); (2, 2), (4, 2); (3, 2), (5, 2);
      (1, 1), (3, 1); (2, 1), (4, 1); (3, 1), (5, 1)
   (b) (2, 5), (4, 5); (2, 3), (4, 3); (2, 2), (4, 2); (2, 1), (4, 1)
   (c) A rhombus has four congruent sides. There is one pair of coordinates: (2, 2) and (4, 2).
   (d) The rhombus from part (c) has four right angles, so it is also a square. There is one pair of coordinates: (2, 2) and (4, 2).

Section 15.1

17. Access the emanipulative *Coordinate Geoboard*.
   (a) The triangle has two sides of length 4 units. One side is vertical and another is horizontal, so the triangle contains a right angle. It is an isosceles right triangle.
   (b) The triangle has one obtuse angle and two congruent sides. It is an obtuse isosceles triangle.

Section 15.1

18. Access the Geometer's Sketchpad® activity, *Perpendicular Lines*. You will see two graphed lines. Notice the lines are perpendicular to each other. You can change the slope of $\overline{OA}$ by clicking and dragging the red dot. The slope of the perpendicular line is given.
   (a) If the slope of one line is 0.941, then the slope of the perpendicular line is -1.062.
   (b) If the slope of one line is -0.355, then the slope of the perpendicular line is 2.814.
   (c) If the slope of one line is 9.625, then the slope of the perpendicular line is -0.104.

Section 15.1

19. Create a coordinate system such that the base of the pole is the origin, and the pole lies on the positive *y*-axis. The wires can be thought of as lines, two of which have positive slopes and two of which have negative slopes.

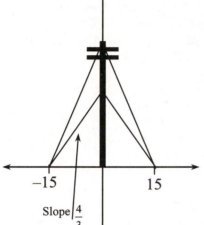

(a) To find the point at which the shorter set of wires attaches to the pole, we need to find the *y*-intercept of the line with slope $\dfrac{4}{3}$ that passes through the point $(-15, 0)$. We will use the point-slope form to write the equation of the line.

$$y - y_1 = m(x - x_1)$$

$$y - 0 = \frac{4}{3}(x + 15)$$

$$y = \frac{4}{3}x + 20$$

The *y*-intercept occurs when $x = 0$. Therefore, the shorter set of wires attaches 20 m above the ground.

(b) The right triangle formed by the pole, ground, and short wire has a height of 20 meters and a base of 15 meters. The hypotenuse (the length of the wire) can be found using the Pythagorean theorem.

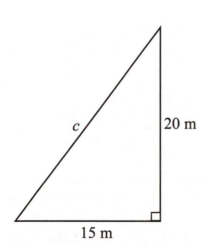

$$a^2 + b^2 = c^2$$

$$15^2 + 20^2 = c^2$$

$$225 + 400 = c^2$$

$$\sqrt{625} = c$$

$$25 = c$$

Therefore, each of the short wires is 25 meters long.

(c) The height of the pole is the height of a right triangle with a base of 15 meters and a hypotenuse of 50 meters. We use the Pythagorean theorem to find the height.

$$a^2 + b^2 = c^2$$
$$15^2 + b^2 = 50^2$$
$$b^2 = 2500 - 225$$
$$b = \sqrt{2275}$$
$$b \approx 47.70$$

Therefore, the height of the pole is approximately 47.70 meters or 4770 cm.

(d) The slope of one of the longer wires is the slope of a line through the points (0, 47.70) and (−15, 0). We use the slope formula.

$$\text{Slope} = \frac{y_2 - y_1}{x_2 - x_1}$$
$$= \frac{0 - 47.70}{-15 - 0}$$
$$\approx 3.18$$

Therefore, the slope of one of the two longer wires is about 3.18, and the slope of the other wire is about −3.18.

Section 15.1

20. The amount by which the highway rises is 10 meters. The horizontal distance from the base of the ramp to the overpass is 150 meters.

$$\text{Percent grade} = \frac{\text{Highway rise}}{\text{Horizontal distance}} \times 100\%$$
$$= \frac{10 \text{ m}}{150 \text{ m}} \times 100\%$$
$$= 0.0\overline{6} \times 100\%$$
$$\approx 6.667\%$$

Thus, the ramp has about a 6.667% grade. That is, the highway rises approximately 0.06667 meters for every 1 meter of horizontal distance.

Section 15.1

21. (a) $\overline{PO}$ and $\overline{RT}$ are both horizontal, and thus parallel, so $\angle QPO \cong \angle SRT$ since they are corresponding angles.

$\angle O \cong \angle T$ since they are both right angles. By the AA Similarity Property, $\triangle PQO \sim \triangle RST$.

(b) Because $\triangle PQO \sim \triangle RST$, corresponding sides are proportional. That is, we know $\dfrac{y_1}{y_2} = \dfrac{x_1}{x_2}$. If the means are interchanged, we have $\dfrac{y_1}{x_1} = \dfrac{y_2}{x_2}$, which is what we wanted to show.

(c) The slope of $\overline{PQ} = \dfrac{y_1}{x_1}$, and the slope of $\overline{RS} = \dfrac{y_2}{x_2}$.

Because we know from part (b) that $\dfrac{y_1}{x_1} = \dfrac{y_2}{x_2}$ we see that the slopes of $\overline{PQ}$ and $\overline{RS}$ are equal. Therefore, the slope of the line l is independent of the pairs of points selected.

Section 15.1

22. If P, M, and Q are collinear with M between P and Q, then $PM + MQ = PQ$. Calculate the distances, using coordinates $P(x_1, y_1)$, $M\left(\dfrac{x_1 + x_2}{2}, \dfrac{y_1 + y_2}{2}\right)$, and $Q(x_2, y_2)$, as shown on the next page.

$$PM = \sqrt{\left(\frac{x_1 + x_2}{2} - x_1\right)^2 + \left(\frac{y_1 + y_2}{2} - y_1\right)^2}$$

$$= \sqrt{\left(\frac{x_1 + x_2 - 2x_1}{2}\right)^2 + \left(\frac{y_1 + y_2 - 2y_1}{2}\right)^2}$$

$$PM = \sqrt{\left(\frac{x_2 - x_1}{2}\right)^2 + \left(\frac{y_2 - y_1}{2}\right)^2}$$

$$MQ = \sqrt{\left(x_2 - \frac{x_1 + x_2}{2}\right)^2 + \left(y_2 - \frac{y_1 + y_2}{2}\right)^2}$$

$$= \sqrt{\left(\frac{2x_2 - x_1 - x_2}{2}\right)^2 + \left(\frac{2y_2 - y_1 - y_2}{2}\right)^2}$$

$$MQ = \sqrt{\left(\frac{x_2 - x_1}{2}\right)^2 + \left(\frac{y_2 - y_1}{2}\right)^2}$$

$$PM + MQ = \sqrt{\left(\frac{x_2 - x_1}{2}\right)^2 + \left(\frac{y_2 - y_1}{2}\right)^2} + \sqrt{\left(\frac{x_2 - x_1}{2}\right)^2 + \left(\frac{y_2 - y_1}{2}\right)^2}$$

$$= 2\sqrt{\left(\frac{x_2 - x_1}{2}\right)^2 + \left(\frac{y_2 - y_1}{2}\right)^2}$$

$$= 2\sqrt{\frac{(x_2 - x_1)^2 + (y_2 - y)^2}{4}}$$

$$= \frac{2\sqrt{(x_2 - x_1)^2 + (y_2 - y)^2}}{2}$$

$$PM + MQ = \sqrt{(x_2 - x_1)^2 + (y_2 - y)^2}$$

Because $PQ = \sqrt{(x_2 - x_1)^2 + (y_2 - y)^2}$, we see that $PM + MQ = PQ$, so P, M, and Q are collinear. Also, $PM = MQ$, since they both equal $\sqrt{\left(\frac{x_2 - x_1}{2}\right)^2 + \left(\frac{y_2 - y_1}{2}\right)^2}$.

Section 15.1

23. (a) Point (2, 1, 3): Move forward 2 units along the x-axis. Move right 1 unit parallel to the y-axis. Move up 3 units parallel to the z-axis.

   (b) Point (−2, 1, 0): Move backward 2 units along the x-axis. Move right 1 unit parallel to the y-axis.

   (c) Point (3, −1, −2): Move forward 3 units along the x-axis. Move left 1 unit parallel to the y-axis. Move down 2 units parallel to the z-axis.

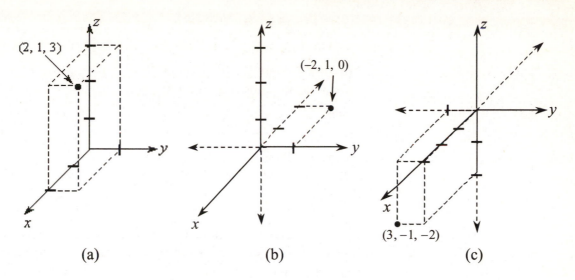

(a)   (b)   (c)

Section 15.2

22. To find the equation of the circumscribed circle, find the center and the radius of the circle. To find the center of the circle, find the circumcenter of the given triangle by finding the intersection of the lines containing the perpendicular bisectors for two sides of the triangle.

Line containing the perpendicular bisector of $\overline{AC}$:

$$\text{Midpoint of } \overline{AC} = \left(\frac{-5-1}{2}, \frac{4+2}{2} \right) = (-3, 3)$$

$$\text{Slope of } \overline{AC} = \frac{4-2}{-5+1} = \frac{2}{-4} = \frac{-1}{2}$$

The line containing the perpendicular bisector of $\overline{AC}$ will contain $(-3, 3)$ and will have a slope of 2.

$$y - 3 = 2(x + 3)$$
$$y = 2x + 9$$

Line containing the perpendicular bisector of $\overline{AB}$:

$$\text{Midpoint of } \overline{AB} = \left(\frac{-1-1}{2}, \frac{8+2}{2} \right) = (-1, 5)$$

$$\text{Slope of } \overline{AB} = \frac{8-2}{-1+1} = \frac{6}{0} = \text{undefined}$$

The line containing the perpendicular bisector of $\overline{AB}$ will contain $(-1, 5)$ and will have a slope of 0.

$$y - 5 = 0(x + 1)$$

$$y = 5$$

Solve the system of equations $y = 2x + 9$ and $y = 5$. Substitution yields the following:

$$5 = 2x + 9$$

$$-4 = 2x$$

$$-2 = x$$

Thus, $y = 2(-2) + 9 = -4 + 9 = 5$. The center of the circle has coordinates $(-2, 5)$.

Use the distance formula to find the radius of the circle. Use the coordinates of the center of the circle and any of the three vertices of the triangle, $(-1, 2)$, for example.

$$\text{Circle radius} = \sqrt{(5 - 2)^2 + (-2 - (-1))^2} = \sqrt{9 + 1} = \sqrt{10}$$

Thus, the equation of the circle is $(x + 2)^2 + (y - 5)^2 = 10$.

Section 15.2

23. Each side of the triangle contains two of the vertices. Use the vertices on each side to create the line equation. One line will contain $(0, 0)$ and $(1, 5)$. One will contain $(0, 0)$ and $(-4, 3)$. The third will contain $(1, 5)$ and $(-4, 3)$.

Line equation through (0, 0) and (1, 5):

$$\text{Slope} = \frac{5 - 0}{1 - 0} = \frac{5}{1} = 5$$

$$y - y_1 = m(x - x_1)$$

$$y - 5 = 5(x - 1)$$

$$y = 5x - 5 + 5$$

$$y = 5x$$

Line equation through (0, 0) and (-4, 3):

$$\text{Slope} = \frac{3 - 0}{-4 - 0} = \frac{3}{-4} = \frac{-3}{4}$$

$$y - y_1 = m(x - x_1)$$

$$y - 3 = \frac{-3}{4}(x - (-4))$$

$$y = \frac{-3}{4}x - 3 + 4$$

$$y = \frac{-3}{4}x$$

Line equation through (1, 5) and (–4, 3):

$$\text{Slope} = \frac{3-5}{-4-1} = \frac{-2}{-5} = \frac{2}{5}$$

$$y - y_1 = m(x - x_1)$$

$$y - 5 = \frac{2}{5}(x - 1)$$

$$y = \frac{2}{5}x - \frac{2}{5} + 5$$

$$y = \frac{2}{5}x + \frac{23}{5}$$

Section 15.2

24. The line containing the median, $\overline{AD}$, will pass through point A, which has coordinates (3, 7) and point D which is the midpoint of $\overline{BC}$. The midpoint of $\overline{BC}$ is $\left(\frac{1+11}{2}, \frac{4+2}{2}\right) = (6,3)$, so use (3, 7) and (6, 3) to create the equation of the line. Find the slope first and then use the point-slope form of the line equation.

$$\text{Slope} = \frac{3-7}{6-3} = \frac{-4}{3}$$

$$y - y_1 = m(x - x_1)$$

$$y - 3 = \frac{-4}{3}(x - 6)$$

$$y = \frac{-4}{3}x + 8 + 3$$

$$y = \frac{-4}{3}x + 11$$

Thus, the equation of the line containing the median is $y = \dfrac{-4}{3}x + 11$.

Section 15.2

25. The line containing the altitude, $\overline{PT}$, will pass through point P, which has coordinates $(3, 5)$ and will be perpendicular to the line containing $\overline{RS}$. The slope of $\overline{RS}$ is $\dfrac{-3-1}{7-(-1)} = \dfrac{-4}{8} = \dfrac{-1}{2}$, so a line perpendicular to $\overline{RS}$ will have slope $= 2$. Use the point $(3, 5)$ and slope $= 2$ to create the equation of the line containing the altitude $\overline{PT}$.

$$y - y_1 = m(x - x_1)$$
$$y - 5 = 2(x - 3)$$
$$y = 2x - 6 + 5$$
$$y = 2x - 1$$

Thus, the equation of the line containing altitude $\overline{PT}$ is $y = 2x - 1$.

Section 15.2

26. (a) To find the total cost, in dollars, multiply 4.50 by the number of people and then add the fixed cost of 200.00.

Number of People	30	50	75	100	n
Total Cost, y	335	425	537.5	650	$4.5n + 200$

(b) If x represents the number of people and y represents the total cost, then the linear equation is $y = 4.5x + 200$.

(c) The slope of the line is 4.5 since the equation is in slope-intercept form. ($y = mx + b$, where m = slope.) The slope represents the cost per person since for every additional person, the total cost increases by $4.50.

(d) Once again, in the slope-intercept form of the line, $y = mx + b$, where b is the y-intercept. Therefore 200 is the y-intercept of the line. It represents the fixed cost. It must be paid no matter how many people there are.

Section 15.2

27. (a) By the Solutions of Simultaneous Equations Theorem, the system of equations will have infinitely many solutions if the lines are coincident. This will occur when the slopes and y-intercepts are the same. Write each equation in slope-intercept form.

$$ax + by = c \quad \Rightarrow \quad y = \frac{-a}{b}x + \frac{c}{b}$$

$$dx + ey = f \quad \Rightarrow \quad y = \frac{-d}{e}x + \frac{f}{e}$$

If the slopes are the same, then $\dfrac{-a}{b} = \dfrac{-d}{e}$ or $ae = bd$.

If the y-intercepts are the same, then $\dfrac{c}{b} = \dfrac{f}{e}$ or $ce = bf$.

(b) There will be no solution if the lines are parallel, but noncoincident. This will occur when the slopes are the same but the y-intercepts are *not* the same. Consider the slope-intercept form of the lines in part (a). If the slopes are the same, then $ae = bd$. If the y-intercepts are not the same, then $ce \neq bf$.

(c) There will be one solution if the lines intersect in exactly one point. This will occur if the lines have different slopes. If the slopes are not the same, then $ae \neq bd$.

Section 15.2

28. Sketch the x- and y-axes. Begin measuring each angle at the positive x-axis. Recall how the quadrants are numbered.

Quadrant II	Quadrant I
Quadrant III	Quadrant IV

(a) Rotate 45° counterclockwise and plot the point 5 units along the terminal side of the angle. The point will be located in Quadrant I.

(b) Rotate 125° counterclockwise and plot the point 3 units along the terminal side of the angle.

(c) Rotate 170° clockwise since the angle is negative and plot the point 1 unit along the terminal side of the angle.

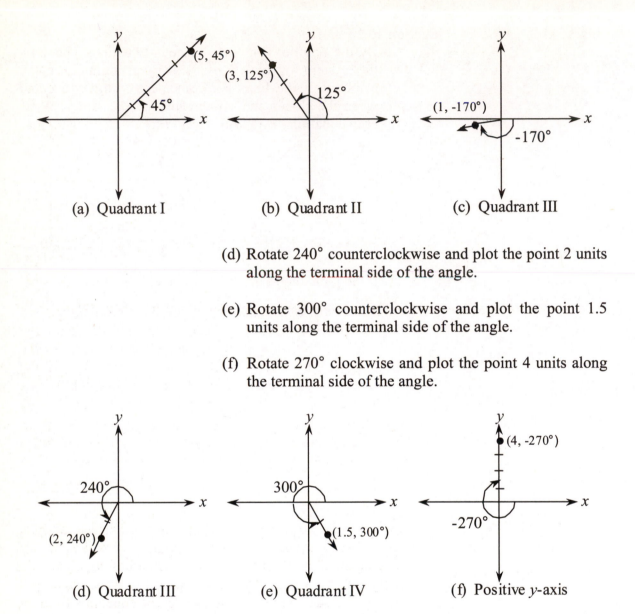

(a) Quadrant I (b) Quadrant II (c) Quadrant III

(d) Rotate 240° counterclockwise and plot the point 2 units along the terminal side of the angle.

(e) Rotate 300° counterclockwise and plot the point 1.5 units along the terminal side of the angle.

(f) Rotate 270° clockwise and plot the point 4 units along the terminal side of the angle.

(d) Quadrant III (e) Quadrant IV (f) Positive y-axis

Section 15.2

29. The point P has coordinates (x, y). From the coordinates given, we can find the lengths of the legs of each triangle formed. See the following diagram:

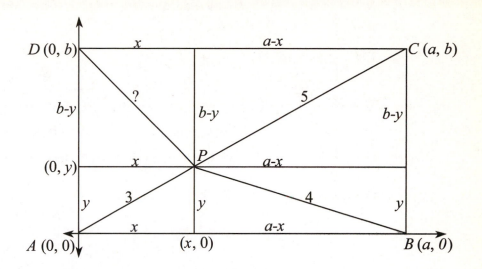

By the Pythagorean theorem, we can set up equations for appropriate triangles.

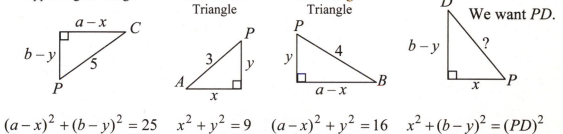

Upper Right Triangle	Lower Left Triangle	Lower Right Triangle	

$$(a-x)^2 + (b-y)^2 = 25 \qquad x^2 + y^2 = 9 \qquad (a-x)^2 + y^2 = 16 \qquad x^2 + (b-y)^2 = (PD)^2$$

It is impossible to solve for each variable because we have five unknowns and only four equations. We will try to find a combination of the first three equations to obtain the equation we want. In the equation we want, there is a $(b-y)^2$ term. Begin by subtracting the equations from the upper right triangle and the lower right triangle, which will eliminate the $(a-x)^2$ term.

$$(a-x)^2 + (b-y)^2 = 25$$
$$\underline{-[(a-x)^2 + y^2 = 16]}$$
$$-y^2 + (b-y)^2 = 9$$

Now add the equation $x^2 + y^2 = 9$ to eliminate the y^2 term.

$$-y^2 + (b-y)^2 = 9$$
$$\underline{x^2 + y^2 = 9}$$
$$x^2 + (b-y)^2 = 18$$

Thus, since $x^2 + (b-y) = (PD)^2$, and $x^2 + (b-y)^2 = 18$, we know that $(PD)^2 = 18$, so $PD = 3\sqrt{2}$.

Section 15.2

30. Use a variable. Let p represent the number of people who attend the dance. The total cost to put on the dance consists of the fixed costs for the band and advertising plus the variable costs for every person attending. Total cost = $400 + $100 + 2p = $500 + 2p$.

(a) If tickets sell for $7 each, then $7p$ represents the revenue generated when p people attend the dance. The class will "break even" when their total cost is the same as the revenue. Set up an equation and solve for p to find the number of people required to attend.

$$\text{Total Cost} = \text{Revenue}$$
$$500 + 2p = 7p$$
$$500 = 5p$$
$$100 = p$$

Therefore, 100 people must attend the dance for the class to break even.

(b) If tickets sell for $6 each, then $6p$ represents the revenue generated when p people attend the dance.

$$\text{Total Cost} = \text{Revenue}$$
$$500 + 2p = 6p$$
$$500 = 4p$$
$$125 = p$$

Therefore, 125 people must attend the dance for the class to break even.

(c) For the class to earn a profit, their total cost plus the desired $400 profit must equal the revenue.

$$\text{Total Cost} + \text{Profit} = \text{Revenue}$$
$$500 + 2p + 400 = 6p$$
$$900 = 4p$$

$$225 = p$$

Therefore, 225 people must attend the dance in order for the class to make a \$400 profit.

Section 15.2

31. (a) Graph both equations. One is a circle centered at the origin with radius 1. The other is a line with slope $\dfrac{1}{2}$ and y-intercept 1. The circle and line intersect in two places, so expect two solutions.

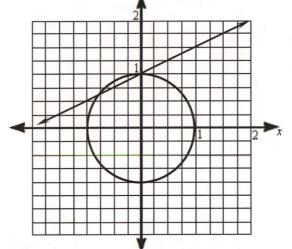

(b) Substitute $y = \dfrac{x}{2} + 1$ into $x^2 + y^2 = 1$ and solve for x.

$$x^2 + \left(\frac{x}{2} + 1\right)^2 = 1$$

$$x^2 + \frac{x^2}{4} + x + 1 = 1$$

$$\frac{5x^2}{4} + x = 0$$

Factor that quadratic expression: $x\left(\dfrac{5}{4}x + 1\right) = 0$.

Set each factor equal to 0 and solve. If $x = 0$, then $y = \dfrac{0}{2} + 1 = 1$, so one solution is (0, 1). If $\dfrac{5}{4}x + 1 = 0$ or

$$x = \frac{-4}{5}, \quad \text{then} \quad y = \frac{\frac{-4}{5}}{2} + 1 = \frac{-4}{10} + 1 = \frac{3}{5}, \quad \text{so another}$$

solution is $\left(\frac{-4}{5}, \frac{3}{5} \right)$.

Section 15.3

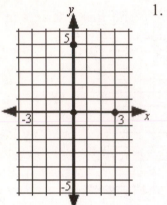

1. (a) Plot the points in a coordinate system as shown to the left. Notice all three points are on an axis, so two sides of the parallelogram can be perpendicular. One way to complete a parallelogram is by creating a rectangle. Do this by plotting a point at (3, 5) as shown in figure (i). If one side of the parallelogram is on the x-axis, then the opposite side must be horizontal as shown in figure (ii), so plot a point at (−3, 5). If one side of the parallelogram is on the y-axis, then the opposite side must be vertical as shown in figure (iii), so plot a point at (3, −5).

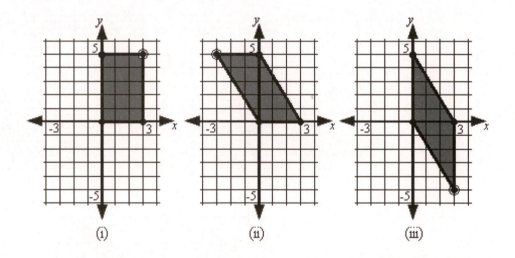

(i)   (ii)   (iii)

(b) Plot the points in a coordinate system as shown.

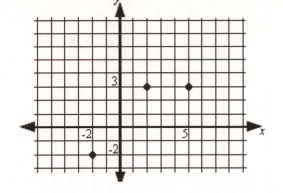

Notice two parallelograms can be created by making sure a pair of opposite sides are horizontal. Plot a point at (−5, −2) or (1, −2) as shown in figures (i) and (ii), respectively. The third parallelogram can be formed by placing a point at (9, 8) as shown in figure (iii).

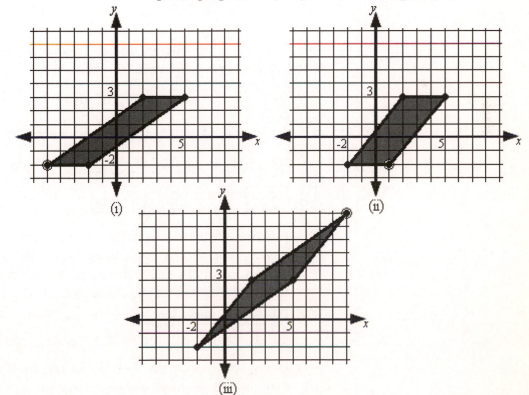

Section 15.3

2. (a) The points are plotted in the following figure (i). Notice a horizontal segment that is 5 units long can be drawn through points (−2, −1) and (−3, −1) while a vertical segment that is 5 units long can be drawn through (3, −1) and (3, 4). These segments are perpendicular. To create a square, the other two sides must each be 5 units long. One must be horizontal and the other must be vertical so that opposite sides are parallel and equal in length. If a point is placed at (−2, 4), then a square is formed.

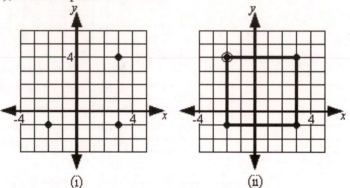

(i)   (ii)

(b) The points are plotted in the following figure (i). A segment drawn between (0, −2) and (2, 1) has a slope of $\dfrac{1-(-2)}{2-0}=\dfrac{3}{2}$ and a length of $\sqrt{(2-0)^2+(1-(-2))^2}=$ $\sqrt{13}$ units. A segment drawn between (−3, 0) and (0, −2) has a slope of $\dfrac{-2-0}{0-(-3)}=\dfrac{-2}{3}$ a length of $\sqrt{(0-(-3))^2+(-2-0)^2}=\sqrt{13}$ units. Notice the produce of these slopes is −1, so they form a right angle. The fourth point must be chosen so that two pairs of parallel sides are formed. If we start at (−3, 0), then rise 3 units and run 2 units, the coordinates of the point we land on are (−1, 3), and that point is $\sqrt{(-1-(-3))^2+(3-0)^2}=\sqrt{13}$ units from (−3, 0). Using the coordinates (−1, 3) as the fourth point, we can verify a segment drawn between (−1, 3) and (2, 1) has a slope of $\dfrac{1-3}{2-(-1)} = \dfrac{-2}{3}$ and a length of $\sqrt{(2-(-1))^2 + (1-3)^2} = \sqrt{13}$ units. A square is formed if the fourth point is $(-1, 3)$.

(i)   (ii)

Section 15.3

3. (a) Keep in mind that a square has four equal side lengths. To plot point C, move a units along the positive x-axis and a units in the positive y-direction to the point (a, a). Point D is on the y-axis, a units from the origin, so it has coordinates $(0, a)$.

    (b) Because a rectangle has four right angles, and two sides coincide with the x-axis and y-axis, the other two sides must be horizontal and vertical. Therefore, point G will have the same x-coordinate as point F and will have the same y-coordinate as point H. Point G has coordinates (a, b).

Section 15.3

4. (a) Notice one vertex of the triangle is at the origin, so the coordinates of point Q is $(0, 0)$. One leg is on the x-axis and the other is on the y-axis. Since $QR = 6$, point R is 6 units from the origin on the positive x-axis, so R has coordinates $(6, 0)$. Since $QS = 4$, point S is 4 units from the origin on the positive y-axis, so S has coordinates $(0, 4)$.

    (b) From part (a), we can conclude Q has coordinates $(0, 0)$, R has coordinates $(a, 0)$, and S has coordinates $(0, b)$.

Section 15.3

5. (a) X is at the origin, so it has coordinates $(0, 0)$. $\overline{XZ}$ is on the x-axis and is 8 units long, so Z must have coordinates $(8, 0)$. We know Y is in Quadrant I and $XY = YZ$, so Y is on the perpendicular bisector of $\overline{XZ}$. Since the altitude from Y has length 5, the coordinates of Y are $(4, 5)$.

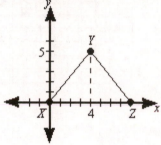

(b) Since the triangle is isosceles, Y is on the line of symmetry, which in this case, is the y-axis. The altitude is 5 units long, so Y must have coordinates of $(0, 5)$. $\overline{XZ}$ is on the x-axis, situated so that X and Z are equidistant from Y and are 8 units apart. Place X at $(-4, 0)$ and Z at $(4, 0)$.

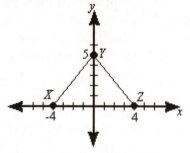

Section 15.3

6. Plot the points in a coordinate system and connect the points to form quadrilateral *RSTU* as shown next.

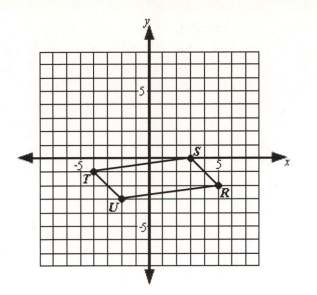

Quadrilateral *RSTU* is a parallelogram if both pairs of opposite sides are parallel. Find and compare the slopes of $\overline{RS}$ and $\overline{UT}$ as well as $\overline{ST}$ and $\overline{RU}$.

Slope of $\overline{RS} = \dfrac{0-(-2)}{3-5} = \dfrac{2}{-2} = -1$

Slope of $\overline{UT} = \dfrac{-1-(-3)}{-4-(-2)} = \dfrac{2}{-2} = -1$

Slope of $\overline{ST} = \dfrac{-1-0}{-4-3} = \dfrac{-1}{-7} = \dfrac{1}{7}$

Slope of $\overline{RU} = \dfrac{-3-(-2)}{-2-5} = \dfrac{-1}{-7} = \dfrac{1}{7}$

By calculating the values of the slopes of each side, we can conclude $\overline{RS} \| \overline{UT}$, since their slopes are equal, and $\overline{ST} \| \overline{RU}$, since their slopes are equal. Thus, *RSTU* is a parallelogram.

Section 15.3

7. Plot the points in a coordinate system and connect the points to form quadrilateral *ABCD* as shown to the left. Quadrilateral *ABCD* is a rectangle if it has two pair of

opposite sides parallel and one right angle. Find the slope of each side.

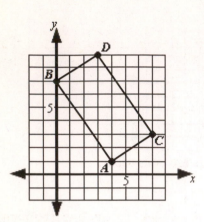

Slope of $\overline{AB} = \dfrac{7-1}{0-4} = \dfrac{6}{-4} = \dfrac{-3}{2}$

Slope of $\overline{BC} = \dfrac{9-7}{3-0} = \dfrac{2}{3}$

Slope of $\overline{CD} = \dfrac{3-9}{7-3} = \dfrac{-6}{4} = \dfrac{-3}{2}$

Slope of $\overline{DA} = \dfrac{1-3}{4-7} = \dfrac{-2}{-3} = \dfrac{2}{3}$

$\overline{AB} \| \overline{CD}$, since their slopes are equal. $\overline{BC} \| \overline{DA}$, since their slopes are equal. Thus, *ABCD* is a parallelogram. The product of the slopes of $\overline{AB}$ and $\overline{BC}$ is $\dfrac{-3}{2} \cdot \dfrac{2}{3} = -1$, so $\overline{AB} \perp \overline{BC}$. Thus, *ABCD* is a rectangle since it is a parallelogram with one right angle.

Section 15.3

8. (a) The midpoint of $\overline{AC} = \left(\dfrac{-3+3}{2}, \dfrac{6+2}{2} \right) = (0,4)$. Thus, the coordinates of *M* are (0, 4).

   (b) The midpoint of $\overline{BC} = \left(\dfrac{5+3}{2}, \dfrac{8+2}{2} \right) = (4,5)$. Thus, the coordinates of *N* are (4, 5).

   (c) The slope of $\overline{MN} = \dfrac{5-4}{4-0} = \dfrac{1}{4}$.

   The slope of $\overline{AB} = \dfrac{8-6}{5-(-3)} = \dfrac{2}{8} = \dfrac{1}{4}$.

   Notice the slopes are the same.

   (d) Use the distance formula to find the lengths of the segments.

   $MN = \sqrt{(5-4)^2 + (4-0)^2} = \sqrt{1+16} = \sqrt{17}$.

   $AB = \sqrt{(8-6)^2 + (5-(-3))^2} = \sqrt{4+64} = \sqrt{68} = 2\sqrt{17}$.

   Thus, $MN = \dfrac{1}{2}AB$.

Section 15.3

9. If the diagonals of the rectangle are congruent, then the distances from A to C and B to D are the same. Use the coordinate distance formula to check.

$$AC = \sqrt{(a-0)^2 + (b-0)^2} = \sqrt{a^2 + b^2}$$

$$BD = \sqrt{(a-0)^2 + (0-b)^2} = \sqrt{a^2 + b^2}$$

Since $AC = BD$, the diagonals are congruent.

Section 15.3

10. Recall that the median of a triangle is the line segment joining a vertex to the midpoint of the opposite side. Consider a diagram of $\triangle ABC$.

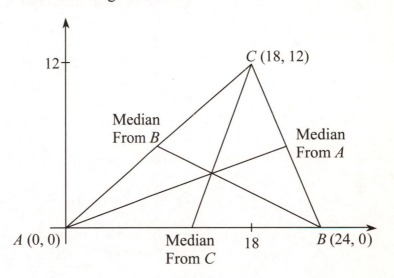

(a) To find the equation of the line containing the median from vertex A, we need the coordinates of the midpoint of $\overline{CB}$.

$$\text{Midpoint of } \overline{CB} = \left(\frac{18+24}{2}, \frac{12+0}{2} \right) = (21, 6).$$

The line will contain the midpoint (21, 6) and the vertex (0, 0). Find the slope of the line containing the points (0, 0) and (21, 6) then use the point-slope equation of a line.

$$m = \frac{6-0}{21-0} = \frac{6}{21} = \frac{2}{7}$$

$$y - y_1 = m(x - x_1)$$

$$y - 0 = \frac{2}{7}(x - 0)$$

$$y = \frac{2}{7}x$$

The equation of the line is $y = \frac{2}{7}x$. We will follow a similar procedure for parts (b) and (c).

(b) Midpoint of $\overline{AC} = \left(\frac{0+18}{2}, \frac{0+12}{2} \right) = (9, 6)$.

The line will contain (9, 6) and the vertex (24, 0).

$$m = \frac{6-0}{9-24} = \frac{6}{-15} = \frac{-2}{5}$$

$$y - 0 = \frac{-2}{5}(x - 24)$$

$$y = \frac{-2}{5}(x - 24)$$

Thus, $y = \frac{-2}{5}x + \frac{48}{5}$ is the equation of the line.

(c) Midpoint of $\overline{AB} = \left(\frac{0+24}{2}, \frac{0+0}{2} \right) = (12, 0)$

The line will contain (12, 0) and the vertex (18, 12).

$$m = \frac{12-0}{18-12} = 2$$

$$y - 0 = 2(x - 12)$$

$$y = 2(x - 12)$$

Thus, $y = 2x - 24$ is the equation of the line.

(d) The intersection of the lines in parts (a) and (b) can be found by substitution.

$$y = \frac{2}{7}x \text{ and } y = \frac{-2}{5}x + \frac{48}{5}$$

$$\frac{2}{7}x = \frac{-2}{5}x + \frac{48}{5}$$ Multiply each side by 35.

$$10x = -14x + 336$$

$$24x = 336$$

$$x = 14$$

$$y = \frac{2(14)}{7} = 4$$

Therefore, the intersection point is (14, 4). This intersection point lies on the line from part (c) if and only if (14, 4) is a solution to $y = 2x - 24$. Substitute (14, 4) into the equation to see if the equality holds.

$$4 \overset{?}{=} 2(14) - 24$$

$$4 \overset{?}{=} 28 - 24$$

$$4 = 4$$

Thus, the point (14, 4) lies on the line $y = 2x - 24$.

(e) The medians all intersect at the same point. Therefore, they are concurrent.

(f) This point is called the centroid.

Section 15.3

11. For quadrilateral *PQRS*, the diagonals are the segments $\overline{PR}$ and $\overline{QS}$. Use the distance formula to determine whether $\overline{PR} \cong \overline{QS}$.

$$PR = \sqrt{[(a+d)-a]^2 + [(b-d)-b]^2}$$

$$= \sqrt{d^2 + (-d)^2}$$

$$= \sqrt{d^2 + d^2}$$

$$= \sqrt{2d^2}$$

$$PR = |d|\sqrt{2}$$

$$QS = \sqrt{[(a+c+d)-(a+c)]^2 + [(b+c-d)-(b+c)]^2}$$
$$= \sqrt{d^2 + (-d)^2}$$
$$= \sqrt{d^2 + d^2}$$
$$= \sqrt{2d^2}$$
$$QS = |d|\sqrt{2}$$

Therefore, because $PR = |d|\sqrt{2} = QS$, we have $\overline{PR} \cong \overline{QS}$.

Section 15.3

12. (a) Since $AB = BC$, we know that the distance from point $A(0, 0)$ to $B(a, b)$ is equal to the distance from $B(a, b)$ to $C(c, 0)$.

$$AB = \sqrt{(a-0)^2 + (b-0)^2} = \sqrt{a^2 + b^2}$$

$$BC = \sqrt{(c-a)^2 + (0-b)^2} = \sqrt{(c-a)^2 + b^2}$$

Since $AB = BC$, we have the following:

$\sqrt{a^2+b^2} = \sqrt{(c-a)^2 + b^2}$	Square both sides
$a^2 + b^2 = (c-a)^2 + b^2$	Subtract b^2
$a^2 = (c-a)^2$	Multiply
$a^2 = c^2 - 2ac + a^2$	Subtract a^2
$2ac = c^2$	
$2a = c$	

Thus, c = 2a.

(b) The median from B intersects the midpoint of $\overline{AC}$.
The midpoint of $\overline{AC} = \left(\dfrac{0+c}{2}, \dfrac{0+0}{2} \right) = \left(\dfrac{c}{2}, 0 \right)$. Since c

$= 2a$, the midpoint is $\left(\dfrac{2a}{2}, 0 \right)$ or $(a, 0)$. Therefore, the

median from B is vertical, since point B and the point of intersection of the median from B and the x-axis have the same x-coordinate. The vertical median is perpendicular to the horizontal segment $\overline{AC}$.

Section 15.3

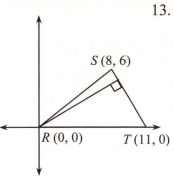

S (8, 6)

R (0, 0)   T (11, 0)

13. Draw $\triangle RST$. To find the equation of the line containing the altitude from vertex R, we need to find the line through the vertex, R, and perpendicular to the opposite side. To accomplish this, we need the slope of the opposite side, and we will use the fact that the product of the slopes of perpendicular lines is -1.

(a) The side opposite vertex R is $\overline{ST}$. The slope of $\overline{ST}$ is

$$\frac{y_2 - y_1}{x_2 - x_1} = \frac{0-6}{11-8} = \frac{-6}{3} = -2.$$ Therefore, we know a line perpendicular to $\overline{ST}$ will have slope $\frac{1}{2}$ since

$(-2)\left(\frac{1}{2}\right) = -1$. Thus, the equation of the line through

$R(0, 0)$ with slope $\frac{1}{2}$ is $y - 0 = \frac{1}{2}(x - 0)$, or $y = \frac{1}{2}x$.

(b) The side opposite vertex S is $\overline{RT}$. The slope of $\overline{RT}$ is

$$\frac{0-0}{0-11} = 0.$$ A line with slope 0 is a horizontal

line. A line perpendicular to $\overline{RT}$ must be vertical. Recall that all vertical lines are of the form $x = n$, where n is a constant. The vertical line must pass through $S(8, 6)$, which has x-coordinate 8. Therefore, the line containing the altitude is $x = 8$.

(c) The side opposite vertex T is $\overline{RS}$. The slope of $\overline{RS}$ is

$$\frac{6-0}{8-0} = \frac{6}{8} = \frac{3}{4}.$$ A line perpendicular to $\overline{RS}$ will have

slope $\frac{-4}{3}$, since $\left(\frac{3}{4}\right)\left(\frac{-4}{3}\right) = -1$. Therefore, the

equation of the line through $T(11, 0)$ that has slope $\frac{-4}{3}$

will be $y - 0 = \frac{-4}{3}(x - 11)$ or $y = \frac{-4}{3}x + \frac{44}{3}$.

(d) To find the intersection of the lines $y = \dfrac{1}{2}x$ and $x = 8$, substitute for x to obtain $y = \dfrac{1}{2}(8) = 4$. Therefore, the point of intersection occurs at $(8, 4)$. If $(8, 4)$ lies on the line $y = \dfrac{-4}{3}x + \dfrac{44}{3}$, then substituting 8 for x and 4 for y will yield a true statement.

$$4 \overset{?}{=} \dfrac{-4}{3}(8) + \dfrac{44}{3}$$

$$4 \overset{?}{=} \dfrac{-32}{3} + \dfrac{44}{3}$$

$$4 \overset{?}{=} \dfrac{12}{3}$$

$$4 = 4$$

Therefore, $(8, 4)$ lies on the line.

(e) The altitudes intersect at the orthocenter.

Section 15.3

14. Refer to the picture in the textbook. Label the intersection of the diagonals as point E. If the diagonals of the parallelogram bisect each other, then point E will be the midpoint of $\overline{AC}$ *and* the midpoint of $\overline{BD}$. Find the midpoints of both of these segments.

$$\text{Midpoint of } \overline{AC} = \left(\dfrac{0 + a + b}{2}, \dfrac{0 + c}{2} \right) = \left(\dfrac{a + b}{2}, \dfrac{c}{2} \right)$$

$$\text{Midpoint of } \overline{BD} = \left(\dfrac{b + a}{2}, \dfrac{c + 0}{2} \right) = \left(\dfrac{a + b}{2}, \dfrac{c}{2} \right)$$

Notice that the midpoint of $\overline{AC}$ is the same as the midpoint of $\overline{BD}$. We can conclude that point E, the intersection of the diagonals, is the midpoint of both diagonals. Therefore, the diagonals of a parallelogram bisect each other.

Section 15.3

15. (a) In $\triangle PQR$, point P has coordinates $(0, 0)$. Since the line l is perpendicular to $\overline{QR}$, and we know the coordinates of $Q(a,\ b)$ and $R(c,\ 0)$, we find the slope of the line

segment $\overline{QR}$ and recall that any segment perpendicular to it will have a slope which is its negative reciprocal.

Slope of $\overline{QR} = \dfrac{0-b}{c-a} = \dfrac{-b}{c-a}$. Slope of $l = \dfrac{c-a}{b}$.

(b) To find the intersection of lines l and m, we need to solve the equations simultaneously. The equation of line m is $x = a$, since it is a vertical line passing through $Q(a, b)$. The equation of line l is $y = \dfrac{c-a}{b}x$, since from part (a), we know that the slope is $\dfrac{c-a}{b}$ and the y-intercept is 0. Substituting, we have $y = \dfrac{c-a}{b}(a)$ where $x = a$ and $y = \dfrac{(c-a)a}{b}$. Therefore, the lines l and m intersect at the point $\left(a, \dfrac{(c-a)a}{b}\right)$.

(c) Since n is perpendicular to $\overline{PQ}$, and we know the coordinates of $P(0, 0)$ and $Q(a, b)$, we can find the slope of $\overline{PQ} = \dfrac{b-0}{a-0} = \dfrac{b}{a}$. The slope of a line segment perpendicular to $\overline{PQ}$ will have slope $\dfrac{-a}{b}$.

Section 15.3

16. An equilateral triangle has three congruent sides. Consider a square lattice. Construct a triangle and assume it is equilateral. Because the horizontal side has an arbitrary length, we can use a variable. Let $2a$ represent the length of the horizontal side. Notice $2a$ must be a whole number, since it is the distance between two dots. The other two legs of the triangle must also have length $2a$. Let b represent the height of the triangle. Notice that b must also be a whole number, since it is the perpendicular distance from a vertex to the base of the triangle. With the construction of the height, two right triangles are formed, each with height b, base a, and hypotenuse $2a$. By the

Pythagorean theorem we have the following:

$$a^2 + b^2 = (2a)^2$$

$$a^2 + b^2 = 4a^2$$

$$b^2 = 3a^2$$

$$\frac{b^2}{a^2} = 3$$

$$\frac{b}{a} = \sqrt{3} \quad \text{This is an irrational number.}$$

Since a is a whole number and $\frac{b}{a}$ is irrational, b must be irrational. If b were rational, then $\frac{b}{a}$ would be rational by the closure property of rational number division. This contradicts the assumption that b is a whole number. Therefore, b is irrational and will not connect a vertex with the base. We conclude that an equilateral triangle with a horizontal side cannot be formed on a square lattice.

Section 15.3

17. Use a variable to represent each girl's age. Let x represent the older girl's age and y represent the younger girl's age. Then, since the sum of their ages is 18, $x + y = 18$. Since the difference of their ages is 4, $x - y = 4$. Solve simultaneously by adding the two equations.

$$x + y = 18$$

$$\underline{x - y = 4}$$

$$2x = 22$$

$$x = 11$$

Since $x + y = 18$ and $x = 11$, $11 + y = 18$, so $y = 7$. Therefore, the ages of the two girls are 7 and 11 years.

Section 15.3

18. Let x represent the number of bicycles that pass the house. Let y represent the number of tricycles that pass the house. Since every bicycle has two wheels, the number of bicycle wheels that pass by is $2x$. Since every tricycle has three wheels, the number of tricycle wheels that pass by is $3y$.

Only seven riders pass by, so $x + y = 7$. There were a total of 19 wheels that passed by, so $2x + 3y = 19$. Solve this system of two equations by substitution. $x + y = 7$ so $x = 7 - y$.

$$2(7-y)+3y=19$$
$$14-2y+3y=19$$
$$y=5$$

If $y = 5$, then $x = 7 - 5 = 2$. Therefore, there were 2 bicycles and 5 tricycles.

Section 15.3

19. Let x represent the amount of money Mike invested, and y represent the amount of money Joan invested. Since they invested $11,000 together, $x + y = 11,000$. After Mike triples his investment and Joan doubles hers, the total value of their investment is $29,000, so $3x + 2y = 29,000$. Solve the system by substitution. We know $x + y = 11,000$, so $x = 11,000 - y$.

$$3(11,000-y)+2y=29,000$$
$$33,000-3y+2y=29,000$$
$$33,000-y=29,000$$
$$4000=y$$

If $y = 4000$, then $x = 11,000 - 4000 = 7000$. Therefore, Mike invested $7000, and Joan invested $4000.

Section 15.3

20. Let x represent the number of quarters spent, and y represent the number of dimes spent. Since the value of a quarter is 25 cents, the total value of x quarters is $0.25x$ dollars. Likewise, the total value of y dimes is $0.10y$ dollars. Since $16.25 was paid, $0.25x + 0.10y = 16.25$. She used all 110 coins, so $x + y = 110$. Solve the system by substitution. $x + y = 110$, so $x = 110 - y$.

$$0.25(110-y)+0.10y=16.25$$
$$27.5-0.25y+0.10y=16.25$$
$$27.5-0.15y=16.25$$
$$11.25=0.15y$$
$$75=y$$

If $y = 75$, then $x = 110 - 75 = 35$. Therefore, she had 35 quarters and 75 dimes.

Section 15.3

21. (a) Consider a simpler problem. Construct a 2 × 3 rectangular network of paths. Label each vertex. In a table list the length of the path from A to each vertex and the number of paths from A to each vertex.

From A to	Length of Path	Number of Paths
P	1	1
Q	2	1
R	3	1
S	4	4
T	3	3
U	2	2
V	1	1
W	2	1
X	3	3
Y	4	6
Z	5	10

As an example, the next diagram illustrates all of the paths from A to Y.

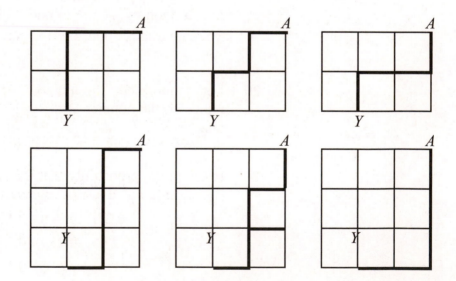

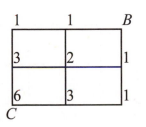

On the 2 × 3 rectangular network of paths, label each vertex with the number of paths you found to it from A. Notice that the number of ways to get from A to each vertex is the sum of the number of ways to get from A to the vertices directly above and to the right for example. This can be generalized to the case where we have a 4 × 3 rectangular network of paths. Therefore, there are 35 paths of length 7 from A to C.

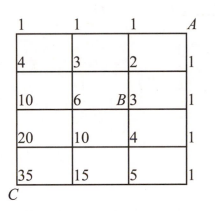

(b) By the Fundamental Counting Principle, the number of paths from A to C through B is the product of the number of paths from A to B and the number of paths from B to C. The number of paths from A to B is 3. To find the number of paths from B to C, draw a 2 × 2 network and label the vertices as we have done previously. There are 6 paths from B to C. Therefore, there are 3 × 6 = 18 paths from A to C through B.

(c) Find the probability that the path will go through B by considering the ratio comparing the number of paths from A to C through B to the total number of paths from A to C. From parts (a) and (b) we know the ratio is $\frac{18}{35} \approx 0.51$.

SOLUTIONS - PART A PROBLEMS

Chapter 16: Geometry Using Transformations

Section 16.1

29. (a) If A' is the image of A under the translation, we must move 2 units down and 2 units right. This translation is denoted by $T_{AA'}$.

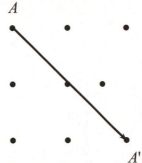

(b) To describe a rotation, specify the center of rotation and an angle. The center, O, must be equidistant from A and A'. The only three such points are along the diagonal of the lattice from the lower left to the upper right. Three possible rotations that take point A to A' are shown.

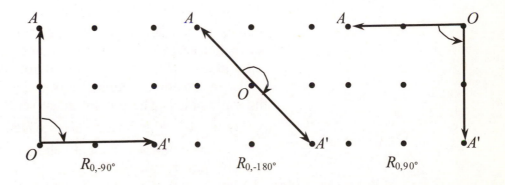

$R_{0,-90°}$ $R_{0,-180°}$ $R_{0,90°}$

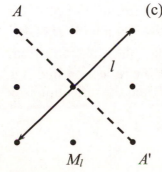

(c) Connect A and A'. The line of reflection must be perpendicular to this segment joining the point A and its image A'. Since the segment $\overline{AA'}$ is the diagonal of the square lattice, the reflection line is the other diagonal.

(d) The glide reflection is formed by translating A along $\overrightarrow{XY}$ to $A*$ and then reflecting it over glide axis l parallel to the directed line segment of the translation. In this case, the translation line and the reflection line must both be vertical or horizontal.

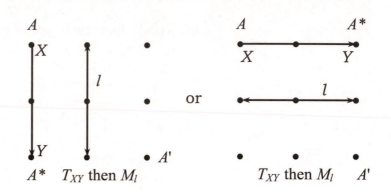

Section 16.1

30. (a) Notice that $\overline{AB}$ and $\overline{A'B'}$ are not parallel. Since a line is translated to a parallel line under a translation, there is no translation that maps $\overline{AB}$ to $\overline{A'B'}$.

(b) Since the center of rotation is equidistant from each point and its image, the center of rotation must be A. Under the rotation, A cannot move since A and A' are the same point. The rotation must send the rest of the points on $\overline{AB}$ to its image, $\overline{A'B'}$, which is the same as $\overline{AB'}$. Thus, point A is the only choice for the center of rotation. The rotation is $R_{A,\,-90°}$

(c) The line of reflection must be perpendicular to the line joining any point and its image. Since A and A' are the same point, consider the line joining B and B'. Because $\overleftrightarrow{BB'}$ is vertical, the line of reflection must be horizontal. Therefore, the reflection line is a horizontal line passing through A, and the reflection is M_l.

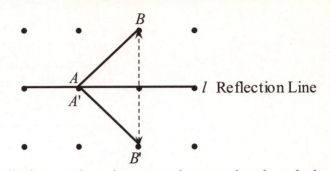

(d) Recall that each point must be translated and then reflected over a line parallel to the directed line segment of the translation. Notice that since A and A' are the same point, if we translate A in any direction and then reflect it over a line which is parallel to the direction of translation, we will never transform A to A'. Therefore, there is no glide reflection that maps $\overline{AB}$ to $\overline{A'B'}$.

Section 16.1

31. For each part, plot the triangle and its image.
   (a) The image of $A(2, 3)$ is $A'(3, 2)$, the image of $B(-1, 4)$ is $B'(4, -1)$, and the image of $C(-2, 1)$ is $C'(1, -2)$. This transformation is a reflection with respect to the line $y = x$.

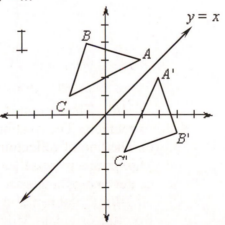

   (b) The image of $A(2, 3)$ is $A'(3, -2)$, $B(-1, 4)$ is $B'(4, 1)$, and $C(-2, 1)$ is $C'(1, 2)$. This transformation is a rotation of $-90°$ about the origin: $R_{0, -90°}$.

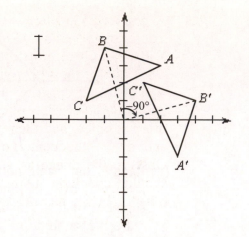

(c) The image of $A(2, 3)$ is $A'(4, 0)$, the image of $B(-1, 4)$ is $B'(1, 1)$, and the image of $C(-2, 1)$ is $C'(0, -2)$. This transformation is a translation. Each point is translated 2 units to the right and 3 units down.

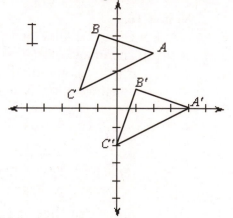

Section 16.1

32. Access the eManipulative, *Rotation Transformation.* Manipulate a collection of pattern blocks by changing the center and/or angle of rotation. Move the center very close to the object and observe how far the image rotates from the original. Move the center very far away from the object and observe how far the image rotates from the original. The farther away the center of rotation is from the object, the greater the distance the image is from the original.

Section 16.1

33. Access the Chapter 16 Geometer's Sketchpad® activity, *Size Transformation*. An object and its image are given for a particular size transformation. You are able to click on the center of the size transformation and move it. You are also able to change the scale factor. Explore these options by moving the center of the size transformation close to the original object and then far away. Change the scale factor and adjust the center of the size transformation again. Observe the image as you explore different options. You should conclude that moving the center of a size transformation has no effect on the size of the image. It does, however, change the location of the image.

Section 16.2

15. (a) We know that $\overrightarrow{PQ}, \overrightarrow{BB'}, \overrightarrow{XX'},$ and $\overrightarrow{AA'}$ are equivalent directed line segments. Thus, by the definition of the translation T_{PQ}, we have $\overline{PQ} \parallel \overline{BB'} \parallel \overline{XX'} \parallel \overline{AA'}$, and $\overline{PQ} \cong \overline{BB'} \cong \overline{XX'} \cong \overline{AA'}$. Since $\overline{BB'}$ and $\overline{XX'}$ are parallel, congruent, opposite sides of quadrilateral $BB'X'X$, we know that $BB'X'X$ is a parallelogram. Since $\overline{BB'}$ and $\overline{AA'}$ are parallel, congruent, opposite sides of quadrilateral $BB'A'A$, we know that the quadrilateral is a parallelogram.

    (b) Line $\overleftrightarrow{B'X'} \parallel \overleftrightarrow{BX}$ and $\overleftrightarrow{B'A'} \parallel \overleftrightarrow{BA}$, since these lines contain opposite sides of parallelograms $BB'X'X$ and $BB'A'A$, respectively. However, since through B' there can be only one line parallel to $\overleftrightarrow{BA}$, we conclude that $\overleftrightarrow{B'X'}$ and $\overleftrightarrow{B'A'}$ must be the same line. So, $A', X',$ and B' are collinear.

Section 16.2

16. Because a translation is an isometry, we know it preserves distances. Therefore, in ΔPQR and $\Delta P'Q'R'$, $PQ = P'Q'$, $QR = Q'R'$, and $RP = R'P'$. Since three corresponding sides are the same, by the SSS Triangle Congruence Property, we know that $\Delta PQR \cong P'Q'R'$. Therefore, since corresponding parts of congruent triangles are congruent, each pair of

corresponding angles is congruent. Thus, translations preserve angle measure.

Section 16.2

17. Rotations are isometries, and isometries preserve angle measure. Notice that $\angle 1$ and $\angle 2$ are corresponding angles when parallel lines p and q are cut by transversal m. Thus, $\angle 1 \cong \angle 2$. Since isometries preserve angle measure, $\angle 1 \cong \angle 3$ and $\angle 2 \cong \angle 4$, so by substitution we know that $\angle 3 \cong \angle 4$. Since $\angle 3$ and $\angle 4$ are congruent corresponding angles, we know $p' \parallel q'$. Therefore, rotations preserve parallelism.

Section 16.2

18. Since A, B, and C are collinear and B is between A and C, we know that $AB + BC = AC$. Consider the reflection that maps A to A', B to B', and C to C'. Since reflections are isometries, and isometries preserve distance, we know that $AB = A'B'$, $BC = B'C'$, and $AC = A'C'$. Therefore, by substitution, we have $A'B' + B'C' = A'C'$, so points A', B', and C' are collinear.

Section 16.2

19. Reflections are isometries and therefore preserve angle measure. If $p \parallel q$, then corresponding angles, $\angle 1$ and $\angle 2$, are congruent. Since reflections preserve angle measure, we have $\angle 1 \cong \angle 3$ and $\angle 2 \cong \angle 4$, so by substitution we know $\angle 3 \cong \angle 4$. Therefore, since corresponding angles are congruent, we know $p' \parallel q'$.

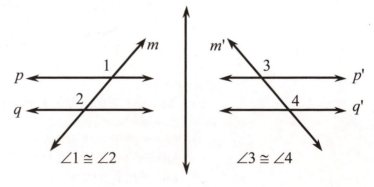

Reflection Line

Section 16.2

20. An isometry maps segments to segments and preserves distance. Consider $\triangle ABC$ and $\triangle A'B'C'$. We know that $\overline{AB} \cong \overline{A'B'}, \overline{BC} \cong \overline{B'C'}$, and $\overline{CA} \cong \overline{C'A'}$. Since three pairs of corresponding sides are congruent, we know that $\triangle ABC \cong \triangle A'B'C'$ by the SSS Congruence Property. Thus, isometries map triangles to congruent triangles.

Section 16.2

21. (a) Since between any two points there is at most one line, there can be only one translation that maps P to Q, namely T_{PQ}.

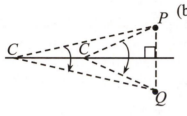

(b) As an example, consider points P and Q. Notice that the center of rotation can be any point along the perpendicular bisector of $\overline{PQ}$. There are infinitely many rotations that transform P to Q. Each has center of rotation C on the perpendicular bisector of $\overline{PQ}$ and an angle of rotation congruent to $\angle PCQ$.

Section 16.2

22. (a) To find the center of the size transformation, construct lines through each point and its image. The center of the size transformation will be the point where the lines $\overleftrightarrow{P'P}$ and $\overleftrightarrow{Q'Q}$ intersect. The point O is the center of magnification.

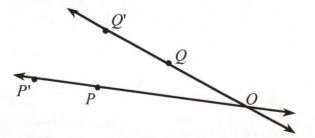

(b) Since $OP' > OP$ and $OQ' > OQ$, the scale factor, k, is greater than 1.

(c) Construct lines through each point and its image. The intersection point of the lines is the center of the size transformation.

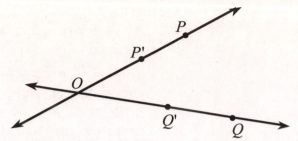

Since $OP' < OP$ and $OQ' < OQ$, the scale factor, k, is less than 1.

Section 16.2

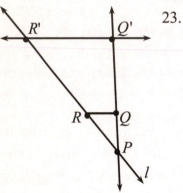

23. The center of the size transformation will be on $\overleftrightarrow{QQ'}$, and it will be the point P where $\overleftrightarrow{QQ'}$ intersects line l. Since the center of the size transformation, P, is on l, and point R is on l, the transformation of R is also on l. If we connect points R and Q and transform $\overline{RQ}$ using $S_{P,k}$, then the line containing $\overline{R'Q'}$ will be parallel to $\overline{RQ}$, since size transformations preserve parallelism. Therefore, the point R' must be the intersection of l and the line through Q' parallel to $\overline{RQ}$.

Section 16.2

24. Let R be the point of intersection of line l and $\overline{PP'}$. Let S be the point of intersection of line l and $\overline{QQ'}$.

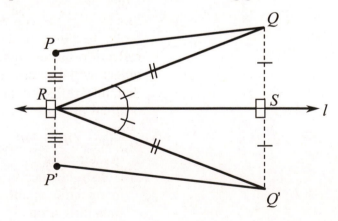

Then $\overline{QS} \cong \overline{Q'S}$ and $\angle QSR \cong \angle Q'SR$ by definition of reflections. We know that $\overline{RS} \cong \overline{RS}$. Therefore, $\triangle QSR \cong \triangle Q'SR$ by SAS. Since corresponding parts of congruent triangles are congruent, we know that $\overline{RQ} \cong \overline{RQ'}$, and $\angle QRS \cong \angle Q'RS$.

By the definition of a reflection, we know that $\angle PRS \cong \angle P'RS$, so $m(\angle PRS) = m(\angle P'RS)$.
Since $m(\angle PRS) = m(\angle PRQ) + m(\angle QRS)$, and
$\qquad m(\angle P'RS) = m(\angle P'RQ') + m(\angle Q'RS)$, we have
$\qquad m(\angle PRQ) + m(\angle QRS) = m(\angle P'RQ') + m(\angle Q'RS)$.
Also, $m(\angle PRQ) + m(\angle Q'RS) = m(\angle P'RQ') + m(\angle Q'RS)$
$\qquad$ (since $\angle QRS \cong \angle Q'RS$.)
After subtracting $m\angle Q'RS$, we have $m\angle PRQ = m\angle P'RQ'$ so $\angle PRQ \cong \angle P'RQ'$.

Finally, since $\overline{PR} \cong \overline{P'R}$, by definition of a reflection, $\angle PRQ \cong \angle P'RQ'$, and $\overline{RQ} \cong \overline{RQ'}$ from above, $\triangle PRQ \cong \triangle P'RQ'$ by SAS. Therefore, by corresponding parts, $\overline{P'Q'} \cong \overline{PQ}$, so $P'Q' = PQ$.

Section 16.2

25. Access the Chapter 16 eManipulative, *Compositions of Transformations*. Create a non-symmetric combination of pattern blocks. Click on the reflection button to create the image of your with respect to a line. Click on the line to move it closer to the original object, then click on the reflection button again. Another line will appear and the object will be reflected with respect to that line. Notice that this reflected object has the same orientation as the original object. They look alike. We can conclude that an object reflected about two parallel lines will have the same orientation and appear the same as the original object. A translation would accomplish the same thing as the two reflections.

Section 16.3

1. (a) P' is the image of P under H_A, as shown in the following figure. P'' is the image of P' under H_B. P''' is the image of P'' under H_C. Finally, P is the image of P''' under H_D. Thus, $H_D(H_C(H_B(H_A(P)))) = P$.

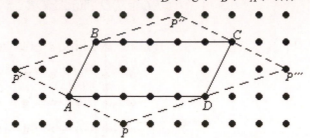

(b) Q' is the image of Q under H_A, as shown in the following figure. Q'' is the image of Q' under H_B. Q''' is the image of Q'' under H_C. Finally, Q is the image of Q''' under H_D. Thus, $H_D(H_C(H_B(H_A(Q)))) = Q$.

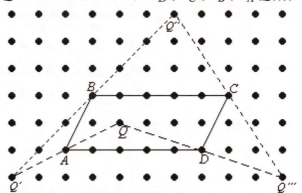

(c) The combination of four half-turns, of a point using the consecutive vertices of a parallelogram as centers of rotation, maps the point to itself.

Section 16.3

2. Recall that isometries preserve distance. Each pair of corresponding sides are the same length, however $BD \neq B'D'$ and $AC \neq A'C'$. No isometry can be found that will map a segment to a segment that has a different length, so this is impossible.

Section 16.3

3.   (a) The reflection, $R_{B,90°}$, maps $\triangle ABC$ onto $\triangle A'B'C'$. The size transformation, $S_{O,1/2}$, maps $\triangle A'B'C'$ onto $\triangle A''B''C''$ as shown in the following figure.

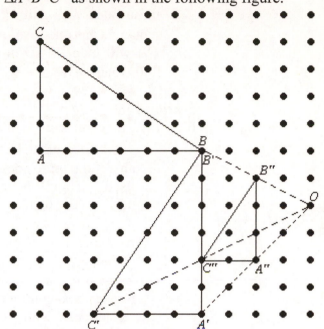

   (b) A rotation followed by a size transformation is a similitude. Similitudes map triangles to similar triangles, so $\triangle ABC \sim \triangle A''B''C''$.

Section 16.3

4.   To show $\triangle ABC \cong \triangle ADC$, the transformation should take A to A, B to D, D to B, and C to C.

   (a) A half-turn will not take A to A or C to C, so a half-turn cannot be used.

   (b) The translation T_{BE} will take B to E and E to D, so the translation cannot be used.

   (c) A 90° rotation with E as the center of rotation will not take A to A, since A is not the center of rotation. Thus this rotation cannot be used.

   (d) The kite has reflection symmetry with respect to $\overleftrightarrow{AC}$, so M_{AC} will take A to A and C to C, since they are on the line of symmetry. Reflections preserve distance, so B maps to D and D maps to B. Thus, M_{AC} can be used to show $\triangle ABC \cong \triangle ADC$.

Section 16.3

5. Because points E, F, G, and H are midpoints of the sides of the rectangle, we know $\overleftrightarrow{EG}$ and $\overleftrightarrow{FH}$ are lines of symmetry for the rectangle. Reflections with respect to these lines, M_{EG} and M_{FH}, will map $ABCD$ onto itself. A rectangle has one rotation symmetry of 180°, so a half-turn, H_P, will map $ABCD$ onto itself. Certainly, one complete 360° rotation, $R_{P, 360°}$, will also work.

Section 16.3

6. (a) Three lines of symmetry for the regular hexagon are $\overleftrightarrow{AD}$, $\overleftrightarrow{BE}$, and $\overleftrightarrow{CF}$. Thus, a reflection with respect to any of the three lines will map the regular hexagon onto itself. Three possible reflections are M_{AD}, M_{BE}, and M_{CF}. Every regular hexagon has 5 rotation symmetries, therefore, $R_{O, 60°}$, $R_{O, 120°}$, $R_{O, 180°}$, $R_{O, 240°}$, and $R_{O, 300°}$ are rotations that map the regular hexagon onto itself. Certainly, $R_{O, 360°}$ will also work.

   (b) In part (a), we listed three reflections that map the regular hexagon onto itself. There are three additional reflections, with respect to the lines through the midpoints of pairs of parallel sides that will also map the regular hexagon onto itself. Thus, there are 6 reflections and 6 rotations, for a total of 12 isometries that map the regular hexagon onto itself.

Section 16.3

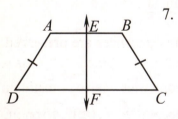

7. Let E be the midpoint of $\overline{AB}$ and F be the midpoint of $\overline{DC}$. Notice $\overleftrightarrow{EF}$ is a line of symmetry for the isosceles trapezoid. Since reflections preserve distance and angle measure, M_{EF} is an isometry that will map $ABCD$ onto itself. Any 360° rotation about any of the four vertices will also work, so $R_{A, 360°}$, $R_{B, 360°}$, $R_{C, 360°}$, and $R_{D, 360°}$ are all possible isometries.

Section 16.3

8. (a) For each of the red rectangles, a triangle has been translated from one end to the other, thus creating parallelograms that are not rectangles, but maintaining equal areas.

(b) The red area in figure (3) is simply a translation of the red area in figure (2). Since translations preserve areas, the two areas are equal.

(c) In figure (3), there are two red parallelograms separated by a dotted segment. From figure (3) to figure (4), two triangular areas, each with one side along the dotted segment, have been translated to the opposite side of their respective parallelograms. Since translations preserve areas, the resulting parallelograms are equal in area to the originals. From figure (4) to figure (5), two triangular areas have been translated from the outside of each small square to fill the insides of the small squares. Since translations preserve areas, the resulting square areas are equal to the areas of the respective parallelograms.

(d) The area of the red square region in figure (1) is equal to the sum of the areas of the red square regions in figure (f).

Section 16.3

9. Let M be the midpoint of diagonal $\overline{AC}$, then H_M is the half turn centered at M.

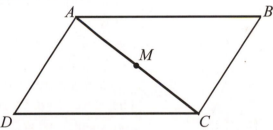

Since H_M is an isometry, we know distances are preserved. We have $H_M(A) = C$ and $H_M(C) = A$. Since $ABCD$ is a parallelogram, $\overline{AB} \| \overline{DC}$. Isometries also maintain parallelism, so $H_M(B)$ is on $\overleftrightarrow{CD}$ since $H_M(\overleftrightarrow{AB}) \| \overleftrightarrow{AB}$ and C is on $H_M(\overleftrightarrow{AB})$. Also, $H_M(B)$ is on $\overleftrightarrow{AD}$, since $H_M(\overleftrightarrow{BC}) \| \overleftrightarrow{BC}$, and A is on $H_M(\overleftrightarrow{BC})$. Therefore, $H_M(B)$ is the intersection of $\overleftrightarrow{CD}$ and $\overleftrightarrow{AD}$, so $H_M(B) = D$. $H_M(\triangle ABC) = \triangle CDA$, so $\triangle ABC \cong \triangle CDA$.

Section 16.3

10. (a) From Problem 9, we know $H_M(\triangle ABC) = \triangle CDA$, so $\triangle ABC \cong \triangle CDA$. Therefore, $\angle CDA \cong \angle ABC$, since they are corresponding parts of congruent triangles. We proved previously that consecutive angles of a parallelogram are supplementary. We know then that $m(\angle DAB) + m(\angle ABC) = 180°$, and $m(\angle BCD) + m(\angle CDA) = 180°$.

By substitution, since $\angle CDA \cong \angle ABC$ we know that $m(\angle DAB) + m(\angle CDA) = m(\angle BCD) + m(\angle CDA) = 180°$. Therefore, $m(\angle DAB) = 180° - m(\angle CDA) = m(\angle BCD)$, so $m(\angle DAB) = m(\angle BCD)$, and $\angle DAB \cong \angle BCD$. Opposite angles of a parallelogram are congruent.

(b) From Problem 9, $H_M(\overline{AB}) = \overline{DC}$, so $\overline{AB} \cong \overline{DC}$. Similarly $\overline{AD} \cong \overline{BC}$.

Section 16.3

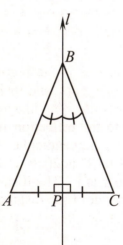

11. Let P be a point on $\overline{AC}$ so that $\overline{BP}$ is the bisector of $\angle ABC$. Let l be the line $\overleftrightarrow{BP}$. Since isometries maintain angle measure, $M_l(A)$ must be on $\overrightarrow{BC}$. We know $AB = BC$, so $M_l(A) = C$. Thus, $M_l(\triangle ABP) = \triangle CBP$, since B and P are on the reflection line, so $M_l(B) = B$ and $M_l(P) = P$. Therefore, $\triangle ABP \cong \triangle CBP$. Since corresponding parts are congruent, $\overline{AP} \cong \overline{CP}$, and $\angle BPA \cong \angle BPC$. Notice that these two angles are also supplementary, so they must both be right angles. Thus, B is on the perpendicular bisector of $\overline{AC}$.

Section 16.3

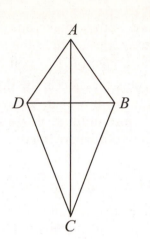

12. (a) In kite *ABCD* construct diagonals $\overline{AC}$ and $\overline{DB}$. From Problem 11, we know that *A* is on the perpendicular bisector of $\overline{DB}$, and *C* is on the perpendicular bisector of $\overline{DB}$. Therefore, $\overline{AC} \perp \overline{BD}$.

(b) The kite will have reflection symmetry if there is a reflection that maps the kite onto itself. We know that $\overline{AC} \perp \overline{BD}$. Because isometries maintain distance and angle measure, $M_{AC}(B) = D$ and $M_{AC}(D) = B$. Since *A* and *C* lie on the reflection line, $M_{AC}(A) = A$ and $M_{AC}(C) = C$. Therefore, $M_{AC}(ABCD) = ADCB$, and the kite has reflection symmetry.

Section 16.3

13. (a) Let *A* be any point that is *x* units from line *r*. Since translations are isometries, they preserve distance. Therefore, the distance from *A* to *A'* where $A' = M_r(A)$ is 2*x*. Similarly, if *A'* is a distance of *y* from line *s*, then the distance from *A'* to *A"* where $A" = M_s(A')$ is 2*y*. The distance from *A* to *A"* is $2x + 2y = 2(x + y)$. Because $\overline{AA"} \perp r$, $r \parallel s$, and $\overline{A'A"} \perp s$, by properties of reflections and parallel lines, we know that *A*, *A'*, and *A"* are collinear. Hence M_r followed by M_s is equal to translation $T_{AA"}$. Since *A* was an arbitrary point, M_r followed by M_s is $T_{AA"}$.

(b) In a reflection, the reflection line is the perpendicular bisector of the segment joining a point and its image. If we were to translate the point to its image, then it would move perpendicular to the reflection line. The direction of the translation is perpendicular to both *r* and *s*. The distance from *A* to *A"* is $2(x + y)$ from part (a). The distance from *A'* to *s* is *y*. The distance from line *r* to line *s* is $x + y$. Therefore the distance for the translation is 2 times the distance between *r* and *s* , or $2(x + y)$.

Section 16.3

14. (a) Consider Example 16.13. If we want to make cue ball A carom once and hit ball B, we reflect A over the side we want to hit and connect the image of A to point B. The point at which $\overline{A'B}$ intersects the side is the point at which we aim. In this problem, however, we want ball A to carom off two sides before hitting ball B. We will need two reflections to figure out where to aim.

Pick any two consecutive sides off which to carom the ball. For example, choose the bottom and right side. Let l be the line containing the right side, and m be the line containing the bottom side of the pool table. Reflect B with respect to l to point B', where $B' = M_l(B)$.

Next reflect B' with respect to m to point B'', where $B'' = M_m(B')$. If we connect A to B'', then we can find point P, where $\overline{AB''}$ intersects the bottom side of the table. If we connect P to B', then we can find point Q, where $\overline{PB'}$ intersects the right side of the table. By aiming the ball at point P, the following successful shot will occur.

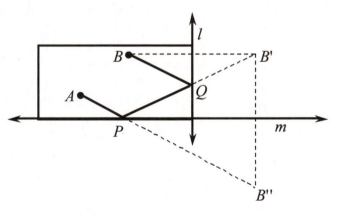

(b) See the following figure. By the definition of a reflection, we know that $\overline{BS} \cong \overline{B'S}$, and $\angle BSQ \cong \angle B'SQ$. Since $\overline{SQ} \cong \overline{SQ}$, we have $\triangle BSQ \cong \triangle B'SQ$ by SAS. By corresponding parts, we know that $\angle 1 \cong \angle 2$. By vertical angles, $\angle 2 \cong \angle 3$. By substitution, $\angle 1 \cong \angle 3$, so the angle of incidence is equal to the angle of reflection.   Similarly, $\triangle B'PT \cong \triangle B''PT$ by SAS and $\angle 4 \cong \angle 6$. Therefore, the angle of incidence is equal to the angle of reflection for the first carom. If ball A hits P in a straight shot, then it will bounce off Q and hit ball B.

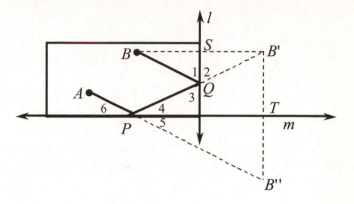

Section 16.3

15.   Consider $S_{A,\frac{b}{a}}$. Since size transformations preserve angle measure, the square $ABCD$ would have image $A'B'C'D'$, which is also a square but with side lengths $a\left(\dfrac{b}{a}\right) = b$.

$A'B'C'D'$ would be congruent to $EFGH$. By the definition of congruent shapes, if two shapes, in this case squares, are congruent, then there is an isometry, J, which will map $A'B'C'D'$ to $EFGH$. Therefore, the combination of $S_{A,\frac{b}{a}}$

and J is the desired similarity transformation.

NOTES

NOTES

NOTES

NOTES

NOTES

NOTES

NOTES

NOTES

NOTES

NOTES